Government Lawlessness in America

Government

EDITED BY

New York   OXFORD UNIVERSITY PRESS

Lawlessness in America

THEODORE L. BECKER and VERNON G. MURRAY

London   Toronto   1971

To our government officers whose pride
rests upon the knowledge that the
American freedom they treasure
dearly depends upon their
official humility

CONTENTS

II Military

III Prisons

IV Courts

VII In Pursuit of a Remedy

THEODORE BECKER

An Introduction to the Problem of Government Lawlessness

There they sat; tens of millions of Americans. What were they doing? Simply watching Chicago police surge into throngs of Americans—clubbing some senseless and gassing some blind. Yes, a portion of the street crowd was frizzy-haired hippies, Yippies, and trippies. But most of those protesters were not. Yes, some spat vile insults and hurled revolutionary (and revolting) material at policemen. But most did not. Most, in fact, were custom-tailored clean-cutters: teachers, suburbanites, reporters, students. Some, as a matter of fact, were official delegates to the Democratic National Convention. But *all* types were assailed by police. Could that comatose army of tele-viewers believe its eyes? Could this be *American* police in an *American* city?

As expected, the far-out news media compared the entire Chicago police force to a horde of locusts and the underground press portrait of Mayor Daley made the latter-day Dorian Gray look like a modern-day cosmetics ad. But what was really depressing for the ordinary American citizen was to find the rank-and-file respectable and reputable news media (television networks, radio, popular magazines, and big city newspapers) agreeing in large part with the underground tracticians. Few members of the working press denied the ugliness of the incident; what remained were a large number of perplex-ing questions. Who was "responsible" for this outrage? How many police (if any) had committed *unjustifiable* acts of violence against how many inno-cent people?

An ad hoc commission was established (in typical American fashion) and, as usual, it was packed with a sizable complement of "the establishment." What was not typical, however, was the result. Rather than being a back-lash, or a whitewash, the product (The Walker Report) was a trenchant indictment of (a) a large number of Chicago policemen and (b) the Daley Administration's handling of the preconvention negotiations with the leaders of the planned demonstrations.

When added to a parallel set of reports on the 1967 summer riots, plus the

1968 campus confrontations, many pieces of a grim mosaic were ready for assembling. But the piece needed to fit them together was missing. The Walker Commission provided the necessary two words: "police riot." What lends this concept intrigue is its tinge of paradox. Police are supposed to contain riots, not enflame them. But the large cache of information on police action in these reports made it painfully clear that police, *some* police, provoke and stoke riots by systematically violating established laws. The Negro community in America had been saying this for ages. But it took the crimson debacle in Chicago, marked by a black absence, to make the problem of police lawlessness visible to white America. That there is some degree of police corruption (payoffs, kickbacks, graft) has been widely believed for some time. But these were allegations of a different, and perhaps more deadly, form of police outlawry.

If some policemen acted against and outside the law, they would be police outlaws. If they did this in regular fashion, and if their acts were contrary to tenets of the fundamental organization of society, then their acts would be truly anti-social. Such acts would be as rebellious as those perpetrated by the most rabid revolutionaries, who also aim to shred the underlying legal fabric of society by illicit force. When it is claimed that this is, indeed, done systematically and regularly, we have charges amounting to police rebellion bordering on police anarchy.

Two major problems many people face is whether to believe the charges at all, and if so, to what extent. Which assertions are credible, which incredible? Even blue-ribbon panels like the Walker Commission, after extensive hearings, seem to be subject to common mistrust about their findings. After all, a jury of twelve Chicagoans (despite the contemporary popularity in some circles of the notion of police riot) decided to acquit eight Chicago policemen on charges brought by the U.S. Government that they had denied large numbers of demonstrators their civil liberties. Evidence sufficient to persuade some of the truth of a matter is not sufficient unto others.

But the police are not the lone officials in American government who have been subjected recently to such wholesale complaints of lawlessness. Police are highly visible members of government and are therefore more vulnerable to exposure and criticism. Furthermore, if they flaunt laws, they may blaze a trail of blood that photographs well in living color. Still, almost all phases of government in America have come under similar criticism lately. As the allegations have mounted in number and intensity, so has the degree of disaffection in many American citizens: among themselves and with their government.

Thus government lawlessness, its existence and the potential extent of it, is, among other things, a problem in believability. That is one of the main reasons for this book. For we hope that the selection of materials and the way in which they are arranged will be convincing that government lawlessness is a real problem and that it is serious because it is so extensive and runs so deep.

WHAT AND WHO TO BELIEVE

One response to a collection such as this may be that too many of the items are simply anecdotal. One, two, or three instances of something are only one, two, or three instances of something: a few scattered felonies are not a crime wave. Another response to the message of this anthology (which is that the problem is real, not fake) may be that even if the evidence of governmental lawlessness is abundant enough, and does establish a pattern, the evidence is still invalid. In other words, the alleged menace is not to be believed: it is the concoction of fanatics; the fantasy of paranoids; the propaganda of extremists. That may be true, but *we* believe that this book, in content *and* method, lends a lot of weight to the contrary.

First, we have taken care to choose articles that describe a variety of offending practices in a variety of government offices. To outline police outlawry, for instance, we did not accumulate a dozen articles on the so-called Chicago "police riot." Instead, we chose articles that allege that there is a vast area of illicit behavior, including excessive use of police force, widespread police harassment, police defiance of Supreme Court decisions, and systematic police perjury. And though it was not as simple to find as many charges against other governmental agencies and branches, the articles collected here state a multitude of ways in which illicit behavior is practiced on all levels of government.

Second, we think that the way in which these articles have been arranged helps to prove that governmental lawlessness is indeed a major contemporary American problem and that it is not a product of illusion, delusion, or collusion. We have proceeded on the assumption that the convergence of diametrically divergent perspectives intersects at or near a point of truth. It's something like the parable of the blind men and the elephant. Each blind man touched a different part and assumed it was the whole: to one, the elephant was a trunk; to another, a huge foot; to a third, a thin tail; to a fourth, a floppy ear. Because the information was not pooled, the individual accounts of the elephant's appearance had many blind spots. The obligatory moral to the story is that each man sees reality from its own disadvantage point. However, if all of us put each blind man's report together, the reports would describe to us what an elephant looked like: nothing more or less than an elephant!

Similarly, it would be foolish for us to deny that commentators on highly inflammatory political issues frequently are the proud possessors of highly impaired vision. Their clarity of sight is strongly influenced by their background, their experience, and their values. So, to create as precise and objective description of what might be "out there" (elephants or government outlaws), one should select observers from as conflicting points of view as possible (in terms of backgrounds, experiences, and values).

Thus, we have tried to include in each section of this volume official government reports or statements; news articles from the leading newspapers and wire services in the nation; scholarly papers; articles and stories from the mass media (*Time, Newsweek, Look*); and articles and squibs from the well-underground presses and out-of-sight mimeograph machines. We have come to believe that when so many strangers (if not antagonists) have seen so much of a similar thing, it probably exists. Whether we call it an elephant or government lawlessness matters little. It is certainly large enough to be noticed.

THE MORE VIOLENT FORMS

The first section, on police lawlessness, was the most difficult one to collate. Perhaps the major reason for this was that there is a tremendous bulk of literature available. Moreover, it was even tougher to decide which arrangement made the most convincing and vivid pastiche.

So as to demonstrate the jaggedness on the edge of the issue, we framed the section on police with two barbed attacks—one at the beginning and one at the end. The first is an excerpt from Tom Hayden's *Rebellion in Newark* and the other a pamphlet honed by the New York Black Panther party demanding that sister Joan Bird be cut free.

Hayden, is a well-known younger-elder of New Left politics. Thus, much of what he says is either shunned or shunted aside by the establishment and by a near unanimity of the silent majority. But it is important to note that Hayden's description of the agony in Newark, during the summer of 1967, was largely substantiated by an elite study commission a year or so later. Hayden's brief is a gruesome account of rampant, random, and lethal police action against the black community in Newark; the Governor's Select Commission echoes his charge, though with less relish. We have included the concluding part of the commission's remarks to demonstrate the extremely close rapport between the two reports. We could have done the same with any major urban riot or campus uproar, that is, juxtapose a highly militant description with a subsequent establishment-oriented set of findings and recommendations that were in substantial agreement. But the most varied accounts were on the 1968 Chicago street scenes.

Thus, following the Newark materials are three items that depict and analyze the Chicago melee. The first was published in *Time* immediately following the Democratic Convention. Following that are excerpts from the Walker Report and a warning from ex-United States senator Wayne Morse. It didn't seem necessary to look to the primary victims for further elaboration on what happened in Chicago.

But bitter accusations of abuse of the policeman's license to exercise force are not restricted to city riots and mass politics. Actually, the issue of "police brutality" is concerned chiefly with day-to-day activities—and particularly in slums, ghettos, and inner-cities. In fact, we could have compiled a bulky book on this topic alone; there are enough individual horror stories for the finding—some true, some fabulous. But little good would have come from that. For those who believe already that such police lawlessness is the rule, and not the exception, it would only re-arouse their passions and harm their ability to conceive of solutions. And the disbelievers would have retained their sociological atheism.

Instead, we have turned to the world of Academe and a book by Professor David Bayley entitled *Minorities Confront the Police*. One subsection is called "Police Brutality," but, happily, it is neither an invective against police departments in general nor against the specific one studied, that of Denver. Bayley discusses the breadth and depth of the "issue" of police brutality without a single reference to swine . . . which, nowadays, is a feat worth mentioning. Instead, Bayley points out, succinctly and cogently, some complexities of "police brutality" from the point of view of the police, the minorities, and from those who are desperately trying to understand.

However, one point worth highlighting here is that 27 per cent of the Denver Police Department admitted, in a questionnaire administered to them by Bayley, that they had personally "witnessed an incident which they considered involved harassment or the excessive use of force [by their fellow officers]." Twenty-seven per cent! That might indicate quite an epidemic of police outlawry, and it should go a long way in persuading even the most adamant skeptic that police malconduct exists—and by the gross. For it is rare that police confess this to outsiders. The contrary, in fact, is true. Police deny that brutality and harassment are everyday phenomena in the cities of America. And, what is worse, they do this under oath in response to specific charges . . . to the lingering embarrassment of the administration of justice. In support of this allegation, we have included a chapter from Paul Chevigny's recent book *Police Power* that contends that police perjury is far from a sometimes thing. Indeed, as the reader will see, Chevigny, a nationally prominent civil rights lawyer, states that police "distortion of fact" at trial is "the most pervasive" of all police abuses.

So, it is in light of these two measured pieces (by Bayley and Chevigny) that we included several articles detailing specific police malconduct and lawlessness. The first is by James Alan McPherson. It indicts the Chicago Police for systematic harassment and excessive use of force against the Blackstone Rangers. Next is an elaborate brief against the Chicago Police for the "assassination" of Fred Hampton and Mark Clark (Black Panther leaders in Illinois) in late 1969. It should be added that much of this was substantiated by a special Federal grand jury in Chicago in the spring of 1970. Following is Murray Kempton's description of a more typical and less sensational act of police harassment against a black community (in this case, Harlem).

To follow up this trio of specific accusations of illegal hassling, threats, and violence are several short items suggesting that more systematic police lawlessness exists on a coast-to-coast scale. A *Newsweek* article concerns itself with a growing suspicion that there is, indeed, a police policy to do in the Black Panther party before it becomes a serious nationwide political threat; and an article from the *East Village Other* wonders whether various "busts" from L.A. to New York are simply coincidence. The New York *Daily News* found out that Abbie Hoffman was wondering about it too.

One of the most effective ways police collect information about groups they believe a threat to public safety is to infiltrate them with undercover agents. No one disputes the effectiveness of this tactic and only a few demand a total cessation of its practice. However, serious temptations exist in these cloak-and-dagger roles for police work that are not condonable and are illegal. If the police vaccine causes the same disease it was thought to prevent, one might wonder whether it should be used any longer. For instance, it is said that police are allowed to commit crimes while undercover in order to gain the confidence of those under surveillance. Even more serious is the accusation that police act as ring-leaders or instigators of incidents that blossom into events that police abort viciously—sometimes injuring innocent people. And when these allegations add evidence that uniformed police *know* that their own fellows are fomenting the trouble (at least partially), then a serious question arises as to who is to blame for the situation in the first place. There is a great difference between instigation and investigation. We have included two pieces on this part of the problem—one an article from the *East Village Other* and the other a report from the New York Civil Liberties Union. Their narration is frightening if true, and alarming even as a serious contention of further instances of unchecked police lawlessness in our cities—and throughout the nation.

The penultimate two articles in the police section raise two other issues of police malconduct. The first treats the problem of wiretapping by the FBI. Identical charges are leveled against many other federal and local "law enforcement" agencies, but this one, by Fred Cook, details methods and rationalizations employed by the most highly respected police bureau in America. The second article discusses the observations of a team of Yale law students who were permitted to station themselves among the New Haven police for the duration of the summer of 1966. Their job was to see to what extent police obeyed orders of the Supreme Court of the United States concerning the rights of suspects under arrest (the *Miranda* decision). Their report is not very heartening, for months after the decision, and after much had been written and explained about it, Professor Michael Wald and his associates observed that police compliance with the law of the land (the giving of *all* instructions required by the *Miranda* decision) had increased from zero to all of 33 per cent. It was very slow compliance and there was great promise that it would always be far from total, in letter, and certainly in spirit. This is a serious allegation of substantial police lawlessness from a highly credible source.

Two other components of government with potentially high visibility for outlawry are military and prison authorities. Many of their illegal acts, however, have been less than sensational since they are obscured by the towering and towered walls of their institutions.

As for the military, its disobedience of the law it defends has become notorious only recently. This is probably owing to (1) the unpopularity of the Vietnam conflict; (2) an increasing public dissatisfaction with general military priorities; and (3) the periodic mobilization and unleashing of National Guard units for search and destroy missions in some of our cities and on some of our campuses. All in all, there has been a growing public awareness of possible military tendencies to take the law into its own hands. The overkill in Newark and Detroit, the air raid on Berkeley, the eradication of the Kent State Sanctuary, and the steady tatoo of cruelty and denial of human rights to prisoners in military stockades have brought military credibility and legitimacy into greater question than ever before.

As for prison officials, a series of recent exposés and jailyard strikes are making it more and more obvious that our penitentiaries may be even worse than we admitted in the past. Many Americans expect that a pack of brutes will (and perhaps should) police the insides of prisons. But our basic law insists that imprisonment is itself punishment (a loss of freedom) and that prisons are not places for further sadistic and unreasoned punishment. We are hearing, with sickening regularity, that the opposite is true. Certain groups of people—certain types of prisoners—are reporting heavy punishment while in prison, quite beyond what our law permits.

The civil rights movement and the resistance to the draft by a host of bright, energetic young Americans, who are committed to ideals, as well as terms behind bars, has resulted in an unprecedented prison invasion by the middle class. They have been struck by the treatment meted out to themselves and some fellow inmates, and they have been reciting the existence of ignominious (and illegal) conditions with extraordinary eloquence. Their ranks have been swelled by a staggering number of teenage marijuana fiends, who also depict a reality gap between their legal rights and official practices and procedures. This is a reportorial coalition of the scions and critics of American affluence, and they have become the most elegant group of cell-dwellers since the French Revolution.

No one dares suggest that prison officials are privileged to disregard the laws of this nation, much less the canons of common decency. What demands attention (and probable action) are so many claims from so many disparate sources that our jailhouses nurture torturers, boldly contemptuous of American jurisprudence and the American legal system.

The sections on the military and the prisons defy logical order. Each contains reports from many sources, official and unofficial. They cannot be ordered historically as these conditions have always existed. And there are no sectional factors involved, since the military is a national establishment and the alleged crimes of our penal system are found from sunny California, to Atlanta, to the District of Columbia, to Fun City. All one can do is select some of the more graphic descriptions. In other words, the selections in these sections of this volume speak for themselves. The reader is invited to read them and reflect on the squalid and degraded life they say exists for all too many American citizens when American officials act without regard for the American law they have sworn to uphold.

A MORE GENTLE ANARCHY

So much for the problem of government lawlessness in our military and paramilitary institutions; these are allegations of very grave offenses—with terrible physical consequences. But they are by no means the only claims of flagrant disdain of the law, perpetrated under the color of law. There are statements of far more subtle instances, far more difficult to detect, but nonetheless real. These are practices of malconduct in the more "dignified" offices of government. But, then, white-collar crime is always more "sophisticated" than the blue (or khaki)-collar kind.

For example, if administrators, public and private, engage in illegal practices, it is less likely that they will receive their legal come-uppance for their misbehavior. There are several reasons for this immunity. The main one is that their malpractice can be covered by the shroud of "discretion." But there are limits to administrative discretion—there is "abuse of discretion" and there are times when this abuse is as intentional as the use of excessive force by a policeman. It is just more difficult to *know* that it was done intentionally.

One peculiar kind of administrator, white-collar variety, is the judge. Judges (and justices) are not usually considered administrators, but they are. Their job, quite simply, is to interpret and apply general laws in relation to specific factual disputes. This is the quintessence of all administration, judicial and otherwise.

The fact of the matter is that judges are only highly specialized and peculiarly attired administrators with rather rigorous rules to guide their decisions. But what is most important, what is critical to all the deference and respect judges are justified in commanding from people, is that they are supposed to be models of *impartiality* and *objectivity* while hearing a case and making a decision. To help guarantee freedom from bias, there must be every assurance that each judge is totally *independent* from other agencies of government. This means that every judge must be utterly inaccessible to undue influence from other government officials and that judges *should never consider issues from the government's point of view*. An umpire, an arbitrator, and a judge must be neutral in their view of the facts in order to make the game fair, and to keep the participants from flaring up at each other. It is this freedom from the government's perspective that is a basic component of the judicial role and that is the sense and essence of judiciousness. When a judge spurns this aspect of his office and oath he is in violation of that law which describes, allows, and authorizes him to act. A judge who fails to be neutral is a fugitive from legitimacy. He reigns, but he must be overthrown.

There have been several highly publicized showcase trials in recent years. Among these are the Number Trials: the Boston Five (Doctor Spock, et al.); the Chicago Eight, then Seven ("The Conspiracy"); and the Panther Twenty-One, then Thirteen; etc. From the perspective of the defendants and their sympathizers, these have been "political trials" from beginning to end, with the quotation marks symbolizing (a) the political motivations of all the government officials concerned and involved and (b) the façade of legality covering the prejudiced nature of the courtroom proceedings. As for the judges in these cases, there are abundant accusations that each of them were highly biased in their personal attitudes toward the various defendants from the outset. In each trial there is voluminous information that lends support to the charge that each judge allowed his prejudice to sway him from the performance of his duty, and as that occurred, he acted against the law that required him to maintain impartiality and an independent spirit.

It is certainly no easy task to distinguish actions of a judge that are (a) clearly within the confines of his judicial role, (b) errors in judgment committed in good faith (even judges make mistakes), and (c) abuses of discretion with malice aforethought. However, many people are beginning to feel that there may well be patterns of behavior so obviously biased and so systematically in favor of the government against defendants that they can substantiate an indictment against the judge charging him with criminal intent to convict. In the eyes of many people, including many who wish to *conserve* our system, "probable cause" exists to cite these judges as "outlaws."

But judges in well-publicized political cases are only the most flagrant illustrations of outlawry. There is the so-called "government's judge"—a man who almost never finds defendants innocent—a man who treats police testimony as gospel truth. It is said that there are substantial numbers of these men, disguised as umpires, who desecrate the black robes they don. The problem is to find out if and where they exist—and to remove and possibly penalize those that might exist; such is the gravity of their malfeasance.

In the section on judicial lawlessness we have placed several articles that, if true, give us a montage of judges systematically acting against the law or in contradiction to their legally imposed responsibility of impartiality and independence.

The first piece, by Jerome Skolnik of the University of California, was plucked from the staff report to the National Commission on the Causes and Prevention of Violence. The task force that did the research was established after the rash of urban disturbances that made the summer of 1967 extremely hot. Although the public was alerted to the function police lawlessness may have played in instigating and maintaining much of the disorder at that time, few people were alerted to the way in which the courts may have increased the general level of disregard for law and order that prevailed in those heated moments. Professor Skolnik alleges various ways in which judges broke the law of the land in a feeble and misdirected effort to restore order. The bill of particulars in his indictment hints strongly at a judicial-like Strangelovean logic of destroying in order to save, that is, break the law in order to preserve respect for it. Tom Hayden noticed the same sort of thing during the Great Newark Unrest—so we've included some of his more vivid prose.

The second selection on the judiciary also complains of a frontal assault by judges on a superior law. The scene is not the American North but the American South, and the alleged violators are judges of higher appellate courts, rather than lower trial courts. According to the author of this essay (a civil liberties lawyer), the court system in the South, in its haste to slow down or foil changes in institutionalized racism, became an almost impassable trail to social justice.

The remaining articles on the judiciary have more to do with what we call "political trials," or with specific instances of potential judicial repression on an individual basis. The reader will find a few cases that many professional observers believe to be the most clear-cut cases of judicial prejudice to be found in the history of American jurisprudence. The description of Judge Ford's alleged bias against the Boston Five is taken from an article that appeared in the *New Yorker* magazine. The description of what happened in the Chicago Conspiracy case, called by many the leading travesty on American justice *ever,* is from a special supplement on that trial in the *New York Review of Books.* We have also included some of the spicier exchanges between Judge Julius Hoffman (no relation to Abbie) and Bobby Seale, Chairman of the Black Panther Party. A third case worth including is the allegation of near criminal passivity on the part of Judge Joseph Karesh, in the murder trial of Officer Michael O'Brien in Oakland in 1967. Last, is the celebrated trial of LeRoi Jones. Together these four proceedings should make some people understand what is meant when someone speaks of political "trials." They also may help the reader understand the invective reserved for American legality—typified by the Black Panther article on "The American Way of Justice???"

Many other accusations of *administrative* outlawry are levied against those in civvies. It is said to exist in all federal, state, and local bureaus and departments and it is claimed to operate in almost every type of proceeding. It is widely stated, for example, that welfare workers, to "enforce" benefit provisions, break and enter premises of recipients, intimidate them with false legal threats, and withdraw payments with scant semblance to due process. Patterns of racial discrimination in almost every sort of public health and welfare organization are also charged frequently—and successfully. Unfortunately, relief is not only dear, but it simply reverses individual decisions that might be discriminatory. Criminal charges are rarely pressed (and are, indeed, nearly impossible to press) against the wrongdoers. The worst that befalls government outlaws is official or unofficial censure, mere wrist-slapping.

Perhaps one of the most notorious examples of administrative outlawry is the strike or "sick-in" by public employees. This defiance of law is becoming as much a part of contemporary life in America as the steady increment in violence in our cities, and it is every bit as illegal as any other crime in our streets. Each garbage man, every transit worker, and each teacher who participates in these mass refusals to work violates the law and does so with full knowledge that this is so. When sanctions are taken, an extraordinary measure, they are almost always taken against one or two leaders, and the tabloids herald the leaders as martyrs of the day. Rarely is action taken against the rank and file, even while they are breaking the law. This tokenism in law enforcement is still another type of illegality (lack of prosecution where it is a duty to prosecute) within the law-enforcement establishment. The Newark teachers' strike in 1970 is perhaps a change in the right direction, for approximately two hundred teachers were jailed for picketing in defiance of a court order enjoining them from such activities.

The pictures are not pretty at all. The photos of grinningly defiant public workers—brandishing their signs and wallowing in smug self-righteousness— are a collage of administrative lawlessness running unchecked. The laws they scorn have been passed in this, our "democratic" society. They are being broken only because a large number of organized people (though they are a small minority of all) believe they should be. They are doing this, in truth, to extort pay raises and fringe gains at the expense of a paralyzed and frightened society. The health, safety, and public welfare of the community is disregarded, if not placed beneath contempt. Yet few photos show policemen wading into these groups to prevent them from disrupting traffic (a minor inconvenience)—as was frequently the police justification for forcibly dispersing anti-war demonstrators in the late 1960's. The reason for this discrepancy may well be that individual policemen are in personal agreement with the demands of their fellow governmental employees and opposed to the views of anti-war demonstrators. Is it a case of unequal protection of the law? Is it unequal persecution by the law?

The section dealing with assertions of administrative lawlessness starts with a well-documented chapter from Omar Garrison's *Spy Government*. It occurred to us that it would amaze the reader to discover that a bureau as seemingly innocuous and benign as the United States Post Office could be the subject of a charge of domestic spying. Similar blurbs on the CIA, or some other super-secret arm of the law, wouldn't amaze anyone much these days. But when even the post office might be in on the James Bond act, then perhaps it is time to flex our panic-button finger.

Why would postal authorities feel it necessary to violate strict laws and official regulations against fiddling with the mails? One can sympathize with a sense of urgency gripping authorities whose own personal safety might be in danger (the police) or whose reason for existence included ultra-sensitive matters (national security) so that they might believe extra-legal measures necessary in a tight moment. But post office officials? Whatever could possess *them* to break the law?

One of the best explanations for all such potentially aberrant behavior, in ordinary, run-of-the-mill bureaucracies, is an article by Stephen Waldhorn. Waldhorn outlines his theory of the pathology of the bureaucrat and provides numerous instances of what he means and how it works. In many ways, his article provides an intriguing framework by which one can better understand many of the items that follow it. And those that follow detail a great range of complaints about administrative malfeasance in office: from Adam Walinsky's report on official lawlessness in non-enforcement of anti-discrimination laws, through Stuart Nagel's elaboration on how welfare agents operate well outside the limits of their legal boundaries, through Judge Jerry Pacht's opinion on administrative lawlessness practiced by the Board of Regents of the University of California (the Angela Davis case) through Ralph Nader's accusations of administrative outlawry (with attendant corroboration from his "Raiders"), to a similar allegation against the Pentagon by Senator William Proxmire (in his capacity as chairman of the Joint Committe on Economics of the U.S. Congress).

Senator Proxmire's questions about suspected muzzling of witnesses, *prior* to their appearance before his committee, involved the Lockheed C5A investigation. He referred to evidence that defense department officials were trying to hamper a witness from presenting evidence about the Pentagon's shockingly inept handling of a huge contract. We have included a lengthy excerpt from the transcript of that hearing where Senator Proxmire suggests that another federal law may have been violated—that is, the forbidding of interference with government witnesses *after* their cooperation with a congressional probe. What is most enlightening about this piece is its illumination of the ingenious rationales bureaucracies could use to disguise such lawlessness, should it exist.

Another type of administrator coming under increasing attack is the *prosecutor*. For prosecutors are administrators who possess important and wide discretion—including power to clamp down hard on radical political leaders through a wide variety of legal tools. One device is to resurrect excessively vague or long forgotten laws to arrest and harass and sap the energies and monies of political leaders of unacceptable (to the prosecutor) groups. When done intentionally, it is unequal protection of the law, and thus an illegal usage of power. Moreover, it is well known in legal circles that prosecutors frequently overcharge certain types of people so they can then "bargain" them into confession and/or jail; this is also beyond their legal power and is lawlessness pure and simple.

We have included an interesting law-review article by James D. Barnett that poses many of the legal problems involved in these questionable prosecution practices. Barnett's essay should make it clearer that some of the contentions in the articles following his are not as incredible and fantastic as one might like to believe. Also, since it might be a bit hard to swallow that prosecutors willfully falsify evidence, we thought it would be wisest to make this point through the medium of two U.S. Supreme Court opinions. Thus, we've included the decisions of *Miller v. Pate* (1967) and *Giles v. Maryland* (1967) to support the claim that it does indeed happen. And, we've included a statement by an eminent Negro jurist to demonstrate that prosecutors can be as contemptuous of judges as some of our more outrageous private anarchists. What the reader must bear in mind, though, is that as reprehensible as these prosecutorial acts might have been, the only available remedy was to liberate the D.A.'s victims. No really effective sanctions were levied against the prosecutors themselves.

Nor did any disadvantage accrue to General Lewis Hershey for his acts above and beyond the call of law and order. As Director of the Selective Service, it was mandatory for him to respect the bounds of what the law empowered him to do. Yet, as most people know, General Hershey capriciously re-legislated the Selective Service Act in 1967 to punish demonstrators against the Vietnam War. Through a letter directed to all local draft boards, Hershey recommended that all "misguided registrants" be re-classified as "delinquents" and that any prior deferments be canceled. This action, ultimately, came under scrutiny by the federal courts and was found to be without legal authorization. We have included relevant portions of the legal decision.

Yet, American boys were incarcerated in the Army and remained there against their will. And though this robbed them of their personal freedom to be that which they were, of years of their youth, and perhaps even worse, of their faith in the American system, no sanction was every taken against General Hershey. Indeed, his retribution was to be kicked upstairs—with a velvet boot.

Another point of administrative lawlessness raised by many people lately involves *inaction* by administrators, in dereliction of their legal duty, and which leads directly to frustration and indirectly to violence. The big question is whether such sins of bureaucratic omission are intentional, and if so, whether the ensuing violence is the responsibility of the bureaucrats. Of course, this was a major burden of proof on the defense in the famous Chicago Conspiracy case, that is, that Mayor Daley and his administration willfully, and with no charitable afterthought, deviously developed a situation that led to inevitable police repression. Instead of using defense arguments from that trial, we have decided to include portions of the "Sparling Report," which issued from a group of concerned citizens, headed by Dr. Edward Sparling, former president of Roosevelt University. We've also included a similar argument about administrative lawlessness as drawn from a book entitled *Berkeley: The New Student Revolt*.

But even as non-uniformed public administrators may systematically skirt the law for reasons they consider justifiable, we also hear of violations of the law by many *elected* officials as well: governors legislators, city councilmen, etc. And they, too, seem to do it with utter impunity.

BLATANT INSURRECTION IN THE SOUTH

The best illustrations of how elected officials manage this on a large-scale basis are how southern politicos have cooked up a twentieth-century insurrection against the supreme law of the land. The Supreme Court, as America's ultimate tribunal, commanded the South to desegregate its educational facilities in 1954. Yet it is often charged that many Dixie officials subject to this law, just the same as any other Americans, continue to circumvent and circumcize this law in every imaginable way and through very imaginative means.

We decided to arrange the articles selected for this section historically, despite the fact that the accusation of official rebellion in the South made it seem that southern leaders are men for all seasons. The reason for noting their persistence through time is that the Court expressly told the South to integrate as fast as was reasonably possible. The assertions in the following articles make it appear that there has been scant deference to the wishes of the Court.

Thus, the first article by former Michigan governor G. Mennen Williams describes the challenge to the Democratic party in 1957 (Little Rock). It doesn't seem as though his party (the southern wing) was up to it. The next article, from a 1961 edition of *Time*, alleges a web of official anarchy in the South spun to entangle Freedom Riders in a network of harassment and physical risk to life and limb. Following that, a *former* history professor at the University of Mississippi, who dared write a book entitled *Mississippi: The Closed Society* (he now teaches elsewhere), presents a systematic analysis of what he believes was a calculated official rebellion against legitimate federal authority. This book was published in the dark age of 1963. The next article, another by Paul Chevigny, is a lengthy indictment of the methods (Mississippi, c. 1965), of state and local officials designed (1) to deny the black citizens of the state the right to vote and (2) to intimidate and punish the many young Americans who came there to help delta blacks gain and enjoy their rights. To update the matter and spotlight the certainty that this is not a medieval tale, but a living drama, we have included another article (by a Professor at the University of Alabama) providing evidence that Southern ingenuity is boundless in nature and energy in its determination to reduce the duly considered, legislated, and adjudicated laws of the land to meaningless drivel.

If we were to end this section by implying Southern resistance to desegregation is the sole instance of sustained or spasmodic legal insurrection against American law by local elected officials, we would do double disservice: to the Confederacy and our point. For there are numerous other instances. Defiance of Supreme Court orders, for one, is not limited to desegregation. The study by Robert Birkby, a professor at Vanderbilt University, is convincing that the non-compliance in Tennessee to the Court's decision on bible-reading was (and may still be) widespread. And there is reason to believe that this decision gained little adherence in northern and midwestern portions of the USA as well.

For our main point in this section is that local and state officials throughout the land act in a plethora of ways that are illegal, as long as they feel that these illegal means justify their sanctimonious ends. Where local sentiment is strong against any political view, or a group opposes the community's prevailing way of life, there is data aplenty to support an inference that an intricate conspiracy will be framed by local authorities to eliminate these threats by any means available. The complaint reads that members of this conspiracy include many members of the local establishment, in and out of government. We have included a group of articles, all from newspapers, that seem to add up to a strong suspicion that this complaint may have a large kernel of truth to it: consisting of the action of a governor, whimsically demanding the immediate arrest of a fifteen-year-old rock-festival patron (for his lack of respect), the persecution of a local radical doctor on some technicality, the "vamping" of an off-base anti-military coffeehouse, or threats by political leaders against judges who have been lenient on sentencing student activists, a frightening pattern emerges.

All rebels and anarchists do their thing with gusto and self-righteousness. The aroma of law makes its smell none the sweeter, and perhaps even more pungent.

THE IMPACT OF GOVERNMENT LAWLESSNESS

To the extent that we have stumbled onto a real flaw in the American art of governance, we have stumbled to the edge of a new American tragedy. The problem is not so much in the bare existence of a substantial amount of official anarchy as it is in the latent (and perhaps more insidious) effect it is having on the American people.

While in Los Angeles late in 1969, I was about to enter the south side of City Hall and I chanced to glance up. There, chiseled over the entrance, was a quote from Cicero. It read: "He that violates his oath profanes the divinity of faith itself." I had long suspected my own view that official lawlessness could be highly deleterious to any government was not a unique revelation, but I had no idea it had been around for two millenia. Of course, Cicero's view is a trifle more metaphysical than my own. I am not interested in the profaning of "faith itself"; my interest is in a more earthy kind of fidelity. Americans may still trust in God, but it is becoming more and more apparent that they are having less and less confidence in our system of government.

In the latter part of the 1960's, a phrase came to dominate much of the critical literature on the Johnson Administration and its policies. This phrase was "credibility gap," which was as newsworthy as another grand canyon, that between generations. Although the use of this phrase was usually directed toward President Johnson's administration—and the President him-self—it seems to me that it also described, quite accurately, a new, entirely different crisis in loyalty toward our governmental system. This crisis exists among substantial segments of our population—particularly the young—and particularly among them, those in college or just out of college.

Their anguish stems from the chasm between the expressed ideals of the American dream and the glaring factual inconsistencies of that dream. In-deed, to many in our future elite, the journey to American perfection has become a "bad trip." Any system is, of course, a close correspondence be-tween the words that express its goals and ideals and the actual practices and procedures in pursuit of them. Any system, and all its subsystems, find discrepancies between the ideal and the real. When it is infrequent or due to error, minor adjustments are sought; when it happens consistently, it pre-cipitates a crisis in the "efficiency" of the system and drastic remedies must be considered in order to avert disaster. When these discrepancies are the result of intentional actions, punishment or expulsion should be demanded by those in the system. When these intentional acts are widespread and systematic, and those in the system do not *act* to remedy the situation, talk of revolution becomes commonplace in some circles.

In America, the business world is rife with such hypocrisy—the promises of advertising are flimsy façades, easy to penetrate. The American family ideal has become a ruin, what with one-third of all marriages being shat-tered (and who knows how many more verging on collapse). And religion, which promises so much and delivers so little (particularly regarding the ideals of brotherhood and equality of opportunity), has come under greater and greater attack of late. Thus government is not the only institution in contemporary America that has come to be seen by many young Americans as being hypocritical at best, and evil at worst.

What the credibility gap means, as regarding the whole government sys-tem, is that we are dealing with deeply set, increasingly noticeable political cynicism. There is a tremendous amount of political alienation among many (if not most) of our very best students—among many of those upon whom America must count on to keep it strong and on a progressive path both at home and abroad. They find the establishment, the system, untrue to its own espoused goals and to its own espoused procedures, regulations, laws, and ordinances. Small wonder, then, that they scoff at slogans mouthed by government politicians entreating "law and order." Such outstanding and frequent breakdown of law and order within government itself can only increase the possibility of complete breakdown in the legitimacy of American government. That is why these alleged crimes (and when committed, they are crimes) by government officials are so severe a problem and why we must seriously consider entirely new structural checks as remedies.

It is important to recall that only several reported instances of potentially illegal behavior were necessary before Congress legislated the crime of crossing state lines to incite riots. It doesn't take much to get Congress to pass legistlation cracking down on rebels *outside* government. It shouldn't take more for Congress to restrain and punish those inside. In fact, it could be argued that it should take less of a threat of its happening to get remedial legislation for the latter crime, because of the potentially more subversive nature of its effects. In any event, it is surely time to ponder solutions to the problem, although some people have already contributed noteworthy thought along these lines.

TOWARD A SOLUTION

Eldridge Cleaver's contribution to America's button brigades is the classic aphorism that "if you are not a part of the solution, you are a part of the problem." And though most people settle into the problem groove, there is an increasing flow of words concerning what must be done about government anarchy. Some of the material is optimistic, some pessimistic. Some writers advocate playing by the rules of the game; some cry out for revolution. Some crave violence, some non-violence. Some see the best remedies as legal ones. Some feel the solution will grow in grassroots politics. The gamut of critics straddles all walks of political life from reactionary through the most vitriolic unofficial anarchist, and their view of solutions is similarly disparate.

It is not too surprising that government cliques, even though similarly aware of this problem, fail to see the truly pressing need for drastic reform. Moreover, they demonstrate great resistance to suggestions about external checks on governmental lawlessness. The usual recommendation of those in government is for better informal self-policing, though there is occasional agreement that some structural change by an offending agency might help to diminish the scope of the problem.

The first four items in the section on remedies present a few notions on how police can better police the police. They are by no means the sum total of suggestion for police control—they are, though, interesting ones we have run across lately. They reflect the problem and the present state of hope (or despair) in finding a satisfactory panacea. The following two articles are responses to two other instances of widely charged governmental lawlessness (the Newark Riot of 1967 and the flowering state of such practices throughout our prison system). The first is a set of recommendations for internal change of the New Jersey municipal court system as proposed by a select commission in 1968. The other is a professorial plea for some rethinking on how we should think about convicts which, if translated into law, would take a long stride toward eliminating systemically inspired unlawful punishments and debasements meted out in so many prisons.

Of course, there are many diehard cynics who are not overly enthused with the idea (dare we call it propaganda?) that self-correction is the best way to curb governmental anarchy. This is not to say that they consider self-imposed internal checks a total loss or that they believe that the establishments of each agency are absolutely incapable or unwilling to work a substantial diminution of lawlessness among some of their fellows and subordinates. But, pessimists that they are, they feel that inner reform would fall far short of the degree of effective restraint they would like to see imposed on the government. So they would like to supplement the self-reform by external checks as well. And, it is difficult to deny some validity to their fears and to much of the wisdom inherent in their recommendations.

Since contemporary America still bears great resemblance to that America one wag once defined as a "government of the lawyers, by the lawyers, and for the lawyers," one type of external check for which many feel greater and greater affinity are the courts. The essay by Steven Waldhorn argues that far more "legal intervention" will be necessary to curb the evil of "pathological bureaucratic" activities. He outlines a multitude of ways in which courts can be employed to accomplish this. To bolster this argument, we've taken the liberty of including a recent New Jersey appellate decision which forebade the state's attorney general from stimulating local police to trespass on political freedom. American courts have traditionally limited executive overzealousness in coping with what the executive considers demonic threats to public safety. Of course, there are many instances where American courts have *not* curbed the executive under similar circumstances.

Furthermore, and more directly to the point of this book, although the established criminal system may be used to prosecute a government offender for an alleged violation (rather than to simply restrain him), and indictments can be returned, one must turn wizard rather than researcher, in order to discover them in any quantity. They are, to be sure, the exception to the rule. We have included an article from the *Los Angeles Times,* noteworthy for the fact that such an indictment was the *first* of its kind in Los Angeles. For those searching the midnight skies for glittering omens, this might provide a sliver of hope. And as indictments of government officials for government anarchy are rare, their conviction on such charges is a rarity among rarities. But the absurdity of absurdities, one which might even dismay the most optimistic legal beagle, came in a *New York Times* news article reporting the conviction of an Arkansas warden who sanctioned unmentionable atrocities on prisoners. The sentencing judge decided to impose a paltry fine and forego *any* prison term for what many might believe to be an outrageously dubious reason. We have included an article explaining the judge's reasoning, which will add to the belief that even those convicted of governmental lawlessness of extraordinary heinousness are treated gingerly by their compatriots in the establishment.

It is not surprising then, that many concerned over the problem of government lawlessness are less than enthusiastic about the courts as a government watchdog, witness the acquittal of the four patrolmen indicted for murder in the infamous Algiers Motel incident. These are turning their heads to calls for extended community action of nonviolent *and* violent sorts.

Waldhorn notes that there are numerous ways in which community action can be and has been effective against a variety of administrative agencies throughout the United States. He suggests how this effectiveness can be increased. We have also included some other articles showing that young people are seeking methods to meet escalating police "busts" against their mushrooming subculture. One article describes the activities of "People's Defenders" in Los Angeles (Venice Beach) while another narrates the community reaction in the East Village (N.Y.C.) following the so-called "Tompkins' Park Debacle" of May 30, 1967.

Unfortunately, community action—particularly the non-violent breed— is bitterly chided by people most aggrieved by acts or systems or government lawlessness. But a few eloquent spokesmen for non-violence remain, despite the tragedy of Martin Luther King. Perhaps the leading advocate for peaceful community action is Cesar Chavez. Therefore, we have included an article describing his position along these lines.

But violence, as a response to government lawlessness, retains a strong appeal. And it is preached and practiced in a variety of ways. One way is *within* the system. This is the use of force to restrain government lawlessness by the use of the "citizen's arrest." And though many might scoff at the potential success of this tactic, we have included an article on one of the most highly successful attempts at citizen's arrest in recent years, that of Reies Tijerinas's courthouse raid in New Mexico in 1968. Though certain to raise the level of violence in the confrontation between government and some citizens, "citizen's arrest" seems infinitely superior a method to solving the problem than one calling for guerilla warfare and calculated acts of terror. As examples of the rhetoric of violence, we have included LeRoi Jones's famous Evergreen poem and a *Newsweek* article describing the reactions of certain black leaders in Detroit to the acquittal of Detroit Patrolman Ronald August in 1969 for murder charges against him arising out of that same Algiers Motel incident.

We conclude this section—and the book—on an optimistic note. For there has been one method that has worked very well in certain parts of this world and which many people believe to be extremely useful for curbing government lawlessness. We refer to the Scandanavian Ombudsman technique. We didn't think it necessary to choose an essay that went into great length on the merit of the proposal because we think there is so little chance that an alien method would be widely adopted in America. There has been great debate, but only Hawaii, of the fifty states, has seen fit to give the method a try up to the time this book is going to press. Besides, let us face the truth; it is a device that has limited practice even in Denmark. The problem of government lawlessness—as alleged to exist in America—needs far more than a simple Ombudsman. It needs a lot of imagination to drum up a lot of solution. But since necessity is the mother of invention, we need first to agree that the necessity exists. That is the burden of this book.

Frankly, we are not very impressed by any single proposal, in and of itself. Each has a gram of value to it, but each is woefully insufficient of itself. Such is the evaluation of the *Chicago Journalism Review* as they considered the available remedies to curb alleged police lawlessness—and thought of ways to improve them. Worse still, some proposed solutions would probably result in a more loathsome disease than the malady they are supposed to overcome. Being true to the tenets of wishy-washy liberalism, we suggest that many flowers be allowed to bloom. We know that the man who popularized this pleasant metaphor, Mao-Tse-Tung, is not considered by too many to be a wishy-washy liberal, but he must have once suffered a lapse into a chronic revisionism that produced this ill-starred doctrine. In any event, we happen to think that *all* remedies should be recommended (short of terrorism and guerilla warfare), and that many groups are necessary, working along a wide front, to bring about a deep and abiding set of changes in our laws and in our political system so that "government outlawry"—or "official rebellion"—might be greatly diminished, if not eliminated.

We also think that other changes in the law and the system are sorely needed before any of this can be accomplished. Primary among the changes that are essential would be a Uniform Government Outlaw Law that must be drafted, submitted to, and passed by state legislatures. Also, we must have a federal law that protects against such situations that are federal in nature or of an essentially interstate character. We are aware that there already are laws on the books that can encompass many of the crimes committed by government officials *if* they are prosecuted. However these laws have been around for a long time and they have lacked enforcement. One option is to pressure the existing mechanisms to execute these laws. But it is harder to influence bureaucracies than to force legislatures to admit the existence of this evil and to pass one omnibus bill to take care of it. Special machinery, new machinery, streamlined machinery, must be constructed to cope with it. When machinery has been unused for so long, the rust may be too thick to clean without damaging the machinery itself. Democratic, not bureaucratic, politics is the only truly effective way.

By stating the problem in all its perplexing complexity, we hope this book can become a part of some future solution. For we guess that we are more trapped by the system than we would like to be; copping out would be far more fun. Perhaps that's why we included Tom Wolfe's description of Ken Kesey's greatest performance. Ah, if only we could all really say: ". . . Hawonkafuckit . . . friends . . ."

I   POLICE

TOM HAYDEN

Excerpts from *Rebellion in Newark*

. . . The two troopers . . . looked at each other. Then one trooper who had a rifle shot Jimmy from about three feet away. . . . While Jimmy lay on the floor, the same trooper started to shoot Jimmy some more with the rifle. As he fired . . . he yelled "Die, you dirty bastard, die you dirty nigger, die, die. . . ." At this point a Newark policeman walked in and asked what happened. I saw the troopers look at each other and smile. . . .

The trooper who shot Jimmy remained . . . took a knife out of his own pocket and put it in Jimmy's hand.

Shortly after three men came in with a stretcher. One said, "they really laid some lead on his ass.". . . He asked the state trooper what happened. The trooper said, "He came at me with a knife.". . .

[We remained where we were] for about fifteen minutes, then I got up and walked to the window and knocked a board down, — and — came over to the window. One state trooper and two National Guardsmen came to the window and said, "Come out or we are going to start shooting.". . .

A National Guardsman said, "What do you want us to do, kill all you Negroes?" I saw a Newark policeman say: "We are going to do it anyway, we might as well take care of these three now." I saw the Newark policeman go over to——, point a pistol at his head and say: "How do you feel?" Then he started laughing. . . .

For anyone who wonders whether this is an exaggerated youthful horror story, the photographs of James Rutledge's chest and head are available from his mother. There were forty-five bulletholes in his head and body.

Clearly the evidence points to a military massacre and suppression in Newark rather than to a two-sided war. This was not only the conclusion of the Negroes in the ghetto but of private Newark lawyers, professors of constitutional law and representatives of the state American Civil Liberties Union. They have charged that the police were the instrument of a conspiracy "to engage in a pattern of systematic violence, terror, abuse, intimidation, and humiliation" to keep Negroes second-class citizens. The police, according to the lawyers' statement, "seized on the initial disorders as an opportunity and pretext to perpetrate the most horrendous and widespread killing, violence, torture, and intimidation, not in response to any crime or civilian disorder, but as a violent demonstration of the powerlessness of the plaintiffs and their class. . . ."

Thus it seems to many that the military, especially the Newark police, not only triggered the riot by beating a cab-driver but then created a climate of opinion that supported the use of all necessary force to suppress the riot. The force used by police was not in response to snipers, looting, and burning, but in retaliation against the successful uprising of Wednesday and Thursday nights.

Items from *Report for Action*
GOVERNOR'S SELECT COMMISSION ON CIVIL DISORDER OF NEW JERSEY

The amount of ammunition expended by police forces was out of all proportion to the mission assigned to them. All police forces lacked an adequate system of ammunition control. No proper procedures had been established for dispensing and accounting for the expenditure of ammunition. The use of personal weapons by members of the Newark Police Department created special problems in this area and should be condemned.

The technique of employing heavy return fire at suspected sniper locations proved tragic and costly.

The heavy firing by police elements against suspected snipers makes it difficult to determine the extensiveness of sniping. There may have been some organized sniping activity once the riot had reached its Friday peak.

There is evidence of prejudice against Negroes during the riot on the part of various police and National Guard elements. This resulted in the use of excessive and unjustified force and other abuses against Negro citizens.

The damage caused within a few hours early Sunday morning, July 16, to a large number of stores marked with "Soul" signs to depict non-white ownership and located in a limited area reflects a pattern of police action for which there is no possible justification. Testimony strongly suggests that State Police elements were mainly responsible with some participation by

From *Report for Action*, Governor's Select Commission on Civil Disorder of New Jersey, 1968, p. 143.

National Guardsmen. These raids resulted in personal suffering and economic damage to innocent small businessmen and property owners who have a stake in law and order and who had not participated in any unlawful act. It embittered the Negro community as a whole at a time when the disorders had begun to ebb.

The evidence presented to the Commission does not support the thesis of a conspiracy or plan to initiate the Newark riot.

Dementia in the Second City

The assault from the left was furious, fluky and bizarre. Yet the Chicago police department responded in a way that could only be characterized as sanctioned mayhem. With billy clubs, tear gas and Mace, the blue-shirted, blue-helmeted cops violated the civil rights of countless innocent citizens and contravened every accepted code of professional police discipline.

No one could accuse the Chicago cops of discrimination. They savagely attacked hippies, yippies, New Leftists, revolutionaries, dissident Democrats, newsmen, photographers, passers-by, clergymen and at least one cripple. Winston Churchill's journalist grandson got roughed up. *Playboy's* Hugh Hefner took a whack on the backside (*see Press*). The police even victimized a member of the British Parliament, Mrs. Anne Kerr, a vacationing Laborite who was Maced outside the Conrad Hilton and hustled off to the lockup.

Creative Warlord

"The force used was the force that was necessary," insisted Police Superintendent James Conlisk Jr. He could point to the fortunate fact that no one was killed. He also pointed out—almost with pride—that the casualties included 152 cops. Yet the cops' excesses during the Democratic Convention were not basically Conlisk's doing. Chicago is Mayor Richard J. Daley's satrapy.

Daley takes a fierce, eccentric pride in Chicago. For 13 years, he has ruled his province like a Chinese warlord. The last of America's big-city bosses, the jowly, irascible mayor has on the whole been a creative autocrat, lacing his megalopolis with freeways, pulling in millions in federal spending.

Daley is also something of an original. In a city with as robust a tradition of political corruption as Boston or New York, he has maintained a pristine record of personal honesty. Yet, like any other expert monarch, he has always known where and how to tolerate corruption within his realm. The son of a sheet-metal worker, Daley grew up in the gritty district of Bridgeport, where he continues to live in a modest bungalow. After starting out as a secretary to the city council at 25, Daley scrambled upward through the party ranks. Hence his understanding of Chicago's muscles and nerves is deeply intuitive. But it is growing archaic, as the mayor's lines to the Negro community atrophy and he continues to rule in the personalistic style of a benevolent Irish despot of the wards.

Daley nonetheless retains formidable influence within the Democratic Party. Thanks to his control of the state government and delegation, King Richard is one of the most assiduously courted Democratic politicians in the country. As Robert Kennedy said last spring: "Dick Daley means the ball game."

It was through such clout that he secured the Democratic convention for Chicago. However, Lyndon Johnson and other party leaders are equally to blame. They wanted the convention in Chicago this year in large part because they felt that it was the one city where the authorities could deal successfully with the planned disruptions. Daley thought so as well.

Bristling Camp

Some Democratic officials sensed disaster. First an electrical workers' strike ruined prospects for adequate television coverage of the streets, which Daley may not have wanted anyway. The strike, called 14 weeks before the convention, also prevented the installation of telephones and seriously impeded the candidates' operations. Then, nine days before the convention opened, drivers for the city's two major cab companies struck. Racial violence, which mercifully never erupted, was a real prospect. So were angry demonstrations by the young.

But the mayor had his way with the party. "Law and order will be maintained," he repeated ritualistically. He put his 11,900-man police force on twelve-hour shifts, called up more than 5,000 Illinois National Guard troops. In addition, some 6,500 federal troops were flown in. Daley turned Chicago into a bristling armed camp, with a posse of more than 23,000 at the ready. The convention hall was protected by barbed wire and packed with cops and security agents. WELCOME TO PRAGUE, said demonstrators' signs.

No Amenities

Daley refused the protesters permission to sleep on the grass of Chicago's Lincoln Park, a 1,185-acre expanse on the North Side. Critics of the cops

pointed out that the site was ideal for the dissidents; it would also have
been ideal for the police, who could have left the kids alone and stood
guard on the fringes of the park until the soldiers of dissent got bored and
left or until the convention was over. It might not have worked out that way,
since many of the protesters were fiercely determined to find trouble, but
at least the notion offered a better chance of avoiding violence. Had Daley
been gifted with either humane imagination or a sense of humor, he would
have arranged to welcome the demonstrators, cosset them with amenities
like portable toilets, as the Government did during the Washington civil
rights march of 1963. Instead, Daley virtually invited violence.

The police were not unhappy. Daley had prepared them last April, in the
wake of the riots following Martin Luther King's assassination, when he
ordered the cops to "shoot to kill" arsonists and to "shoot to maim or cripple"
looters. Chicago police theoretically receive regular in-service riot training,
but in fact the training consists largely of reading general departmental
orders rather than intensive drilling.

Bloodletting

Fortunately, there was no shooting. The demonstrators constantly taunted
the police and in some cases deliberately disobeyed reasonable orders. Most
of the provocations were verbal—screams of "Pig!" and fouler epithets. Many
cops seemed unruffled by the insults. Policeman John Gruber joked: "We
kind of like the word pig. Some of us answer our officers 'Oink, oink, sir,'
just to show it doesn't bother us." The police reacted more angrily when
the demonstrators sang *God Bless America* or recited "I pledge allegiance
to the flag."

In some of the wilder fighting, the demonstrators hurled bricks, bottles
and nail-studded golf balls at the police lines. During the first three days,
the cops generally reacted only with tear gas and occasional beatings. But
on Wednesday night, as the convention gathered to nominate Hubert
Humphrey, the police had a cathartic bloodletting. Outraged when the
protesters lowered a U.S. flag during a rally in Grant Park beside Lake
Michigan, the cops hurled tear gas into the crowd.

The demonstrators, bent upon parading to the convention hall (Daley
had refused a permit), regrouped in front of the Hilton, where they were
surrounded by phalanxes of cops. Police warned the demonstrators to clear
the streets, waited for five minutes for several busloads of reinforcements to
arrive. And then the order was given.

Violent Orgy

Chicago cops are built like beer trucks. They flailed blindly into the crowd
of some 3,000, then ranged onto the sidewalks to attack on-lookers. In a

pincer movement, they trapped some 150 people against the wall of the hotel. A window of the Hilton's Haymarket lounge gave way, and about ten of the targets spilled into the lounge after the shards of glass. A squad of police pursued them inside and beat them. Two bunny-clad waitresses took one look and capsized in a dead faint. By now the breakdown of police discipline was complete. Bloodied men and women tried to make their way into the hotel lobby. Upstairs on the 15th floor, aides in the McCarthy head-quarters set up a makeshift hospital.

The onslaught ended half an hour later, with about 200 arrested and hundreds injured. Elsewhere, the confrontation continued through the night. Then at 5 a.m. on Friday, with the convention ended, eleven policemen swarmed up to the McCarthy headquarters. They claimed that the volun-teers had tossed smoked fish, ashtrays and beer cans at the helmeted cops below. With neither evidence nor search warrants, they clubbed McCarthy campaign workers. One cop actually broke his billy club on a volunteer's skull. Daley stood by his angry defense of his cops' conduct against the "terrorists," who, he snarled, "use the foulest of language that you wouldn't hear in a brothel house."

The demonstrators had chanted the night before: "The whole world is watching!" And it was. Newspapers and television commentators from Moscow to Tokyo reacted with revulsion to the orgy of violence in Ameri-ca's Second City. Thanks to Mayor Daley, not only Chicago but the rest of the U.S. as well was pictured as a police state. That impression may be unfair to a handsome and hospitable city, but it will linger long after Dick Daley's reign.

Items from The Walker Report

A SUMMARY

During the week of the Democratic National Convention, the Chicago police were the targets of mounting provocation by both word and act. It took the form of obscene epithets, and of rocks, sticks, bathroom tiles and even human feces hurled at police by demonstrators. Some of these acts had been planned; others were spontaneous or were themselves provoked by police action. Furthermore, the police had been put on edge by widely published threats of attempts to disrupt both the city and the Convention.

From *Rights in Conflict* by the Walker Commission, pp. 1-11. Bantam Books, Inc., 1968.

That was the nature of the provocation. The nature of the response was unrestrained and indiscriminate police violence on many occasions, particularly at night.

That violence was made all the more shocking by the fact that it was often inflicted upon persons who had broken no law, disobeyed no order, made no threat. These included peaceful demonstrators, onlookers, and large numbers of residents who were simply passing through, or happened to live in, the areas where confrontations were occurring.

Newsmen and photographers were singled out for assault, and their equipment deliberately damaged. Fundamental police training was ignored; and officers, when on the scene, were often unable to control their men. As one police officer put it: "What happened didn't have anything to do with police work."

The violence reached its culmination on Wednesday night.

A report prepared by an inspector from the Los Angeles Police Department, present as an official observer, while generally praising the police restraint he had observed in the parks during the week, said this about the events that night:

> There is no question but that many officers acted without restraint and exerted force beyond that necessary under the circumstances. The leadership at the point of conflict did little to prevent such conduct and the direct control of officers by first line supervisors was virtually non-existent.

He is referring to the police-crowd confrontation in front of the Conrad Hilton Hotel. Most Americans know about it, having seen the 17-minute sequence played and replayed on their television screens.

But most Americans do not know that the confrontation was followed by even more brutal incidents in the Loop side streets. Or that it had been preceded by comparable instances of indiscriminate police attacks on the North Side a few nights earlier when demonstrators were cleared from Lincoln Park and pushed into the streets and alleys of Old Town.

How did it start? With the emergence long before convention week of three factors which figured significantly in the outbreak of violence. These were: threats to the city; the city's response; and the conditioning of Chicago police to expect that violence against demonstrators, as against rioters, would be condoned by city officials.

The threats to the City were varied. Provocative and inflammatory statements, made in connection with activities planned for convention week, were published and widely disseminated. There were also intelligence reports from informants.

Some of this information was absurd, like the reported plan to contaminate the city's water supply with LSD. But some were serious; and both were strengthened by the authorities' lack of any mechanism for distinguishing one from the other.

The second factor—the city's response—matched, in numbers and logistics at least, the demonstrators' threats.

The city, fearful that the "leaders" would not be able to control their followers, attempted to discourage an inundation of demonstrators by not granting permits for marches and rallies and by making it quite clear that the "law" would be enforced.

Government—federal, state and local—moved to defend itself from the threats, both imaginary and real. The preparations were detailed and far ranging: from stationing firemen at each alarm box within a six block radius of the Amphitheatre to staging U.S. Army armored personnel carriers in Soldier Field under Secret Service control. Six thousand Regular Army troops in full field gear, equipped with rifles, flame throwers, and bazookas were airlifted to Chicago on Monday, August 26. About 6,000 Illinois National Guard troops had already been activated to assist the 12,000 member Chicago Police Force.

Of course, the Secret Service could never afford to ignore threats of assassination of Presidential candidates. Neither could the city, against the background of riots in 1967 and 1968, ignore the ever-present threat of ghetto riots, possibly sparked by large numbers of demonstrators, during convention week.

The third factor emerged in the city's position regarding the riots following the death of Dr. Martin Luther King and the April 27th peace march to the Civic Center in Chicago.

The police were generally credited with restraint in handling the first riots —but Mayor Daley rebuked the Superintendent of Police. While it was later modified, his widely disseminated "shoot to kill arsonists and shoot to maim looters" order undoubtedly had an effect.

The effect 'on police became apparent several weeks later, when they attacked demonstrators, bystanders and media representatives at a Civic Center peace march. There were published criticisms—but the city's response was to ignore the police violence.

That was the background. On August 18, 1968, the advance contingent of demonstrators arrived in Chicago and established their base, as planned, in Lincoln Park on the city's Near North Side. Throughout the week, they were joined by others—some from the Chicago area, some from states as far away as New York and California. On the weekend before the convention began, there were about 2,000 demonstrators in Lincoln Park; the crowd grew to about 10,000 by Wednesday.

There were, of course, the hippies—the long hair and love beads, the calculated unwashedness, the flagrant banners, the open lovemaking and disdain for the constraints of conventional society. In dramatic effect, both visual and vocal, these dominated a crowd whose members actually differed widely in physical appearance, in motivation, in political affiliation, in philosophy. The crowd included Yippies come to "do their thing," youngsters working for a political candidate, professional people with dissenting political views, anarchists and determined revolutionaries, motorcycle gangs, black activists, young thugs, police and secret service undercover agents. There were demonstrators waving the Viet Cong flag and the red flag of revolution and there were the simply curious who came to watch and, in many cases, became willing or unwilling participants.

To characterize the crowd, then, as entirely hippy-Yippie, entirely "New Left," entirely anarchist, or entirely youthful political dissenters is both wrong and dangerous. The stereotyping that did occur helps to explain the emotional reaction of both police and public during and after the violence that occurred.

Despite the presence of some revolutionaries, the vast majority of the demonstrators were intent on expressing by peaceful means their dissent either from society generally or from the administration's policies in Vietnam.

Most of those intending to join the major protest demonstrations scheduled during convention week did not plan to enter the Amphitheatre and disrupt the proceedings of the Democratic convention, did not plan aggressive acts of physical provocation against the authorities, and did not plan to use rallies of demonstrators to stage an assault against any person, institution, or place of business. But while it is clear that most of the protesters in Chicago had no intention of initiating violence, this is not to say that they did not expect it to develop.

It was the clearing of the demonstrators from Lincoln Park that led directly to the violence: symbolically, it expressed the city's opposition to the protesters; literally, it forced the protesters into confrontation with police in Old Town and the adjacent residential neighborhoods.

The Old Town area near Lincoln Park was a scene of police ferocity exceeding that shown on television on Wednesday night. From Sunday night through Tuesday night, incidents of intense and indiscriminate violence occurred in the streets after police had swept the park clear of demonstrators.

Demonstrators attacked too. And they posed difficult problems for police as they persisted in marching through the streets, blocking traffic and intersections. But it was the police who forced them out of the park and into the neighborhood. And on the part of the police there was enough wild club swinging, enough cries of hatred, enough gratuitous beating to make the conclusion inescapable that individual policemen, and lots of them, committed violent acts far in excess of the requisite force for crowd dispersal or arrest. To read dispassionately the hundreds of statements describing at firsthand the events of Sunday and Monday nights is to become convinced of the presence of what can only be called a police riot.

Here is an eyewitness talking about Monday night:

> The demonstrators were forced out onto Clark Street and once again a traffic jam developed. Cars were stopped, the horns began to honk, people couldn't move, people got gassed inside their cars, people got stoned inside their cars, police were the object of stones, and taunts, mostly taunts. As you must understand, most of the taunting of the police was verbal. There were stones thrown of course, but for the most part it was verbal. But there were stones being thrown and of course the police were responding with tear gas and clubs and everytime they could get near enough to a demonstrator they hit him.
>
> But again you had this police problem within—this really turned into a police problem. They pushed everybody out of the park, but this night there were a lot more people in the park than there had been during the previous night and Clark Street was just full of people and in addition now was full of gas because the police were using gas on a much larger scale this night. So the police were faced with the task, which took them about an hour or so, of hitting people over the head and gassing them enough to get them out of Clark Street, which they did.

But police action was not confined to the necessary force, even in clearing the park.

A young man and his girl friend were both grabbed by officers. He screamed, "We're going, we're going," but they threw him into the pond. The officers grabbed the girl, knocked her to the ground, dragged her along the embankment and hit her with their batons on her head, arms, back and legs. The boy tried to scramble up the embankment to her, but police shoved him back in the water at least twice. He finally got to her and tried to pull her in the water, away from the police. He was clubbed on the head five or six times. An officer shouted, "Let's get the fucking bastards!" but the boy pulled her in the water and the police left.

Like the incident described above, much of the violence witnessed in Old Town that night seems malicious or mindless:

> There were pedestrians. People who were not part of the demonstra-tion were coming out of a tavern to see what the demonstration was . . . and the officers indiscriminately started beating everybody on the street who was not a policeman.

Another scene:

> There was a group of about six police officers that moved in and started beating two youths. When one of the officers pulled back his

nightstick to swing, one of the youths grabbed it from behind and started beating on the officer. At this point about ten officers left everybody else and ran after this youth, who turned down Wells and ran to the left.

But the officers went to the right, picked up another youth, assuming he was the one they were chasing, and took him into an empty lot and beat him. And when they got him to the ground, they just kicked him ten times—the wrong youth, the innocent youth who had been standing there.

A federal legal official relates an experience of Tuesday evening.

> I then walked one block north where I met a group of 12-15 policemen. I showed them my identification and they permitted me to walk with them. The police walked one block west. Numerous people were watching us from their windows and balconies. The police yelled profanities at them, taunting them to come down where the police would beat them up. The police stopped a number of people on the street demanding identification. They verbally abused each pedestrian and pushed one or two without hurting them. We walked back to Clark Street and began to walk north where the police stopped a number of people who appeared to be protesters, and ordered them out of the area in a very abusive way. One protester who was walking in the opposite direction was kneed in the groin by a policeman who was walking towards him. The boy fell to the ground and swore at the policeman who picked him up and threw him to the ground. We continued to walk toward the command post. A derelict who appeared to be very intoxicated, walked up to the policeman and mumbled something that was incoherent. The policeman pulled from his belt a tin container and sprayed its contents into the eyes of the derelict, who stumbled around and fell on his face.

It was on these nights that the police violence against media representatives reached its peak. Much of it was plainly deliberate. A newsman was pulled aside on Monday by a detective acquaintance of his who said: "The word is being passed to get newsmen." Individual newsmen were warned, "You take my picture tonight and I'm going to get you." Cries of "get the camera" preceded individual attacks on photographers.

A newspaper photographer describes Old Town on Monday at about 9:00 p.m.:

> When the people arrived at the intersection of Wells and Division, they were not standing in the streets. Suddenly a column of policemen ran out from the alley. They were reinforcements. They were under control but there seemed to be no direction. One man was yelling, "Get them up on the sidewalks, turn them around." Very suddenly the police charged the people on the sidewalks and began beating their heads. A line of camera-

men was "trapped" along with the crowd along the sidewalks, and the police went down the line chopping away at the cameras.

A network cameraman reports that on the same night:

> I just saw this guy coming at me with his nightstick and I had the camera up. The tip of his stick hit me right in the mouth, then I put my tongue up there and I noticed that my tooth was gone. I turned around then to try to leave and then this cop came up behind me with his stick and he jabbed me in the back.
>
> All of a sudden these cops jumped out of the police cars and started just beating the hell out of people. And before anything else happened to me, I saw a man holding a Bell & Howell camera with big wide letters on it, saying "CBS." He apparently had been hit by a cop. And cops were standing around and there was blood streaming down his face. Another policeman was running after me and saying, "Get the fuck out of here." And I heard another guy scream, "Get their fucking cameras." And the next thing I know I was being hit on the head, and I think on the back, and I was just forced down on the ground at the corner of Division and Wells.

If the intent was to discourage coverage, it was successful in at least one case. A photographer from a news magazine says that finally, "I just stopped shooting, because every time you push the flash, they look at you and they are screaming about, 'Get the fucking photographers and get the film.'"

There is some explanation for the media-directed violence. Camera crews on at least two occasions did stage violence and fake injuries. Demonstrators did sometimes step up their activities for the benefit of TV cameras. Newsmen and photographers' blinding lights did get in the way of police clearing streets, sweeping the park and dispersing demonstrators. Newsmen did, on occasion, disobey legitimate police orders to "move" or "clear the streets." News reporting of events did seem to the police to be anti-Chicago and anti-police.

But was the response appropriate to the provocation?

Out of 300 newsmen assigned to cover the parks and streets of Chicago during convention week, more than 60 (about 20%) were involved in incidents resulting in injury to themselves, damage to their equipment, or their arrest. Sixty-three newsmen were physically attacked by police; in 13 of these instances, photographic or recording equipment was intentionally damaged.

The violence did not end with either demonstrators or newsmen on the North Side on Sunday, Monday and Tuesday. It continued in Grant Park on Wednesday. It occurred on Michigan Avenue in front of the Conrad

Hilton Hotel, as already described. A high-ranking Chicago police commander admits that on that occasion the police "got out of control." This same commander appears in one of the most vivid scenes of the entire week, trying desperately to keep individual policemen from beating demonstrators as he screams, "For Christ's sake, stop it!"

Thereafter, the violence continued on Michigan Avenue and on the side streets running into Chicago's Loop. A federal official describes how it began:

> I heard a 10-1 call [policeman in trouble] on either my radio or one of the other hand sets carried by men with me and then heard "Car 100 —sweep." With a roar of motors, squads, vans and three-wheelers came from east, west and north into the block north of Jackson. The crowd scattered. A big group ran west on Jackson, with a group of blue shirted policemen in pursuit, beating at them with clubs. Some of the crowd would jump into doorways and the police would rout them out. The action was very tough. In my judgment, unnecessarily so. The police were hitting with a vengeance and quite obviously with relish. . . .

What followed was a club-swinging melee. Police ranged the streets striking anyone they could catch. To be sure, demonstrators threw things at policemen and at police cars; but the weight of violence was overwhelmingly on the side of the police. A few examples will give the flavor of that night in Chicago:

"At the corner of Congress Plaza and Michigan," states a doctor, "was gathered a group of people, numbering between thirty and forty. They were trapped against a railing [along a ramp leading down from Michigan Avenue to an underground parking garage] by several policemen on motorcycles. The police charged the people on motorcycles and struck about a dozen of them, knocking several of them down. About twenty standing there jumped over the railing. On the other side of the railing was a three-to-four-foot drop. None of the people who were struck by the motorcycles appeared to be seriously injured. However, several of them were limping as if they had been run over on their feet."

A UPI reporter witnessed these attacks, too. He relates in his statement that one officer, "with a smile on his face and a fanatical look in his eyes, was standing on a three-wheel cycle, shouting, 'Wahoo, wahoo,' and trying to run down people on the sidewalk." The reporter says he was chased thirty feet by the cycle.

A priest who was in the crowd says he saw a "boy, about fourteen or fifteen, white, standing on top of an automobile yelling something which was unidentifiable. Suddenly a policeman pulled him down from the car and beat him to the ground by striking him three or four times with a nightstick. Other police joined in . . . and they eventually shoved him to a police van.

"A well-dressed woman saw this incident and spoke angrily to a nearby police captain. As she spoke, another policeman came up from behind her and sprayed something in her face with an aerosol can. He then clubbed her to the ground. He and two other policemen then dragged her along the ground to the same paddy wagon and threw her in."

"I ran west on Jackson," a witness states. "West of Wabash, a line of police stretching across both sidewalks and the street charged after a small group I was in. Many people were clubbed and maced as they ran. Some weren't demonstrators at all, but were just pedestrians who didn't know how to react to the charging officers yelling 'Police!' "

"A wave of police charged down Jackson," another witness relates. "Fleeing demonstrators were beaten indiscriminately and a temporary, makeshift first aid station was set up on the corner of State and Jackson. Two men lay in pools of blood, their heads severely cut by clubs. A minister moved amongst the crowd, quieting them, brushing aside curious onlookers, and finally asked a policeman to call an ambulance, which he agreed to do. . . ."

An Assistant U.S. Attorney later reported that "the demonstrators were running as fast as they could but were unable to get out of the way because of the crowds in front of them. I observed the police striking numerous individuals, perhaps 20 to 30. I saw three fall down and then overrun by the police. I observed two demonstrators who had multiple cuts on their heads. We assisted one who was in shock into a passer-by's car."

Police violence was a fact of convention week. Were the policemen who committed it a minority? It appears certain that they were—but one which has imposed some of the consequences of its actions on the majority, and certainly on their commanders. There has been no public condemnation of these violators of sound police procedures and common decency by either their commanding officers or city officials. Nor (at the time this Report is being completed—almost three months after the convention) has any disciplinary action been taken against most of them. That some policemen lost control of themselves under exceedingly provocative circumstances can perhaps be understood; but not condoned. If no action is taken against them, the effect can only be to discourage the majority of policemen who acted responsibly, and further weaken the bond between police and community.

Although the crowds were finally dispelled on the nights of violence in Chicago, the problems they represent have not been. Surely this is not the last time that a violent dissenting group will clash head-on with those whose duty it is to enforce the law. And the next time the whole world will still be watching.

SENATOR WAYNE MORSE

The Police State

It is well, perhaps, that the sad spectacle of events surrounding the 1968 Democratic Convention linger with us, however painful. Like few other events in American history, the battle of demonstrators and police in the Chicago streets has left us with questions so fundamental in their importance and so awesome in their implications that they plead the urgency of a national debate.

What is the role of the police in a free society? How far may enforcers of the law go before they are outside the law? From forcible suppression of dissent in the streets, how far away is suppression of dissent on the airwaves, in the newspapers and periodicals, in the streets and in our homes?

These are some of the questions raised by events in Chicago, and we must answer them now.

Americans are often fond of saying that we have "a government of laws and not of men." In Chicago, the axiom was reversed. The policeman is responsible for apprehending persons in apparent violation of the law. He cannot make laws. He cannot decide guilt. He cannot punish. He cannot administer retribution for ideas and actions that offend him personally. As Justice Holmes wrote, "If there is any principle of the Constitution that more imperatively calls for attachment than any other, it is the principle of free thought, not free thought for those who agree with us but freedom for the thought we hate."

The basic tactics of a police state—suppression of lawful dissent by force, punishment without due process—are death to a free society. Employment of such tactics, no matter where or under what circumstances, constitutes a grave threat to the very existence of that society, and the actions cannot go unchallenged. What happened in Chicago is an appalling portent of things to come. The portent must not be ignored. Within one week of the Chicago demonstrations, a group of off-duty, civilian-clothed policemen in New York attacked a handful of black militants awaiting lawful trial in a court of this land. It was an assault for which those policemen are as liable under the law as any other perpetrators of assault. When the protectors of the public

From *Law and Disorder*, Myrus and Joseph, Chicago 1968. Reprinted by permission.

become the public threat itself, the days of democracy are numbered. The concept of an orderly system of laws, justly conceived and justly administered, crumbles.

That there was provocation and incitement of the police in Chicago is incontrovertible. But the issue is whether or not there was action taken by some members—and I emphasize *some* members—of the Chicago police force that was in excess of their lawful powers. Millions witnessed these events on television here and throughout the world. There is no question that illegal assault by the police occurred, that their legal powers were exceeded, and that members of the Chicago police force, in the heat of passion, assigned themselves the roles of law enforcer, jury, judge and punisher.

As one who taught courses in the law of arrest, and for years taught the law of criminal procedure, I find it indisputable that the law of arrest does not give any law-enforcement officer the right to do more than arrest. The meaning of arrest within our legal codes is clear: it means to bring the accused person under custody, and once under custody and restraint, the police have no right beyond that point to engage in actions that amount to assault and battery. Any policeman who engages in that kind of outrage is exceeding his police authority, and his action must be restrained. The alternative to such restraint is replacement of the rule of law by the rule of the jungle and personal whim.

It is, at best, a dangerous hypocrisy to approve the punishment of demonstrators by unlawful means while simultaneously shouting for law and order. Justice is negated by unjust means, the law is crushed in the hands of vigilantes, and we find ourselves facing anarchy in pious masquerade as law enforcement. Demonstrators should be punished for their missteps, and the police must be punished for theirs, and by due process. In my home state of Oregon, officials who authorize or condone illegal police activities, such as occurred in Chicago, would be subject to recall.

The police state is neither able nor willing to recognize itself as such. Rarely can we find any member of the populace who approves of a "police state," and seldom do those who applaud illegal use of police power cast themselves in the role of the oppressed. When freedom of dissent and lawful assembly topples, it topples for everyone, and due process gives way to the vigilante route of mock justice and simple revenge. In the gradual evolution of a police state, the institutions of government become covert and indistinguishable. The lines of appeal disappear, responsibility is diffused, representation of the people is abandoned. The courts become simply an arm of the police, without regard for individual rights. The institution of government becomes a monolith, oppressive in its presence and irresponsible in its actions.

To assume that this cannot happen here is to ignore recent history. The report of the National Advisory Commission on Civil Disorders pointed out in detail that the role of the police in ghetto society is increasingly abrasive and unresponsive to the problems of the ghetto dweller.

The Chicago confrontation shows us that friction between citizens and police not only is at explosive proportions in the ghetto, but is now a significant factor in the broad middle class, affecting both young and old, white and black. The channels of communication and the foundations of respect between many citizens and the police are breaking down, and it is my belief that this disintegration is of paramount danger to the country.

We cannot learn the lessons of Chicago soon enough.

DAVID H. BAYLEY AND HAROLD MENDELSOHN

Police Brutality

The most dramatic charge that can be made against the police in their relations with the public is that of brutality. Most of the urban riots in recent years have had an alleged incident of police brutality as the pretext. Certainly charges of police brutality are not uncommon; they are reported almost daily in newspapers and on radio and television. While most people are aware of the issue, it is much more important to minorities. Forty-six percent of the majority population said they had heard charges of police brutality. Among Negroes 68% said they had heard such charges, and among the Spanish-named, 59%. Most people, regardless of community, got their information through the news media. However, the proportion of people in the minority communities who heard the charges from friends or neighbors was much greater than among Dominants. Where only 4% of the Dominants obtained their information from friends and neighbors, 30% of the Negroes and 12% of the Spanish-named had done so. Moreover, whereas only 4% of the Dominants had personal experience with police brutality, 9% of the Negroes and 15% of the Spanish-named had. There can be no doubt that minority communities are much more attuned to the issue than the majority community.

The police are aware of the charge too, indeed more than anyone else. Like the public, the mass media are their best source of information—22% cited this source. The next more important source was fellow police officers, who correspond to the "friends and neighbors" of the minority people. For policemen, like minority people, "police brutality" is an issue which is in the air they breathe; it is the stuff of daily conversation among their peers. Officers cited as their next most important sources of information about charges of police brutality, minority people, suspects, and arrested persons.

Before one can really deal with the issue, it is important to be clear about what "police brutality" is. It is not a straightforward category. Holding a suspect and beating him with a rubber hose would certainly be brutality. But is arm-twisting in order to get a person to enter a patrol car? Are threats, such as gestures with gun or nightstick, brutality? Bayard Rustin once said: "I don't know a Negro family that has not had a member who has not met with physical or spiritual brutality on the part of the police."[1] If brutality is synonymous with mistreatment of any kind, then verbal abuse, ridicule, malicious humor, denigrating epithets, and elaborate condescension would all qualify. People can certainly be hurt as deeply by being dismissed with contempt as by being struck or manhandled. In order to cope with the difficulty of defining police brutality, we asked respondents what they meant by it. As one would expect, the vast majority thought of the use of physical force, the doing of bodily harm. Most revealing, however, were the answers from minority people. Thirteen percent of the Negroes and 15% of the Spanish-named listed as police brutality not listening to the other side of the story, taking situations into their hands without consideration for the people involved, unfair use of authority and misuse of law. Furthermore, 3% of the Negroes and 5% of the Spanish-named cited unfriendliness, suspicion, and prejudice. Only 4% of the Dominants thought of these other activities as constituting police brutality. In fact, among Dominants the second most popular response (14%) was to deny that police brutality existed or to argue that force was necessary or that the charge was trumped up by criminals. Another 8% of the Dominants argued that, though physical mistreatment was what they meant by police brutality, it was for the most part provoked by the people dealt with by the police. In other words, Dominant citizens can hardly imagine brutality in any form other than physical violence, and many of them believe the whole issue is overdone. The gap between minority and majority perspectives revealed by these responses should give pause to even the most optimistic reformer of majority-minority relations.

1. Thomas R. Brooks, "Necessary Force—Or Police Brutality?" *New York Times Magazine*, December 5, 1965, 65.

One is justified in concluding that when people hear the phrase "police brutality," they have in mind by-and-large physical assaults. This is the meaning that will be adopted in the following discussion.

It should also be noted that police brutality is not just a descriptive category. Rather, it is a judgment made about the propriety of police behavior. Not all examples of the use of physical force by policemen are instances of brutality. The phrase connotes that what the police have done is unjustified, not required by circumstances. Since the use of the phrase implies a judgment, people may disagree profoundly about whether a particular incident, even though it involves the obvious use of force, is a case of brutality. Any discussion of police brutality is therefore encumbered by confusion about whether it applies to more than physical assaults and also by disagreement over what circumstances absolve the police from blame. Just as the content of police brutality is a function of perspective, and in turn, a consequence of social position in the community, so judgments about the circumstances that exculpate the police are also a function of perspective. The phrase "police brutality" must be used with great care, and people should not be at all surprised to discover that minority groups weigh it much differently than does the majority community.

The willingness to believe charges of police brutality leveled by minority individuals varies dramatically among ethnic groups. Only 8% of the Dominants said they were prepared to believe the frequent charges. Among Negroes, on the other hand, 37% said the charges were true, and among Spanish-named, 39%. The police were even more skeptical of minority charges than was the Dominant community as a whole: 88% of the officers said that less than 5% of the charges were true. Whatever the amount of truth actually in the charges, the fact remains that a world of difference separates the perspectives of the minority and majority communities on this issue. Minority people are prone to believe; majority people are prone to discount. The result is that majority people dismiss minority claims as exaggerated; minority people conclude they cannot get a sympathetic hearing from the majority community.

Analysis shows no evidence that class affects whether a person has heard charges of brutality or his willingness to accept them as true. Ethnicity, not class, is the deciding variable. We do find, however, that Negro and Spanish-named men are more apt to have heard of police brutality than women. This may simply mean they are more sensitive to the issue than women.

Over twice as many Negroes as Dominants and over twice as many Spanish-named as Negroes claimed that they or someone in their family had been badly treated by the Denver police. The proportions were 4% for Dominants, 10% for Negroes, and 24% for the Spanish-named. The nature of the bad treatment varied according to ethnic group. Physical brutality in some form was more prominent among Negroes and Spanish-named. Sixty-one percent of the Negroes and 63% of the Spanish-named who had been badly treated gave this as their reason; only 26% of the Dominants said physical brutality was the problem. Moreover, whereas 36% of the Dominants thought that their bad treatment was a matter of the police being unfair or unwarranted in their action, only 22% of the Negroes and 21% of the Spanish-named gave this as their reason. Thus, minority individuals experience a higher incidence of what they consider to be bad treatment and the forms this treatment assumes are more serious than those experienced by Dominants. Physical abuse is more commonly experienced by minorities.

Analysis reveals no important associations between having experienced bad treatment and social background. Class is unrelated to the incidence of bad treatment. This finding gives credence to the charge of well-to-do Negroes with professional status that they are subjected to the same kind of humiliations that all Negroes experience. Professional attainments do not hide the color of their skins. Young Negro men (teen-agers and twenty-one to thirty years old) have a higher incidence of being badly treated than older people. This may indicate that they are in fact singled out for harassment more often than others or that they have a much greater sensitivity to the slights of police contact.[2] Whichever the explanation, young Negroes have had experiences with the police that do not dispose them favorably toward policemen.

It should be noted that the vast majority of minority people have *not* been badly treated by the police. This does not excuse the bad treatment which has been meted out, but it does put into perspective the magnitude of the problem. Responses from the intensive survey of minorities reveal a more somber picture. Among the minority members who had contact with the police, 60% of the Negroes and 45% of the Spanish-named said the treatment was all right. Another 8% of the Negroes and 7% of the Spanish-named said it was all right but cold and distant. Twenty-seven percent of the Negroes and 36.8% of the Spanish-named said they had been treated with disrespect, cursed, manhandled, or roughed up. Thus, while most minority people cannot complain about discriminatory police treatment at first hand, many of them can—and the proportion is far larger than among Dominants. These facts are hardly a matter for congratulation of policemen.

When unfair police treatment of minorities is being discussed, what seems to be troubling minority people most is not the outright use of an unwar-

2. Teen-age Negroes have complained about being harassed by the police. They complained especially about being treated as eternal objects of suspicion, frequently being stopped for questioning or treated curtly, authoritatively, or rudely. See *The Denver Post*, August 22, 1967, p. 2.

ranted amount of force. Rather, they are more concerned about harassment in the form of street interrogations and arrests on spurious grounds. For example, in the intensive minority survey, when respondents were asked to specify the ways in which police made life more difficult for Negroes and the Spanish-named, the most common complaint was that of harassment (21% of Negroes and 26% of Spanish-named). Outright brutality was fourth in the Negro list, accounting for 4% of the total, and fourth in the Spanish-named list, accounting for 4% of the total. In short, minorities are sensitive about their position; they know they are peculiarly visible. Policemen reinforce this feeling when they appear to single minority people out for special attention. Even if policemen were, therefore, to abandon any form of physical coercion directed at minority people, wariness of the police would continue to remain strong among minorities as long as the police appeared to be looking upon them with chronic suspicion.

Policemen proved to be surprisingly candid about their own personal experience with police brutality. Fifty-three percent of the officers said that they had personally witnessed an incident that someone might consider to constitute police brutality. A third of these incidents the officers dismissed as involving the necessary, and justifiable, application of force, usually in connection with making an arrest. But it is significant that 27% of all officers interviewed had witnessed an incident which they considered involved harassment or the excessive use of force. Curiously enough, the proportion of personal experience with "brutality" is approximately the same among policemen as it is among minority people.

PAUL CHEVIGNY

The Police and Society

. . . The anatomy of street-corner abuses is unchanging. The policeman on the beat sees his job to be one of maintaining tranquillity and perpetuating the established routine. Any person out of the ordinary is suspicious; if he is recognizably deviant, then he is potentially criminal. Potentially criminal also, and a severe threat to good order, is any challenge to the policeman's authority. A challenge may come either from the deviant, simply by his failure to respond to an officer's order, or from the ordinary citizen who is openly defiant. In either case, the challenge will be met by anger and one or more weapons out of the arsenal of legal sanctions, from a summons up through summary corporal punishment. Criminal charges, beginning with disorderly conduct and ranging up to felonious assault, are commonly laid to cover the actions of the policeman and to punish the offender. In the eyes of the police, arrest is practically tantamount to guilt, and the police will supply the allegations necessary for conviction; the courts are treated as a mere adjunct to their purpose. Distortion of the facts becomes the most pervasive and the most significant of abuses. The police ethic justifies any action which is intended to maintain order or to convict any wrongdoer (i.e., anyone actually or potentially guilty of crime). In studying search and seizure, for example, we found that the police tend to justify a search made "in good faith"—really looking for a crime—regardless of whether it is a lawful search or not. Once again, the facts are distorted so as to justify the search in the eyes of the courts, although there is less distortion in connection with house searches than with searches of persons on the street.

We have seen that some abuses do not precisely fit our conception of the tendencies in police behavior that give rise to abuses—those, for example, which are committed for personal reasons like family revenge or professional advancement. Although it is significant that these are the abuses which are generally condemned by policemen themselves, it is important to observe that such actions shade off subtly into duty-oriented abuses, because the Department encourages the man to identify himself with his authority. Other abuses, such as those that occur during mass police action, seem to be similar in origin to ordinary street abuses, but are distorted out of all recognition by mass frenzy. Finally, a few abuses are chronic because they are systematically encouraged by the Department. In condoning systematic abuses, the Department itself acts upon much the same rationale that the individual policeman uses to justify isolated street abuses. When the Department authorizes an action in violation of due process, such as a roundup of prostitutes, it does so to preserve order ("a clean city") and to harass a group of people who are considered undesirable. The chief difference between isolated and systematic abuses is that there is less distortion of the facts about the latter, because the individual officers find it unnecessary and thus make no attempt to cover their own actions. Except in the case of systematic harassment, then, distortion of fact is the thread that runs through all abuses, however different they may seem. The distortion of fact, and indeed every abuse, is rationalized by the need to maintain authority and catch wrongdoers.

The tendencies in police behavior which give rise to abuses do form a sort of "police character": a man, suspicious of outsiders, who is concerned with order, reacts aggressively to threats to his authority, and regards every attempt to control that authority with cynicism. Other authors have attempted to mold this character, or a similar one, into a sociological or psychological framework. Neiderhoffer, for example, has analyzed the policeman according to the characteristics of an "authoritarian personality." For our purposes, terms like this are tautological; the word "authoritarian" either reiterates what we know already about policemen, or else it is irrelevant. To get at the roots of police behavior, I should have to go to a deeper psychological level, and the fragmentary nature of the evidence collected here, together with the fragmentary nature of the available psychological studies, prevents me from performing the task adequately. It is enough here for us to know that the characteristic police reactions are a logical product of the police role (e.g. maintaining order) and the traditions of the Department (e.g. secrecy).

The important point for us here is that police abuses *do* form a pattern, and that they reveal one aspect of police character. Police abuses are a set of consistent responses in similar situations, and not very surprising responses at that. The policeman identifies with the office with which he is vested, and considers a threat to that office the most serious of threats to good order. It is misleading to say that his views are unlawful or unethical. They may participate in a different ethic, and perhaps even in a somewhat different law from the criminal law of the modern, liberal state, but unquestionably there are ethics and law at work here. It is a "good guys versus bad guys" ethic, free of the strictures of procedure: the person who is "wise to a cop" has no respect for authority and deserves to be punished. Deviants are undesirable, and the police should ride herd on them to keep them from intruding on the rest of society. A criminal ought to be caught and put in jail the quickest way that one can get him there.

Is this really such an unfamiliar canon of ethics? Doesn't it rather ring of the opinion reflected in most of our newspaper editorials and shared by thousands of citizens? We should realize that the appeals courts asks an extraordinary act of will from the policeman. They ask him to be concerned solely with "enforcing law," not with simply catching wrongdoers. It is an abstract distinction that most of us treat with the same suspicion as does the policeman, and the policeman continues to ignore it partly because we encourage him to do so.

Max Weber distinguished between the substantive rationality and the formal rationality of legal systems. A substantively rational system obeys generally consistent, if poorly articulated, norms of ethics and law. The formally rational legal system is more coherent and logically consistent. It is the typical system of a society governed by an impersonal bureaucracy dealing at arm's length with citizens. Our criminal law is becoming increasingly rational in the formal sense, as economic and political relations become more abstract, while the police continue to adhere to a kind of substantive rationality. Formal rationality is increasing partly because the rough rules of the police are simply inadequate to the social changes taking place in our society, and to the ideal of equal justice. The conflict in which the police are placed—between their own code and the formal code—is the conflict of modern city administration, and indeed, of the people who live in the cities. The question which the citizens of New York, and of every city which pretends to a liberal administration, must ask themselves is whether they would rather have the police follow their old-fashioned rules, or whether they really want the police to adhere to the formally rational (and substantively different) rules of due process of law. It is clear that there is something in most of us that does not want the police to change; the landslide vote against a civilian review board demonstrated that, if nothing else. We want efficiency, quick work, order above all, though we claim to want due process and equal justice as well. Without basic changes to eliminate the obvious injustices in our society, we cannot expect to have all these, but if all else fails, we think we would like to preserve at least the appearance of order ("peace and quiet"). It is for the police to play the tough, no-nonsense half of this conflict. The enlightened feel a little guilty about their own impulse to coerce respect by force, and it is easier for them to turn the police into a whipping boy than to admit to such instincts themselves. The police do all the "wrong" things—club people who are outcasts or defiant of authority—but the unfortunate truth is that much public disapproval of their actions is sheer hypocrisy. Many, perhaps most, citizens feel that it is desirable for a policeman to coerce adherence to his code by punching a "wise kid" or ransacking an apartment without a warrant. They hide from themselves the fact that every act which coerces obedience from a man by unlawful means is by definition an act of oppression. For people who accept such practices, much as they may recoil from the consistency with which they are applied by the police, virtually no abuses are recorded in this book.

For legislators and judges the police are a godsend, because all the acts of oppression that must be performed in this society to keep it running smoothly are pushed upon the police. The police get the blame, and the officials stay free of the stigma of approving their highhanded acts. The police have become the repository of all the illiberal impulses in this liberal society; they are under heavy fire because most of us no longer admit so readily to our illiberal impulses as we once did.

The welter of statutes intended to control morality by penalizing the possession of some contraband, or the act of vagrancy or loitering, pointedly reveals the hypocrisy in the administration of our laws. The legislature passes such statutes, knowing quite well that their enforcement encourages a host of police abuses, including unlawful searches, dragnet arrests, and systematic harassment. The links between these abuses and morals legislation is no accident; the impulse in each is the same. It is the drive to legislate the lives of others and to force them to adhere to an accepted mode of life; that impulse cannot be enforced without abusing the rights of citizens.

Viewed in this light, the distortions of fact by policemen, which we have pronounced at once the most dangerous and the most pervasive of abuses, do not seem quite so shocking or unnatural. Lying is a bridge between the substantively rational rules of the police and the formally rational ones of the criminal law, by which the first are made to appear to conform to the second.

The actions of the police probably embody a natural tendency of any group of bureaucrats, working out in the field where their decisions have low visibility, to avoid the effect of restrictive regulations that conflict with existing practices. . . . The effects of the conflict between rule and practice are more dramatic in the case of the police than of other bureaucrats because the victims of their practices wind up in jail, and more prolonged and exaggerated because of the traditional solidarity and secrecy of the police. Like many other minor bureaucrats before them, however, the police continue to adhere to their old customs because they know that their superiors and much of the rest of society approves. They have no motive to change.

Up to this point, I have made little effort to choose between the substantively rational rules of the police and the formally rational rules of the courts. Even without a choice between the two, the distortion of facts by the police is an inherently dangerous practice. In our society, law enforcement officers are expected to respond to civilian legal directives, and if they fail to do so, then the power of society to change its laws is significantly decreased, and the police in effect control the criminal law. But the covert adherence to another set of laws is not nearly so serious if in fact those laws are superior to, or just as good as, the stated law. If the formally rational rules are unworkable or unnecessary, to avoid them is a relatively minor failing, because in the long run the laws themselves will probably change. . . . The problem [of value judgments about the effectiveness of the formal rules] cannot be ignored entirely if we are to understand the effect of police abuses. We must at least look a little more deeply into the formal rules.

Let us consider, as an example, the requirements of "probable cause" for an arrest and search. The limitations of probable cause are established to make sure that the police arrest only people whom a neutral and rational observer would suppose to be guilty. A system of dragnet arrest and search would probably catch more persons carrying contraband than the application of probable cause, but the courts attempt to make a prior judgment so that those who are obviously or probably innocent will not be harassed. Any rule that relaxes the requirements of probable cause necessarily lowers the standards of suspicion and tends to include more innocent persons. As we have seen, police methods, when they depart from probable cause, do tend to punish innocent people together with the guilty. The point for use here is that the courts have made a policy judgment to exclude as many arrests of the innocent as possible, consistent with catching the obvious criminal. The rule of the courts, apart from being formally rational, also embodies a substantively rational rule *different* from that of the police, and the formal nature of the rule is intended to control police action and enforce the underlying substantive principle. The substantively rational police rule favors investigation so long as it is done in good faith, a policy judgment which is properly for the courts rather than the police to make because the courts are better equipped to strike the balance between investigation and freedom. The police rule inevitably favors investigation—favors the authorities, in short. It is apparent, then, that the rule of the courts is not dryly logical or lacking in practical effectiveness, but is simply based on a judgment different from that of the police about the needs of society.

There are two principles underlying such procedural rules: first, that the elaboration of legal rules is properly a matter for the courts, and second, that the balance is properly struck on the side of personal liberty. Our society is suspicious of both these principles; it finds the police easier to grasp than the court rules. Though the incidence of police abuses may be reduced by institutional reforms, the police rules cannot change finally until society decides to disapprove of them. More citizens must come to accept the principle that the term "law enforcement" refers to enforcement of the laws and not to the arrest or harassment of defiant or deviant citizens. More citizens must come to accept the principle that all police abuses constitute the enforcement of a private code by unlawful means and that, as such, they are inherently oppressive. Too many people, in fact, understand this already and yet secretly (or openly) approve the acts of the police because they fear the defiance of others as much as do the police. They recognize that nearly every form of defiance of an authority, whether it be from a "wise" teen-ager, from the hippie way of life, or finally, from an open revolt by students or black people, is a demand for a new way of life both social and economic. They fear that demand for change enough to use force to oppose it, and unless that fear disappears, they will continue to condone police acts of oppression, and police rules will not change.

The saddest aspect of police abuses is that they defeat their avowed purposes. The rationalization for street abuses is that they create or at least maintain respect for authority. Punishment for the wise guy is supposed to "teach him a lesson," but the system of police abuses creates only contempt for authority. A man, and especially the already defiant black man in this country, does not feel respect when he is clubbed, when he is charged with a crime, and when he loses his only job because he has been convicted. Words cannot convey the despair, the hatred, induced by a system which injures a man and then brands him as a criminal. It is not enough to say that the behavior of all the administrators involved—the officer, his superiors, the prosecutor, the judge—is understandable. The system within which the police work is evil, for the simplest of reasons: because it injures people and destroys their respect for the legal process. It is not for nothing that ghetto people have chosen police abuses as the symbol of oppression; it is because they actually *are* acts of oppression.

This brings us back to the importance of police abuses and the urgency of the problem they present. They are hardly the only act of oppression in our cities, but they are the easiest to recognize. The anger they instill is part of the fuel for the violent uprisings in our cities during the past five years. As an indispensable condition for ending those uprisings, the police must change their allegiance from a private code to a publicly recognized rule of law, and it is only when society itself demands this change that it will take place.

JAMES ALAN MCPHERSON

Chicago's Blackstone Rangers

Few uniformed policemen walk the streets in the Woodlawn area. Those who do are black. Most white policemen drive through the area in cars, usually accompanied by a black officer. Most of the policemen in the area seem to be young. They are, for the most part, polite, and a little cold. On occasion one notices a parked patrol car with two hard-faced white officers in the front seat and the barrel of a shotgun framed in the window between them. Only then does one remember the tension which is supposed to exist between the police and the black community. It is present, but it is not racial; at least not in the traditional—black-white—sense of the word.

Black people, if Blackstone Rangers can be called representative of black people, feel a tension between black policemen and themselves. It is a feeling of mistrust, of discomfort. Rangers do not seem to be under continual

From *The Atlantic Monthly*, June 1969, pp. 93-96. Copyright © 1969 by the Atlantic Monthly Company, Boston, Mass. Reprinted by permission of the author.

harassment from the police, but it is a fair assumption that they, or at least their leaders, are being watched by other blacks. If one sits too long in a restaurant with a Ranger of any status within the organization, he will eventually become aware of another black sitting in the next booth, sipping an eternal cup of coffee. Perhaps he is merely enjoying his coffee; perhaps he is a plainclothesman on the job. In any case, Rangers find it more relaxing to converse inside the Center or in one of their other meeting places.

"It shouldn't be called the Police Gang Intelligence Unit," says Mickey Cogwell, one of the Main 21 (the leadership of the Blackstone Rangers). "It should be called the Gang *Stupid* Unit because they are so stupid. If they really wanted to get us, they would wait until we commit crimes and then arrest us. Instead, they try to stop us from doing anything."

Mickey Cogwell is another busy man. Among the Main 21, he is recognized as the Ranger leader with the most business ability. For this reason Ranger president Jeff Fort put him in charge of West Side business operations of the Blackstone Nation. Cogwell is intelligent, and his directness suggests honesty and candor. He wears a black derby and a blue turtleneck sweater and talks very fast. He has had considerable experience with the Gang Intelligence Unit. He has been arrested more than sixty times.

"Every time people do things for us the G.I.U. tries to publicize it so that donators get bad publicity," Cogwell says. "It doesn't want the Rangers and Disciples to have a peace treaty because it threatens the security of their jobs. I feel that the G.I.U.—black men—use the Rangers and the rivalry between us and the D's to make their work more important to the system."

Cogwell believes that the members of the G.I.U. have extra-police powers. According to him, they can go into the Cook County Jail whenever they want; they have easy access to the press whenever they want to publicize stories about the Rangers; they have the help of the power structure in Chicago; and they can even influence judges. "Suppose one of the younger cats go out and does something and is put in the Cook County Jail. They will be offered a chance to get out if they swear that they were told to do something by one of the older Rangers, by one of the Main," he says. "The police have realized that they can't break up the Stones now. They might have done it four or five years ago, but now all they can do is arrest the Main. But Stone will still go on. In order to break us up, they will have to arrest everyone from the Main down to the peewees.

"If the police pick up a Stone, we take the number of the car, call a lawyer, and follow the car to the station," Cogwell states. "We wait in the halls until the lawyer comes. Then we try to find out what the bond is. If it's not too high, we try to raise it. But most bonds are set too high." He attributes the high bonds to intervention by members of the G.I.U. and the influence they seem to have over judges. . . .

While the Rangers can, in many instances, be considered a kind of spontaneous para-police force in their efforts to show the strength of their organization, there is another consideration to place in focus: are the police, specifically the members of the Gang Intelligence Unit, themselves a parapolitical force? This question is important in a very singular respect. It is evident that the Blackstone Ranger Nation is not interested in voluntarily *helping* the police: all of their activities which may be called helpful to the police seem to arise, unavoidably, from their efforts to keep the name of the Ranger organization safe from adverse publicity or else to demonstrate the tremendous power and community appeal, at least among the young, of the Blackstone Ranger Nation. In both of these areas the activities of the Gang Intelligence Unit seem to contribute the necessary pressure or motivation. The relative ease with which its members operate within the police department and the cooperation they receive from the State's Attorney's Office and the Cook County Jail, the influence they seem to have in the courts, and the easy willingness of the press to publicize incidents about the Rangers all suggest that members of the Unit have more than ordinary police powers.

For example, in December of 1968 after Jeff Fort was found guilty of contempt of Congress and released on $5000 bond, he was arrested by members of the G.I.U. on an old charge: failure to pay a $50 fine for a previous disorderly conduct arrest. The arrest warrant was issued on March 17, 1967. The eight G.I.U. officers who arrested Fort arrived at his home carrying axes, prepared to break down the door. They had no search warrant, but they searched his apartment and found a .22 caliber gun. Fort was charged with failure to register the gun.

Marshall Patner, the white Chicago lawyer who walked out of Senator McClellan's investigation of Poverty Program funding of a Ranger project with his client Jeff Fort last summer, has been in a position which enabled him to observe the activities of the Gang Intelligence Unit firsthand. "The question is," he says, "whether the police run the whole show. The G.I.U. can say 'no bond' to the judges, and no bond is given. Judges listen to them. State's attorneys listen to them."

Patner is paid by the Kettering Foundation to provide legal counsel for Rangers in general and Jeff Fort in particular. A 1956 University of Chicago Law School graduate, he quit his job as head of the appellate and test case division of the Legal Aid Bureau of Chicago to help William W. Brackett, who served as counsel for the Reverend John Fry before the McClellan Committee. Fry is a white clergyman whose church, the First Presbyterian, housed one of the Rangers' training centers funded by the Office of Economic Opportunity through a local grass roots group. The Woodlawn Organization (T.W.O.). The church thought Fort should have a black lawyer, but Fort preferred Marshall Patner.

"As a lawyer," Patner says, "I don't see my function as looking over a client to see what he's doing. I see these people as needing defense because they are being picked on for offenses which other people wouldn't be charged with, and subject to high bond just because they are Rangers." Since the McClellan hearings, Marshall Patner has received angry letters and telephone calls suggesting that he should be put into a concentration camp. . . .

"The police are definitely out to get the Stones," Carl Banks, a Ranger teacher, tells me at the Black P. Stone Youth Center, "especially since Nixon got in. Every time a black gets arrested, if he's from this neighborhood he's treated like a Stone. His bond is hiked up, he's harassed." Banks's voice changes to anger. "They don't want the Stones to have anything." He crushes a cigarette butt with his foot. "They want to keep us right down here on the ground."

"Why do you think they're out to get you?" I ask him.

Banks lights up another cigarette. "Some people in the area are still scared of us. This neighborhood used to be terrible, especially for strangers. Now all that's changed."

"How has it changed?"

"Stone run it," he says. "There's less fighting now. Stones are keeping dope and faggots out of the neighborhood. We even try to keep prostitutes out."

I follow Carl Banks over to the stage where the drums are assembled. It is time for his practice session. "We want to represent to the kids that this is our neighborhood," he continues; "we love it, it's all we got. We want the kids to feel the same way. We try to instill some dignity and pride in them. That's what the P. stands for."

"Are the kids forced to join?" I ask.

Carl considers this. He beats out a roll on one of the drums before answering. "It might have been that way in the old days," he admits. "But there's no pressure now. That's why we're going slow now. The older brothers aren't as active as they should be, some of them are drifting away. Having the peewees with us is OK, but we really need the adults to get our program going good."

"How do you get the kids to join?" I ask.

"They just come in," Banks says. "This is the only place open at night for kids to attend. There's nothing else in the area that's open except the Y.M.C.A. on Seventy-first Street." . . .

Congressman Abner Mikva, a white reformer who has fought the Daley machine, was elected to his first term in Congress last November from the Second Congressional District of Chicago, which encompasses the Woodlawn part of the South Side. He is considered by many people in Chicago to be something of an expert on Ranger affairs. Over coffee in his home on South Kenwood Avenue, Mikva offers some of his impressions of the group.

"I'm not a pro-Ranger. If someone commits a crime in the area and if he is a kid, the victim will assume that he's a Ranger, but if the Rangers had committed all the crimes they have been charged with, there would probably have to be at least 100,000 of them, or they would have to be some of the most energetic criminals who ever lived," he says. "I don't think they are civic-minded young reformers. I think that many of them are so alienated that it will be a hard job trying to bring them back into the mainstream. But even if you could bust up the gang structure, it would cost more to keep these kids apart than it would cost to help them do something constructive."

Unlike most groups of young, organized blacks, the Rangers do not seem to be primarily racially oriented. If they believe in any form of black power at all, it's the physical energy which they are attempting to harness in the black community and the economic power which, they believe, will come through constructive uses of that energy. If they hold any political philosophy at all, it is truly a grass roots one: they want to wrest control of their community not so much from the power structure as from the control of an older generation of blacks. They have a large number of the young people; now they are attempting to expand their source of energy by moving into the black, middle-class neighborhoods. And it is in such areas that the limitations of the Ranger appeal are tested. It is within these areas that class lines become more apparent.

Abner Mikva admits the reality of these class lines which contribute to polarization in the black community. "In other neighborhoods they really are recruiting, but these are different kinds of kids. They're middle-class, with two parents in the home—home-owning parents—not kids from broken families. The Rangers are scaring the daylights out of them. And unfortunately, some of the white churchmen are helping them. I get violent mail, more from the black community than from the white, asking: 'What are you doing defending the Rangers?'

"Some people in the South Woodlawn and Oakland areas would say that the police are too easy on the Rangers," he observes. "Some parents believe that they should crack some skulls. They're scared to death. And these are *black* people. This shows that it's not so much a color thing between the police and the Rangers. I can't recall any time over the last two years when I saw two white policemen alone in a car in the community. They're mostly black and white teams now. Or, if there are two white policemen, they don't respond to street calls. A good part of the G.I.U. is black, and some of these men have done community work in Woodlawn or with Operation Breadbasket. Some of them are militant, but they're against the Rangers because they're policemen and for obeying the law." Mikva feels, however, that the police do create a problem in the black community, in spite of the sameness of color. "The police insist on using direct, terrorist, violent methods and only succeed in polarizing people. They force people like myself to come out pro-Ranger because of their tactics. I come out saying more in defense of the Rangers than I would like to. . . .

LILLIAN S. CALHOUN

The Death of Fred Hampton

THE PANTHERS AND THE REST OF US

The crash and flicker of pre-dawn gunfire, a cache of weapons, two dead black men—they were familiar scenes for police and the Black Panther Party. Yet this time, the shots that killed Fred Hampton, 21, and Mark Clark, 22, in Chicago on December 4 somehow began to echo around the world. To the surprise of the police, the Panthers, and the press, they gave the community a brief burst of illumination, by which it tried again to see itself.

Most easily seen was the doubt. There was doubt that Cook County State's Attorney Edward V. Hanrahan's police had shown "bravery . . . restraint . . . and discipline" in a search for illegal weapons, as Hanrahan himself insisted. And it spread to doubt in law enforcement, doubt in ourselves, doubt—especially—that doubt could ever be resolved. "This is a tragic story for Chicago," was the view of Clayton Kirkpatrick, editor of the *Chicago Tribune* and a staunch supporter of law and order.

Officials, journalists and revolutionaries were not prepared for the changing public mood: Hanrahan's announcement of a heroic police raid against "vicious" Black Panthers, press photographs of 18 seized weapons (including, police said, one sawed-off shotgun), the personal accounts of the policemen themselves—it was the route that Hanrahan had taken successfully as a crimebusting federal district attorney.

But this time, black Alderman A. A. (Sammy) Rayner charged that the killing of Panther Chairman Hampton was an "assassination." Nine Congressmen called for an independent investigation. Thousands of local black students mourned. The white mayor of suburban Maywood (where Hampton grew up) demanded murder indictments against Hanrahan's raiders. Ralph Abernathy, Jesse Jackson and Dr. Spock eulogized Hampton and joined 5,000 persons at a memorial service.

From *Chicago Journalism Review*, Vol. 2, No. 12, Dec. 1969, p. 13. Reprinted by permission.

For many, doubt about Hanrahan's story revived doubts about the scores of police raids and the twenty deaths of Panthers in the past three years. Hanrahan hit the issue squarely:

"I would have thought our office is entitled to expect to be believed in by the public. Our officers wouldn't lie about the act. I'm talking about the credibility of our officers here and myself."

At first, the news media too misjudged the public mood. First reports flatly accepted the police definition of the incident as a "shootout." *Chicago Today* blared: "Panther bosses killed in cop shootout."

It was a familiar case of journalistic doubletalk, since doubt was present even in the city rooms where those first stories were written. One *Sun-Times* reporter quit when editors buried his story—the first report that the location of bullet holes in the Panther apartment did not square with the police version of the raid.

Another editor told a group of reporters who wanted to dig deeper that "nobody would be interested in it."

Yet, a week later, local newsmen rushed to catch up with the story, seeking rumored witnesses and charting investigations. *Chicago Today* was declaring, in a front page editorial: "Mr. Hanrahan should step aside" from investigations of the raid.

It wasn't that the media were whipping up the citizenry, as Hanrahan had charged: the media were being pushed by the community—especially the black community, some of whom even sought a 6 p.m. to 6 a.m. "curfew" for whites in black neighborhoods. Loudly and more clearly than ever before, the community was saying that it didn't trust the system.

Why was the doubt spreading?

Partly, there was the physical evidence which challenged the police story; partly the universal dread of midnight raids; partly the contradictions in the policemen's story; partly the account which the Panthers themselves gave of the incident; partly the growing numbers of Panther raids and deaths nationwide. As the Panthers' general counsel, Charles Garry of San Francisco, put it: "I have satisfied myself that there is a national scheme by the various agencies of government to destroy and commit genocide upon members of the Black Panther Party."

Beside the specifics of Hampton's death, doubt grew because the clichés police and the news media had applied to Fred Hampton and the Black Panthers clashed wildly with reality.

"I firmly believe," said a top cop in the state's attorney's office, "that 95 per cent of the blacks are terrorized by these Black Panthers, and are just afraid to open their mouths." Yet in all of Chicago these past weeks, only one black leader, United States District Judge James B. Parsons, was heard to defend the police against the Panthers. The newfound unity of the black community against the raid was striking indeed, embracing even Mayor Daley's loyal black aldermen.

"It's about time," the state's attorney's policeman had said, "that people stand up and be counted as to what they believe in."

And forty black mail carriers in uniform raised their fist in solidarity before filing through the apartment where Hampton was slain.

"I see this," said law enforcement professor, A. C. Germann, a consultant to the U.S. Department of Justice, "as just a kind of normal, routine police operation. Police have never worried too much about legality, or morality, or compassion. The aim has been getting the job done, like American business-men."

If one looked at the talented prosecutor who applied Mafia-busting tactics to Chicago's militant gangs and the revolution-minded Panthers, or at James (Gloves) Davis, one of the police raiders, who said on television that he was a "colored" officer and who earned his nickname as an old-style cop who beat troublemakers while wearing black gloves, or at the inertia of the news media in explaining the raid and the Black Panthers or at the shrewd silence of Mayor Daley—if one looked at the city at work, it was possible to see in the death of Fred Hampton a great threat to the routines of the old order, and first stirring of the new.

Last June, in testimony before the Senate Permanent Investigations Sub-committee, Fred Hampton said:

"I just went to a wake where a young man had been shot in the head by a pig. And you know this is bad. But it heightens the contradictions in the community. These things a lot of times organize the people better than we can organize them ourselves."

ADDING UP THE EVIDENCE

The killing of Fred Hampton was widely debated partly because the apartment where he was slain was later opened to the public by the Black Panther Party. Thousands of persons, black and white, saw some of the evidence on the walls of the apartment. Here, Christopher Chandler describes that evidence.

Cook County State's Attorney Edward V. Hanrahan described it as a blazing gun battle that erupted when police officers, attempting to serve a warrant, were attacked by members of the Black Panther Party.

Anyone who visited the apartment at 2337 West Monroe Street is forced to the conclusion that the state's attorney is lying, or at best speaking from ignorance. Whatever happened during the barrage of gunfire at 4:44 a.m.

CONTRADICTIONS IN POLICE ACCOUNTS OF THE RAID

This is an imperfect chart made by imperfect people that is, at least, not trying to confuse anyone. Everything on it was said at least once by the person to whom it is attributed. Don't hold us responsible if present statements they make don't match with these. Even Edward V. Hanrahan now admits that a machine gun was used inside the Panther apartment.

Barbara A. Boyer

	Official Tribune account	Panthers	Jalovec	Davis	Carmody	Ciszewski	Groth	Neighbors
Number of men	14	At least 14 inside, 150 outside on roofs, cordoning the street	15	14	14	13	14	Police all over, up on roofs with machineguns and carbines, street cordoned off
What Police Said	This is the police. We have a warrant.	*Knock-Knock* "Who's there?" "Tommy" "Tommy who?" "Tommy gun!"						"Open up, brother." "Who is it?" "Police."
Who Answered Knock	A man	Not said	Women & men	A woman	Nobody	Heard firing first	A woman	Nobody — firing began after knock and orders to open up
First Shots	Panthers, through the front door	By police at the front	Woman with shotgun at rear	Woman with shotgun in living room	Heard them from front	Unknown person fired shotgun through back	Woman with shotgun sitting on bed in living room	Don't know
Police Entrance	Front first	Front first	Back door	Not said	Rear window	Back door		Don't know
Lights	Off	Off	Off	Off	On	On	Off	Don't know
Police on Roof	No	Yes	Yes	No	No	No	No	Don't know
Machinegun	No	Yes	Yes	No	No	No	Yes	Yes
Length of fight	15 minutes — 3 pauses	Brief — one pause	10 or 12 minutes	10 to 15 minutes	Unknown	5 minutes	15 minutes — 3 pauses	Eight minutes — with one brief pause

on December 4, it could not have been a "battle" in the sense of two sides shooting at each other.

Simply viewing the bullet-torn walls of the apartment has been a deeply disturbing experience for thousands of citizens who have filed through the apartment, because the overwhelming evidence is there for all to see.

Police massed a heavy concentration of machinegun and shotgun fire at one living room wall and into two bedrooms. There was little if any return fire.

There have been countless calls for an investigation, and it appears there will be several. But no "blue ribbon" citizens committee can hope to "restore confidence" for anyone who has walked past those punctured walls.

Who knocked on which door, how the firing began, who fired what at whom and why remain uncertain. But from the physical evidence at the scene, examined the day of the raid and several times subsequently, the following is as nearly accurate a reconstruction of the circumstances as is possible at this time.

The Front Door

There are two bullet holes in the door that opens into the living room. One shot was fired from the anteroom into the living room while the door was slightly ajar. It is four feet from the ground and was apparently made by a .45 calibre bullet. A second hole, about a foot and a half below the first, appears to have been made by a shotgun firing from the living room out into the hallway. It was fired at a sharp angle, with the load (police say it was a solid rifle load deer slug fired from a shotgun) lodging at the angle of the ceiling in the southwest corner of the anteroom. The angle suggests that whoever fired the shot was prone on the living room floor right in front of the door.

According to the police version, the shotgun blast was fired through the door, narrowly missing them as they entered the anteroom. They then plunged through the door into the darkened living room. The blast could have "narrowly missed" the officers. But it seems improbable that any two officers, greeted by a shotgun blast, would break down the door and jump into a dark room. The police version made no mention of the shot fired into the living room. A more likely hypothesis seems to be that the first shot was fired by police. Mark Clark was killed by a bullet in the chest, and the top hole in the door would be about the height of Clark's wound, if he were standing behind the door, where his body was found in a pool of blood. After that shot either Clark or someone else in the room, perhaps on the mattress on the living room floor, got off one wild shot through the door into the anteroom ceiling.

The Living Room

The south wall of the living room contains 42 closely stitched bullet holes, mainly from a machine gun but with a few holes probably made by a .45 calibre weapon. They penetrate the wall (which borders on the north bedroom) and some of them penetrate all the way into Hampton's rear bedroom. One pattern of machinegun fire is clearly visible, forming an arch across the wall and back again, about three feet from the floor. The shots were fired from two positions—the living room doorway and the middle of the living room—so that some bullets were firing diagonally into the wall and some were perpendicular to it. There is also one possible bullet hole in the northwest corner of the room.

The police version has two shotgun blasts being fired at the policemen from the bed in the southeast corner of the room. One policeman wounds the girls on the bed and wheels to slay Clark. In the officially sanctioned account given by Hanrahan's men to the *Chicago Tribune*, one policeman sends machinegun fire into the south wall and down the hallway as covering fire. In the television version which Hanrahan staged for WBBM-TV, one policeman fires single shot blasts from his machinegun into the wall in response to shots being fired out of the north bedroom.

No shotgun blasts could have been fired from the bed in the southeast corner of the room—or, if they were, they somehow failed to leave a trace. There is no evidence of anyone firing out of the middle bedroom, except for one very questionable hole in the northwest corner of the living room. The more likely hypothesis indicates at best a disregard for human life, for it suggests that the wall was riddled to subdue anyone within who might have contemplated firing.

The Back Door

The kitchen door, leading onto the small porch, was apparently forced—the lock still hangs from the door. The south kitchen window and the west window in Hampton's rear bedroom were broken from the outside. There were two long ladders lying in the back yard. There is no evidence of any shots reaching the kitchen or dining room or bathroom. Four shoutgun blasts were apparently fired from the entranceway between the kitchen and the dining area—two hitting high up on the far wall of Hampton's bedroom, one hitting low on that wall, and one blasting through both closets and lodging in the upper northeast wall of the middle bedroom. There are gunshot holes in a neighboring shed which come from the general direction of Hampton's window.

The police version involves a complex series of exchanges of gunfire, including three shots fired at one officer as he comes through the kitchen door, and shotgun blasts being fired from the bedroom into the bathroom door. This version was supported by three photographs purporting to show three gunshot holes in the kitchen door frame, and a bathroom door riddled with bullets. However, the photos, furnished to the *Tribune* by the state's attorney's office, were fraudulent. The holes in the kitchen door frame were nail holes. The "bathroom door" was in fact the north bedroom door that had been riddled by police machinegun fire.

The gunshots in the shed have not been mentioned in any police account, and may in fact be police bullets from the hallway or shots that had been there for some time. There is not one shred of evidence that anyone fired at policemen entering the rear.

The police apparently broke into the kitchen and proceeded to the dining room without meeting any opposition. They then fired into both bedrooms, although when or why is impossible to judge. They may or may not have broken Hampton's bedroom window after scaling one of the ladders to the window ledge, and may or may not have then fired directly down into Hampton's bed. The only direct evidence for this is the fact that the bedroom window was broken from the outside in.

. . .

The Pathologists' Reports

Hampton was killed by a bullet which entered his skull about two inches above the midpart of the right eyebrow. The direction of the bullet was downwards and toward the middle, lodging in the base of the skull behind the nose. Another bullet entered at a point just below the right ear, on the same angle as the first, and emerged on the left side of the voice box in the front of the neck. Two other bullets grazed his arms. The bullets came from above, at about a 45 degree angle.

The official coroner's autopsy will not be released until an inquest is held. In the meantime, Coroner Andrew Toman has described the wounds differently to the newspapers. The above findings are based on a part of an autopsy conducted by Dr. Victor Levine, former chief pathologist for the coroner's office and two other pathologists. Their findings indicate that a bullet has been removed from Hampton's skull. Dr. Levine said he had talked to a "high authority" in the coroner's office who told him the bullet had been removed and sent to the police crime laboratory. Dr. Toman said, "That is a dirty lie."

The independent autopsy shows that Hampton was shot from above, substantiating the view that he was shot while in bed, either by a man in the doorway or on a ladder outside the window. The police version states that Hampton was found dead in bed. The question of the missing bullet remains a mystery.

WHO, WHAT, WHERE, WHEN—AND WHY

With the authorities reluctant to discuss the details of the raid, reporters and citizens sought more information, along the way picking up bits of fact and fast-spreading rumor. Brian Boyer, the first newsman to discover the discrepancies between the police account and the physical condition of the apartment was asked if he could explain how and why the raid occurred, and how the state's attorney and his police felt about the wave of criticism. Here is his report.

The phone number at the State's Attorney's office is 542-2900. If you call that number and ask for the boss, Edward V. Hanrahan, or his assistant, Dick Jalovec, you get a slight man with a Mr. Chips voice. His name is Mel Mawrence, and now he is the public relations man for the office. He used to handle O. W. Wilson, the chain-smoking professor who became chief of Chicago's police after the Summerdale scandals.

Mel has not been feeling well these pleasant, early winter days because the man he calls his master has not been feeling well. It has not been ill health that has stricken his preoccupied master, because Hanrahan is a rugged, handsome Irishman with none of the Irish vices. At least he doesn't have any of the usual ones. What's made a former acolyte like Ed feel so bad is that his own number one man, Dick Daley, hasn't been going out front to tell the people how much he's behind him. He's got the feeling that he's been abandoned by all his good buddies, just because of a stupid mistake.

Even at St. Giles Church in Oak Park that Sunday he knew people were looking at him and wondering. Ed doesn't swear, but he sure as hell wanted to speak up and tell the newspapers what he thought about them. He'd stood 1,000 bullets up on end in even rows and showed them all those guns and a sawed-off shotgun and they still hadn't understood what he was talking about. They talked about how Fred Hampton was 21 and murdered in bed and about why he'd sent his men in early in the morning like they didn't know what kind of people Black Panthers were.

On the morning of the shooting, State's Attorney Edward V. Hanrahan met for three hours with his special assistant, Richard S. Jalovec, and the policemen who made the raid. Then Hanrahan gave his statement to the press. It said:

"This morning, pursuant to a search warrant, state's attorney's police attempted to search the first floor apartment at 2337 W. Monroe Street to seize sawed-off shot guns and other illegal weapons stored there. Our office had reliable information that this location was a depot for such illegal weapons gathered by members of the Black Panther Party.

"As soon as Sgt. Daniel Groth and Officer James Davis, leading our men, announced their office, occupants of the apartment attacked them with shotgun fire. The officers immediately took cover. The occupants continued firing at our policemen from several rooms within the apartment.

"Thereafter, three times Sgt. Groth ordered all his men to cease firing and told the occupants to come out with their hands up. Each time, one of the occupants replied, "Shoot it out," and they continued firing at the police officers. Finally, the occupants threw down their guns and were arrested.

"The immediate, violent criminal reaction of the occupants in shooting at announced police officers emphasizes the extreme viciousness of the Black Panther Party. So does their refusal to cease firing at the police officers when urged to do so several times.

"Fortunately only one police officer was wounded. We wholeheartedly commend the police officers for their bravery, their remarkable restraint and their discipline in the face of this Black Panther attack—as should every decent citizen in our community."

To Mr. Hanrahan's dismay, "every decent citizen of our community" did not respond as he was expected to—because the story told by Hanrahan and his police officers was redolent with contradictions and lies, because the physical evidence at the apartment seemed similar to a massacre scene, and because the Black Panther Party outmaneuvered Hanrahan in the press.

In fact, there were those who thought the state's attorney had revealed the face of a national police conspiracy to harrass, imprison, and murder dissenters in a developing fascist state.

There is a lot of mail on Mel's desk and some of it is for Mr. Hanrahan and some of it is against him but he's thoroughly sick of it all. There is something going on in Chicago if not in the entire United States with the sit-ins and the demonstrations and half a million people going to Washington against the war despite Mr. Nixon doing a pretty good job. Mr. Nixon is doing everything that he can to get out of that war with some shreds of dignity left and then Pinkville comes up and they start comparing what just happened here in Chicago with whatever it really was that went on there. The Tribune certainly has some decency left and doesn't convict anybody before all of the evidence is presented in court for there weren't any people there from the newspapers and nobody knows everything about it except 14 or 15 men who came out of this office.

That Bobby Rush and his other people are probably out doing something

right now about whatever it is they call social contradictions and the role of
vanguard being to heighten them. They don't even know what this country
is all about if they haven't ever had anything to do with it.

If social reality can be read by its contradictions, this case provided a
primer.

In January, 1969, the new prosecutor brought an activist concept to the
state's attorney's job.

In addition to presenting evidence in criminal cases, and investigating
crimes, the activist concept meant surveying and pressuring youth gangs—
largely black—which were becoming politicized at the time.

There is nothing wrong with a prosecutor assembling a police unit and
conducting raids. Thomas Dewey ascended to the governorship of New
York by creating a special prosecutions unit and smashing Murder, Inc.

But Dewey's was an effort against the criminal underworld, not a political
organization, however threatening it might be to officialdom.

Hanrahan's "war on gangs," confined primarily to black youth groups (including the Panthers), already has drawn the ire of the black community—
and white liberals. Hanrahan's predecessor had resisted City Hall pressure
to initiate a similar gang war, believing that a prosecutor's job was to prosecute cases, not engage in aggressive police work.

After the Panther raid, Hanrahan denied that he was after gangs as such,
but the previous efforts of his men—and many of his comments—disputed
him. Addressing a group of young girls in the Neighborhood Youth Corps,
he referred to gang members as "animals unfit for society." He was met with
jeers, snickers, and hisses by the street-smart audience.

"I'm trying to take the romance out of gangs and let the brutality show
through," he said in a recent interview with the *Daily News*.

"It's one thing to call gangs Mad Latins or Maniac Africans, but when
you see their conduct is like that of a vicious animal there is nothing desirable about that. Nobody in their right mind would approve that kind of
conduct and they shouldn't approve the name."

The strategy for Hanrahan's efforts against the gangs was copied from the
city's gang intelligence unit, which supplied the nine policemen for the
special prosecutions unit. The strategy had three parts:

Surveillance—by constant monitoring of the whereabouts of gang leaders,
grilling jailed gang leaders, and using informers.

Case building—by setting traps, buying witnesses and informers, and
careful police work.

Gang destruction—by picking off the leaders with arrests and jail sentences
based on the above, or by violence if they can be egged on to strike at
police.

These procedures are not unusual, and a prosecutor has a lot of discretion if the society approves. Geoffrey C. Hazard, a judicial researcher for the American Bar Foundation and an expert on prosecutors describes the discretionary powers of the prosecutor as "tremendous."

"In that respect, this is a government of men, not laws," Hazard said. "The only effective constraint is other interests who may scream about this—interests who have some power at their disposal."

A special problem in Chicago is that counter-pressures from minority and special interest groups are not felt as strongly as they should be. They are particularly weak when the object of prosecution appears as irresponsibly dangerous as the Panthers appears to be.

Hazard said that the prosecutor's job "should require great political sophistication, but Hanrahan is wielding a meataxe."

Thomas A. Foran, U.S. Attorney doesn't like gangs and actively detests the Panthers, but he privately described Hanrahan's war on gangs to newsmen as a "racist purge."

But Hanrahan had his own ideas, and to accomplish them he brought Jalovec with him from the U.S. attorney's office. Jalovec is a politically ambitious 29-year-old lawyer whose goal, says a friend, is to be mayor.

Hanrahan and Jalovec handpicked the men they wanted for the Special Prosecutions Unit—four other assistant state's attorneys and nine aggressive men drawn originally from the Chicago police department's gang intelligence unit and its anti-subversive squad.

The state's attorney's police has been regarded as a soft job, but this unit, bearing Hanrahan's personal stamp, was to be different. The men were selected for their skills. They included a thirst for action and experience in surveillance and harrassment of gang youth. At least one of the policemen chosen, James (Gloves) Davis, was among the most hated and feared men on ghetto streets.

It seemed to Hanrahan and Jalovec that the Black Panther Party was a natural object of their attention—especially since the FBI and the Justice Department both had told police officials that the party was the nation's most dangerous threat.

There is no reason to think that Hanrahan disagreed.

The Panthers are black, Maoist revolutionaries and prophets of self-defense who shoot back when they are faced by police with guns.

Mel keeps wondering about what's going on in that apartment on Madison Street with all the people going through and the Panther kids telling all of them the bullet holes show that Fred got murdered in his sleep. He'd like to go through himself even though Mr. Hanrahan's a good man and wouldn't lie if he could help it. Mel thinks there is something strange going on and in all his life he's never seen anything like it before. Those Yippies and those revolutionaries stirred up something like this last year when they caused all that trouble when the Democrats were here but there were a lot more of them and they didn't tote guns around and talk about shooting back and how if America doesn't change they were going to destroy it. Just the SDS did and they got their heads cracked and that is that.

In 1969, up until the fourth day of the twelfth month, two Panthers had died in armed confrontations with Chicago police, and more than a dozen had been shot. In the same battles, two policemen died and many others were injured. "War against the gangs" started to look like "war against the Panthers."

But the Chicago Police Department—along with the FBI—was receiving the glory for tangling with the Panthers. The police had become Panther-phobic on November 13 when the Party and Chicago police engaged in a predawn gun battle in an abandoned hotel at 5801 South Calumet which left two dead policemen and one dead Panther.

One of the police victims was a 22-year-old John J. Gilhooly, scion of a well-established police family. His father, John J. Sr., has been with the department for 29 years, with the Englewood District automotive division. His uncle, Alphonse Gilhooly, is on the police detail that guards the home of Mayor Richard J. Daley. His brother-in-law, Gary M. Olson, is a police-man in the Gresham District.

Relations between Panthers and the police were strained, to say the least.

If law enforcers had wanted to find revenge, they knew about the apart-ment at 2337 West Monroe which the FBI helped to keep under surveillance. They knew that Fred Hampton and his Minister of Defense, Bobby Rush, slept there when they were in town and that, true to the Panther code, guns were usually near.

According to the search warrant that Hanrahan got for the raid, informants saw sawed-off shotguns in the apartment on December 1 and 2. Possibly they were FBI informants.

Hanrahan told Jalovec and Sgt. Daniel Groth to map out the raid, accord-ing to Mel Mawrence, the prosecutor's public relations man. They used a drawing of the apartment floor plan. They assembled enough deadly force to subdue an Army platoon—including at least one submachine—even though, according to one official in the Chicago police department, the state's attor-ney's men haven't had to fire a shot in nine years.

The search warrant was obtained at 4:45 p.m. on December 3, the day before the raid. The man who granted it to Sgt. Groth was Judge Robert Collins, formerly Hanrahan's first assistant at the U.S. attorney's office.

When everything was ready, Hanrahan was briefed at home, according to Mawrence.

The Chicago Police Department was not told of the raid in advance. Police agencies are wary about leaks—and about competition from each other.

One vehicle the plainclothes police took to the apartment was an Illinois Bell Telephone truck, according to neighbors and one reporter who arrived when it was all over.

How many men participated in what followed is an open question.

The official version is that 14 policemen, five of them black, were involved. But a persistent rumor and some published newspaper accounts put the total at 15. If there was a 15th man, there are rumors that he is either a relative or friend of the slain officer Gilhooly.

Mel gets out of his chair a little when Mr. Hanrahan comes walking briskly through and Dick Jalovec comes right in back of him but younger and bigger and he tries to be cheerful despite all of the troubles and doesn't worry about what might happen if he lands out of a job. If somebody comes asking if this office and any of its men had anything to do with revenge we've let too much evidence go to the press and we've got to protect the rights of the defendants.

I'd tell them and I do tell them that this case is closed until we are in front of a proper grand jury and court that understands what the problems of a prosecutor are and the urgent need as expressed by Mr. Mitchell to stop the Black Panther activities and a certain reality that to run for higher office a man like Mr. Hanrahan must make a good mark and he is also a devoted kind of individual who comes in early and stays to after 7 each night.

At 4:44 a.m., when the nine human beings inside the apartment were asleep, men outside the apartment had stationed themselves with machine guns and high powered carbines atop nearby buildings and at the front and rear entrances to the apartment, according to neighbors. The state's attorney says that no men were placed on the roof tops.

Later, when the guns stopped firing—the police estimate they fired more than 300 shots—Hampton and Mark Clark were dead. In police custody were Brenda Harris, Verlina Brewer, Blair Anderson, and Ronald Satchel (all critically wounded), and Debra Johnson, Louis Trulock and Harold Bell. All were charged with attempted murder of the policemen, and a variety of other charges were placed against them. Bonds of up to $100,000 were set against their release, and only Debra Johnson, eight months pregnant with Hampton's child, could be immediately bailed out.

It is interesting to note that with the exception of Trulock, the Panthers were all in their late teens and early 20's. The average age of the known policemen was 39. Rush said on a radio interview that he thought generational conflict as much as racial fear was responsible for the raid. He charged that the police, Jalovec, and Hanrahan, had planned and carried out a murder.

A great many in Chicago's black community, which is 31 per cent of the population, and thousands of others whose skins are white, seemed willing to believe that the Panther's charges might be true.

This social fact is as important as the version that will be adopted by a "blue ribbon" committee before it's all over; it may indicate that the society is irreparably split.

MURRAY KEMPTON

The Harlem Policeman

August has been cooler than the mismanagers of our affairs deserve. Its breezes have blown away that summer madness which was the proximate cause of the Harlem riots. Peace has returned to the largest of our colonies and, with it, public notice has departed; and those two oppressed minorities, the American Negro and the American policeman, stand facing one another, alone as they have always been.

New York's Mayor Wagner came home from Spain when the Harlem troubles were at their worst, and, a few minutes after he landed, expressed his absolute confidence in the performance of his police, an opinion formed before he could have asked a question. That night he went on television to remind the people of Harlem that attendance at the World's Fair was declining and the city's hotels only half-filled because tourists were being frightened away by reports of violence in the streets. The riots are over now; the hotels are filling up again. But Mayor Wagner had made the point: the poor have a duty not to afflict the comfortable. There were Negro riots a few days later in Rochester, in upstate New York; the police quieted those, too, and their city council rewarded them by granting the $1,000 average annual pay rise which policemen have agitated for for years.

The Harlem riots never escaped the boundaries of that ghetto. They were, in fact, so massively contained that most New Yorkers knew of them only from television and the prints, as Englishmen know of the troubles in British Guiana.

From *The Spectator*, Aug. 14, 1964, pp. 201-2. Reprinted by permission.

The afternoon of July 15, a group of Negro adolescents were idling outside their summer school on East 74th Street and fell into a quarrel with the janitor of the apartment-house next door. He was watering the front steps and turned his garden hose upon them. One boy, James Powell, ran up the steps to pursue the janitor, who escaped inside and bolted the door behind him. Powell pounded on the door; nothing up to that point had been more excessive than schoolboy games are. And then Police Lieutenant Thomas Gilligan came out of a television repair store near the scene with pistol drawn; Powell came down the steps towards him and Gilligan fired three times. He asserts that the first shot was a warning fired to young Powell's side. It is the accepted privilege of policemen, in emergencies in New York, to fire a warning shot in the street and in a crowd. Gilligan says that thereafter Powell came at him with a knife and that he shot him first in the arm and then, when Powell came on, in the body—fatally.

There appears to have been a small public disturbance then; all that was significant in any witness's memory was the voice of one Negro girl crying to those policemen who came running to Gilligan's aid: "All right, go ahead, kill another nigger." Gilligan was taken to a station house; the District Attorney's office was still questioning witnesses when his brother policemen told him to go home. "We sometimes hold a policeman," a police inspector said, "but not in a case of justifiable homicide like this one."

It was an extraordinary and summary judgment. Lieutenant Gilligan is a large man; Powell was a small fifteen-year-old. A knife was found near Powell's body; but no witness except Gilligan has publicly remembered seeing it in Powell's hand. The image of a boy who is struck in the arm in which he holds a knife and still brandishes his weapon and charges forward is not one that would convince everybody. Still, Gilligan was set loose, and by the weekend, seven blocks of Harlem rang with the bricks and bottles of their riotous inhabitants and the gunfire of the police. One man was killed and in all a hundred-odd persons, fifty of them policemen, were treated for injuries. The police, granted their methods and their resentments, are credited with acting reasonably well even by their critics.

But the essence of that scene was remembered acutely by Dr. Kenneth Clark, the Negro sociologist:

> It was a different crowd from any I have ever seen at riots like this one. It had the tone of that girl at the junior high school who kept yelling, "Come on, kill another nigger." A sort of taunting quality. Men would walk by the cops and say, "Hey, whitey, here's one of us to shoot." I'm sure that anyone there who was white would identify with the police. I know I identified with that crowd.
>
> I kept wondering why the city hadn't sent in more white cops. I walked four blocks before I found my first Negro cop. There were ten

white ones standing on a corner bunched together and scared. And, then separated from them, as far apart as both groups could get, there were three Negro policemen. They couldn't have been better segregated.

What was stranger still was how different they looked. The white ones were doing the best they could to look like cops, straight, stiff and firm. And the Negroes were doing their best to look like anything but cops; they were lounging and slouching and altogether acting like they were just out on the corner.

Now it is over, and the life of the Harlem citizen with the policeman who is to him the only visible symbol of and focus for his resentments goes on as it did. The nature of that relationship is described in the words of one twenty-one-year-old Negro:

> Everything in this dump is a big laugh to the cops unless you kill a cop. Then they don't laugh. I had a cop walk up to me a couple of days ago. You know what he said? "Move over!" They have the street blocked up and he's going to tell me you can go around them. I said, "Hell if I do!" He said, "I'll slap your black ass." I told him, "That's one way you'll know if you're living or dying." He just looked at me. I said, "Why don't you say it? You want to say nigger so bad."

> Everything has been resolved except the case of Lieutenant Gilligan, which is still before a grand jury. One must assume that society will support the police here as it does in all small things. But they would seem to deserve more than absolution from their sins and indifference to the indignities which, more than the rest of us, they share with the Negro. "It is our job," their Commissioner has said, "to deal not with the causes of these things but with their results."

Too Late for the Panthers?

Is there some sort of government conspiracy afoot to exterminate the Black Panthers? The black revolutionaries themselves are convinced of it—and have long used such charges as part of their propaganda against capitalist white society and its "pig" police. Last week, in the wake of yet another bloody shoot-out between the cops and the Panthers, the talk of conspiracy —or, at the least, systematic harassment—began to find a larger and more sympathetic audience than ever before.

The latest skirmish in the guerrilla war between the gun-toting Panthers and the police took place in Los Angeles. The cops' mission, authorities said, was to search Panther headquarters on the edge of the Watts ghetto for a suspected cache of illegal weapons. To bring off the job, the police department assembled a 300-man task force and moved in on the building just before dawn. The result was a four-hour gun battle in which both sides exchanged hundreds of shots. At one point, the police tried to get at the Panthers by dynamiting the roof of their headquarters. The cops also used helicopters—to scout the neighborhood for Panther reinforcements—and even wheeled up an armored personnel carrier, borrowed from the National Guard.

Outnumbered and outgunned, the Panthers finally hoisted a white flag. And when the police finally got into the building, they found what they said they had come for: an arsenal of weapons including two submachine guns, a dozen carbines and rifles, eight pistols, a score of homemade bombs and thousands of rounds of ammunition. Six Panthers (and three policemen) were wounded during the fight and thirteen militants arrested.

The Los Angeles episode came just four days after a deadly confrontation between the police and the Panthers in Chicago in which two top Illinois leaders of the party were killed (*Newsweek*, Dec. 15). The two incidents prompted an unprecedented outcry—and not just from the Panthers and their allies on the far left. Liberals of impeccable credentials, including Whitney Young Jr. of the Urban League, attorney Joseph L. Rauh Jr. of Americans for Democratic Action, and Adlai Stevenson III, the Illinois State Treasurer and U.S. Senate candidate, called for investigations of the police action against the Panthers, whose hierarchy around the country has been all but decimated over the past year.

The pressure brought a prompt response from the government. In Washington, the Justice Department denied that it had ever had a "policy of concerted activity with local police in order to harass any members of the Black Panther Party." And Justice did agree to a preliminary Federal investigation of the Chicago incident. The U.S. investigation won't be the only one. At the weekend, a dozen organizations, including the NAACP Legal Defense Fund and the American Jewish Congress, were planning to set up a committee of inquiry to look into the question of alleged police harassment of the Panthers.

There is no doubt that the police around the nation have made the Panthers a prime target in the past two years—but whether there is any sort of systematic approach to it all is highly questionable. "I doubt seriously that there is anything organized on a national scale," says one former high-ranking Federal lawman. "But there could be inspiration."

The Justice Department makes no secret of the fact that it maintains a special intelligence unit to keep tabs on the Panthers; and the FBI follows standard procedures for exchanging information with local law enforcement agencies. "If we hear that the Minutemen or the DAR or the Black Panthers are caching submachine guns," said one FBI source last week, "it's absolutely incumbent upon us to pass that on to local police." Last summer, FBI chief J. Edgar Hoover described the Panthers as "the greatest threat to the internal security of the country" among all black extremist groups.

Not that local authorities need much prompting from anyone where the Panthers are concerned. The Panthers' whole stance is based on unrelenting hostility to all established authority, especially "the pigs." Recently, the Panthers have tried to downplay their gun-barrel politics and introduced a free breakfast program for children, but in ghettos around the country, cops grumble about sniping and other hit-and-run assaults that they blame on the party. What's more, police raids on Panther hide-outs generally do turn up frightening arsenals—and the Panthers' insistence that they arm only for self-defense is less than persuasive to many officials.

While Panthers and police practice self-defense, the party's ranks are dwindling. Federal officials estimate that there are no more than about 1,500 Panthers scattered in roughly 40 chapters around the country. Few of the Panthers' leaders remain at liberty. Chairman Bobby Seale, 32, is in custody along with thirteen others in connection with the alleged execution of a suspected Panther informer—and Seale also faces trial on charges stemming from the 1968 Chicago convention riots. Defense Minister Huey Newton, 27, is serving a two- to fifteeen-year sentence for killing a policeman.

Third-ranking Panther Eldridge Cleaver, 34, the Minister of Information, fled the country rather than return to jail for parole violation (but has made some tentative inquiries about returning to the U.S. from exile in Algeria). National Chief of Staff David Hilliard, 27, was arrested recently on charges of threatening President Nixon's life during an antiwar speech, and last week Hilliard was convicted on a two-year-old gun charge. In New York and New Jersey, nearly a score of Panthers are being held in connection with an alleged plot to blow up department stores. A list compiled by the Los Angeles ACLU indicates at least a dozen Panthers have been killed since the fall of 1967, and Panther lawyer Charles Garry puts the toll since January 1968 at more than double that number.

The Chicago and Los Angeles confrontations with the police have produced substantial community support for the Panthers—much of it from people who have no use for the party's primitive, polemic Marxism. In L.A., nearly 6,000 people massed on the steps of City Hall to back the Panthers' right to survive. The rally was called by a coalition of community groups including the NAACP, Urban League and the Conference of Black Elected Officials. The pro-Panther movement gained some impetus when Assistant

Police Chief Robert Houghton, who commanded last week's predawn raid, conceded: "I don't know whether this was the best tactic."

Chicago police stood behind their essential story of the fifteen-minute gun battle that resulted in the deaths of Illinois Panther chieftain Fred Hampton, 21, and Mark Clark, 22. But an unofficial autopsy sponsored by the Panthers suggested that Hampton may have been killed while asleep. The controversy was heightened when the conservative *Chicago Tribune* ran two misleading photos supplied by the police, and a local TV station put on a half-hour reconstruction of the gun battle, based entirely on the police version of the affair. While mourners filed past Hampton's bier, hundreds of other citizens, black and white, accepted the Panthers' invitation to a "death tour" of Hampton's blood-stained apartment; many came away angry or in tears and pressed dollar bills in the hands of the Panther guides.

The Chicago and Los Angeles shootouts have already won the Panthers more publicity than they ever had before—and perhaps more sympathy. But the party is so depleted that it may never be able to exploit its new-found fame.

DAN KATZ

Police Review, National Coincidence

When the violence erupted in Tompkins Square on Tuesday afternoon, Allegra Perhaes was sitting in the locked-arm circle on Hoving Hill with her two children—Michael, age 7, and Marissa, 6—in her lap. "When the cop fell over into the group and the night sticks started swinging," she recalls, "I got scared and tried to get up and run, carrying my children. And all of a sudden, here was this cop cursing at me—'get those little pricks out of here,' like that—and then he took his little club and hit me twice, on the arm and leg. I couldn't believe it, and I still have the bruises—I just cried, that's all I could do. I just couldn't believe it."

The police having somehow allowed her to leave the area, Mrs. Perhaes immediately contacted the ACLU, who instructed her to lodge a formal complaint with the Civilian Complaint Review Board. Appearing before the Board's headquarters, at 201 Park Avenue South, Mrs. Perhaes accidentally

From *The East Village Other*, 6-15/7-1, 1967, p. 3. Copyright 1969 by The East Village Other, Inc. Reprinted by permission.

confronted the officer who had struck her: "I'll never forget that man's face," she recalls, "and I straightaway bent over to read the number on his badge. He covered his chest with his hand and demanded that I tell him my name." Failing to get the officer's badge number, Mrs. Perhaes asked for an interview with Lieutenant Mullins, who was handling the complaints from the Tompkins Square riot.

Lieutenant Mullins registered her complaint in detail and then informed her that all the Tompkins Square complaints were to be handled as one group rather than a separate complaint; Mullins later told EVO that the complaints were being slotted together because they had all derived from the same "geographical area." He further told EVO that, "offhand," he calculated that a total of seven Tompkins Square complaints had been registered with this office. Each separate complainant will be informed of the disposition of his case, Mullins said; his final report on the question of brutality in the Tompkins Square Memorial Day riot, however, will be handled as one case to itself.

"It all seemed pretty well planned out, to me," Mrs. Perhaes commented, speaking of the way the cops handled the riot. "Nobody really knew what was happening, just all of a sudden there was all that violence, and then everyone was crying—just crying, all the police were dragging people away to the paddy wagons."

Allegra Perhaes, incidentally, does not consider herself a hippie: "I was probably the only square there, in fact—I even had shoes on and I was dressed pretty conventionally. But those people around me, those beautiful flower people—they were holding my babies' heads away from the night sticks, guarding them. . . ."

The Memorial Day beatings and arrests, subsequent near-riots, and the general cop-community relationship scene seems to have its historical counterparts. The tactics of the cops remind us of past incidents; somehow, we've been through this movie before.

Like in 1961. Washington Square Park had been the traditional Sunday gathering grounds of West Village folksingers and listeners for 17 years, and for the 14 of them that permits were necessary, they were issued with no hassle. So when Izzy Young, of the Folklore Center, was refused a permit on April 6, 1961, it was decided that the singers would march on the park the following Sunday.

It was Parks Commissioner Newbold Morris who had ordered his staff not to issue permits to any but "bona-fide" musical groups. He further ordered that all musicians without a permit were to receive a summons.

The following Sunday, April 9, the kids showed up, with guitars and dulcimers. The cops arrived with clubs. 10 singers were arrested, including novelist Harold Humes. The clubs were used.

A few days later, Young received a letter from Richard Ballantine, of Ballantine Books, stating that he saw the Sunday bust, and that he would "testify, under oath, that the police were brutal to the extreme. I saw, from a distance of 10 feet, two police officers knock a man to the ground, kick him while he was prostrate and offering absolutely no resistance, and hit him on the head with a club. I saw a young girl, less than five feet tall, and in all probability weighing less than 100 pounds, who had to be carried away by friends, as she had been beaten severely about the head with clubs. I saw that, to the best of my knowledge, the crowd never, at any point, attacked the police." As could be expected, the New York *Mirror* ran two-inch banner heads the day after the bust, screaming, 3000 BEATNIKS RIOT IN VILLAGE!

Why did the nightsticks fly? Why the ban in the first place? Commissioner Morris claimed that he wanted to make the park "more attractive." He accused the singers of "trampling all over the grass, flowers, and shrubs." But, since the Washington Square folksingers always played in or near the fountain, a completely concrete area, and this day was no exception, Morris' explanation was clear-cut bullshit.

Other theories began to arise. The musicians claimed that the ban was an attempt to drive "beat types" from the Village, in order to benefit real estate interests, including New York University. The musicians believed that the real estate people saw them as a liability, keeping the rents "low" ($100/ month for a 60-year-old two-room apartment with cockroaches is LOW?), and preventing the City from running an avenue through the Park. OK, so maybe the real estate people WERE that naïve, believing that the kids were keeping the rent down. MAYBE the real estate people were paying off Morris and the cops, to get the beats out. Just maybe.

It was obvious, later, that the nationwide publicity surrounding the Washington Square Park incidents made Greenwich Village the most popular tourist attraction in New York. After all, why go to a foreign country, when you can visit an alien culture, right in your own backyard? The Macdougal Street Mirth Merchants, some of whom were in business before the ban, most of whom moved downtown at the right time, cleaned up, and are STILL cleaning up. Isn't it possible that a few of them could have foreseen the results of such publicity before the ban and the bust? . . . This all looks pretty gross, man.

Indeed, the Rev. Howard R. Moody of the Judson Memorial Baptist Church, a former Marine combat pilot and a friend of Young and the folk-singers, implored, "We want the Mayor to know we want a thorough investigation. If there's corruption—a payoff scandal—we don't want it hushed up. The people from the coffee-houses are being grossly mishandled."

As far as the brutality goes, the only statement wending its way forth from officialdom, was one from Police Commissioner Murphy: "My department doesn't use unnecessary force." He said he would investigate complaints, and that's the last anybody heard of it. Isn't it possible that Commissioner Murphy was a fink?

Meanwhile, pressure was being placed on Morris to lift the folksinging curb. He said that he would "look to public opinion before deciding to reconsider the songfest ban." A day later, he said that he doesn't have a large enough staff to conduct a survey on public sentiment. He agreed, however, to consider the sentiments expressed in letters written to him by Villagers. A week later, the Post ran a story about the mounds of unopened letters in Morris' office, and quoted him as saying, "Look, I'm not running a poll here, you know." The folksinging ban continued.

On April 15, the Salvation Army held a concert in Washington Square Park. The concert featured 15 bands and 700 bandsmen. Morris issued the permit.

Various groups and individuals within the Village, some opposing the ban and some favoring it, were actively attempting to influence public opinion and the Park officials. Community opinion rapidly polarized, and it became clear that what some of the older Village residents objected to was not the singing, but rather, the presence of Blacks among the new "beatniks." Thus, the cops and the parks department had managed to get the Village to fight itself. Make different groups of undesirables hate each other, and they'll kill themselves off.

All the while, officials continued to spew forth the same familiar trash. Police Inspector William F. Reel produced this gem: "They're schemers. They come there (to the Park) looking to get arrested."

On May 1, the cops beat more heads.

Both Young and the ACLU by now had complaints and petitions registered in State Supreme Court, to overrule Morris' ban. Mayor Wagner strongly supported Morris, while Congressman John Lindsay and others supported Young's petition. On May 5, Young told the Times, "We have been trying to fight this thing legally, but, so far, the cards seem to be stacked against us." He proceeded to send telegrams to President Kennedy, his little brother, Rockefeller, Stevenson, Cardinal Spellman, and Bernard Baruch, asking for help. He got none.

On May 8, 600 sang-in at the Park, without instruments, and on May 13, Wagner finally permitted the kids to sing and play between 3-6 p.m. on the 14th. An anti-sing group, composed of organizations such as the American Legion, the Knights of Columbus, the PTA, the Holy Name Society, the Village Businessmen's Association, and a Cub Scout Pack, threatened a demonstration if the ban was dropped.

Singing was permitted sporadically by the good graces of Wagner, Morris, and the cops, until August 7, when the Appellate Division of the State Supreme Court reversed a lower court decision on Young's petition. The Appellate Division stated that Morris acted improperly, and re-asserted the right of human beings to sing. At certain times.

And so the crisis ended. Or rather, and so the Village ended. For the incredible amount of publicity turned the West Village into a multi-million-dollar coney-island freak show, where innocuous uptown and cross-country tourists flocked to waste their time and money watching beatniks. And guess who got rich.

This pattern seems to be a recurring one, in all areas where hippie or underground communities begin to develop. First, the cops pull one atrocity on flimsy pretense, like the Memorial Day Tompkins Square Affair. This serves a number of purposes. It brings the first surge of publicity. It puts the longtime residents of the area up-tight, like, we don't mind you living here, but man, you just put heat on the place. It provides the excuse to put more cops on the beat, which always tenses a situation. Take a walk along Avenue A near the Park tonight, and see enough cops for a be-in. All this cop-created tension, plus the summer heat, plus the frustration of pavement life, creates a bad scene. If the cops get their way, from this point on, the different community groups can be pitted against each other, killing each other off. The cops actually become keepers of the peace. And the end result is always the same; the uptown pseudo-hips cash in on the new tourist attraction, and the hippies have to look for a new home.

Similar occurrences took place on the Sunset Strip last winter. On November 13, the cops lied to the press, declaring that 1500 teenagers were wandering the streets, armed with molotov cocktails. The first major action of the police, using the lie as emotional springboard, and the ridiculous 10:00 curfew as a legal one, occurred on November 20, when 47 flower children (well, sort of) were busted. The problem, of course, was that the liquor-serving rock joints, now able to bring in the under-21 kids who could dance, but not drink, charged minimums of $2.50, too steep for a couple of dances and a coke. As a result, the kids walked the streets in throngs, an act perceived by the exploitative rock merchants as a threat to their business. The cops, while babbling about protecting law and order, were actually protecting the wealthy burn artists. Only naïveté says this is coincidental.

Albert Mitchell, owner of the Fifth Estate coffee-house, and a staunch supporter of the Strip hippies, declared that "This is a classic power struggle between the wealthy real estate business interests and the bohemians. We will never give up. We will not be steam-rollered out of town."

LA County Suprvisor Ernest E. Debs leans all the way back in his padded swivel chair, and munches, "We will never surrender the area to a bunch of wild-eyed beatniks."

So the war is on.

On November 21, over 400 city, county, and state cops subdue a crowd of 1,000. Fifty more are busted. The Times reports that the enforcement of the curfew began on the demand of nightclub owners and restaurant owners, who said their businesses were hurt by "gangs of unruly juveniles." On November 28, the Times reports, "400 baton-swinging, armed officers marched shoulder-to-shoulder down Sunset Blvd., shoving the protestors into side streets, and clubbing them on the pavement. Youths shouted, 'Who do cops protect? MONEYMAKERS!' "

By December 5, 337 arrests on the curfew charge had been made. In three weeks' time.

On December 12, cops entered a private hall, in which was taking place a meeting to protest police action, and asked one of the kids for his ID. Albert Eason Monroe, 57-year-old Executive Director of the Southern Cal ACLU, informed the kid he had a legal right not to show the cop ID disclosing age. Monroe was booked on "SUSPICION OF INTERFERING WITH A POLICE OFFICER."

The important point is that the burn merchants run the Strip. The burn merchants run the West Village. Burn merchants run North Beach. Information seems to indicate that they are gaining control of the Haight (to be documented in the next EVO). It looks like a variation of the same shit beginning in the East Village; Memorial Day was just the beginning.

Certain questions have to be answered. Why did the cops bust up a peaceful situation in the Park, beat people, arrest people, cause a riot, all over the noise complaint of one urinal cleaner? The business potentials have been outlined above. If this is the case, who's paying the cops? Or is it plain, uncorrupted fascism?

Last week, the press reported that a white hippie girl was stripped and attacked by Puerto Ricans in the Park. People who were on the scene, however, declare that the chick danced in front of the crowd, dared them to grab her, and took off her blouse herself. Good publicity, realizing that the press would write "white girl attacked by Puerto Ricans." The motive? Perhaps to pit the hippies against the Puerto Ricans. Maybe an excuse for more cops. SPECULATON: Who put her up to it?

The thing we have to do is refuse to be used in their game of political exploitation. We must refuse to resist them on the streets and in the park—they want us to demonstrate, non-violently, of course. This is publicity. If we can stay off the streets and out of the park for a few weeks, they'll be powerless. If we want the Lower East Side as a place to live and play, let's not fall into their trap. Stay indoors, go uptown, go out of town, but be INVISIBLE. The alternative is a sideshow.

Anyway, now they know how many holes it takes to fill the Albert Hall.

EDWARD BENES

Yips See "Pattern of Frameups"

"We break enough laws; the police don't have to resort to these tactics to make arrests," yippie leader Abbie Hoffman said yesterday. He accused the police of planting narcotics in the East Village haunts of his followers.

Looking tired after spending Saturday in Federal Court, where he answered an indictment for conspiracy to riot during the Democratic National Convention in Chicago, followed by his appearance on Sunday in Manhattan Criminal Court on a gun charge, Hoffman threatened reprisals against the latest alleged police harassment.

"I have no idea how we can defend ourselves. We don't want to set up barbed wire fences around our establishments the way they did in Chicago," he said.

"But I assure you, we will take every legal means and use every counter demonstration method to offset this effort by the police—which violates law, order and ethics—to break up the renaissance of the people," he told reporters at 338 E. Sixth St.

Two of Hoffman's followers pointed specifically to a "certain police pattern" which has uncovered "planted narcotics" in two hangouts used by the yippies. Both finds were made Sunday.

Ed Sanders, 29, owner of the Peace Eye Bookstore, 147 Ave. A., near Ninth St., said he found two glassine envelopes containing a white powder which might have been heroine, secreted in the toilet in the rear of the store.

Sanders said he should have photographed the evidence and called his lawyer, but instead, fearing police action, flushed the contents down the toilet.

Paul Krassner, 36, editor of the *Realist* and one of the founders of the so-called renaissance movement, summed up the feelings of the yippies.

"We used to be afraid of pickpockets who took stuff out of our pockets, now we must be on the alert for people putting things into our pockets," he said.

In another development, three lawyers charged that undercover police-

From the New York *Daily News*, March 25, 1969, 16. Reprinted by permission.

men mixed with demonstrators Saturday night outside the New York Times building on W. 43d St. The lawyers accused the cops of trying to create trouble by passing out cans of spray paint and stink bombs to yippies.

PEGGY KERRY

The Scene in the Streets

On the evening of December 9th, a demonstration was held near the Waldorf-Astoria Hotel to protest President Nixon's appearance at the hotel to receive the National Football Foundation's award as "the year's most accomplished and distinguished American."

The demonstration took place outside the Bankers Trust Company Building. By the time I arrived at 5:15 p.m. it was impossible for the marshalls to ask for any sort of a moving picket line—there were too many people. Barriers kept demonstrators out of the street and divided them from the steadily increasing number of policemen and readily recognizable plainclothesmen. The plainclothesmen were the only non-uniformed people allowed in the street apart from the press, Peace Parade Committee marshalls, legal observers from the Lawyers Guild, and observers from the Civil Liberties Union. Some in the crowd carried anti-war signs, but the majority of the signs read "Free Huey Newton" and "Avenge Fred Hampton." People chanted pro-Panther and anti-war slogans. It was a very vocal but peaceful group assembled to protest the policies of the Nixon administration. It must have numbered 3-5,000.

Charge for the Flag

At about 6:15 p.m. a red flag was hoisted on the Bankers Trust Building flag pole. Very little was made of this incident and it wasn't until a police officer pointed to it that I noticed it at all. He pointed up at it and ordered it down. Lee Evers and his wife were a short distance away from the flagpole and observed that "six policemen made their way through the demonstrators, lowered the cloth, and took two men along with them into the police lines . . . and for no reason we could distinguish, the police beat the

From *The Scene in the Streets* by Peggy Kerry. The New York Civil Liberties Union, Dec. 1969, pp. 7-21. Reprinted by permission.

two men with their clubs, and drew blood. It was a horrible sight. We were astounded. The men fell to the ground and were dragged along the gutter [and] across Park Avenue." John Kelley, a graduate student from Columbia University, said he was standing directly behind the flagpole beside the two men arrested. "I really don't know what they were doing to be arrested. They weren't even standing in the way of the cops as they came barrelling through the barricade, knocking over three people and, in flying wedge formation and with nightsticks ready, rushed the steps to the flagpole. One of the men beside me threw up a victory peace sign. This must have been what prompted the arrest. The police looked very angry and emotional. Two policemen grabbed a man, clubbed him over the head and dragged him down the steps. A friend of his followed him and the police grabbed the friend too. It was a senseless act of violence."

Robin Ellis, a young man who had formerly worked for the Southern Christian Leadership Conference, said he saw the police car carrying the two arrested men on Park Avenue. One of the men arrested, a middle-aged pacifist, raised his fingers in a peace sign as he looked out of the window at the crowd. "The cop in the front seat just turned around and hit him," Robin said. The man hit said, "I gave the peace symbol to the demonstrators through the car window and the tough holding me slugged me with his club across the face. I thought at the time that my nose was broken. The thug was in plain clothes."

Incident at the Barricades

The flagpole incident incensed the crowd, and many epithets were directed at the police. One of the police barricades at 48th Street was knocked down and, according to Neil Conan of WBAI, police went through the barricade and arrested several people. One witness says, "A contingent of police wielding clubs attacked a group of demonstrators, running into them, and coming up with their prey, a youth with his arms covering his head." A young girl said, "Three to five plainclothesmen pinned this demonstrator to a car and beat him up. The plainclothesmen were interrupted for a short time by a uniformed cop who kicked the demonstrator in the groin and proceeded to beat him up. The uniformed policeman left and the demonstrator was taken away by two of the plainclothesmen."

Barricades were knocked down several times, perhaps accidentally or perhaps intentionally by angry demonstrators. At no time when this happened did I observe demonstrators rush into the street.

Glenn Kolleeny, whose father is an NYCLU cooperating attorney, was arrested during one such incident at the barricades.

"Two kids, one next to me, were pushed by the crowd so that the barrier was overturned again. Police in the street grabbed me even though I was still on the sidewalk," Glenn reported. "A policeman pulled me into the street and put me in a headlock. I started yelling, 'I'm not resisting.' Three other cops came over, circled around me and started clubbing me. They had pulled off my glasses. One cop was clubbing at my head. I was bleeding from my nose and face. All the time I was being dragged to the island in the center of Park Avenue. Half way across, one of the three cops hit me squarely across the top of my head while I was being held in the headlock."

Milton Beller of the Office of the Corporation Counsel of the City of New York was standing by the Fifth Avenue Peace Parade sound truck when the barricade at 48th Street was knocked down. "I don't know if this was done intentionally or whether it occurred accidentally because of the large crowd pushing up against the barrier. In any case, a number of policemen came charging into the crowd, many, but not all, with their clubs in hand raised to the levels of their heads. The crowd grew panicky and many ran back from the barrier as the police came in. The police grabbed some people and started beating them, some with their fists and some with their clubs. A boy of 17 standing near me when the barrier went down was beaten for no apparent reason. He clearly was not responsible for any trouble at the barrier. One policeman grabbed him and started beating him with his fists. He was not arrested. After a few seconds the policeman just left him and started running after some other people.

"I saw other people being beaten. Some were arrested and others were not. It appeared to me that the police were just beating people at random with no clear indication that the people they were attacking had committed an illegal act. I saw none of the people being attacked fight back or attempt to hit the police. Most attempted to protect themselves by covering their heads or tried to run."

The Counter-Demonstration

Between 50th and 51st Streets on Park Avenue, a pro-Nixon demonstration was held at the same time as the anti-Nixon demonstration. About 50 people carrying signs reading "Welcome Nixon," "Nixon's the One" and "Tell it to Hanoi" were marching in a picket line which was well guarded by the police. Anyone who tried to stop and watch was hustled on by the police.

A black taxicab driver stopped to talk with three blacks dressed as astronauts who were part of the counter-demonstration. "I must stress that my intention was not to prevent them from picketing but to persuade them to reconsider," he said. He was told to join the pickets or move on and he joined them. "I was not obstructing the marchers but was only talking to those people who were willing to talk to me. Suddenly I was grabbed by four police and forcibly removed from the spot. When I protested, I was thrown against a wall, frisked, threatened with arrest and verbally abused."

Use of Plainclothesmen

There were many plainclothesmen in clusters on Park Avenue who would disappear into the crowd from time to time. They wore blue jeans and ski or army jackets. Pauline Rosen of Women's Strike for Peace observed from the speakers' platform atop the Fifth Avenue Peace Parade panel truck "two instances of men in grey windbreakers grab demonstrators [and] begin to beat them. They kept punching and beating them. One of these men turned the demonstrator over to the police after he was finished with the beating. These men, most of them wearing grey windbreakers, some wearing Moratorium buttons and even carrying black and red flags were seen with the uniformed police."

Shelley Ramsdell of the Moratorium Committee also noted that the plainclothesmen were "confused in their policies. Moratorium buttons and Vietcong flags just don't go together. That's how some people were easily identified as plainclothesmen."

Others were not so easily identifiable. Ann Yellin of Women's Strike for Peace said that she saw a group of ski-jacketed men beat up several demonstrators. Her first reaction was that this was an attack by a rightist group. Later when the demonstrators were turned over to the police, she realized who the ski-jacketed men were.

On one occasion, the plainclothesmen could not even recognize their own. Jonah Raskin, who was later clearly identified as a demonstrator and severely beaten later on in the 17th precinct, was at first mistaken for a plainclothesman outside of St. Patrick's. "He's one of ours," he overheard a plainclothesman beside him say.

In many cases, the plainclothesmen did work uniformed police could have done—they made arrests. Demonstrators were always concerned as to who these men were and what right they had to make arrests. One man said, "Soon after 6 p.m. I saw two men wearing army fatigue jackets dragging a man from the crowd, and striking at everyone around them with blackjacks. They pulled the man behind the Bankers Trust Building, and continued to attack people who wanted to know who they were and why they were arresting the man. I followed them and saw two uniformed police come to their assistance and drive most of the demonstrators away with random blows of their nightsticks."

Sheila O'Conner of the James Madison Constitutional Law Institute also witnessed this incident. "I saw two men in brown jackets dragging a young man along the ground and back into the passageway which leads to 49th Street. His coat and shirt were pulled up because of the dragging so that his bare body scraped the cement. At no time did the men identify themselves as policemen to those who came to discover why he was being treated in such a manner."

John Kornbluth of the Moratorium Committee also saw two plainclothesmen striking a demonstrator with blackjacks.

One person who was arrested by plainclothesmen said that he was standing on 48th Street near the Bankers Trust Building with some friends when a group of eight plainclothesmen passed them saying "Power to the People!" "They had crew-cuts, were all different ages and just looked uncomfortable in their clothes. So we said, 'Oink, Oink. Smell the pigs!' And they just attacked us and started beating us up."

At no time was it possible to find out the badge numbers of plainclothesmen. Sandy Scott, an NYCLU observer, said that a policeman told her it was possible to obtain numbers from plainclothesmen simply by asking. On no occasion when she or others tried did they meet with success.

An Attempt To get Police Numbers

David Schwartz, an observer for the Lawyers Guild, says that one demonstrator "called out to someone to read off the badge numbers of officers who were assaulting demonstrators [on Fifth Avenue]." According to one witness, the demonstrator than approached a policeman and, while trying to read his number, asked "What are you doing?" "The policeman said 'That's one of the motherfuckers.' and grabbed [the demonstrator] who was led away." David Schwartz reports that the demonstrator did not resist arrest, but the police threw him headfirst into the bus. Friends of the demonstrator who witnessed the arrest were clubbed and one girl said that "a policeman picked up a metal litter box and threw it straight into my chest, knocking me to my hands and knees. Friends in the crowd pulled me away from the officer."

Break-Up of Parts of the Demonstration

It was about 7:15 p.m., shortly after we no longer heard sirens in the direction of Fifth Avenue, that the police began herding all demonstrators standing at 49th Street and Park Avenue west towards Madison Avenue. Sandy Scott reports that "the police gave no answer when people asked why they could not return to the demonstration site." The only people allowed in the direction of Park Avenue were people who stated to the police that they condemned the anti-war demonstration. TPF officers came through the arch of the Bankers Trust Building and pushed people off the steps that only a moment before they had been allowed to stand on. There were policemen at the corner of 49th Street and Madison Avenue breaking up the groups of demonstrators into different directions and telling them to go home.

As they were being pushed up 49th Street, Sandy Scott reports that she heard a girl crying hysterically. She was a high school student who had come with two friends. In the confusion of being pushed up the street, one friend had knocked over a barricade. According to the High School student, her friend was beaten and dragged off by the police.

While police on Park Avenue were herding demonstrators towards Madison Avenue, the demonstrators around Saks were being driven down Fifth Avenue or east along side streets. Nancy Garden, an observer for the Civil Liberties Union, reports, "There seemed to be a pattern of inconsistency among the police, perhaps deliberate, perhaps simply genuine confusion on their part. Over and over again, one cop would say, 'You can't go down this street; but you can on the other side.' One would get to the other side, however, and find one could not. Some policemen were adamant about 'Moving along'; others less so. Some seemed to be doing their best to avoid confrontations with demonstrators; others seemed to be seeking them out."

· · ·

Later Incidents along Fifth Avenue

The police seemed bent on clearing Fifth Avenue of demonstrators. Three young men were standing on the corner of Fifth Avenue and 49th Street at about 7:50 p.m. when a police officer approached one of them.

"He grabbed my upper left arm," Howard LaCasa, a New York City school teacher, reports, "and told me to come with him and not make a sound. My friend began to follow me and the officer, noticing him, ordered him to 'Get the hell out of here.' I was quite surprised and shocked at being approached and grabbed by the officer and asked him where he was taking me and why. He replied that I had better go with him. My reaction was to say 'No' until I knew the reason why I was being treated in this manner. The officer indicated that I had better go with him as he tightened his grip on my left arm. I was led to Rockefeller Plaza where there were considerably fewer people present. All this time I remained holding the sign (an anti-war sign indicating how many U.S. soldiers have been killed in Vietnam). We then turned off Fifth Avenue and into the Plaza, the officer was now holding me by the back of the neck. At this time he was saying, 'I told you twice to get away from the corner' (meaning 49th Street and Fifth Avenue). This was not so. I was only on the corner for a few minutes and there were no police on that side of the street and none approached me or signalled me in any way. He then grabbed me by the collar, shoved me against the wall and said, 'I'll bust your fuckin' head in if you don't drop the sign.' I then repeatedly asked what I had done and he repeated twice in an angry aggressive tone, 'Drop the sign or I'll smash your fuckin' head in,' all the time holding me by the collar against the wall. I was terrified that he meant every word he said and by the third time he threatened me, I dropped the sign and said that I dropped the sign now let me go. He did not release me right away. It was not until after he noticed that I was staring at his badge number that he released me. He told me to leave in a direction which was away from where my friends and the crowds were standing and told me that he better not see me downtown anymore that evening."

This was not the only sign-collecting incident during the evening. Don Hazen of the Human Resources Adminstration reports that "at one point, one block west of the Waldorf at approximately 48th or 49th Street, a large group of Tactical Police Cops were grouped. As groups reached that point, being pushed in that direction by cops from the rear, the T.P.F. group decided to collect all banners. Then they proceeded to run up to any individual with a sign or banner and ripped the banners out of their hands. Any person who expressed confusion at this approach and attempted to hang on to their signs or banners was rapped on the arms and chest with clubs. The cops then brought all their acquisitions over to a police van where they gleefully jumped on the banners and signs, destroying them, and then threw them into the vans."

John McIlwain, a legal observer for NYCLU, reports that about 8 p.m. "as we moved down Fifth Avenue following some young demonstrators who called out remarks to the police, suddenly, for no apparent reason, the cops broke into a run across Fifth Avenue just as we crossed 48th Street heading south. As I followed I saw one officer club a demonstrator on the head in a doorway of a building and then run on, leaving the demonstrator crumpled on the ground."

The window breaking spree had long since ended and yet the police still continued to club and arrest at random. A large police bus moved slowly down the east side of Fifth and it was into this bus that John McIlwain watched "demonstrators who had been arrested, pushed, shoved, jabbed and unnecessarily roughed up."

The Panel Van Incident

Roger Tyndell, whose son was arrested in the following incident, recounts the following:

> At approximately 8:25 p.m. I was walking in company with my wife and daughter toward 5th Avenue and 48th Street.
> Groups of policemen were breaking up knots of people who were leaving the peace demonstration area on Park Avenue and urging them to move on. A few minutes earlier we had witnessed several arrests and beatings. I was struck by the fact that the police in these cases were using force indiscriminately. One young man was straddled after a chase by a policeman and struck with his riot stick. . . .

As we reached the S.E. corner of Fifth Avenue we observed a policeman threatening another young man with his riot stick as he advanced
on him. . . .

At about this time the sound truck used by the Fifth Avenue Peace
Parade Committee, a rented panel truck, drove past, travelling south on
Fifth Avenue. The driver thrust his hand out of the driver's side window
in the shape of a V, signifying peace. He called out words which I recall
as "This is what Richard Nixon's fascist police are going to be like, and
don't you forget it."

The truck was in motion all of this time. No profanity had been used,
no particular persons had been addressed. There were people in motion
on either side of Fifth Avenue and people preparing to use the cross-
walks, all of them in the company of or not far removed from policemen.
There seemed to be policemen everywhere.

Immediately after this utterance and while the vehicle was still in
motion, a helmeted policeman rushed past me and my daughter brandishing his riot stick in pursuit of the vehicle. This was the signal for a rush.
People in the crowd, myself included, yelled "Stop! Leave them alone!"
It was clear that people were alarmed by the imminent action of the police who now converged rapidly on the truck. The truck slowed down
and pulled over toward the curb in response to the sudden movement of
police. From a position I had maintained off the S.E. corner of 48th
Street and Fifth Avenue I could see a policeman beating in the driver's
side window with his stick before the vehicle had come to a full stop.

Ruth Silber, an employee in a law office, said she saw eight or nine policemen club the top of the truck. They pulled open the back door, one person
was literally hurled from the van into the startled onlookers. The others were
pulled out and, after them, shopping bags with leaflets and peace buttons
which were strewn over the sidewalk and street.

Don Hazen of H.R.A. was also present and observed that "a number of
cops arrived, and pounced on the truck like crazy animals, smashing it with
their clubs and ripping open the back doors and smashing whatever and
whoever was inside. The group of cops dragged at least three individuals
away from the truck, using force and their clubs very freely."

David Brauner, a young lawyer, saw the driver dragged from the truck.
He observed "no conduct on the part of any occupant of the vehicle which
justified their arrest and absolutely no provocation to justify the violent manner in which they were handled or the willful destruction of their property
by the officers."

Hendrick Hertzberg of the *New Yorker* said, "No one I saw resisted; on
the contrary, the attitude of those arrested was, if anything, supplicating."

According to one couple at the scene they spoke to the police captain in charge on two occasions, "calling his attention to what appeared to be police beating of unresisting citizens and violent misuse of private property." He assured them he was in control of the situation.

Yet the situation was one in which occupants of the van were beaten and arrested and one member of the Peace Parade Committee passing on the street at that point was arrested for asking what had happened to the van. Onlookers and legal observers were pushed away from the scene. It was only after persistent questioning that we were able to ascertain to what precinct those arrested were being taken.

All arrested in the van incident were thrown into the police bus which had been moving slowly down Fifth Avenue. Across from the van I witnessed the beating of a youth who had been singled out by the police as he walked down Fifth Avenue. Two policemen pulled him in front of the bus and clubbed him for a minute or so. Then, while still clubbing him on the back, they pushed him up the steps of the bus.

In the Precincts

Sixty-eight people were arrested on that evening between 6:00 and 9:00 p.m. All defendants were taken to the 14th, 17th or 18th precincts to be booked. Some were brutally beaten after their arrests. Many defendants state that they were punched, beaten and kicked while hand-cuffed. Some said they were kicked in the face and beaten with blackjacks. In several instances people in cars behind the police vans were witnesses to the brutal beatings.

The National Lawyers Guild under the direction of Mary Kaufman attempted to provide lawyers for all arrested. In many cases, even when clients asked for a Guild lawyer, they found it difficult to obtain permission to see one as they did not know his name.

At the 17th precinct the doors were closed to lawyers after the arrival of two Guild attorneys and two private attorneys. At the 14th precinct it took two hours for the Guild lawyer to be allowed in. Paul Chevigny, an NYCLU staff attorney, was the only attorney permitted in the 18th precinct. After he had seen two clients, they were moved to the 17th precinct. Chevigny saw them again on release. In the interim they had been systematically, severely and protractedly beaten.

Parents whose children had been taken to a hospital for treatment often found it difficult to obtain the name of the hospital and sometimes found it almost impossible to determine whether their children were in the precinct or in a hospital.

Many defendants were badly in need of medical care, but were required to wait several hours before being taken for treatment.

Many waited several hours before they were allowed to make their one phone call. Often the arresting officer made it for them rather than allow them to use the phone themselves.

Of the 68 arrested early that evening, only nine were arraigned in night court. Bookings in the precinct took an unusually long time.

CLAUDIA DREYFUS

George Demmerle: The Pig Wore a Dayglow Helmet

When we're not being accused of perverse smut peddling, the charge most often slung at underground journalists is that we're hopelessly paranoid. Like a few weeks ago I was talking to this fellow, Bernie the Reform Democrat, about my fears that the government may be launching a full scale attempt to muffle the media, over and underground. "Nonsense," said Bernie, "Nixon wouldn't dare mess with the big shots at NBC, CBS and the *New York Times*. You're just paranoid!"

The next day I ran into my friend Lance, the immaculate male model "Dahrl-ling," he gushed, while brushing my cheek ever so delicately, "why don't we go somewhere and refresh ourselves?" I had been reading some very exciting Ralph Nader kind of stuff and began rapping about the dangers of insecticides and artificial foods. "Nonsense, Darh-ling," snipped Lance as he sipped a glass of Diet Pepsi, "You're just paranoid!"

And then there's Dr. Parataxis, a well-known psychoanalyst who hangs around a West Village pub.

Parataxis was rather uptight about the possibility of violence at the Washington Moratorium. "Whether or not there's violence in D.C.," I said, "I think that it's important for people to go down to the March. America is really beginning to look like Nazi Germany and I think people should show that they're not Good Germans."

"Nonsense," the analyst said condescendingly, "how can you compare the United States to Germany? It's a bad war, oh yes. But the Americans don't go around slaughtering whole Vietnamese villages. They're not committing genocide. Frankly, I must say, you have strong paranoic tendencies."

So, it was with a certain perverse satisfaction that I noted the following item in last Thursday's *New York Times:* "BOMBING SUSPECT FREED MINUS BAIL: DIE MAKER MAY BE INFORMER OR COOPERATIVE WITNESS."

"One of four persons originally held on high bail in a plot to bomb governmental and corporate buildings has been freed without bail in Federal Court with the Government's consent.

"The government refused to say yesterday why it had consented on Tuesday to a motion by *George Demmerle,* who had been held on $50,000 bail, to be released on his own recognizance. Frequently in such cases the defended is either an underground informer or one who has decided to cooperate with the authorities."

George Demmerle . . . George Demmerle . . . George Demmerle. I knew the name. CLICK! Of course, he was the tall, forty-ish guy known around the East Village as "Prince George Crazy" and "George Crazie." I had met him once and at the time, had kind of accused him in print of piggery.

Flashback to last August's Nagasaki Day Parade to End the War in Vietname. Over fifteen thousand New Yorkers had braved the summer heat to march against Southeast Asian murder. But when the marchers arrived at the Central Park Bandshell, instead of the expected program of anti-war songs and speeches, they found the stage siezed by a group of Crazies and members of Walter Teague's American Committee to Aid the National Liberation Front. Every time a speaker from the Fifth Avenue Peace Parade Committee would begin his rap, Crazies and Teagelets would commence shouting him down with chants of "Power to the People," "The Stage belongs to the People," and "Get the C.P. (Communist Party) off the stage!" Fist fights and scuffles were constantly breaking out between Peace Parade Committee marshals and the usurpers. Every now and then a disruptor would begin blasting the audience on a portable phonograph and amplifier set with horrible scratchy sounding Vietcong marching songs. The audience below simply responded to the panadomonium with chants of their own: "You're all agents" and "Get the pigs off the stage." But there were other marchers, many of them new to the peace movement, who rather than participate in insane internicine warfare, simply got up and left the park.

And on stage was this huge man who was sort of leading the madness. The man was striking because of his costume: a shocking pink satin cossack shirt, an orange day-glow helmet, and a freaky acid smile. Around him was large coterie of Crazies who would follow him in any chant he cared to start. The man's name was "Prince George Yippie" alias "George Crazie" alias "George Demmerle."

Bravely, I approached Prince George and asked him why the Crazies had come to disrupt the Nagasaki Day Demonstration. Was there not a rightwing rally somewhere where Crazie efforts might prove more productive? Georgie boy looked at me suspiciously and answered: "We Crazies have been trying to get up here for years. But the Fifth Avenue Peace Parade Committee is dominated by the CP and they won't let any other view get a forum. We feel that the Parade Committee should be more militant, so we're going to force them to be so. The Movement shouldn't be holding peace rallies we shouldn't be out in the streets!"

Did Prince Crazy think his disruption would cause a split in the Movement? "Oh no, I don't think we're splitting the Movement," Crazie George replied. "We go around making enemies, so that the Parade Committee can gain support. Besides, we're not into organizing."

The demonstration ended as it had begun: with scuffles, curses and chants. But afterwards, as I sat talking with Michael Luckman, the Parade Committee's press relations man, a young nurse approached us with a very interesting story. This lady had come to the demonstration with the Medical Committee for Human Rights and, in the course of providing medical aide, she spotted three Crazies flashing badges and handing papers to two well-known Red Squad super-sleuths. Could she identify any of the three? She said she could. So Mike had her look through photographs of the demonstration and the girl did come up with one positive identification: George Demmerle.

That week EVO printed the story, complete with the nurse's revelations. It was that week that East Village Crazies broke off all friendships with EVO staffers. It was that week that our hallway was plastered with Crazie stickers. It was that week that my mailbox was filled with notes saying: "Prince George Crazie was here. He wants to talk with you."

Figuring that George either wanted to beat the shit out of me or play me some Vietcong music, I decided to ignore the messages. Now I wish I hadn't been so hasty. It might have been interesting to hear old George be indignant at my accusation of his pigdom.

When news of Prince George Crazies finkery burst into the headlines, many of his East Village acquaintances reacted with genuine shock. "George must have freaked out last week or something," explained Bill Etra, a photograper for RAT. "I mean, I just can't believe that was an agent all along. It's really hard for me to conceive of an police agent being tripped out constantly. And George always went around as if he was on one big, big trip."

RAT's Art Director, Paul Simon disagreed: "As soon as I heard that four people were arrested for these bombings, it struck me that if any one of them actually was guilty, it would *have* to be Crazie George. Cause he was the craziest person I had ever met. But as soon as we learned that there was a police informer among the defendants, I immediately thought of George— for the very same reason."

Friends of George Demmerle describe a vague collage of events to explain his character. George was the guy who sat at Yippie planning meetings playing with his own toy bombs. George was the guy who showed up at the

Alternate U. costume party dressed as a dead Green Beret. George was the guy whose brother said that he always thought he had very right-wing politics.

Jeff Shero, RAT's editor, only knew George Demmerle from Yippie meetings. "Whenever there was a meeting," Shero recalled, "He'd get up and say to people, 'Anyone who wants to get arrested, come with me.' A lot of people thought he was very cool and very radical. In retrospect, it appears that George was trying to get a lot of people busted."

"It's funny," said Jeff thoughtfully, "he always struck me as a guy who was over thirty-five, flipped out and having fun with his life. I guess he wasn't having much fun after all."

FRED J. COOK

The FBI Nobody Knows

The pressure for convictions and the awesome reputation of the FBI both combine at times to foster actions that are carried out with scant regard for individual or human rights. The right of the individual to privacy, his right to be secure in his home and his person unless the law can show adequate reason for intruding upon him—this philosophy, the basis of the Bill of Rights, in view of many the most precious contribution the American system has made to Western civilization—is regularly flouted in the FBI's preoccupation with obtaining convictions at whatever cost. Wiretapping, for instance, has been repeatedly held by the federal courts to be illegal, and the evidence so obtained has been banned. Yet the FBI admittedly wiretaps. It contends that it does so only in security, in espionage, cases in which the welfare of the nation conceivably may be at stake, but "security" obviously is an elastic term that can be stretched to cover a wide swath of suspicion. Does the FBI, in fact, limit its electronic eavesdropping only to bona fide spy-security cases in which the eavesdropping is partially legitimized by approving orders from the central Bureau or the Attorney General? Jack Levine contends it does not.

"In each of the FBI field offices," he stated in his report to the Justice

Department, "there are carefully concealed rooms in which the wiretaps are monitored. Access to these Sutech (Technical Surveillance) Rooms is limited to the SAC, ASAC, and those Agents in each field office who are assigned to the monitoring. The information received from wiretaps is credited to 'informants' which are designated by symbols and numbers. These inform- ant records are kept in top-security files in the field offices. . . . It is a matter of common knowledge among the Bureau's Agents that much of the wire- tapping done by the field offices is not reported to the Bureau. This is the result of the pressure for convictions. A still greater number of taps are not reported by the Bureau to the Attorney General or to the Congress."

Expanding on this statement in a subsequent interview over radio station WBAI in New York, Levine pointed out that the FBI, with its power and prestige, has little difficulty in establishing a close liaison with telephone companies throughout the nation. This simplifies its task of electronic eaves- dropping, since the easiest, most foolproof way to tap a telephone is to "bridge" a pair right in the telephone exchange into which subscribers' lines feed. If the tapping is done in this way, even the most suspicious or the most concerned telephone user could never prove it, for an expert could check his line until Doomsday without discovering a thing, as there would be no actual, physical tap of the line anywhere near the premises. Hence a cozy relation between telephone officials and the FBI—a fact of life that may almost be taken for granted—eliminates all possibility of detection and, in Levine's words, lets the FBI "use the company's trunk lines with the coop- eration of the company officials."

The FBI, Levine said, "recognizes that much of this sort of dirty law enforcement and security work is illegal, but they feel that without it they'll be hampered in getting the information they need." This is, of course, the crux of everything. In a really important case, in which the approval of Bureau headquarters in Washington could be obtained, a formal application to tap would be made through channels, and the illegal act would be per- formed with as great an appearance of legitimacy as the orders of authority could give it. But, said Levine, "in many instances, the agents in charge of the various field offices feel that it would be better to go ahead and tap a phone, let's say, without clearing it through FBI headquarters because of the concern which they have for building up their conviction statistics and getting valuable information. There are many cases in which illegal activity is going on in the Bureau field offices in which it is not cleared."

Levine said he had been "interested in finding out from the agents in the office where I was working whether all the taps that were going on in the Detroit office had been approved either by the FBI's headquarters in Wash- ington or the Justice Department. And I found out from talking to the agents who monitored the taps that many of these cases are not approved and are not known by Bureau officials or by any one in the Justice Department."

A similar invasion of privacy is sometimes practiced on a person's mail. The FBI and the Post Office Department, brethren in the federal stable, usually work closely together. "This is not widely known," Levine said in his radio interview. "Neither the Post Office Department nor the FBI likes to advertise the fact that this is going on. But in incoming mail, particularly, it's easy for the FBI, through contacts that they have at the local post offices, to keep a close watch on this. They *generally* will not open mail unless it's a case that they're very, very concerned with. In the ordinary criminal security case, it's very doubtful whether the FBI would actually open someone's mail. But if the case was important enough and the information was reliable enough, they'd do it and will."

To wiretapping and mail surveillance, the FBI adds what is known in the Bureau as a "bag job." This is nothing less than the entering of a person's home in his absence without a search warrant, in direct violation of the Fourth Amendment to the Constitution. "This is very often resorted to," Levine said, "although it's generally unknown that the FBI engages in this kind of practice." Bag jobs were, he said, "done every day in the Bureau."

Evidence obtained in such illegal fashion cannot be used, of course, in a court trial unless it can in some way be legitimized. It can be utilized, however, for investigative leads, and information so gained can be used to pressure confessions. It is obvious, too, though Levine emphasized that he had never heard of the FBI's fabricating a case, that secret knowledge so gained is easily subject to abuse and could conceivably enable an agent, if he were unscrupulous enough and if the pressure for a conviction were strong enough, to build a chain of evidence to fit the needs of his case.

Levine had never worked a bag job, he said, but he told how it is done: "My roommate was working on a big tire theft case out in Detroit, and he and another agent were assigned to pick someone's lock and search this person's premises for evidence of participation in the crime. Here's the way a bag job works. You, the agents, are instructed—and this is given in our FBI training course in Washington—on these so-called jobs that you are on your own. In other words, you're working inside a bag; this is how they get the name. If you're found trying to break into an apartment or a building by the local police, let's say, who sometimes are unaware that the FBI is going to be there on that particular night, and if you're arrested and there's any publicity on this, then you're on your own and the FBI, you know, will deny that you had any authority to do that."

Knowledge of such techniques and intimate acquaintance with the inner mechanics of the FBI brought Jack Levine to conclusions that conflict starkly with the agency's public image. "I don't know whether the FBI has ever deliberately fixed a case," he said in his radio interview, "but I will say this: There's almost an obsession in the FBI with conviction statistics and with trying to—well, I think they have a very strong prosecutive personality, let us say. Generally I would say the FBI does not attempt, on an equal basis, to find evidence of innocence as it does evidence of guilt, and I think that this type of mentality or attitude can lead, or might or could conceivably lead, to some . . . in some investigations to innocent people being convicted of crimes or of lack of loyalty."

Under such circumstances, Levine decided that a long career in the FBI was not for him. He knew, too, that if he was going to quit he must quit soon; for among his fellow agents he saw many who would like to get out but were trapped by the long years they had spent in the Bureau and the family responsibilities they had acquired. Determined not to become such a victim, Levine wrote out a brief letter of resigntaion, stating his intention of returning to New York and resuming the practice of law. The resignation was accepted without prejudice, a significant point, on August 4, 1961. Jack Levine, in effect, had obtained his honorable discharge.

MICHAEL S. WALD *et al.*

Interrogations in New Haven: The Impact of *Miranda*

The Supreme Court decision in *Miranda v: Arizona* has been a touchstone of debate over the rules protecting the rights of suspects. The debate, begun even before *Miranda,* ranges from courts to police academies, from law reviews to popular magazines. Myriad claims regarding the likely impact of the ruling on law enforcement and "crime in the streets," are bandied about. Although the controversy has been singularly lacking in facts to support any position,[1] some critics of the decision are sufficiently upset to recommend a constitutional amendment reversing the decision.

From *The Yale Law Journal,* Vol. 76, pp. 1521-1648. Reprinted by permission of The Yale Law Journal Company, Fred B. Rothman & Company and the authors.
1. This has been recognized by many of the participants in the controversy. *See, e.g.,* Brief for New York as Amicus Curiae at 21-24, Miranda v. Arizona, 384 U.S. 436 (1966). *See also Developments in the Law—Confessions,* 79 *Harv. L. Rev.* 935, 945 (1966), opining, characteristically, that the factual questions are "unanswered and perhaps unanswerable."

Impressed by the need for systematic answers to the questions and claims cast up by the controversy, we undertook a study of the implementation and effect of *Miranda*. The core of the effort involved stationing observers at the New Haven, Connecticut, police headquarters around the clock for an eleven-week period during the summer of 1966. These observers witnessed all the interrogations conducted by the police during this period. In addition to the observations, interviews provided additional data for our study of the likely impact of *Miranda*, supplying the perspectives of the various participants in the criminal process—the detectives, prosecutors, defense lawyers, and suspects themselves.

The project attempts, essentially, to evaluate the claims that interrogations are inherently coercive and that *Miranda* will susbtantially impede successful law enforcement.[2] Four general questions are explored: What is the interrogation process like? What has been the impact of *Miranda* on the suspect's willingness to cooperate? How important are interrogations for successful solution of crime? Finally, what would be the impact of a lawyer in the stationhouse? The practical problems of implementing the decision are explored only briefly. No attempt is made to defend or attack the value judgments underlying the positions involved.[3] For some people, our approach is probably irrelevant, although, we hope, interesting. *Miranda* can be supported without any knowledge of the potentially adverse effect of the

---

2. The decision raises questions about the constitutional basis of the holding, the competence of the Court for such specific rule-making, the values underlying the decision, the effects the decision will have on law enforcement, and the problems of implementation.

The approach of this study is directed to the positions taken by those critics and supporters of the decision whose arguments are based on factual issues, since these are the only testable ones. While supporters of *Miranda* rely primarily on constitutional and value arguments, they also claim that interrogations are coercive and unnecessary. *See* 384 U. S. at 436-60; N. Sobel, *The New Confession Standards* (1966).

The critics claim Miranda will severly hamper law enforcement. This position is set forth in the brief for government in Westover v. United States, 384 U.S. 436 (1966), at 17: "We start from the premise that it is essential to the protection of society that law-enforcement officials be permitted to interrogate an arrested suspect." It was adopted by the dissenters in *Miranda:* "There is every . . . reason to believe that a good many criminal defendants who otherwise would have been convicted . . . will now . . . either not be tried at all or will be acquitted. . . ." 384 U.S. at 542 (dissenting opinion of White, J.). This position has been advocated by many commentators.

3. Various value positions underlie the claims of both critics and supporters. For example, the supporters claim interrogations without warnings threaten human dignity and that a system without such safeguards is unjust. The critics, on the other hand, assert that law-abiding citizens are the primary people about whom to be concerned and that they should not be denied protection in order to safeguard rights of "known" criminals.

decision: some commentators argue that the constitutional bar against compulsory self-incrimination is absolute and decisive;[4] others contend that to promote overall justice in the criminal process we must provide warnings to suspects, regardless of impact.[5] However, most critics and supporters alike rely on factual as well as value positions. This study attempts to provide some data for their discussion.

. . .

Changes in Police Behavior

To test whether our presence substantially affected police behavior, we tried to find out how the police acted before and after our observations. We interviewed 40 persons who had been interrogated during the four months preceding and following our three-month study.[6] We asked them to describe the same features of their interrogations that our observers recorded in the police station. Assuming that the process might be perceived differently from the suspect's perspective, we also interviewed 20 of the people whom we saw questioned last summer. By asking them questions to which we already had answers, we could tell how much, and on what points, their reports differed from those of our observers. This factor could then be applied to the interviews with the other suspects to estimate how accurate their reports were likely to be.[7]

Almost half of the interviewed suspects whom we had observed described their interrogations differently than our observers. The discrepancies followed no pattern; some even reported the process more favorably, saying, for example, they had received *Miranda* warnings when our observer had not recorded any such warnings. However, most respondents reported a more hostile interrogation than our observer recorded. Two suspects reported falsely that they were hit at the Detective Division. From this evi-

---

4. This position is inherent in the majority opinion in *Miranda* 479. *See also* E. Griswold, *The Fifth Amendment Today* 75 (1955).

5. Weisberg, *Police Interrogation of Arrested Persons: A Skeptical View*, in *Police Power and Individual Freedom* 153, 179-80 (C. Sowle, ed., 1962).

6. We had hoped to be able to interview a larger number of suspects. Unfortunately, we were denied access to the state prison and reformatories and this limited our sample to those people in jail or on probation. Many of those that were on probation were hard to find. It was not until we obtained the services of a former convict, now working for the Legal Assistance Association, that we were able to locate any defendants whatsoever. Fortunately, a number of those interviewed had been arrested several times over the past five years so we were able to get a comparison over a fairly long period.

7. This is, of course, a crude test. However, since the test indicated there was no significant change, problems with the test do not affect the validity of the findings.

dence, it seems probable that the responses of the people questioned before and after our observation period were also somewhat inaccurate.

Yet, even if we do not assume any exaggeration by the groups we did not observe, their description of the process was so similar to what we did observe that we feel justified in assuming our presence did not markedly affect the detectives' behavior.[8] If there were any changes, they appear to have been in the interrogation tactics used by the police. As we discuss below, during the summer the atmosphere at interrogations seemed generally friendly or businesslike to our observers; the police employed very few tactics such as threats, promises or trickery. From the reports of those we interviewed it appears that the detectives frequently displayed a more hostile air before and after our months of observation. The police told suspects more often that they would be "worse off" if they did not talk, played down the seriousness of the crime, swore at the suspects, and made promises of leniency. However, last summer we did find such tactics used frequently in the cases which the police considered most serious. The large proportion of serious crimes in the unobserved sample may therefore account for the more frequent use of such tactics.

Our belief that our presence had but slight effect is further supported by the impressions of our observers. Initially, our presence was viewed skeptically. The detectives treated us with suspicion, greeted us by silence, and locked the observers out of the detective headquarters when they left. Within two weeks, however, the attitudes of the detectives had changed markedly. They became friendly with the observers, talked and joked freely, and gave us free run of the station. The people on the night shift particularly seemed to enjoy having someone to talk with.

Aside from their apparently unguarded behavior, several other factors suggest that the police acted naturally after the first few weeks. The detectives frequently did not follow the letter of the law, and often gave no warnings despite our presence. As the summer progressed they also became more candid in their conversations. They tried, for instance, to justify, not to hide, their various prejudices.[9] Some detectives also admitted that coercive inter-

8. From these interviews we learned that interrogations had been conducted in the same rooms throughout. Almost all interrogations were about the same length as our summer average. No suspect indicated he had been denied a lawyer, either before or after *Miranda*, although a number of post-*Miranda* suspects indicated no warnings had been given them. This was also true during the summer. Even before *Miranda* most suspects were allowed to call friends and relatives, and were offered cigarettes and food. Only six of the people reported they had been treated badly; the others said their treatment was "o.k."

9. Almost all of the detectives were extremely biased against Negroes. However, this bias, while often voiced, was seldom evidenced during the interrogations.

rogations were sometimes useful, though this was invariably qualified—"of course, it doesn't happen any more."[10]

. . .

ADHERENCE TO LEGAL NORMS

Physical Coercion

We saw no undue physical force used by the detectives.[11] From what we sensed about the attitudes of the detectives in both divisions, we doubt that many of them would employ force as a calculated tool to pry out a confession.[12]

In the first place, neither division often needs a confession badly enough to beat someone up for it, because both usually have so much evidence when they arrest suspects and because the crimes are not generally very serious. Second, few of the detectives are calculating or ruthless in their attempts to extract a confession. They find interrogating a challenging game in which they try hard to outwit the suspect. But few are such crusaders against crime that they feel physical violence is justified to get a confession.[13]

Giving Advice of Rights

According to the detectives, before Miranda suspects were advised that they might remain silent and that anything they said could be used against them.[14] The Miranda decision therefore meant that the detectives had only

10. For a similar conclusion for a different police department see J. Skolnick, *Justice Without Trial* 36 (1966). Skolnick's presence was less likely to affect behavior since he was with the police only sporadically.

11. At the Detective Division the policemen sometimes were forced to subdue an unruly suspect, but this was accomplished without relish. None of the detectives ever threatened violence overtly, though a few appeared threatening whenever they lost their tempers. We were not present in the police cars between the time suspects were arrested and when they arrived at the Detective Division headquarters, but there was no evidence that they were taken elsewhere for questioning or that they were physically abused before being brought to the station.

12. Of course, our presence may have affected their behavior. Several of the detectives in the Detective Division said that they had transferred from the Special Services Division because they "didn't like the way things were done over there." One candidly told an observer that he had left the Special Services Division because they used too much force on suspects. In one case during the summer, a Special Services detective used excessive force in arresting a woman suspect. Other isolated incidents of such conduct were disclosed to us through several conversations with detectives.

13. Special Services belies the generalization. In this division most of the detectives seemed to feel they were the protectors of the public against vice and morals offenders.

14. Our impressions during the two weeks of observation before Miranda were that suspects were rarely warned and never at the outset of questioning.

to include advice about counsel to fulfill the new requirements. The new rules were not adhered to in most of the cases we observed—nor were the old. Despite the presence of our observers in the police station, the detectives gave all the advice required by *Miranda* to only 25 of 118 suspects questioned. Nonetheless most suspects did receive some advice; only 22 per cent of the suspects were not advised at all of their constitutional rights. The most frequently given warning was the right to silence—90 of the suspects were told. While only 51 were advised that anything they might say could be used against them, 81 were told they had a right to counsel, but only 27 of their right to appointed counsel.

The detectives clearly gave more adequate advice later in the summer, however, as they became more accustomed to the *Miranda* requirement; much of the non-compliance may therefore have been transitional. (See Table 1.) During the two weeks of June after *Miranda* less than half the suspects received a warning which included more than half the elements of the *Miranda* advice,[15] but by August more than two-thirds of the suspects

Table 1

ADVICE OF RIGHTS, BY MONTH, FOR ALL INTERROGATIONS[16]

Advice of Rights	Month			Total
	June	July	August	
0–2 warnings	14	31	14	59
3–4 warnings	9	22	28	49
Total	23	53	42	108
Full *Miranda* advice	0	8	17	

Not ascertained: 2
Not questioned: 9

Chi Square significant at .05 level.

15. The detectives may have had little chance to adjust to the *Miranda* decision in June.
16. In this table, as in others throughout the article, we will often divide the measure of the adequacy of the advice given the suspect into two categories. The category of less adequate warnings includes those in which the detective told the suspect nothing about his right, or gave him one or two parts of the four-part *Miranda* warning. In nearly every case in this category the detective advised the suspect of his right to silence and/or to counsel. The category of more adequate warnings includes those incorporating three or four parts of the *Miranda* advice. The usual three-part warnings included the statement that anything the suspect said could be used against him; the advice of the right to appointed counsel was almost never given unless all other parts of the *Miranda* warnings were also recited.

The last figure on the chart shows the number of interrogations in which the detectives repeated all four parts of the *Miranda* advice of rights.

received such a warning. More important, the number of full *Miranda* statements increased even more dramatically. No suspects received the full *Miranda* statement in June, while more than one-third of those questioned in August received the complete warning.

Undoubtedly the detectives' initial failure to give the *Miranda* advice was partly attributable to ignorance. Although the detectives were told of the decision by their superiors, few of them seemed to understand its requirements. Only one of the line detectives, so far as we could tell, had read the decision by the time we left the stationhouse. Toward the end of the summer, those who took the department's in-service training course began to receive more complete lectures on *Miranda*, so that by the end of last year all the detectives should have known what advice of rights they were required to give. Near the end of the observation period, cards giving the *Miranda* advice were passed out by the department to all the detectives and patrolmen with instructions to read one to each suspect at arrest. At the same time all detectives were given a waiver-of-rights form which they were to have the suspect sign before they questioned him.[17]

These remarks must be qualified for the Special Services Division. There the detectives were more conscious of the letter of the prescribed advice soon after it was promulgated. Consequently, their omissions generally seemed to be intentional.[18]

Despite increasing adherence to the letter of *Miranda*, however, both groups of detectives complied less readily with its spirit. By and large the detectives regarded giving the suspect this advice an artificial imposition on the natural flow of the interrogation—an imposition for which they could see little reason. Most incorporated into their tactical repertoire some sort of hedging on the warnings, when they were given. Some changed the warning slightly: "Whatever you say may be used *for* or against you in a court of law." Often, the detectives advised the suspect with some inconsistent qualifying remark, such as "You don't have to say a word, but you ought to get

17. The card read as follows:

Warning

I am a Police Officer. I warn you that anything you say will be used in a Court of law against you; That you have an absolute right to remain silent; That you have the right to advice of a lawyer before and the presence of a lawyer here with you *during* questioning, and

That if you cannot afford a lawyer, one will be appointed for you free before any questioning if you desire.

18. The detective who had read the decision, and who seemed to understand most fully its implications, was a member of Special Services. Perhaps his knowledge was responsible for that of his comrades.

everything cleared up," or "You don't have to say anything, of course, *but* can you explain how...."[19]

Even when the detective advised the suspect of his rights without these undercutting devices, he commonly de-fused the advice by implying that the suspect had better not exercise his rights,[20] or by delivering his statement in a formalized bureaucratic tone to indicate that his remarks were simply a routine, meaningless legalism. Instinctively, perhaps, the detectives heightened the unreality of the *Miranda* advice by emphasizing the formality of their statement. Often they would bring the flow of conversation to a halt and preface their remarks with, "Now I am going to warn you of your rights." After they had finished the advice they would solemnly intone, "Now you have been warned of your rights," then immediately shift to a conversational tone to ask, "Now, would you like to tell me what happened?"

In the few cases where a suspect showed an interest in finding a lawyer and did not already know one, the police usually managed to head him off simply by not helping him to locate one. Somtimes they refused to advise the suspect whether he should have a lawyer with him during questioning; more often they merely offered him a telephone book without further comment, and that was enough to deter him from calling a lawyer.

What circumstances influenced the detective's compliance with *Miranda*? Only one explanation for the varying compliance by the detectives—other than the change over time—survived statistical testing. For the sample as a whole, persons suspected of more serious crimes were given more adequate advice of their rights than those suspected of less serious crimes.[21] (See Table 2.) Our data showed no statistical relationship between the availability of evidence and the giving of warnings. But if we look only at the 56 suspects accused of more serious crimes, our data suggest—although not to a statistically significant degree—an interesting and highly rational set of priorities for giving the advice of rights. (See Table 3.)

The suspect of a serious crime was most likely to get a more adequate warning in the cases where the police had enough evidence to go to trial, but

19. Sometimes the advice was not given until extensive questioning had occurred.
20. This was usually conveyed by tone or manner of delivery.
21. "Serious" is used here to denote the New Haven detectives' evaluation. To obtain the evaluation, each detective interviewed was given a stack of cards with crimes printed on them and asked to place each under one of four headings: Least Serious, Fairly Serious, Serious, and Most Serious. The average results provided a basis for ranking crimes on an ordinal scale from 1 to 4. "Ordinal" implies that we know only that category (2) is more serious than category (1), not how much more, and that the scale is not absolute. The latter point is important because New Haven has a relatively low rate of violent crimes against the person. On another scale some of the crimes ranged "Serious" by the detectives might appear relatively trivial.

Table 2

ADVICE OF RIGHTS, BY SERIOUSNESS OF CRIME, FOR ALL INTERROGATIONS

| Advice of Rights | Seriousness of Crime | | Total |
	Less Serious	More Serious	
0–2 Warnings	36	21	57
3–4 Warnings	20	36	56
	56	57	113

Not ascertained: 5
Not questioned: 9

Chi Square significant at .01 level

not enough for a conviction. Thus, the police seemed most careful to insure the admissibility of the suspect's statement when they had a case against the suspect but when it was not clear that he could be convicted without an incriminating statement as evidence. The detectives apparently worried less about the admissibility of the statement if the case seemed open and shut. They were also apparently more willing, from sheer necessity, to take a chance on admissibility when they did not have enough evidence to get to trial unless the suspect incriminated himself.

This pattern is consistent with the conception of their job which many of the detectives seemed to hold. Perhaps as a result of past experience with the prosecutor's office, they often seemed to feel that their job was to produce some written evidence against the suspect and let the prosecutor handle the case after that. Given the detectives' rather narrow conception of their

Table 3

ADVICE OF RIGHTS, BY EVIDENCE AVAILABLE, FOR SUSPECTS OF
SERIOUS CRIMES

| Advice | Evidence | | | Total |
	Enough To Convict	Enough for Trial	Not Enough for Trial	
0–2 Warnings	10	4	6	20
3–4 Warnings	14	14	8	36
	24	18	14	56

Not ascertained: 8
Not questioned: 9
Less serious crime: 54

Chi Square not significant at .05 level.

part in the criminal process, it would not be surprising to find them more interested in obtaining some kind of statement to present to the prosecutor than in the statement's admissibility at trial.

. . .

THE MOST COERCIVE INTERROGATIONS

Throughout the preceding discussion we have dealt with each aspect of psychological interrogation and adherence to legal norms in isolation, stressing the low level of coerciveness in most questioning. Here, we shall examine the 17 interrogations where the police put most of the elements of psychological interrogation together, isolated the suspect from friends, and disregarded his right to end questioning.

Although we shall call these interrogations "coercive," we should note at the outset that some of them might not be legally coercive under *Miranda* and past coerced-confession decisions.[22] In four of the cases the full *Miranda* warning was given, and the suspect was either allowed to terminate the interrogation or made no attempt to do so. The police used more than three tactics in 16 of the 17 interrogations, and many more in several of them. But under the traditional due process standard for coercion, probably few of these interrogations were coercive enough to invalidate the evidence elicited. For example, the police questioned only two of the 17 for as long as seven hours, and only eight for more than one hour. Even though the detectives' procedures in these interrogations were certainly less than a civil-libertarian's ideal, some of them would have been difficult to challenge successfully in court.

To isolate these interrogations, we used as many as possible of the indexes of interrogation techniques and adherence to legal norms discussed in the previous sections. We felt that we could not consider coercive the detective's failure to offer a suspect amenities. Rather, it was more likely to mean that the interrogation had been short, or that the detective had simply forgotten to make the offer. We also did not use the index of the detective's advice of rights, since we felt that inadequate advice was largely a function of the date of the interrogation.

Five indicators of a coercive interrogation were used: (1) whether the attitude of the police towards the suspect was "hostile" or "ambiguous";[23]

22. On the other hand, suspects in some of the cases not labeled coercive may have been legally coerced into confessing—*e.g.*, some with short interrogations were not given warnings.
23. The latter was included because of our feeling that the ambiguity arising from the use of contrasting adjectives to describe the detectives' conduct may have meant that the detectives had gone to considerable trouble to ensnare the suspect with a tactic.

(2) whether the detectives employed three or more tactics; (3) whether they questioned the suspect for more than one hour; (4) whether they refused to stop questioning after the suspect indicated that he wanted to terminate the interrogation;[24] (5) whether they neglected to tell the suspect he could contact friends or family until after questioning was completed.[25] None of the interrogations in our sample included all five of these indicators; only three interrogations included four of the five. We decided to examine closely the 17 interrogations wherein we found three or more of the indicators.[26] . . . [T]he detectives were hostile or ambiguous, and used three or more tactics, in most of the interrogations chosen by this method. The other three indicators were erratically distributed.[27]

24. We did not include the cases in which the suspect had made no attempt to terminate questioning, since in these cases the detectives had not violated the rules of *Miranda*.
25. We did not include interrogations in which the detectives had simply not told the suspect at all that he could contact friends and family because of our feeling that the failure to mention the privilege was often a mere oversight on the part of the interrogator, or resulted from the brevity of the interrogation. Furthermore, we had noted that when the detectives apparently wanted to prevent the suspect from calling, but also wanted to say that he had been offered the chance to call, they generally advised him after the interrogation.

The detectives virtually never denied a suspect amenities after he had requested them, so we could not use the denial of amenities as an indicator of coercion.

Furthermore, we felt that amenities were sometimes offered, as well as withheld, to induce the suspect to talk, so that it was not clear in any given case what meaning could be attached to the fact that the detectives had not offered amenities. As it turned out, our feelings appear justified; 8 of the 17 suspects selected by the five indicators we used had been offered cigarettes.

26. One or more of these indicators was found in 85 of the 121 interrogations we had watched, but most interrogations included only one or two of them. The large number of interrogations in which one or two indicators of coercion appeared corroborated our earlier conclusion that the detectives employed these devices half-heartedly most of the time.

Our confidence in the value of the method of selecting the 17 interrogations for analysis was increased when we discovered that all seven of the interrogations from which the detectives tried to exclude us were selected by it.

27. One observer conveniently recorded, immediately after the interrogation, a conversation which formed one of these 17 interrogations. We repeat it here to give some of the flavor of the "most coercive" interrogations:

Subject had been picked up at 5 a.m. Car 15 had gone up the street and patrolman had followed to give possible assistance. Subject and another youth came running down the street. Patrolman apprehended subject. Stolen car was then found parked on the street in front of subject's home. Subject was accused of having taken the car. Interrogation proceeded as follows:

Detective: "It's pretty obvious you were in the stolen car. You were running away from it and from the policeman. Taking a car for a joyride [taking a car without owner's permission] is a lot less serious offense than car theft, so relatively what you did was a pretty minor offense. You were running away, we have you I'd say, so it'll go a lot easier for

INTERROGATIONS

Having isolated these interrogations, we tried to determine why the detectives had been more coercive in them. We found here, as in previous sections, that the detectives interrogated aggressively in serious crimes when they needed evidence to insure the suspect's conviction, when they needed the name of an accomplice, or when they felt the suspect could help them clear other crimes. In nine of the 17 interrogations, the police needed a confession or admission to assure conviction.

Five of the remaining eight were directed toward solving other crimes, primarily breaking-and-enterings. In the other three interrogations, we could find no reason for the use of coercion. In each the police had enough evidence to convict before questioning, and the questioning was directed only toward obtaining evidence against the suspect himself.

Almost all the suspects in these interrogations had been arrested for relatively serious crimes. Only five of the 17 crimes were among those ranked

---

you if you just tell me now exactly what you did. You'll be charged with the lesser offense, and the judge will go easier with you if you say: 'I made a mistake, and it won't happen again. . . .' Maybe you didn't even take the car, but were just a rider in it.

If we have to put you on a lie detector, well, that would take a lot of time and expense, and we wouldn't be too happy about that.

So, I'm being honest with you, and now I want you to be man enough to admit what you did. You don't have to tell me about the other guy, just yourself. Will you take a lie detector test?"

Suspect claims he knows nothing. Detective's tone then gets tougher, aggravation enters his voice, and a few flares of temper. Indicates that he doubts the suspect's story. Calls the home of a girl the suspect says he was talking to at the time of the car theft— the line is busy. Threatens to confront the suspect with the girl or her mother. Gets the name of the other kid who ran away from the police, threatens confrontation with him.

Detective: "If the other kid says the car was taken and you took it or were in it, I'll tell the judge how uncooperative you were. It'll be tough on you, and I'll try to give the other kid a break. (A moralistic tone enters his voice.) What were you doing out at 5 a.m. anyhow? We've got you, I'm certain, and you know it."

Then he locks the boy in the wire cage in the main room of the Detective Division. After a minute or two, he returns to the cage and talks to the subject. Buys him a soda. Subject says that only other kids were involved. Detective brings him to the fingerprint room to talk further. Subject says he was sitting on his porch, when the car drove up, some kids got out and ran off. When the patrol car came by, subject ran because he knew the police would pick up anyone around for questioning. Subject says he knows the kids—he gives the detective their first names. Detective says he doesn't want subject to be hurt by a record, so will keep subject out of it if subject's story is true. Will let subject go home if he agrees to come back at 12:30 p.m.

Subject doesn't appear at 12:30 and detective has only the first names of the other kids. Detective says he figures the subject fell asleep, and can always be picked up later. Detective believes him to be telling the truth.

"fairly serious" by the police; the other 12 were all among those ranked "serious" or "most serious."

We found no evidence that the police had used coercion in response to the personal characteristics of the suspects. Nor did they react to hostility from the suspects; in fact, this group of suspects was significantly more cooperative with the detectives than the sample as a whole. The proportion of Negroes and suspects with prior records was not significantly different from the sample as a whole. The 17 suspects were significantly younger than the sample as a whole; all were less than 30 years of age, and nine were less than 21. The large number of younger suspects, however, is probably accounted for by the fact that the crimes involved were more serious than those in the sample as a whole, since younger suspects tended to be arrested for more serious crimes.

The police gave noticeably more adequate advice of rights to these 17 suspects than to the sample as a whole. Eight of the 17 received the full four-part *Miranda* advice, one received three of the elements of the *Miranda* advice,[28] six received one or two of the elements,[29] and only two received no advice at all.

Despite the more adequate advice of rights given these suspects, the police were disproportionately successful in interrogating them. Seven of the suspects confessed; two admitted to their crimes; and two made incriminating statements. Only six of the 17 interrogations were unproductive. By comparison, only 21 suspects in the entire sample of 127 confessed, and only 11 made admissions.[30]

Surprisingly, the police were no less successful in the interrogations where they had given relatively adequate advice than in the others. Of the nine suspects given the full *Miranda* warning or three parts of it, four confessed, one made an admission, and another made an incriminating statement.[31] Similarly, three of the eight suspects given less adequate advice confessed; one made an admission; and one made an incriminating statement.

Our analysis of these 17 coercive interrogations thus indicates that the Court's fears of coerced confessions in *Miranda* are not groundless in New

28. Right to silence; right to counsel; anything he said could be used against him.
29. Usually right to silence and right to counsel, or right to silence alone.
30. Furthermore, some of the uncoerced confessions were virtually spontaneous. The police were not seriously interested in questioning two of the 14 suspects who made uncoerced confessions and three of the nine who made uncoerced admissions. Thus of all of the confessions and admissions which the police sought at all vigorously, one-third (nine of 27) occurred in the 17 coercive interrogations.
31. Although the other three gave no statement, it is not clear that the interrogations were failures. All three were co-suspects with one of those who confessed after being given the full *Miranda* advice. As soon as one of the four confessed, incriminating the other three, the police stopped questioning them.

Haven, despite the lack of coercion in the typical interrogation. Aggressive interrogation pays off in confessions. Moreover, these cases suggest that the *Miranda* advice of rights does not reduce the value of coercion in obtaining confessions.

Free Joan Bird

Joan Bird is one of the two sisters that are still being incarcerated along with the other members of the N.Y. Panther 21. Her ransom (bail) is $100,000.00, as it is with the rest of her comrades. The N.Y. 21 have had seventeen bail hearings and the ransom has still not been reduced. But to understand the "case" surrounding Joan Bird and the rest of the N.Y. 21, one must have a lucid understanding of the fascist repression that is running rampant in America.

On January 17, 1969, at approximately 9:00 p.m., sister Joan Bird, a nineteen-year-old nursing student at Bronx Community College was found in a disabled car parked near the scene of an alleged "sniper" attack on two pigs, cruising in a patrol car on the Harlem River Drive. The sister was taken to the Wadsworth Precinct and held for "questioning."

Sometime in the early morning, brother C. Squire was also questioned by the pig cops. After the pigs conducted a "jive" investigation (the pigs broke into C. Squire's home and brutalized him) brother C. Squire was also arrested.

Saturday, after sometime between 2 and 3 p.m., Lumumba Shakur, along with Panther attorney Arthur Turco, went to the Wadsworth Station to see why sister Joan was being detained without charges. Upon identifying himself, brother Lumumba was immediately surrounded by all the pigs in the precinct and placed under arrest.

At 11:00 p.m., Saturday night, sister Joan, C. Squire, and Lumumba Shakur appeared before super negro judge "Alowishes" Archibald. When Joan entered, she *fell* into the crowded courtroom; it was obvious to everyone present, that she was the victim of the most brutal beating imaginable. She was unable to walk without being assisted. It appeared as if her right ankle was broken. Both of her eyes were blackened and her left eye was swollen and closed. There were abrasions over both eyes and the left side of her face was completely distorted. Sister Joan had been stomped and

From *Black Panther Pamphlet*, 1969. Reprinted by permission of the Black Panther Party.

kicked, numerous times in the stomach and back. Footprints visible all over the sister's coat bore witness to the fact that she had been walked over by the pigs.

When sister Joan hobbled before his "dishonorableooddball" Archiball, the judge was temporarily blinded by the so-called justice he was supposed to represent. When attorneys Lefcourt and Turco made a move to have nigger pig Roland McKenzie indicted for felonious assault, judge Archibald started to mumble. Pig Chief Morton of the Wadsworth precinct came to the aid of both the judge and pig McKenzie by stating that the injuries were incurred when the sister *fell out of the car* and that he was present all the time that sister Joan was held in detention. Attorneys Lefcourt and Turco immediately made a move to have pig Chief Morton indicted for conspiracy and nigger judge Archibald seemed more confused than ever. Ransom (bail) had been set at $20,000.00, each on all three of the defendants.

STATE OF NEW YORK

                                        COUNTY OF NEW YORK

I, Joan Bird, being duly sworn, depose and say:

That I am 19 years of age, and presently a student at Bronx Community College.

That on Friday evening, January 17, 1969, at about nine o'clock p.m., I was in a car on Harlem River Drive, New York City, that was approached by police without provocation. Guns were fired and I remained in the car that was being fired upon. I did not participate in the gunfire. Then one of the police told me to "crawl out of that car bitch," so I proceeded to do as instructed. Then Patrolman McKenzie said "Let me take this: Bitch you better tell me the truth." At this point McKenzie and another dragged me by my arms, while on the ground on my back. McKenzie then with a short black club beat me across my face and head, at which point I became dizzy; I also noticed that my mouth was bleeding.

At this time they put handcuffs on me and turned me over face down to the ground and my hands cuffed behind me. Then they began to kick me and walk on my back and legs. Then McKenzie put a gun to my head and stated "I ought to kill you, you motherfucker," then proceeded to take my right hand fingers and bend them back and said: "You better talk or I'll break your fingers." I screamed. Then they were all talking about how they should take me to the woods in the park and shoot me, and nobody would know the difference. I screamed. Then McKenzie and another picked me up and put me into a car.

On the way to the station house, at about 160th and Edgecomb Avenue, McKenzie got out of the car and stopped a black man and searched him, then put the black man in the car and we proceeded to the 34th precinct.

Then we entered the station house, with the black man. I never saw this man before and I do not know his name, and I never saw him again.

Then I sat downstairs for about 5 minutes, facing the wall, then I was taken upstairs to another room, filled with what I believed to be plain-clothes police. At this time, a tall white plain-clothes police told me: "Unless I tell the truth, I will take you upstairs and throw you out the window and it will look like suicide." This person also stated during the evening that: "I will stick this size 10 up your cunt until it comes out your throat if you don't stop bullshitting."

Also, during the evening, a short, white plainclothes with beige suede shoes, or short boots on, said, "I'd better say that the others with me beat me up or that I tripped." Then on the way to an erroneous address I gave them, the cop who stated he would use his "size 10" stated, "I'm a bastard and unless you tell the truth I'll show you how much of a bastard I can be."

After we returned to the station from the erroneous address, at about 3:30 a.m., a white, heavy-set plainclothes policeman with black rim glasses called me "bitch" and pushed me against the wall and threatened me with his fist closed, and I screamed and he said, "you better shut up, or I'll punch your face in some more." At this time, about 4:00 a.m., I screamed for my mother and they let her come in, they did not do anything to me after that point.

They never asked me if I needed medical attention nor did they allow me to call my attorney. I was not placed under arrest until 19 hours later. I was told I was being held as a material witness, and they were going to let me go home with my mother. They took me to court at about 12:00 p.m. the next day after being held all night. I was still not under arrest.

I finally got to see my attorney, Mr. Arthur F. Turco, Jr., when he arrived at court, 100 Centre Street, N.Y., at about 3:30 p.m. Saturday. He demanded to see me in private, at which time I told him what had happened to me. Then we were called into the courtroom, at which time the Assistant D.A. asked that I be held in 50,000 dollars bail as a material witness, because my life was in danger. Mr. Turco objected to the bail and demanded my immediate release, it was now 19 hours I was being held. He also questioned by whom my life would be in danger by, the police or my own black people? At this time, the judge called both, my attorney and the D.A. to the bench, and he suggested since he could not hold me as a witness the D.A. should arrest me, which he then did. I was not arraigned until 26 hours after I was picked up.

(Signed) Joan Bird

The bail was reduced to $5,000.00 and about a week later, the ransom was met. Sister Joan was bailed out of jail and she continued to work for the people. After convalescing from her brutal torture, she returned to school, with her mind set on being a nurse. But trying to return to the life she knew prior to the bust was totally impossible. Sister Joan and her parents were constantly harassed. The pigs would call all hours of the night and scream obscenity in the phone until they were hung up on. Joan's parents were harassed on numerous occasions.

The pigs would show in person at Joan's home scene, hoping to provoke the Bird family into some irrational act so they could justify vamping on sister Joan again.

Sister Joan was able to survive this constant harassment until the middle of February. On the night of February 27, 1969, our attorneys told us that the pigs were going to arrest sister Joan on the charges of conspiracy to commit armed robbery. When the sister appeared in court the following day for a scheduled hearing she was re-arrested in the courtroom. Once again the ransom was $5,000. Within 24 hours the party had sister Joan on the streets. The pig harassment and intimidation did not cease. The party in New York City was exposing the contradictions and taking the struggle to a higher level. It is interesting to note that the terrorist repression against the party in New York did not escalate until the Free Breakfast for Children Program was just about to be implemented. The national repression against the party was also being taken to a higher level and Sister Joan—withstanding the almost daily repression, remained in the streets as a servant of the people until the wee hours of the morning after April Fool's Day.

On April 2, 1969, fascist pigs kicked down Joan Bird's door and in the presence of her parents, kidnapped sister Joan. Many other Panthers in New York City also had their doors kicked down on this same night . . . but this is the story of the N.Y. Panther 21.

II   MILITARY

Excerpts from Testimony of Representative Mario Biaggi (Democrat, New York) Before House Armed Services Committee

In a report and proposed statement of policy, the committee largely blamed the officers of the Second Marine Division for the tense situation at Camp Lejeune. "The lack of informed, courageous leadership in dealing with racial matters is widening the gulf of misunderstanding between the races," the committee told the commanding officer, Maj. Gen. Edwin B. Wheeler, who has since been assigned to Vietnam on normal rotation.

The report was submitted to the commanding general of the Second Marine Division last April 22 by Col. Louis S. Hollier, head of the Ad Hoc Committee on Equal Treatment and Opportunity at Camp Lejeune. The text of that report follows:

(1)

This committee conducted an extensive examination relative to the subject of equal treatment and opportunity for minority groups within the Second Marine Division with emphasis on the white-black marine relationship. Despite policies emanating from the highest echelons of Government down to and including those of the commanding general and as further expressed by organizational commanders within the division, a racial problem of considerable magnitude continues to exist and, in fact, may be expected to increase.

(2)

There are two major aspects to this problem. First, is that this division and the Marine Corps, are returning marines, both black and white, to civilian society with more deeply seated prejudices than were individually possessed upon entrance to service. These marines are potentially susceptible to the militant doctrines and policies of racial extremists. Second is that conditions exist within the division which could readily cause a minor incident not necessarily containing racial overtones to expand to a major racial confrontation.

From testimony given by Congressman Biaggi to the Special Subcommittee to Probe Disorders on Military Bases of the Armed Services Committee, House of Representatives, September 16, 1969. Reprinted by permission.

93

(3)

The pressures of our society which generally foster prejudice and the impatience, in fact the complete disillusionment of the young black marine with the extent of progress towards the realization of equal treatment and opportunity were recognized and considered as a background for investigation. This report, however, deals specifically with aspects of the problems which exist within the Second Marine Division. These, in summary are:

(a) A general lack of compliance on the part of officers and noncommissioned officers with the existing policies, either by intent, in spirit or through ignorance.

(1) Many white officers and noncommissioned officers retain prejudices and deliberately practice them. The most manifestations lie in the racial stories, jokes and references to and about blacks or black marines. These continue to exist in both official and unofficial contacts. The result is obvious when made within the hearing of a black marine. More insidious, perhaps, is the fact that the attitudes reflected are thus perpetrated among contemporaries and fostered in subordinates. Unfortunately, the major offenders in this regard are among the relatively senior officers and enlisted marines.

(2) Some of the facilities of the local community remain segregated; housing, barber shops, bars and amusement centers. Patronage of these facilities by officers and enlisted personnel of this command is, in fact, condonation of discrimination. In addition, failure to act on valid complaints of segregated facilities, as required by current directives, presently exists and continues to be a source of discouragement among black members of this command.

(b) A major and serious cause of racial tension results from the actions of military police in the Camp Lejeune area. The black marines in your command are the special target for discriminatory actions by the military police. The black marine believes that any incident in which blacks are involved is automatically treated as a racial incident by the military police. They believe that they are brutalized, unfairly and illegally detained and inhumanly treated.

(c) The black marine is particularly concerned that only results, and never causes, are the subject of disciplinary actions on official investigations when black marines are involved. Whether real or imagined, every such incident is a racial incident and is quickly known by every black marine in your command. Any such incident, regardless of how trivial, could flare up into a full-fledged riot.

(d) In the opinion of the black marine, he has no official channel available to him by and through which he can obtain redress for complaints of discrimination. In essence request mast is not accomplishing the purpose for which it was intended. There is a reluctance on the part of your troop leaders, both officers and enlisted, to admit that racial problems exist within a unit or organization. Thus complaints seldom progress beyond company level, if they go that far. In any case, the black marine has no confidence in request mast procedures. He seldom sees any results.

(3) An exception to this broad indictment is in the office of the division inspector. However, only a small percentage of complaints are brought to this source.

(e) Because racial tensions exist within the Second Marine Division, black and white Marines tend to polarize. Action and reaction increase the polarity of white to white and black to black. As and if this trend continues the danger of major racial incident increases.

(f) The black marine exhibits unusual affinity and sympathy for members of his race. Constant exposure to the news of every possible input, relating incidents with racial overtones, spread rapidly throughout the black marine population. Attitudes are drastically influenced regardless of validity of information, with resounding effect throughout the command.

(g) The absence of black representation in official photographs and drawings, such as career planning posters and barbershop (acceptable-haircut pictures), exemplify the subtle prejudice-by-omission and spread an undesirable effect in your command.

(4)

Generally speaking, the young marines, black and white, who live and work closely together and who are both the subject and target of the problem, are striving for mutual accommodation. Their attempts are blocked and frustrated by the officers and noncommissioned officers, who, knowingly or unknowingly, intentionally or otherwise, prevent the full realization of your desired objectives.

(5)

The committee report, Enclosure (1), includes statistics as directed in the appointing letter. It is recommended that they be deleted. They are not only subject to interpretation, or misinterpretation, but more importantly lend credence to allegations that equality of opportunity and treatment do not exist.

(6)

This report is broad in its condemnation. This is purposeful.

(7)

If new policies, or renewed emphasis on existing policies, are to be effective, it is suggested that all units within the Tri-Command be advised of the situation and encouraged to initiate and support corrective action."

If the Ad Hoc Committee report was not a well-kept secret, it was obviously a forgotten document until the *New York Times* published its contents on Aug. 10, more than three months after it was submitted to the commanding general of the Second Marine Division.

My conclusions, however, were reached during my inspection of Camp Lejeune. Yes, racial strife appeared to be both prevalent and explosive. But at the same time, the military command seemed unable to cope with the problem. . . .

Bishop Assails Chaplain System After Visiting Military Prisons

The Most Rev. Antulio Parilla Bonilla, a Roman Catholic Bishop from Puerto Rico who has visited what he called "political prisoners" in 19 civil and military jails over the last four weeks, called yesterday for the abolition of the military chaplaincy.

"The men in the stockades told me they get little spiritual help from the chaplains," the Bishop said at a news conference. "Chaplains are Army men first and churchmen second."

The Bishop's demand was an indirect criticism of Cardinal Cooke, who, as military vicar of the Catholic Church, serves as spiritual leader of Catholics in the armed services and as a kind of bishop to the Catholic chaplains.

A spokesman at the New York Archdiocese described the Cardinal's duties as, in part, making sure the chaplains "give good spiritual service" to servicemen.

Clergy and Laymen Concerned About the War in Vietnam, one of the sponsors of Bishop Parilla's visit, billed it as counter tour to Cardinal Cooke's traditional Christmas journey to American military bases around the world. The spokesman at the Archdiocese said there would be no response to the Bishop's charge.

As an alternative to the chaplaincy system, Bishop Parilla proposed a policy of "free-access" by clergymen in the area surrounding a base to military personnel, including prisoners. Otherwise, he said, military bases remain "closed enclaves" in which conscientious objection can go unrecognized by chaplains.

In 1968, the American Jewish Congress also asked for an end to the chaplaincy and called for its replacement with civilian chaplains paid by their respective faiths. Reform Jewish rabbis voted last June to end compulsory chaplaincy service by their rabbis, a move stemming from objections to the war among Reform rabbinic students.

During the Bishop's tour, which began Dec. 18 in Seattle, he visited 19 jails and stockades and spoke to what he numbered in the "hundreds" of prisoners, including servicemen serving sentences for refusing to obey orders in protest against the war in Vietnam.

He also saw members of antidraft groups, such as the "Milwaukee 14," and members of the Black Panther party. He visited for half an hour with Bobby Seale, the Black Panther leader, who is in the San Francisco county jail.

Prison officials at all but four of the stops permitted Bishop Parilla to see inmates and to speak with them privately or address them as a group. At four military prisons, he was barred and at one he was only allowed to visit the base hospital.

At Fort Dix in New Jersey, the Bishop and several followers were detained by the military police on Monday, searched for identification and photographed after they refused to stop a march toward the stockade, which they had been refused permission to visit.

The group was given a letter saying they would be subject to prosecution if they tried again to gain access to the stockade. The Bishop said yesterday that he would "like to go back," but had made no definite plans.

He said the prisoners had complained of "inhuman" treatment in some prisons and added that he had been "shocked" by the large numbers of blacks and Puerto Ricans in the jails.

Bishop Parilla, who is active in the Puerto Rican independence movement, was auxiliary bishop of Caguas, P. R., until three years ago. He now teaches at the University of Puerto Rico in San Juan.

The Young Lords, the Puerto Rican youth group that occupied the First Spanish Methodist Church last week, declared its support for the Bishop yesterday and said he would address a rally in the Barrio tonight.

Plainfield

On Friday, July 14, while the attention of most officials in the State was still focused on Newark, nearby Plainfield was experiencing incipient disorder. It was centered in a poor, predominantly Negro area. About 13,700 persons, or 28% of the city's population, estimated at 49,000, is nonwhite. A majority of the nonwhites are concentrated in two areas of Plainfield—one in the eastern part, where some 1,700 persons live, and a larger one in the West End, with about 8,000 residents. More than one-third of Plainfield's total unemployment originates in these two areas.

Early in the day, Councilman Harvey Judkins, a Negro, heard rumors that a disturbance was likely, and he relayed these reports to Mayor George F. Hetfield. The week before rumors had circulated through the Negro community that a Negro woman, Mary Brown, had been beaten with handcuffs by the police. The police denied the allegations. The rumor received wide circulation, and produced some tension.

Friday evening, there was a disturbance at the White Star Diner. According to one report that circulated through the community, a white youth struck a Negro youth, Glasgow Sherman, and an off-duty policeman who was present took no action.

Lieut. Daniel S. Hennessey of the Plainfield Police Department testified he saw Mr. Sherman early on Saturday (about 1 a.m.) and Mr. Sherman told him he had been attacked at the White Star Diner, that a car with four or five men had been hit with a Molotov cocktail, that the men got out of the car, and that one of them, "because he was the closest, hit him (Mr. Sherman) in the eye."

An eyewitness, however, told a different story. He said that, after a heated discussion at the diner about alleged recent beatings of Negro women, a Negro youth made a Molotov cocktail and threw it at the car of a white youth. Another Negro, in the company of the white youth, reacted by hitting the one who had thrown the missile.

Also on Friday evening—later than the Sherman incident—approximately 200 Negro youths gathered at the West End Gardens Housing Project to complain about police brutality. Councilmen Judkins and Everett C. Latti-

From *Report for Action*, Governor's Select Commission on Civil Disorder of New Jersey, 1968, pp. 145-52.

more, both Negroes, addressed the group. Although Councilman Judkins told Lieutenant Hennessey that he did not expect any trouble, shortly afterward 40 or 50 youths proceeded to West Front Street and broke windows.

About 12:30 or 1 a.m., on Saturday, at Plainfield Avenue and West Third Street, the police found several 17- and 18-year-olds making gas bombs behind a gas station. The youths fled and the police confiscated the materials— old cloth, gasoline and empty bottles. The violence that night was limited to three or four broken store windows.

SATURDAY

On the afternoon of the following day, Saturday, a group of Negro youths met at the Youth Center with Mayor Hetfield and Councilmen Lattimore and Judkins. The principal complaint was police behavior.

> People were tired of being beaten and pushed around by this police department.

The youths also complained about the lack of recreation facilities and the inadequacy of programs at the Youth Center.

Spurgeon Cameron of the Plainfield Chapter of the National Association for the Advancement of Colored People (NAACP) believes this meeting was one of the two incidents leading to the riot. He said:

> The meeting ultimately broke up . . . because of a sense of frustration because the answers coming forth were not meaningful answers. . . .

Robert Nelson, a youth who attended, testified:

> Hetfield wasn't saying anything. He was saying the same old thing they heard before.

THE DEATH OF POLICEMAN GLEASON

At about 8 p.m. Sunday, several persons reported to the police that a policeman was under attack. The initial reports were discredited because false alarms of the previous night had made them wary. Furthermore, the police had not assigned a foot patrolman to the area in question, and a Negro, who identified himself as a minister, had informed the police that he had not seen a policeman in that vicinity. State Police records indicate that the Plainfield Police Department received notice of the attack on Mr. Gleason at 8:27.

Captain Campbell and a rescue squad of 18 men found Mr. Gleason lying on his back on West Second Street at around 8:30 p.m. His revolver and several rounds of ammunition were missing, but he had been not wounded by bullets. The reason for Mr. Gleason's presence on West Second Street at that time was not resolved by the Commission. Captain Campbell testified that he could not answer that question because of a pending investigation. Mr. Gleason died from the severe beating at 8:45 p.m. at Muhlenberg Hospital in Plainfield.

Mr. Cameron, who had witnessed the beating of Gleason, said that he saw a "white helmet" going down Plainfield Avenue, that he heard four shots and saw a Negro youth stagger and fall. Mr. Cameron further testified:

> As I walked over toward him, (the youth) I vaguely remember the blue uniform of the policeman running back to Front Street.
> . . . I remember seeing him being struck by his night stick by people. . . . I made a couple of vain efforts to get people to stop, all of which was unsuccessful. Eventually, I went limp. Everybody then retreated and I said, "Get the devil out of here." The rescue squad came, picked him up, took him to the hospital. He was still alive.

OTHER SATURDAY NIGHT DEVELOPMENTS

About 9:45 o'clock the same evening, in nearby Middlesex, the Plainfield Machine Company was burglarized and 46 carbines stolen. Based on intelligence reports, the police believed that some of these weapons were in the riot area, along with ammunition that had also been stolen from the company.

Sunday night a perimeter around the area was established by Plainfield police. The police went into the area on special missions, in response to calls for help from persons, and for reconnaisance. Captain Campbell stated that his orders were to hold to a line of containment and not go in and patrol the riot area. Colonel Kelly testified that State Police began to arrive Sunday evening but were not initially committed to the riot area. They maintained checkpoints to patrol the surrounding area.

In view of the heavy State Police commitment to Newark, National Guardsmen were dispatched to the Westfield Armory, to be diverted to Plainfield when necessary. According to Captain Campbell, guardsmen arrived between 11 and 11:30 p.m. By 2 a.m. Monday, National Guard armored carriers and State Police patrols were moving through the riot area. Complete control of the perimeter that the Plainfield police had established was assumed by the National Guard and State Police by 3 p.m. Monday. The State Police and the National Guard set up 29 or 30 posts, and maintained these for the next 36 hours.

By the morning of Monday, July 17, the situation was generally quiet. Captain Campbell testified that all looting was over by Monday evening or Tuesday morning and that the riot had effectively run its course by some time Tuesday. Colonel Kelly agreed with this view of the situation.

On Monday morning, Colonel Kelly returned to Newark from Plainfield and briefed Governor Hughes, Commissioner Paul N. Ylvisaker of the Department of Community Affairs, and other members of the Governor's staff. In the late afternoon, Commissioner Ylvisaker and Attorney General Sills traveled to Plainfield. The Governor was never present in Plainfield during the disorder. . . .

THE SEARCH

. . . The Plainfield police, to their dismay, had not been consulted. Their attitude was summed up by Lieutenant Hennessey, who testified that on Monday he wanted to conduct a search for the stolen rifles and that he spent Tuesday gathering intelligence on where the rifles could be located. He testified that he was prevented from conducting such a search, although it was clear that such plans were discussed.

Colonel Kelly testified:

> We felt that the rifles would never be forthcoming, so we decided and we asked for an opinion (from the Attorney General) could we search, and by the opinion that was given to us we had a right to search under the riot proclamation.

On Tuesday evening there was a planning session to mount a large-scale search operation for Wednesday afternoon. Top commanders of the Plainfield police, the State Police and the National Guard took part. Lieutenant Hennessey testified that he put together all the available intelligence on the possible location of the rifles and drew a map pinpointing two or three specific apartments within the West End Gardens housing project. When the promised weapons did not materialize, the machinery for the search was put into motion.

On Wednesday morning Governor Hughes met with State officials in Trenton to discuss the search. Colonel Kelly was in contact with this group by telephone. He was instructed that the press was to be permitted on the searching expedition, and 10 community representatives were to accompany the searchers. Before Commissioner Ylvisaker and Attorney General Sills left the Governor's office in Trenton, the Governor, according to Mr. Ylvisaker, had some "second thoughts" about the plan, but ultimately he indicated that the search would proceed.

The Governor's proclamation, dated July 17, invoked the Governor's authority during a state of disaster, and authorized the State Police and the National Guard "to search in areas and buildings in order to remove and confiscate firearms, ammunition or explosives." No search warrants were obtained or applied for.

The plan for a search was also announced over a local radio station early Wednesday morning, much to the consternation of the police. Captain Campbell testified that the announcement "was going to negate anything we were after."

More than 100 State Police and National Guardsmen were assigned to the operations and were assembled around noon. Armored personnel carriers of the National Guard were on hand to carry the searchers.

Colonel Kelly testified that he wanted the Plainfield police along as guides:

> The Plainfield Police, Captain Campbell would go in and be in the West End. Lieutenant Hennessey would be in the other homes because he knew where they were and he knew the people. There was another detective from the Plainfield Police Department to assist Lieutenant Hennessey because we didn't know where the homes were. Captain Campbell got the key for the apartments from the superintendent so that we could open doors.

Community teams, made up of local residents were also to go along to observe the search.

Commissioner Ylvisaker testified that, as he arrived on the scene, he was concerned that the heavy complement of forces traveling in armored personnel carriers might look "like an invasion" rather than a search. He objected to the use of the heavy equipment. He testified:

> I jumped out front and said "Stop! In the name of the Governor, stop." . . . I remembered our conversation in the Governor's office . . . that this thing could become a national spectacle and start up the whole thing again. . . . Kelly waved the personnel carriers off to the side. Then it took me two or three minutes to realize a vacuum had developed in command. . . . Finally when I realized nothing was happening, I have a vague memory of giving some kind of signal to Colonel Kelly that the thing ought to start. The jeeps then began coming across the intersection.

Mr. Ylvisaker also testified that he was informed of an agreement providing that there would be no local police in the search parties. Local policemen were ordered off the trucks.

Colonel Kelly's testimony confirms that Mr. Ylvisaker stopped the personnel carriers "in the name of the Governor," and that Mr. Ylvisaker objected to the participation of the Plainfield policemen in the search.

At 1 p.m. the search proceeded, concentrating on the West End Gardens Apartments. According to Attorney General Sills, about 26 locations were searched.

In some cases the search parties were described by witnesses as rude and unruly. Charles Miller, of the Plainfield Human Relations Commission, who accompanied one group, observed troopers break through a window in order to unlock a door, kick over a stuffed chair and break a mirror. He testified that one trooper asked him; "Do you like what you see, friend?" Mr. Miller replied: "Carry on fellows; I am just watching." Mr. Miller added:

> As I got in the hall a State trooper who was carrying an M-1 rifle . . . says, "What the hell are you doing up here?" I said, "I am an observer of this search." He said, "Hell, anybody can put a white armband on." I said, "I am just leaving." At this point, as I turned around, he let me have a butt stroke of the M-1, and I proceeded downstairs more rapidly than I intended to.

The search did not produce any of the 46 stolen carbines. However, Captain Campbell testified that his men found four or five of the stolen weapons in the Evergreen Cemetery near the corner of Plainfield Avenue and Fourth Street sometime Wednesday afternoon and Thursday. The captain further testified that, prior to Wednesday, a combined group of State and local police recovered in the riot area the cartons that contained the stolen carbines and boxes that held the 30-caliber ammunition that had been stolen from the factory.

Following the search, the morale of the Plainfield police fell. The general disapproval of tactics of containment and the handling of the search had frustrated the men. Some 40 Plainfield policemen gathered in a session closed to the press, and threatened to resign "en masse" because they were "left out," "tired" and felt "poorly treated."

Colonel Kelly arrived and addressed the men, and helped to prevent any mass resignation.

. . .

FINDINGS

1. The mob action resulting in the death of a Plainfield policeman was an act of brutality that must be condemned.

2. Under the circumstances that prevailed in Plainfield on Wednesday, July 19, the methods used to conduct the search in the West End Gardens Apartments reflected poor judgment that was widely viewed to be a violation of civil rights. The evidence before the Commission leads to the finding

that there was little, if any, justification for this search which had limited chances of yielding up the missing weapons, which added to the already high tension in the community, and which left a legacy of bitterness among the residents of the searched area.

JOE PILATI

Presidio—They Try To Take Away Your Mind

SAN FRANCISCO—For Johnny Williams, 20-year-old Vietnam veteran from Reno, Nevada, the morning of August 8 was just like every other morning he'd greeted during the preceding 10 weeks in the Presidio stockade. "The guards aren't supposed to wake you up until 4:30, but between 3:30 and 4 they start banging on the doors until it's impossible to sleep any more."

It wouldn't be dawn for an hour or so, another dawn with its inevitable 30 minutes of strenuous physical exercise before breakfast. Johnny Williams stretched out in his bunk, tried to ignore the pounding on the walls and the shouts of "Get up, you bastards!" outside his cell. He was thinking about getting out of the Presidio, silently mulling over the plans he'd been making for the last two months. Standing on line for breakfast at 5 a.m., he knew that within a few hours he might be free—a fugitive once more, but free at least to seek help in San Francisco, where according to the scuttlebutt (reluctantly confirmed by military spokesmen) some 5000 to 10,000 AWOL soldiers roam the streets and try to elude the MPs every day of the week. But Johnny Williams knew that by lunchtime he might not be free. He might be dead.

"There was another guy in there," he said, recalling the stockade at the huge Army post occupying 1400 acres in the northwest corner of San Francisco, "another guy who was repeatedly AWOL. Everyone knew he was a heroin addict. As soon as they got him back inside, they'd send him to the hospital and shoot him up again. I remember having to hold him up while we were standing on line for chow—I'd grab him by the armpits and support him, otherwise he would have collapsed."

"I told this guy that I had to escape. I didn't care if I got shot. I just had to do something." Johnny Williams did something that morning. For more than two hours he crept through the underbrush, wearing only an undershirt and his Army fatigue trousers, eluding the eyes of sentries until finally he crossed the last barbed-wire barrier and found himself standing, dazed and exhausted, in one of San Francisco's public parks adjoining the Presidio complex.

There he befriended two of the city's ever-present "hippie mailmen"—guys his own age who had somehow avoided being impressed into the war machine, who had latched onto fairly decent jobs in the postal service through the simple expedient of passing exams with superb scores which preclude (under civil service regulations) discrimination based on hair length and off-duty social proclivities.

Johnny Williams had already resolved that once he got out of the Presidio, he would try to get out of the country. He had been AWOL "at least nine times" since he was shipped back from Vietnam in the fall of 1967, and each time he'd been recaptured—so that by now he'd been confined in stockades at Fort Lewis, Washington, at Oakland Army Base, and at the Presidio. "The Presidio is the worst by far," he told me later in the afternoon of his escape. "They try to take away your mind. When you're not working, you have to march. When you're not in some kind of formation, you can't talk to the other prisoners. It's next to impossible to get together. But if something doesn't happen real quick to make that place fit for human beings, there's going to be another mutiny."

"Another mutiny" could have even wider repercussions than the sit-down demonstration organized by Presidio prisoners last October after a guard had fatally shot in the back a mentally disturbed 18-year-old private, Richard Bunch, thereby triggering mutiny charges against 27 prisoners. More than half of the prisoners received sentences ranging up to 16 years; in June, 14 of them had their sentences reduced to between six and 12 months, in the wake of a publicity-defense campaign which enlisted support from Senators Alan Cranston (Democrat, California), Charles Goodell (Republican, New York), and other legislators. Three of the "Presidio 27" have reportedly escaped to Canada.

After the slaying of Bunch, prisoners at the Presidio—including the 27—drew up a list of demands in hopes that some of the conditions which led to the shooting might be investigated by influential military and civilian agencies. These demands centered around living conditions (more toilets, wash basins and showers, and sufficient food to feed all prisoners a complete meal three times a day); complete psychological evaluations of all prisoners and guards, rotation of guards who are now working 12-hour shifts; and elimination of shot gun details. In a rambling, hour-long conversation with Johnny Williams on the day of his escape, it became clear that few if any of these grievances had been rectified or even seriously considered by authorities at the Presidio.

"There's a room behind a black door at the Presidio MP office," he said. "It's a little room, about four by eight feet, where they keep as many as 15 guys for days on end, while they're being processed. They keep the lights on all night, so you can't sleep. There's no heat, and it gets pretty cold at night.

You have to beg the guards for a blanket, and lots of times you won't get one. They don't have enough jackets to go around, so they'll send you out to work in fatigues when the temperature is 40 or so. There were guys who caught a cold at least once a week because of this. If you refuse to work, they'll write you up and put you in the box (the maximum security cell block, in which cells have no toilet facilities and no furnishings on the concrete floors except for a cot). Of they'll put you on rabbit chow for 10 days at a time (a diet consisting of bread, water, and lettuce three times a day)."

Johnny Williams had been confined, along with virtually all of the other Presidio inmates, in Building 1213—a white stucco edifice built in 1912 to accommodate 43 persons, but which has a "normal" capacity of 88 today, according to Army spokesmen there. The building's population on the day of the "mutiny," last October 14, was 123 prisoners. According to Williams, at the time of his escape there were "at least 100 prisoners—and that would be rock-bottom. Probably it was more like 130 or so." During the week immediately preceding his escape, he said, "10 or 15 guys had started a hunger strike and hadn't eaten for four days." Grinning, he claimed that "some of them looked much better for not eating the slop."

Williams was drafted in December, 1966, and completed basic training and AIT (advanced infantry training) at Fort Lewis. He was then shipped to the Da Nang region in Vietnam, where he saw combat with the First Infantry Division and received what he called "a superficial bullet wound in my leg" shortly before the end of his first six-month hitch. On his first 30-day leave, he returned to Fort Lewis and "split" (went AWOL) for the first of many times. "After that, it was just court-martial after court-martial and stockade after stockade." At the time of his escape, he said, "I was up for another court-martial because a sergeant asked for my name and I told him, but I didn't say my rank." At one time he had been "up for Spec-4 (Specialist Fourth Class)"; most recently, he had been busted from E-3 (PFC) to the lowliest rank of all, E-1.

Each time Williams went AWOL, he found himself with practically nowhere to turn. His father, a career Army Man, offered no sympathy. He had a girl friend in Nevada, but she had no money. Bay Area draft counselors specializing in military work, whom he contacted after his escape, lost touch with him after he left San Francisco. He may have found his way, by now, to some relatively safe and hospitable environment. I hope so.

"Are there still beatings going on?" Williams repeated my question, then answered it: "Sure, but you don't see them. You hear guys screaming and guards cursing them out after they've peed on the floor, when the guards won't let them out to relieve themselves. I remember one guard in particular, a big beefy guy who'd make guys drink out of the toilet if they were thirsty." Williams's eyes were bloodshot from lack of sleep and he'd keep rubbing them as he shifted about nervously, his voice a dull monotone, his fingers gripping the arm of the chair where he sat. "Some of these things that go on . . . you just can't believe them."

I shook hands with Johnny Williams after we'd finished talking, knowing full well that I'd probably never see him again, and that if he successfully avoided his pursuers, no one in San Francisco—or possibly in his and my native land—would ever see him again. It was still Friday afternoon. The day before, I'd seen dozens of young men in green fatigues standing by a loading dock at the Oakland Army Base, across the bay. All of them had either returned from Nam or were about to be sent there; next to the loading dock was a spruced-up mess hall designated in stark black stencil lettering, "Returnees' Steak House—Open 24 Hours."

Oakland is one of the major debarkation points for the Southeast Asian front. When a unit is shipped there, civilian clothes and regular uniforms are taken away and only fatigues may be worn during the three or four-day period before most arrivals are shuttled to Travis Air Force Base, the last stop before Vietnam. I spoke to several men there who were carrying orders for Vietnam. All were 18 or 19, most were lower-middle-class or working-class kids who had no prospect of attending college, and all were highly skeptical of the "de-escalation." "All the guys being sent home are on short time—they would have been coming home in a matter of weeks, anyway," said one soldier bound for Vietnam. "They're shipping more guys out of here now than they were in June," another GI added.

Meanwhile, back at the Presidio, maybe the brass actually want "another mutiny." Maybe they'll get it. Johnny left a lot of friends behind.

Mutiny in the Presidio

The routine roll call at the Presidio stockade in San Francisco was disrupted last October. Linking arms and singing *We Shall Overcome*, 27 Army prisoners staged a sitdown protest. An hour later, they were hauled off to their cells, charged with mutiny—one of a baker's dozen of crimes ranging from

From *Time*, February 21, 1969, p. 17. Copyright 1969 by Time Inc. Reprinted by permission from *Time*, The Weekly Newsmagazine.

murder to rape punishable by death under the Uniform Code of Military
Justice.

At the outset of their mass trial, a seven-man court-martial board was told
by the presiding law officer that it was a "nonviolent mutiny." Maximum
penalty: life in prison. To simplify defense procedures, the Army will judge
the 25 (two escaped the stockade Christmas Eve) in small groups or individually. Last week the first of the defendants to be tried, Private Nesrey D.
Sood, 26, a father of three from Oakland, Calif., was found guilty. He was
given 15 years at hard labor, forfeiture of all pay and allowances, and an
eventual dishonorable discharge. "I am shocked," said Paul Halvonik, an
American Civil Liberties Union attorney who defended Sood. "Fifteen years
for going out and singing and raising his fingers in a 'V' is absurd." Sood, a
draftee who had gone AWOL last September because he heard that his wife
was neglecting their children back home, was due for discharge at Fort
Lewis, Washington, the week he was arrested.

Alleged Sadism

Halvonik argued that merely refusing to obey an order is not mutiny. Sood,
he said, was simply trying to call attention to his legitimate grievances. The
stockade at times had 140 prisoners crowded into a space allocated for 88,
and rations were sometimes short. The inmates had demanded that military
guards be subjected to psychiatric tests because of alleged acts of sadism.
The protest took place three days after a guard killed a prisoner, Private
Richard Bunch.

After reportedly telling a guard to "be sure to aim for my head," Bunch,
who had been examined by an Army psychiatrist, deliberately walked away
from a work detail. He was killed by a single shotgun blast that ripped his
skull. That night, when the other prisoners vocally protested the shooting,
Captain Robert S. Lamont, 25, disciplinary officer, told them that they were
in danger of committing mutiny.

Shock Effect

At the trial, Lamont testified that he had read to the protesting prisoners
Article 94 of the Military Code, which defines mutiny, "for the shock effect."
He said that he did not read the article that prescribes the penalties for disturbing the peace because his mind was "focused on mutiny." The defense
brought in an acoustical expert who said that the prisoners in the enclosed
courtyard could not have heard Lamont's warning carried over a loudspeaker. The charge of mutiny itself was questioned by Army Investigator
Captain Richard J. Millard. In a report that was never revealed to the court,
Millard wrote: "To charge mutiny, an offense which has its roots in the
harsh admiralty laws of the previous centuries, for demonstrating against

conditions that existed in the stockade, is, in my opinion, a miscarriage of justice."

By week's end, two more privates had been sentenced. Lawrence W. Reidel, 20, was given 14 years, and Louis S. Osczepinski, 21, got 16—presumably because he had two previous AWOL convictions. Both men had been labeled "sociopaths" by their attorneys, but after three days with Army psychiatrists, they were adjudged sane. During the trial, Osczepinski attempted suicide by slicing both his wrists with a razor blade.

Extremely severe judgments in military courts are common. It is a foregone conclusion that those who have been charged will appeal. The first step of the complicated but fairly liberal review procedure is the staff judge advocate, who can approve the sentence, reduce, or dismiss it. From there it goes to Washington. All this takes time, of course, which the accused must spend in prison, since there is no provision for bail in military law. However, despite the rigmarole of court-martial, there is little likelihood that any of the convicted "mutineers" will spend anything like 15 years in jail.

KARL H. PURNELL

The Army's Kangaroo Courts

"Be sure to aim for my head," were the final words spoken last October by Pvt. Richard Bunch, a prisoner at the Presidio stockade in San Francisco. Then, as the young soldier deliberately walked away from a work detail, a guard accepted the challenge and blew off the top of Bunch's skull with a 12-gauge shotgun blast. Reverberations of the shot are still creating shock waves which may finally bring to public view the medieval concepts governing U.S. military penology.

Three days after the killing, a group of other inmates at the Presidio stockade attempted to get a hearing for a list of complaints about life in that overcrowded prison by means of a sit-down protest. For this, they were brought before a court-martial and charged with mutiny. Three of the soldiers received sentences of fourteen, fifteen and sixteen years each at hard labor. The fifteen-year sentence of Pvt. Nesrey D. Sood was reduced by the judge advocate general to two years, partially, it must be supposed, in response to public indignation. Several more trials are now in court and others are pending.

From *The Nation*, April 7, 1969, pp. 432-34. Reprinted by permission.

The harsh sentencing of prisoners, particularly those convicted for offenses with political connotations, and the subhuman conditions of many military stockades, are nothing new in military life. Although the doctrine of crime prevention through severity of punishment has long been discarded by modern penologists, faith in the remedial effects of severe and prolonged discomfort still influences military courts.

Recently, two freshmen Senators, Charles Goodell (R., N.Y.) and Alan Cranston (D., Calif.), have taken action to focus public attention on the abominable conditions in U.S. military stockades. Calling for investigations by the Senate Armed Services Committee, they stated: "The outrageous shotgun killing of Pvt. Richard Bunch at the San Francisco Presidio stockade, October 11, and the disclosures of deplorable conditions at the stockade there which came to light following the sit-down demonstrations by twenty-seven fellow prisoners a few days later, make it imperative that Congress take a close look not only at the Presidio but at military prisons throughout the country." In the House, Reps. Abner J. Mikva (D., Ill.) and R. L. Leggett (D., Calif.) have raised the same issue.

At the Fort Dix stockade in New Jersey, a survey of twenty-seven prisoners just completed by the American Civil Liberties Union (N.J.) shows that guard brutality, overcrowding of facilities and lack of sanitary living conditions have for years been a part of prison life. Refusal to allow prisoners to submit complaints through proper military channels, illegal censorship of mail and continual harassment of prisoners by sadistic guards are "altogether typical," an ACLU investigator disclosed.

For example, one prisoner at Fort Dix recalled that he was ordered to crawl to his sergeant on hands and knees to apologize for a remark he had made. When the soldier refused, he was pushed into a cold shower and then forced outside to stand naked in the winter weather for three hours. Similar stories of guard brutality and barbaric conditions are common in Vietnam, where the immediacy of war creates even less sympathy for prisoners. Serious rioting in both the Army's Long Binh jail ("Ole LBJ") near Saigon and the Marine brig in Danang took place last year when prisoners would no longer endure their harsh treatment.

One reason for the lack of regard for prisoners has been the failure to staff military stockades with qualified persons. At the Presidio, neither the Commanding Officer, Capt. Robert S. Lamont, nor any of the guards had any training for penal work. Department of Defense Instruction No. 1325.4 says: "personnel . . . shall be specifically trained in the control, management and correction of persons." In most cases, young Military Police are simply handed a shotgun and assigned to stockade duty, where the practice of prisoner harassment is soon acquired.

Other regulations assure the prisoners proper living conditions and suitable sanitary facilities. At the Presidio, inmates claim they had to walk through human excrement caused by leakage from the four toilets serving the 180 men. During the weeks preceding the sit-down demonstration, prisoners were getting little food, medicine was unavailable for some of the sick, and guards tormented and beat soldiers who fell into their disfavor. This kind of treatment took a toll of the prisoners: fifty-two suicide attempts have been reported by the Army during the past year and the prisoners claimed there were many more.

Senators Goodell and Cranston believe they may be prying the lid from a Pandora's box in calling attention to the Presidio case. Complaints from twelve other stockades throughout the country have already reached their desks.

While all this is the stuff of which public scandals are made, it may be only the tip of the iceberg as far as military justice is concerned. Less spectacular but equally important to the GI is the spider web of military legal proceedings in which many soldiers are entangled.

With more and more cases tied to dissent from the war in Vietnam, an almost unlimited power of sentencing has enabled military authorities to mount a campaign of terror against those GIs who place conscience above duty. Three major weaknesses in the Uniform Code of Military Justice have become apparent to defense lawyers who try to secure a fair trial for their soldier clients.

Most notorious of these is the exercise of command influence on the decisions of a military court by ranking officers. In court-martial cases, the unit commander decides whether to bring charges. He then appoints the court, the law officer (similar to the judge) and the defense counsel from officers under his command. Finally, he can review the sentence and either waive or reduce it.

With these powers over judge, jury and hangman, the sentencing of soldiers can obviously be subject to the prejudices of the senior officer. Last July, charges were brought against Maj. Gen. Thomas Lipscomb, commanding general of Fort Leonard Wood, for tampering with court-martial trials. Although Lipscomb was cleared (there has never been a conviction on charges of command influence), the allegations of threatening counsel, demanding severe sentences and attempting to intimidate court members, at least dramatized the possibilities for exercising such influence.

Many members of Congress agree that command influence in court-martial cases has been excessive. However, they point to a new amendment to the Uniform Code, aimed at eliminating future command influence. Now, through the efforts of Sen. Sam. J. Ervin, Jr. (D., N.C.), law officers in court-martial cases are placed under the jurisdiction of the judge advocate general. Thus the judicial arm of the services will determine promotions, ratings, etc., for this "independent field judiciary." To become effective August 1, the new regulations are being hailed by many officials as a definite deterrent to undue influence by a commanding officer.

Yet there is reason to suspect that such optimism may be misplaced. Command influence has often come from the judge advocate's office itself. In the case of *United States* v. *Perry and Sparks,* charges of reprisal actions against defense counsel were leveled at the staff judge advocate of Fort McPherson, Ga. The defense counsel claimed the reprisals were taken because he would not follow suggestions on how to conduct a case. Here again, there was no conviction, although a "misunderstanding" was admitted.

Many civilian lawyers with experience in military courts feel the new law will have little effect. "The whole thing is a façade," Charles Morgan, the Atlanta attorney who represents Capt. David Levy, says. Morgan claims the extensive "cooperation" and "rapport" among the officer corps in any military unit will enable command influence to take place. "The judge advocate's office is often the source of the worst kind of influence in court proceedings." To Morgan there will always be a Kafkaesque quality to military trials until the Uniform Code is completely revised and servicemen can be tried in civilian courts.

A second major obstacle to fairness in military trials arises from the ambiguous definitions of improper behavior. When does an officer violate Article 133, prohibiting "conduct unbecoming an officer and a gentleman"? Several protesters of the war in Vietnam have been convicted of "contemptuous words against the President, Vice President, Congress, Secretary of Defense, Secretary of a Department or a legislature of any State," all of which is prohibited under Article 88 of the Code.

In the Presidio case, Sixth Army Commandant Gen. Stanley Larson ignored the recommendation of an Army hearings officer and ordered the twenty-seven demonstrators tried for mutiny. Under Article 94 that is defined thus: "any person who with intent to usurp or override lawful military authority, refuses in concert with any other person, to obey orders or otherwise do his duty or creates any violence or disturbance is guilty of mutiny." Under this definition, charges of mutiny could presumably be brought against two or more drunken soldiers singing *Roll Me Over* loudly enough to create a disturbance.

A third major defect arising from the Uniform Code is the disparity of sentencing among different courts; variations are sometimes grotesque, Pvt. Ray Jones, who deserted and went to Sweden for more than a year after learning he was assigned to Vietnam, got four months at hard labor and a bad-conduct discharge on his return to the United States. When a Senate Armed Services subcommittee on the Treatment of Deserters from Military

Service began to complain about leniency, the Army became tough. In its next case, Pvt. James Arnett, who similarly returned from Sweden after leaving his post, received four years at hard labor.

Historically, the whole problem of maintaining discipline has been in the hands of a soldier's unit commander. Whether the punishment consisted of keel-hauling a mutinous sailor or flogging a soldier for stealing, the affair has traditionally been local. Given earlier conditions of communications and travel, this may have been reasonable; but today, when transporting a soldier to a proper court of law or communicating with a central command is an easy matter, there is little excuse for leaving serious trials in the hands of local military officials.

On the contrary, there is ample reason for sweeping changes. Last year, desertions among the armed services rose sharply to 53,357 or one every ten minutes. More and more soldiers are forming themselves into organizations to protest the inequities of the military system. Attempts to terrorize this new breed of young Americans into submission through the practice of stockade brutality and drumhead courts-martial will be no more successful than Mayor Daley's police were at quelling protesters.

Lieut. (j.g.) Susan Schnall, a Navy nurse who was recently court-martialed for marching in an anti-war parade while in uniform, summed up the feeling of a growing number of young soldiers when she said: "It [the Presidio case] really concerns the right of man to be treated as a human being, not just as a cog in a machine, even if he is in the Army. People ask us how you can have the military without discipline. But the way to maintain discipline is through respect not repression."

R. JOE PIERPOINT

Torture at Fort Dix

Until recently, when the army became embarrassed and took it down, there was a sign over the Fort Dix stockade with the Orwellian message, "Obedience to the Law Is Freedom." As any servicemen with nonconformist views can attest, obedience to military law is impossible. Fighting the system is a near guarantee of a court martial. Yet, there are those with courage who do and many of them wind up in the stockade . . . in this case the Fort Dix

From *New Politics*, Vol. VII, No. 4, April 1968, pp. 5-14. Reprinted by permission.

stockade. This is their story, told through a series of letters sent to the Workers Defense League which is defending a number of the prisoners against charges which carry sentences of as long as 40 years.

After weeks of harassment, intimidation, bad food, overcrowded conditions and beatings, some of the prisoners in the Fort Dix stockade rebelled. The army described the incident to the press as a "minor disturbance" but those who have been singled out as its leaders are charged with conspiracy to incite riot, incitement to riot, rioting, arson and destruction of government property. In army Newspeak, a "minor disturbance."

All those charged with conspiracy are political prisoners—pacifists, American Servicemen's Union organizers, radicals; brave men who have committed the unforgivable sin of thinking for themselves and acting on their consciences. Francis Heisler, National Counsel for the Workers Defense League and a long time defender of anti-war servicemen, once commented that there is always more compassion on the part of a military court martial board for a rapist, a murderer or a thief than for a man who refuses to kill. And these are men who refuse to kill.

On June 5, 1969 at 8:30 p.m., a foot locker fell from the second (top) floor of cell block 67. At about the same time, another foot locker fell from block 66. The windows they fell out of were open but, immediately thereafter, several foot lockers came through other, unopened, windows. The army claims that some mattresses caught fire and some plumbing became unattached. The next day the CID began an "investigation." In fact, it was an attempt to frame those men known to be anti-war. Man after man was brought into the stockade and told that if they would sign a statement charging those the army had singled out as culprits, they would get special favors from the commanding General, including reduction of the charges against them and almost immediate freedom. And, in fact, several prisoners who signed such damaging statements were released from the stockade that evening, although they still had time to serve. Those the army was trying to frame were then placed in disciplinary segregation (solitary confinement).

Who are these men?

Terry Klug, one of the "conspirators" an American Servicemen's Union organizer who worked for a time with Resistance in the Army (RITA) while he was in Paris. Terry returned from Paris and turned himself in to the army of his own free will. Nonetheless, he was charged with desertion. Jesse Moscowitz and Rowland Watts of the Workers Defense League represented him. He was found guilty of desertion and sentenced to three years imprisonment. That conviction will be appealed. The following letter, written prior to the "minor disturbance," demonstrates the courage and depth of idealism of those like Terry Klug struggling for dignity in the army.

Dear Mr. Watts,

I'm not very good at saying thanks so please accept what you find in these lines as an attempt to say the words not only as words, but as a true feeling.

Unfortunately, I'm rather poor. . . . Yet, I think the only way I can pay you back (and by you I mean yourself and all the rest—all the people throughout the world who stand for true freedom and equality) is by remaining as one with those beliefs which I have fought for.

Three years look big. It's a long time to me and I don't mind admitting that I'm scared. . . . I guess I showed my fear in front of all those people who supported me there at the court-martial. But there is something else that I hope I showed at that time. And that was pride. That was the proudest moment in my life standing there in front of the jury . . . and knowing that what I had done was right and knowing that I still had the strength to want to fight back.

I'm presently back in the "cage." My little 8′ by 6′ steel cell. They took all of my belongings away from me and only feed me a diet of bread, water and cold vegetables. They are back at trying to make me break again. It's useless for them to keep trying. It's only an unpleasantness for both sides, I can assure you. But they don't seem to understand.

I look forward to hearing from you and the rest of those whom I consider my people.

Terry G. Klug

Not long after Terry wrote that letter he found himself facing 40 years and six months more in prison, a victim of the army's attempt to silence the growing demand for human rights in its ranks.

While the prisoners in the stockade do not expect to be treated as country club guests, they have a right to expect to be treated as human beings. But the Fort Dix stockade is not just a strict, overcrowded prison. It is a full-fledged chamber of horrors.

The testimony of torture and beating is confirmed in letter after letter from other prisoners. This is a letter sent from the Fort Dix stockade by Carlos Rodriguez.

Dear Friend:

The story I tell you in this letter is 100% fact, I may be court martialed like many others and it is important that my story pierce the ears of the people outside the stockade. Chances are that when you read this I will be taken to court but that is beside the point as long as you discover and can see what the army is really like.

In this testimony I will talk mostly about the Military Police Company working in the stockade. Those most involved are the 532nd and the 759th but the 532nd are, in my opinion, the worst. I think that these

M.P.s., with a few exceptions, must be psychopathic. Certainly their anti-social and immoral conduct would indicate something like that for they are sadists.

If you think that torture is no longer used you are wrong. The army has devised these leather belts which they call straps. Straps are put on your wrists with your wrists twisted behind your back as far as they can go and tied to your ankles and you lie with all your weight on your stomach on the wooden bunk because in that position your chest can't even touch the ground.

With this in mind let me give you a few cases. I'll start with Jimmy Friend (of course that is not his real name because I don't have permission to use it). I was in Mental Hygiene when I looked out the window and saw this prisoner being taken to Segregation. He was being hit on top of the head when all of a sudden he let one go and landed on Sgt. Branhover's face. (Sgt. Branhover is a lifer.) Then they really put it to him. The word from Major Casey was, "Drop him." As I went then to my cell I saw big bruisers go in this cell and they followed Major Casey's orders with enthusiasm. He was in the straps about five or six hours. He was laid on a bunch of boards about eight inches off the ground and every thirty minutes or so he was picked up and let fall hitting his head and abdomen, each time from higher up. As a result the man was unable to use his legs without support, his face was bashed up and he couldn't use his arms. He was in extreme pain in every muscle, bone and pore of his body. How long he endured this completely useless and unbearable pain I don't really know. He was in cell 12 and I was in 14. The next day he processed out of the pound.

June 5th, this is a true report except I don't think the man was put in straps. I was not in the same cell block at the time. His name is Johnny Sanchez and he has been to Viet Nam and risked his life fighting communism and all the NOBLE REASONS the government produces. The man went through many hardships as anyone who has been to Viet Nam knows. When he finally came stateside the man was a complete nervous wreck. I myself once was startled as one day I walked past his cell and there he was shaking as if his life depended on it—perhaps it did. I could go on and talk about the price Johnny Sanchez paid for that war and got nothing out of it but becoming a nervous wreck and I could talk about who is getting the profit from that war, but most people know that now —or they should. Anyway, he was beat up by four guards, taken to the barber shop and all his hair was cut off in front of every single eye in the stockade. I think the army was afraid of a protest against the treatment and conditions in the stockade and they were making an example of Johnny Sanchez of what they could do to anyone who objected or protested. They were saying that if anyone gets out of hand they would get what Johnny got. And by getting out of hand they meant being at the right place at the wrong time, a smile when it's not supposed to be there. Anything as simple as that.

I was out of segregation at the time approximately 2 to 3 hours. Next thing I know there's a disturbance which the army calls a riot. And I'm back in segregation with about twenty other prisoners. Why, I don't know 'till two days later. That's when I find out it's a bum rap—Code 13 (CID investigation). I don't want to discuss this part so much because if I tell too much about the inhuman abuses we suffered here, I know how these people work and they will try to cover their holes. But, I will tell you the report because I heard it from the guards: "NECESSARY FORCE NEEDED AND USED."

Before I proceed let me explain this little saying since it is not rare that you'll see it in reports: (1) When a prisoner hits a guard, of course they will not state who did the pushing or punching first, what the provocation was, etc., and since we are prisoners we have the benefit of the doubt against us and statements will always show the prisoner was at fault. Even guards who don't condone this treatment will not object officially in reports because they have to live with the other guards. (2) When a prisoner refuses to do something, and (3) many times as a means to get even or without any justifiable reason (but they will find one).

Jones, which is his real name, was told by one guard in control, "Don't Smile." A few minutes later, a smile came upon his lips and all of a sudden four guards, as if anticipating his smile came from everywhere. They pounced on this man as never before. When the officers saw what was happening they did nothing but passed on by. When they sent him to the hospital his face—I mean what I'm saying—his face was hardly visible along side the bumps and blood. He was brought back to segregation at night so no one could see. Outcome, the man was not put in the straps but put on Code 11 (very dangerous) which means shower and shave once a week only. The report when he was taken to the hospital was "Necessary Force Needed and Used." You figure it out and don't smile.

This next thing I tell you is absolutely true and I can use the person's real name because it was me, Carlos Rodriguez. I have nothing to hide and here it goes: I've been now in Segregation approximately 35 days. If you don't count the few hours I spent outside on June 5 then I've been here fifty days on this Bum Tip charge. On July 8 I was told to move from Cell Block 77 to Cell Block 85. After some hassle about a foot locker a Gung-ho PFC Cleland threw my clothes on the floor. I then refused to move until someone picked up my clothes and put them back where they belonged. Then Sgt. Himan called me a punk and I smiled in his face and said that he was a punk because he needed all those other guards to back him up. At this time Sp/4 Miller tried to beat me on my back but I noticed him coming and put it towards the wall. Then Sgt. Himan put his hands on me and I tried to protect myself. Sp/4 Miller started punching. Next thing I know all six are trying to put me down. Blows on the head, punches all over but I cover my face. Between all of them they get me down and tie my hands behind my back and begin to put on pressure. More punches on my back, sides, head and, next thing I know Sgt. Himan, to prove he is the man he isn't, puts my head on the floor, left side up, and leaves an imprint of his boot and bump on the other side. They kicked me in the back of my head and put a foot on the back of my neck and applied pressure. All this after they had put my hands behind me and tied them and I was completely subdued. Was it "Necessary"? No. They later start walking me back and try to throw me against the edge of a building but missed. When coming into my cell they punched me, and another prisoner saw them. They tried to put me against the bars of my door but I side stepped. For that I got another imprint on my left side.

So, as you can see, where my story is also leading, I'm talking about Military Police Brutality. Most likely, if you have any insight, you will see why these people Re-Up. Simply because of their inferiority complex that they cannot compete with people on the outside. And really they can't because they'd be by themselves and just the thought makes them shudder.

Bill Brakefield is a pacifist who, earlier this year, sought asylum in the chapel at City College. His efforts to resist being returned to the army failed. Bill was seized by government agents and returned to the army. Here is a letter from him.

Dear Friends,

Abraham Lincoln once said, "To sin by silence when they know they should protest makes cowards of men." I am not a coward; neither are the five other young men who, along with myself are being brought before a general court-martial on consipracy charges for the riot here at Ford Dix Stockade June 5, 1969.

I wish to protest the inhuman treatment we have and are enduring since June 5th. It was the inhuman treatment which caused the rebellion of sixty black, Puerto Rican, and white prisoners here at the stockade!

On June 6, 1969, I was brought down to segregation; some of my friends were already here; some had not yet been brought to segregation. Here is a rough idea of the sort of treatment I received. With three guards in front of me, three behind, and two on either side of me holding onto my arms, I was shoved violently through the door of segregation cellblock 77. I was pushed against the wall, spread-eagle fashion. I was then searched for any weapons I may have concealed (what had I done?) on my person. My arms and legs started to shake involuntarily, my face contorted with the time and strain as the minutes dropped like sweat from my brow. All the while the guards told me not to move or they would enjoy beating my face into the cold, concrete floor of the cellblock.

Finally, after what seemed like hours, a sergeant grabbed my collar at the back of my neck and pulled me up to a standing position. My knees buckled but I would not go to the floor for these pigs; I stayed erect. I was told to get into the shower room and strip. After I had stripped naked and my anus and penis had been checked for possible razor blades to be used against an "innocent guard" I was told to stand in the shower stall. Another sergeant came over to talk to me. He said, "Brakefield, a policeman is going to shoot you dead one of these days." I was going to tell him violence is the tool of the ignorant but I kept my mouth shut.

For the first forty-eight hours all the prisoners who were pending investigation were kept on disciplinary segregation. This is punishment; we had done nothing to deserve this. We were not allowed to smoke, to write, or to speak to anyone.

These illegalities continued until the correctional officer, Major Casey, the man who placed these restrictions on us, took them off. But we have already been punished! Why do we have to go on with this farce? Why does the Criminal Investigation Division of the Military Police have to resort to blackmail and bribery to get signed statements against us?

Please stand up and help us overcome these injustices. Write to your Congressmen, your Senators, and write to the President, please. We need your help. Declare your solidarity to us by writing these people. I, William Brakefield, Terry Klug, Allen Ferrell, William Miller, Thomas Callow, and Jeffrey Russel (who has just become a father) need your help. Please help us.

William Steven Brakefield, Fort Dix, N.J.

There is method to the madness of the army's eat-your-cake-and-have-it-too attitude in referring publicly to the incident at Fort Dix as a "minor disturbance" while charging the men with riot offenses which could put them in prison for most of their lives. The Presidio cases in California in which the men were charged with mutiny earned the army a bad press. What is more, the army is now well aware of the fact that civilians grow quite upset when they learn the reality of stockade conditions. The military appeal for respect for authority is one thing, military justification for brutal, inhuman conditions is quite another. The army would rather not have any publicity about its stockades. Public awareness would certainly lead to public outrage. Terry Klug, in writing about the June 5th events says:

> The military is trying its utmost to keep this happening out of the press and away from the eyes of the people by saying that what happened was a "minor disturbance" and that they now have everything well under control. The facts that I wish to present are that it was not a minor disturbance and the Machine does not now nor will it ever have us under their control. The riot itself proved that the conditions in the stockade were humanly unbearable. Riots do not happen because they are fun to be in; they happen because people, real people, and sensitive people, react to human insensitive treatment. Therefore, I hold it to be the law

makers themselves who are responsible for instigating this riot. If the Machine wants to press charges let them charge those who are truly guilty; the stockade officials themselves. In other words, the Machine should clean its own house because it's filthy.

But the military is not cleaning its own house. It is simply closing the doors and trying to detour the public around it. When the press decided to tour the Fort Dix stockade, the army actually released over 60 prisoners so that it would not look too overcrowded. The reporters were not permitted to talk to the prisoners although they were allowed to have a meal with them —the first and the last decent meal ever served in the Fort Dix stockade.

While the army is aware that convictions obtained by depriving men of their legal rights and through the use of torture and beatings will eventually be overturned, those traditions are so much a part of the military system that they continue to be used. Terry tells something about that:

> After two days [of disciplinary segregation] the Machine realized that we had a beautiful case against them and quickly gave us back most of our privileges. But in the days to come we found out (and have proof) that the stockade commander himself was going through our privileged correspondence to our lawyers, etc., opening them up, reading them and then returning them to us saying that they were not addressed properly or some such nonsense. Those letters he read were pertinent to our cases. Also he would hold up our personal mail for periods often exceeding one week then return them to us with some off-the-wall excuse.

Jeffrey Russell, a pacifist and a Buddhist, sent letters to both the Workers Defense League and the American Civil Liberties Union shortly after June 5, asking for legal representation. His letters were held up for five days and then returned to him on the grounds that they were unmailable. As a result, when Rowland Watts and the WDL went to Fort Dix to interview the men and offer the needed legal assistance, he knew nothing about Russell and did not get to talk to him. This, of course, left Russell without counsel for a prolonged period and gave the military extra time in which to try to break him. Because they were unable to do so, they eventually allowed one of his letters to reach the WDL and Russell now has representation.

This interference with the mail is not confined to letters to lawyers and is not simply used to hamstring legal defense. The military uses this technique to try to break the morale of the prisoners.

Terry Klug has written eleven letters to his girl friend, none of which has she received. Her letters to him, however, have not been interfered with and each is more desperate than the last as she tries fruitlessly to find out what is happening to him. Major Casey, the stockade commander, has actually visited Klug to harrass him about his girl, using crude but effective psychology:

> So Mad Casey strolls through Seg. today and says, "Been receiving letters from the girl lately, Klug?" I politely replied, "Not within the last four or five days, Sir," and he laughed and told me that she's probably come to her senses and found a guy on the outside. That's a hell of a thing to say to a guy who's been in six months. Then he passed Rodriguez cell and said, "We really have you now."

Four prisoners signed a letter that describes another approach to destroying the morale of the men.

> Prisoner Thomas Catlow has been going on a hunger strike because he believes his Basic Human Rights have been taken away from him. He has been railroaded by the Guards in c/b 85 whereupon after being written up by SP/4 Hail, PFC La Flame said it was not good enough to put him on d/s [disciplinary segregation]. He, PFC La Flame, then rewrote it. When Capt. Williams who is considered by himself Judge, Jury and Executioner toured the same c/b [cell block] he approached prisoner Catlow, he read the 508 and told Catlow he was going on d/s. When Catlow replied that the 508 he was reading was not the original and that PFC LaFlame was right behind him demolishing the original Captain Williams' reply was "I don't hear anything." When later brought into the c/b 71 he was not searched by the Guards on Duty at the time. The next day he was shaken down and tobacco was found in his footlocker. He was written up. The doctor, Capt. Pickering, did not give him a physical as is required and later in the day he was put on d/s chow with a physical that was given to him 50 days ago. When Major Casey (The Man) toured the cell block, Catlow told him that he was not informed of the why. Major (The Man) Casey, putting on a smile, said very sarcastically, "Well, we'll inform you one of these days," and kept on walking. Today, the 27th, when he asked for a cup of water that is entitled to him with every meal he was at first refused then later given a cup of water by Sgt. Swack but the water was hot. When he questioned Sgt. Swack he was told "Stick your head in the commode you stupid bastard" and was verbally slandered. A few minutes after that PFC Mathews told Catlow "you are too stupid to think."

Bill Brakefield gives an overall picture of what it takes mentally, morally and psychologically to be a guard in the stockade.

> Dear Friends:
> Having been confined for eight months in the Fort Dix stockade as a political prisoner because of my beliefs, activities and convictions it has

been my pleasure to have met some pretty interesting and fairly disgusting men of rank.

I said it has been my pleasure to have met these men for the simple
reason that without meeting them I would not have known a more interestingly disgusting group in American society anywhere else in my life.

Please take for example one person, a sergeant E-6.

This sergeant has asked me repeatedly to get his name in print, every
day, as the sergeant tours segregation, he jokes with me about writing
him up in an underground anti-military-establishment newspaper that is
located outside the Fort Dix area.

Today the sergeant came through the cellblocks and passed-up my
cell completely. One of the guards who was passing through the blocks
with the seregant turned to me and said the sergeant wasn't speaking to
me because I had hurt his feelings.

This man, Sergeant E-6 Howard (Howie) Davidson, whose feelings
are so easily hurt because his name does not appear in print has many
times disregarded the feelings of others.

Howie has a particularly disgusting habit of putting people in straps.
He thoroughly enjoys this practice of medieval torture.

Brakefield goes on to describe the function of the straps much as Rodriguez
did and says that after Howie has the prisoner in the straps he "likes to
laugh and say, 'talk back to me now you mother fucker.'"

Well, Howie, I have finally written you up. I hope the people who read
this can picture the type of military policeman you and the vast majority
of your friends are.

I might add that it has been a pleasure exposing you to the public and
at the same time asking the public to request your resignation along with
the other "interestingly disgusting men of rank."

The lengths that the Army will go to break a man is dramatically exposed
in a letter from Jeffrey Russell. Jeffrey was married in a Buddhist ceremony
but because it was not a "legal marriage" the army refused his wife any
benefits. She traveled to Fort Dix to be married in the stockade chapel and
Jeffrey's letter described her experiences as a visitor to Fort Dix.

Good Brothers:

When one is locked up in a Maximum-Security Segregation in the Fort
Dix stockade one can only realize that he will be harassed and persecuted.
But, when my wife came to Fort Dix to visit me she didn't expect to be
accosted and molested by the MP's (military pigs) and the CID's (cruel,
insane deviates).

Mrs. Kathleen Russell was staying at the EM guest house here on post
when she first came to Fort Dix. Her first night the MP's tried to arrest

her for being a prostitute. A few days later she and some friends from the Coffee House returned to her room to find it torn apart and clothes scattered everywhere. They also found microphones that had been hidden in the room. Kathy went to stay with the Coffee House people, afraid to stay alone. Once again she was accosted by the MP's and this time they tried to pick her up.

I am not screaming perversion. I am saying that all of this was planned by the army to terrorize her because she is my wife. This may seem low and it is, but this also shows the corruption of tyranny and fascism.

I send greetings from your brothers here.

Om Shahati,
Jeffrey O. Russell

Brutality, coercion and psychological torture have all been used by the army in an attempt to break the spirit of these dissident prisoners. They have failed. The Fort Dix prisoners will probably be court-martialed in late September or early October. They fear that unless there is a strong public outcry, they are likely to be railroaded to Leavenworth. They have legal assistance. What is needed now is massive public support.

ROBERT G. SHERRILL

Andersonville-by-the-Sea

On March 17, a "for official eyes only" memorandum was sent from Wallace H. Robinson, Jr., quartermaster general of the Marine Corps, to the chief of staff, Gen. W. J. Van Ryzin, in which he warned that "a truly explosive situation" exists within the Camp Pendleton, Calif., prison but that "a public disclosure of existing conditions could tend to place the Commandant in an embarrassing defensive position."

He was right on both counts, but he failed to point out that the Pendelton brig—the second largest prison in the Navy apparatus—was continually erupting with riots and brutalities that only the Marine Corps' great luck had kept from reaching the press. Racial tensions in the Marine prison are intense. One riot a few months ago sent twenty men to the hospital.

Accompanying his memorandum was a secret survey of conditions at the Pendleton brig, conducted last March, in which it was officially admitted

From *The Nation*, September 15, 1969, pp. 232-42. Reprinted by permission.

that the prison—a conglomeration of World War II temporary wood-frame buildings and tents, and prefab metal buildings once used as a prisoner-of-war camp—is no better than a concentration camp. The brig was built to handle 400 men. The normal prison population is now 800, and often there are peak loads of nearly 900.

The report is limited to the physical breakdown of the camp. It makes no mention of the cruelties imposed upon the prisoners, but accounts of these were obtained by *The Nation* elsewhere—from Father Alban Rosen, a priest who has done voluntary chaplain work at the base, from U.S. Senators, from men who are deserters from the Marine Corps, and from Dr. Larry McNamee, who served as brig physician for a year.

There are several accounts of prisoners being handcuffed to the steel-mesh fence surrounding the 20-acre camp—handcuffed in a spread-eagle fashion, their feet dangling inches above the ground. On one occasion the sight of a prisoner hanging like that brought about a sit-down mutiny that might have blown up into something much worse than the celebrated Presidio Army base "mutiny," but in this instance cool-headed officers broke it up.

Dr. McNamee, who left the Marine Corps in July and is now doing his residency in Cleveland, came away with many memories of his career as the first and last full-time physician at the Pendleton brig. He recalls a number of prisoners who came to him bruised over their chests and backs, who told of being beaten with taped clubs by the guards. An investigation uncovered the clubs, but nothing was done to the guards. He also remembers the prisoner whose arm had been broken and was in a cast; this young man was ordered to lie down on the ground, and then one of the guards stepped on the cast and smashed it.

On that occasion—it was a time of wholesale punishment, for the prisoners had done something the guards resented—"I saw a prisoner in a down position (with nose touching ground, legs spread-eagled and hands clasped behind back; in other words the prisoner is supported on the ground by his face, chest and toes), and one guard was standing on one foot and another guard was kicking the other foot out further. A foreman was with me and I said, 'go over and stop them—the guy's legs can't spread any further.' But the prisoner himself reacted. He jumped up and kicked at one of the guards and another guard got pushed back by the prisoner. At that point, the second guard ran at the prisoner and kicked him in the chest, knocking him to the ground. Three or four other guards grabbed him, forced his hands behind his back and his face to the ground. He couldn't possibly move. The guard who had just kicked him, now fell on top of him and began pummeling him on the back of the head, hitting him as hard as he could with his fist closed. I mean, really belting him. Before I could get there, somebody else had pulled the guard off. The prisoner was sent to the Ice Box."

The Ice Box is made up of six cages set on an open concrete slab. Prisoners held there are protected from the weather only by bars; the confidential report acknowledges that the Ice Box, which has been in use for years, "is a cruel and unusual punishment." This is incorrect; it is cruel but not unusual. In fact, there is another twist to the Ice Box punishment that the report did not notice: the cages are covered with canvas during the day when it is hot; at night, when it is cold, the canvas is removed. And the nights at Pendleton can be cold indeed.

Another of the specialty facilities is the "Bull Pen," a fenced-in area used for holding prisoners who are being processed. Sometimes as many as thirty men are held in this area and they are kept there up to eight hours. There is no toilet, no urinal or drinking fountain in the Bull Pen. If guards refuse to take them out, they must relieve themselves on the spot. Eight months before General Robinson's survey, Dr. McNamee had sent in a complaint to the base's commanding medical officer about this situation, without results.

Although the report claims that "the double chain link fence which surrounds the main compound is basically sufficient to contain prisoners," it elsewhere notes that "there were 166 escapes during the past year." Although more than 90 per cent of the prisoners are being held on no charge more serious than AWOL, the treatment meted out to them encourages attempts to escape, even at the risk of being shot.

The report continues: "The camp was described by one officer as looking like Andersonville. The following paragraphs are an attempt to graphically describe a most serious situation that could develop into a series of embarrassing circumstances to the Marine Corps if immediate steps are not taken to permit corrective action."

The 1942 vintage building being utilized for all newly confined prisoners undergoing indoctrination and/or awaiting classification is a fire and safety hazard. The two-story barracks building was built as a temporary structure at the beginning of World War II and very little improvement has been made since. The bottom decks are divided into cells utilizing scrap steel bars, etc., that were salvaged when Camp Elliott was closed down.

It was reported that if the prisoner load on the second deck was past a certain level the doors to the cells on the first deck would not open.

There is only one escape hatch on each deck, all the windows and doors being either barred or secured to prevent escape. This particular building and two others like it are notably the best structures in the complex except for a new Maximum Security building which was recently completed.

Even the new building is inadequate; there are 48 cells in this building and only two commodes, the heating is poor and food must be carried from the mess hall and served in the individual's cell which routinely, during the winter, results in cold, greasy food.

In two areas tents are being used for confinement of medium custody prisoners. Oil burner heating is provided for these areas, and the tents are extremely overcrowded, the average footage per man in these tents is about 25 square feet. The standard square footage is 72 square feet per man.

Supervision of these areas presents an additional safety problem. In order to exercise any degree of control over the prisoners it is necessary for the guards to mingle with the prisoners. At night this is obviously an extremely dangerous practice as recently evidenced by a guard being beaten up by some prisoners while he was making his security rounds.

The men who run the brig have put a great deal of imaginative thought into figuring out ways to punish prisoners. One Marine deserter hiding out in Pasadena, Calif., told of the room of mirrors, in which some prisoners were punished by being forced to stand naked all day, sometimes for several weeks, just looking at themselves. Another deserter, interviewed in Whittier, Calif., had been a guard in a correctional custody platoon until he couldn't take it any more. "There's an interview that all prisoners go through," he said. "I've seen twenty or thirty. You hold your sea bag that weighs between 75 pounds and 115 pounds; you hold this over your head and turn in a circle as fast as you can, screaming, 'No, Sir' and 'Yes, Sir.' Once I saw a sergeant climb up on top of two foot lockers and jump on the bag one fellow was holding over his head. The bag fell on his head and he was knocked flat to the floor. It broke his nose and knocked out his teeth."

Father Al, the Franciscan priest, who was stationed at San Luis Rey Mission near Pendleton said: "No matter how bad it is, you can believe just about anything the Marines tell you about the brig. I really don't doubt any of the stories, because of the things I've seen and heard. I've seen faces beaten in. I know about the room of mirrors."

After Dr. McNamee had been treating patients at the brig for a while, and after he had made numerous complaints to his superiors to have conditions improved, he began asking the prisoners who came to him to write down what had happened to them. Here are a few. The original spelling is retained sometimes to convey a more accurate indication of the kind of young men the Marine Corps pushes around in its prisons.

Charles L. Francis set down these troubles on March 3, 1969:

"About 17:30 I was called to the duty hut. I was haveing my gear inventoreid. L/Cpl. Johnson was explaning the rules. He told me to stand at atention on the yellow foot prints in the duty room. I was told to keep my head and eyes to the front. He told me to give him 25 4 count push ups.

When he seen that I was tirering, he wanted them perfect. After he seen that I couldn't complet them he had me stand at atention then he comenced hitting me with a club in the stomach and ribs. He would stop four a few minutes and then say I was eyeballing the area and start the beating again."

The doctor found sufficient cuts, bruises, skinned areas and lumps to support the story.

McNamee made the following report on H. L. Clark (no date):

"States he told corporal he couldn't take any further harassment and then began to cry. He was then hit in the eye, thrown to the ground and kicked in the left hand and left side of the chest."

When he reported to the doctor, he had a three-inch swelling under his right eye, a swollen cheek and bruised ribs.

This one is signed by Pvt. Jimmy L. Milton on March 5, 1969:

"On 2 March 1969 Cpl. DeGross called me to the Correctional Custody office and then he beat me a few times in the chest, then he made me eat four cigaretts and then pushed me out the door.

"Then on the 3 of March 1969 Cpl. DeGross again called me to the duty CC office and then L/Cpl. Johnson and Cpl. DeGross beat me agein, L/Cpl. Johnson dug his finger nails into my forhead and beat me in the chest along with Cpl. DeGross, and this time Cpl. Anderson held his fist at the back of my head and L/Cpl. Johnson then pushed my head back as hard as he could.

"Then they made me get on the deck and then L/Cpl. Johnson kicked me in the head and some one kicked me in the side."

Statement signed by Pvt. Stephen Weddel on February 28, 1969:

"I was called in the duty CC office and L/Cpl. Johnson, Sgt. Blye and another cpl. beat me in the chest with their fist and feet leaving marks on my chest and hurting my ribbs to the point where I can just barely breath."

Statement signed by Pvt. Howard J. Stamm, Jr., on March 4, 1969:

"On or about the 27 day of Feb. I was called into the duty CC instructors office and Cpl. DeGross beat on my chest until I fell backward out the door and he then pulled me back in and continued beating on my chest until I fell down. He choked me and told me to get up he then pushed me out."

Pvt. Charles J. Comiskey received a bloodied and broken nose in the following episode, which he described in a statement signed March 4, 1969:

"I was called into the CC instructors hut and told to stand at attention on some yellow footprints keeping my eyes straight ahead. At that time L/Cpl. Johnson started beating me with a rolled up towel in the face. He then gave me blows to the stumic and karate chops in the neck. When I put my hands up to protect myself instinkivly, he thought I was crazy or something and invited me to hit him back. When I accepted his invitation with a swing and a curse, three of the CC instructors grabed me, beat me, and tied me up continuing the act until the assistant warden came and took me to sick bay."

Statement of Pvt. Peter T. Rood, signed March 5, 1969:

"At approximately 0915 on this date I suffered a cut on the back of my head. I was in the CC instructors hut doing extra P.T. because I couldn't do correct push-ups in the yard due to my back. I had a skiing accident about 1½ months ago. I went off a jump and one ski caught on an open patch of the jump. I tumbled and landed against a tree which was very close to the side of the slope. I struck the tree directly on the small of my back.

"Since then I've had bad, sharp pains in my lower back, accompanied by severe headaches and bad dreams. When I returned from the regular P.T. this morning, my back was sore and I had sharp pains in my spine. I couldn't hold a push-up position so I was told to go into the CC instructors hut.

"Cpl. DeGross forced me to do exercises when I complained about my back. He kicked my feet out from under me and grabbing the back of my shirt pushed me forward to the deck. After several repititions I was left on the deck. Cpl. DeGross kicked me a few times in my side and grabbed my shirt collar, lifting and dropping me in a push-up type exercise. I was then righted and I began to feel dizzy. I began to fall but the corporal held me up. He then gave me a shove and I fell backwards, tripping over something and striking my head on a footlocker, I believe, and I then blacked out and came to when a corpman tried to awake me. Others were in the room but since I was new in the CC area I didn't know them. When I was laying on the deck I overheard the people in the hut discuss what story they were going to tell everyone."

Pvt. Mark S. Sutherlin, a prisoner in the maximum security unit, got into an argument with a guard in October 1968. The result of the argument was this:

"He pushed me and then ordered me to put my tray of food on the floor and eat it there. Well, I didn't feel like being his fool, so I refused agien. So he pushed me agien, nocking my tray of food all over the place, then he came at me swinging his fists, so I swung back. While we fought, he kicked me in my scrotum, it didn't hurt then, but now, and it is also all blue."

It was indeed, as the doctor noted in his memorandum, entirely blue and large and tender.

Pvt. C. W. Mowery, on February 5, 1969, told of being called into the instructors' hut and being ordered to take the prisoner's down position.

"I got down in the prisoner's down position and everyone left except the two CC's that were to make the CC instructor's rack. Then another CC instructor that was just came on duty came into the CC instructors hut and stomped me twice in the back while in the prisoners down position. There were about six CC instructors in the hut when it happened but only two wrote me up. I seen the Major Voigt and he believes what they say I reckon. Anyway he told the Cpl. on duty to sent the assault charge against me to my C.O."

From L/Cpl. Gerald M. Bonnell, January 17, 1969:

"When I came to CC the 14 of January 1969, it wasn't until the next morning when they started beating on me, hitting me in the belly 3 or 4 times and asked me if I would do anything if they did it again, and kicking me in the back by my left shoulder 2 or three times and almost breaking my neck by the jurk of being kicked. They said to get things straight and I got all nervous and confused and couldn't do so that is when they chocked me and picked me almost up off the deck by my neck. I have been a nervous wreck since I joined the Marine Corps. I never said any thing or talked back, or disobeyed the CC instructors or threatened or took a swing at any of them, but yet they treat us like animals and I want out of CC and the Marine Corps."

To that he added a postscript: "Now since I signed this here form it will be a lot harder on me so I want out of CC as soon as possible."

Pvt. Lloyd A. Wyman, in a statement signed September 26, 1968, told of his refusing to run in physical training, as ordered, after which this happened:

"Upon my refusal to run, two of the aforementioned personnel dragged me by the arms in order to make me run. Fortunately, I was able to pull away from them, at which time I was placed in the 'Prisoners Down' position. While in this position, one of the personnel present at the time jumped, landing on his knees in the center of my back. This action was executed with considerable force and caused great pain. It should be known that I have been under treatment and medication for a back problem."

Fifty-three per cent of the prisoners Dr. McNamee tried to have taken for clinical diagnosis or hospital care never got there. Guards could not be spared to escort them but, as Dr. McNamee said, "there was always a guard available to escort prisoners to mow the general's lawn."

Also, Dr. McNamee says that only 15 per cent of the medicine he prescribed for his patients was ever taken by them. One prisoner with gonorrhea was in the brig from October 1968 to January 1969 and was never admitted to the hospital despite repeated efforts by Dr. McNamee to get him there. Dr. McNamee made eight efforts to get a private admitted to a chest clinic for studies, and never succeeded. Sometimes prisoners with temperatures of 102 degrees are forced to take part in daylong exercises.

Boredom takes almost as high a toll as sickness. In a report to the base medical officer, Dr. McNamee spelled out some of the results. "Inmates throw razor blades at one another. Numerous small lacerations have been seen on my confinees as a result of the above. Boredom apparently is the cause of this activity. Boredom also contributes to the incidence of self-inflicted cigarette burns. Two confinees place a lighted cigarette between their forearms to see who could stand the pain longer." Prisoners also catch wild mice and try to keep them as pets; several prisoners are treated each day for bites.

There aren't enough guards to do a proper job. Consequently, security is poor and drugs pass in and out with no trouble. Inmates who can't afford drugs shoot cold water, coffee, Kool-Aid and various medications dissolved in tap water. As a result, one to two cases of serum hepatitis per month are seen at the brig sick bay.

Obviously, to bring the prison facilities and treatment up to a civilized level, a number of things are needed, including money. The Marine Corps is asking for $2.5 million to build additional brig facilities, but they would not be large enough and the old jail would have to be used.

As General Robinson said in his private note to the chief of staff:

"Difficulty is anticipated on this line item before Congress in view of its historic reticence to fund new brig facilities. Senator Stennis in particular has gone on record stating he did not like to build a new facility for the 'bad guys' while the 'good guys' lived in substandard barracks. . . .

"The Senatorial investigation of conditions at the Presidio could serve to assist the Marine Corps in obtaining authorization and funding of this line item at Camp Pendleton, because recognition of a need for more adequate service brigs would help us."

The best and quickest solution, of course, would be to follow the precedent set in 1957 by Gen. David Shoup when he was commandant of the First Marine Division at Pendleton. He simply freed everyone in the brig who was there for something less than a felony—which immediately cleared the prison of virtually every prisoner.

III   PRISONS

GROVER LEWIS

Prisoners of War in Sunny California

"Lawd, I'm just a country boy in this great big freaky city."
—Sir Douglas Quintet.

—Jesse Ritter, who's lived with his large family for about a year in or near this deceptively somnolent seaside community located 20 miles, as the locals have it, "down the Peninsula" from San Francisco, is the kind of strapping, good ol' country boy-made-good that my grandfather in Texas would rightly have called a man of parts.

It's no trick-bag metaphor; it simply indicates a man who transcends a single definition.

Jesse teaches at S. F. State College, where he holds the office of director of freshmen English. At State, he also serves as vice-president of the vigorous (and until recently, strikebound) American Federation of Teachers local.

A four-year Korean-vintage Navy veteran, and a surviving gladiator of the Circus Maximus-like Ph. D. games of various Southern and Midwestern universities as well, Jesse husbands to the needs of a household numbering —not counting a cat and dog—seven members, his kids ranging in age from a para-hip 17 to less than one year old. After 20 years, he's still married to the same woman he started out with, Lorna ("What's doone in the kitchen tonight, Lorna?"), a zaftig earth-mother from Arkansas who loves fiercely to cook and laugh and love those around her.

Outside the office, Jesse leads a strenuous physical life—chopping wood for the fireplace, scrambling along the cliff faces above the ocean a couple of hundred yards from his house—so he leapt at the opportunity to go sailing on Thursday, May 22, when four friends from State's art department—Gary Oberbilling, Joe Halley, Alf Young, and Dennis Beall—invited him to take part in Alf's outrageous environmental-art scheme.

They were going to drive up to Berkeley and borrow a boat, and then they were going to dye the Bay. No shit. Legally, legitimately, they were going to dye the Bay.

> *"Negotiate? What is to negotiate?"*
> —*Governor Ronald Reagan, May 21.*

A skeletal chronology of recent Berkeley municipal calamities and related events might prove useful at this point.

THURSDAY, May 15—In a grisly confrontation that resembled a print of Godard's "Weekend" cut up by Burroughs and re-spliced by someone with the sensibilities of Goebbels, Berkeley police, assisted by Alameda County sheriff's deputies and units of the California Highway Patrol, dispersed thousands of "street people" protesting the demolition and fencing-off of the People's Park, which had been built by volunteers three weeks earlier on a mired vacant lot owned by the University of California. At one point, police were authorized to fire birdshot at rooftop observers and alleged provocateurs of the melee below. U. C. student Allen Blanchard and a non-student visitor to Berkeley from San Jose, James Rector, were among those injured by shotgun charges. In all, 138 persons, including police and civilians, were injured during the disturbance; scores were arrested.

MONDAY, May 19—In behalf of his AFT local, Jesse Ritter addressed a telegram to U.C. Chancellor Roger W. Heyns, formally deploring the violence of the previous Thursday in the South Campus area; copies were dispatched to the Berkeley City Council, Berkeley Mayor Wallace Johnson, and Governor Reagan. The telegram, sent over Jesse's official signature, concluded: "In the name of humanity, call off the dogs of war you have unleashed upon the citizens of a democracy."

—James Rector died of "acute heart failure" at 10:12 p. m. Before his death, surgeons at Herrick Memorial Hospital had removed his spleen, parts of his pancreas, and a kidney. Rector was 25.

TUESDAY, May 20—In the afternoon, ground and air police detachments under the coordinated command of Alameda County Sheriff Frank Madigan routed hundreds of demonstrators, onlookers, and passersby when National Guard helicopters released streams of tear gas in the vicinity of Sproul Plaza; foot forces swept the area, again arresting scores. The tear gas penetrated adjacent classrooms in use, the U. C. infirmary, and a nearby grade school still in session.

—Doctors treating Allen Blanchard for pellet wounds suffered on the rooftop alongside James Rector conceded that the student would be permanently blinded.

—In an autopsy, a forensic suregon removed three double-aught buckshot pellets from Rector's chest cavity. One of them had been lodged in his heart. A double-aught buckshot pellet is larger than a .30 caliber bullet—about the size of a marble.

WEDNESDAY, May 21—At a press conference in Sacramento, Governor Reagan defended the action of police authorities during the People's Park disturbances in Berkeley. "Once the dogs of war are unleashed," he said, "you must expect things will happen, and people being human will make mistakes on both sides."

THURSDAY, May 22—In another public statement, Governor Reagan declared that police shouldn't be blamed for James Rector's death: "He was killed by the first college administrator who said some time ago it was all right to break laws in the name of dissent." A spokesman for the Governor subsequently clarified that Reagan wasn't referring to "anyone in particular."

—At midafternoon, Dr. Jesse Ritter, along with three of his four colleagues from State, and approximately 400 other men and boys, lay face down on the asphalt "grinder" at the Santa Rita Rehabilitation Center far out past the Berkeley Hills near (why, of course) Pleasanton. This was Sheriff Madigan's turf, this "rehabilitation center," and the guards soon made it clear that they relished working over any of the prostrate prisoners who spoke or moved without permission. Jesse lay there for five and a half hours before being "processed" for illegal assembly and failure to disperse—both misdemeanor counts in the Golden State—his arms hugged flat against his sides, the heels of his sneakers slanting up at the frosty blue sky as directed.

"Despite well-meaning, idealistic people, there are people who are hostile."
—U. C. Chancellor Heyns, May 22

So, they tooled across the Bay Bridge from San Francisco at noon on May 22, the five of them from State, to dye the Bay . . . red and orange. It was Alf Young's concept; he was very much into environmental design experimentation lately, and he'd secured the necessary permission from both the Coast Guard and S. F. Mayor Joseph Alioto. To do the dyeing deed, they were going to use Nora Morganroth's five-meter, needle-nosed sloop, which they first had to ferry from Oakland to the Sausalito marina. In whimsical high spirits, anticipating the zany afternoon on the Bay, they drove to Nora's flat near Shattuck Avenue in the South Campus area of Berkeley.

Nora wasn't in, she'd left them a note saying she'd be back, so they stopped at a neighborhood diner for lunch. When they emerged, there was a general commotion in the street, and several National Guardsmen with bayonet-fixed rifles ordered them to move toward the avenue, away from the block where their car was parked. At the intersection, along with a dozen or so other people, they were encircled by Berkeley police, and four of the five were arrested by random selection: "You, you, you, and you. Move!" Inexplicably, Dennis Beall was passed over; he slipped away and immediately contacted the office of Victor van Buorg, the AFT's chief legal counsel.

Musing about the surreal scene back home at Moss Beach the next evening, where I talked with him for hours after he was freed on $800 bail, Jesse recalled with a wry shrug: "The police let straights through, but they singled out hair, particularly, and people like us, dressed, uh, kinky. Hell, we were going sailing." He grinned, wistfully. "We were going to dye the Bay.

"I was handcuffed to a nearly hysterical hippie kid. The bus ride to Santa Rita wasn't bad. We were all nervous, but we could talk among ourselves. All of that ended at the compound. When we got off the bus, a deputy pointed a shotgun at our heads and ordered us to lie face down on the 'grinder'—that's an old Army term for the bare ground. Except that this wasn't bare ground. It was alphalt sprinkled with fine gravel. Within a half-hour, there were about 400 of us lying there; the women, maybe 100 of them, were held in a separate compound. Every 20 minutes, somebody would order us to change the direction of our heads from left to right. After a while, I started tripping on the different colors of the gravel." Thoughtfully, he inspected first the palms, then the backs of his hands. "There was nothing else to do," he said finally.

> "It's a piss-poor consolation, but Sheriff Madigan is dead. He piqued too soon."
>
> —Graffito at S. F. State, May 23

"Sheriff Madigan's men were obviously following a preconceived scenario —playing weird, sadistic military games, I guess," Jesse ruminated, stoking up the fireplace while Lorna fixed dinner and the Ritter kids and their chums barreled in and out of the glass-enclosed living room like banshees on a seek-out-and-destroy mission.

"There've been prisoners of war treated better than we were," he went on. "I personally was prodded and kicked and shoved and chopped on the backs of my legs with a lead-weighted sapper, and cursed and humiliated— we all were—but I was one of the lucky ones, because I recognized right away what was going down. Some of the younger ones in my barracks, though . . ." His voice trailed off.

"There were some pitiful cases, and some funny ones. One of the fellows on the bus was a psychiatrist who'd stepped out of his office for a stroll and was caught up in the sweep on Shattuck. He broke us all up. 'I'm a psychiatrist,' he kept on introducing himself, 'can I help you?'

'Then there was a long-haired kid who'd dropped acid an hour before he was arrested. Amazingly enough, the guards saw that he was freaked or sick or something, and didn't hassle him. When he wandered into our barracks, we scrounged him a cigarette and coaxed him into sitting over in a corner where we could keep an eye on him.

"Some of those younger kids . . . they were so brave, and so vulnerable. In the messhall, one kid got out of line in some slight way, and the guards leaned him head-first against a metal pole and pounded on the pole with their sappers until his nose bled. I quoted Joe Heller to some of the greener kids in my group. You know—'They can do anything to you that you can't keep them from doing.' Most of them had never heard of Heller, but they flashed on that line."

Settling into a deep chair, Jesse shook his head ruefully, wonderingly.

"Those guards, my God, they were"—he groped for the right intensive—"beyond fiction, even Heller's . . . During the hours we spent on the 'grinder,' if you asked to urinate, the deputies would take that as a sign of weakness and needle you beyond endurance—either that, or take you off to one side and beat the living shit out of you in private. One of them said to a very young kid: 'Wanna pee-pee, huh, creep? Well, hold it till it hurts, then piss your pants and we'll beat them dry for you.'

Another guard, a short, red-haired guy—the worst of them all—rousted my barracks at 4:30 a.m.: 'Well, I had me a good night's sleep, you shit-eating perverts. Now I'm ready for some killing.'

"At breakfast, a deputy kept bawling at the line as we filed along: 'If you take it and don't eat it, we'll push your fucking face in it.'

"Gradually, it dawned on me that what was happening to us was torture"—he paused at the word to light a cigarette—"and that the ratio of sub-human punishment meted out to us was in direct proportion to the guards' fear of us. Well, not us, exactly—we were defenseless—but the guards were deathly afraid of what all those barracks full of long-haired freaks stood for.

"Sometimes, in their panicky zeal to play their larger-than-life horror roles to the hilt, the deputies blew their lines. I remember one of them yelling at a slowmoving longhair: 'Awright, you scrubby queer cunt, toes and ass against the wall!'

"Toward morning, the guards circulated the rumor among themselves that the street people were planning to march on the compound to free us. The National Guard circled the camp in jeeps and trucks all night. That was an eerie, godawful sight—to see cops guarding cops.

"Just before we were released at 8 a.m., one of the deputies made us march drill-style, chanting: 'We love the blue meanies! We love the blue meanies!' Another guard congratulated the deputy who'd come up with the idea: 'Hey, great, we'll make them all do that.'"

Jesse restlessly paced around the room before stopping at a window to peer out at the dark ocean. When he spoke again, there was metal in his voice.

"It almost unhinges my mind to say it, but the only humane treatment any of us got at Santa Rita came from the trusties. And each other. And the trusties are criminals."

> *"They can do anything to you that you can't keep them from doing."*
> —*Joseph Heller*

After dinner, the Ritters and some friends and I sat around the snapping fireplace, sipping red table wine. We were in a drowsing poem of a house overlooking the ocean, warm, well-fed, safe, so we liked to think, as the seasonal fog enveloped the beach below. The was was fully 25 miles away, up the Peninsula, north.

The Case of Wesley Robert Wells,
Twenty-seven Years a Political Prisoner

Now, Sir, I will not undertake to argue the legal merits of my case, as I'm sure you are, or will be, thoroughly familiarized with them. I must say, though, that I feel that the Attorney General has been unfair, unscrupulous and unethical, in the prosecution of the case. The Attorney General, for the very same reason a matador waves the red cloth before the eyes of the bull, presented "documentation" of my so-called prison "record" to every court wherein my case was adjudicated, as though it should be—and knowing that it should not be—given judicial consideration. One only has to read the various decisions rendered in the case to see that the Attorney General's unscrupulous and unprincipled tactics were effective, and accomplished his end. In every court wherein the case was adjudicated, the court made judicial observations with respect to my so-called "record."

Now, that the courts have upheld the judgement of death in the case, the State is contending, as it did in all the courts, on the basis of the so-called "record," a unilateral "record," presenting only one side of the story, as always, and doesn't even present that one side accurately or truthfully, that

From *Black Panther* newspaper, September 1969. Reprinted by permission of Black Panther Party.

I have a punishment "Record" of many infractions of prison rules, that I am incorrigible, "a hardened killer," and therefore should be, and must be, put to death, exterminated—presumably for the "protection of society." The fact that the guard involved in the altercation has stated (as reported by Walter Winchell, over his Sunday evening news broadcast) that he, understandably, does not wish me to be executed is completely forgotten or ignored by the State.

Now, Sir, I assure you that I am not the kind or type of man my so-called "record" portrays me to be, nor am I the depraved beast the State contends that I am. I will not undertake to justify, excuse or rationalize my past prison conduct, for I would be one of the first to admit that I have not been a "model prisoner." But I will say, in all sincerity, that during the many years I've spent in prison, I've been conditioned—by necessity, by the law of the jungle—to be tough, to be hard, and at times, even to be mean. I've been forced to fight for my very existence, to employ every means at my disposal for survival, I speak, Sir, the plain unvarnished truth. I've been cynically pitted not only against tough, vicious lifers, prisoners who had no hope of ever being free, and therefore were willing to go to any length, including "putting another prisoner on the spot," to curry favor with the officials, and thus get a "good spot" to do their time, and end their lives on it: and against, as well, wild, young prisoners, striving to make themselves reputations as prison tough guys, but I have also been pitted against ignorant, prejudiced and brutal guards who resented and were antagonized by my independent spirit, my sense of dignity, and sense of justice, and who undertook to break my spirit, and to "teach me my place" as I was told. To accomplish this, I was often unjustly punished, often subjected to all manner of degrading, cruel and inhuman treatment: the "hole," the "lime cure," the "water treatment," the club, and other unspeakable inhumanities.

I first entered prison a young man (19) of high ideals and principles, during my formative years; during a period that might be appropriately termed the "dark age" of prisons and prison administration. Men were sent to prison in those days solely for the purpose of punishment—and they got just that. Little, if any, thought was given to helping the prisoner or to rehabilitate him. The only rule the prison officials knew or practiced in handling of the prisoners was the "rule of the club," the "lime cure," "the water treatment," and the "hole." The prisoner was treated in such a manner as to only bring out the worst in him, to arouse animal instincts; and he would, not infrequently, act and react more like wild, like some depraved beast, than a rational human being.

Those were the days of the con boss system. That is to say, the days when the con bosses ran the prison, and ruled with an iron hand. The con boss had as much power as the guard—and there were some con bosses who had far more power than guards. A con boss could and there were some that did, cause a prisoner's time to be pretty tough. A young prisoner, especially was subject to have his life made really miserable by the con boss unless he was willing and able to fight for his rights, or "drew commissaries" with which to pay off; or unless he was willing to pay off otherwise.

All records were recorded and kept by convicts who had the rating and power of con bosses. If a guard brought you before the captain for some infraction of the rules, the captain would give your card to one of his convict clerks and tell him to write the charge against you. If the "con" clerk happened to be of the opinion that you rated (had influential convict friends), or if he happened not to like the arresting guard, he would write the charge against you so as it would read as a misdemeanor. But, on the other hand, if the "con" clerk, should happen to dislike you, he would more than likely write a minor infraction as to read as a "major felony." Then again, if the infractor were willing and able to pay the price, there wouldn't be any charge entered against him. It wasn't uncommon for a con boss to have a prisoner put in the hole in an effort to force him to submit to his lustful desire; or as payment to some guard for services rendered.

It was during this period, my early years in prison, during the "dark age" of prison administraton, that most of my so-called prison "record" accrued, and cast the die for that which was to follow.

I had been in prison only a short time when I was charged with my first infraction of prison rules; it was for fighting with a prisoner for calling me a nigger. We were brought before Captain Carpenter, and I told him what the fight was. Imagine, if you can, my great surprise, and shock, when the captain said: "Well that's what you are, isn't it!" Can you imagine how I felt to have Captain Carpenter say such a thing to me, and to be forced to take it? His remark not only made me angry, but hurt me very deeply, and shamed me. But I could do nor say nothing about it. I then and there resolved that I would prove to the captain—and indeed, to the whole prison world around me—that I was a man, a man who could take unflinchingly anything, any punishment, any abuse he or his guards could inflict upon me, and still live to leave San Quentin a better man that he was. I do believe that something died in me that day; that a metamorphosis took place. That "Bob" Wells, the man so much has been said and written about, was born. And, due to many long years of ignorant, callous and inhuman treatment, and being forced to live under the law of the jungle, "Bob" Wells, for self-preservation, ruthlessly denied existence to Wesley Wells, the young man who entered prison with high ideals and principles; the young man who was unable to believe that the mere pigmentation of his skin was a badge of inferiority, warranting him with less common courtesy to dream of better things—of a chance in life, of a chance to develop a good mind, and to put it to useful work, to someday be a doctor—as was his mother's wish. After that, after the metamorphosis, for many long, dreadful years, Wesley Wells never had a chance.

After 38 months, I was transferred to Folsom. At that time, I was glad. I thought I would be treated as a man, and would be able to do my time and get out. But, oh, how wrong I was proven to be! Upon my arrival at Folsom I met Captain C. L. Larkin (who later became Warden), a very mountain of a man, weighing about 240 pounds, and about 6 feet 6 inches tall; and without a doubt, the cruelest, most vicious man I ever had the misfortune to meet, and be forced to live with. If there were any prisoner the captain disliked more than another, it was the young San Quentin transfer, who he said caused him all of his trouble. I was called to the Captain's office the first day I entered the prison, and Captain Larkin proceeded to lay down the law to me. "So you think you are a tough nigger, huh?" he said to me, "Well we have ways here to handle tough niggers." He then tells me, "I'll have you eating out of my hand before you leave here." And as I started out of his office, to wait on the "captain's line," as he told me to do, he kicked me viciously—just to convince me, I imagine, that he did "have ways to handle tough niggers." Well, that was my Folsom reception; and the battle between the captain and me was on, he to break me, and have me "eating out of his hand," as he said he would, and I just as determined to prove him wrong.

Though the racial discrimination in San Quentin was bad, it was ultra-democratic in comparison to that of Folsom. For example, most of the colored prisoners were housed in what was known as the "buzzard roost," in Number One Building; and were the last ones to enter the mess-hall. They had to stand against the mess hall wall and watch and wait until the complete prison body entered the mess-hall and was served, before they could enter the mess hall. Having been reared from an early age in West Los Angeles, in a rather democratic neighborhood, I found the racial discrimination of the prisons extremely galling, and due to my inability to submit to it without showing my resentment, I soon incurred the hostility of the prison officials in general, and aggravated the animosity of Captain Larkin in particular. I will not undertake to relate the many abuses, the many injustices, the cruel and inhuman treatment accorded me by the prison officials of Folsom, for to do so would necessitate me writing a book. But I feel it to be in the interest of justice and I would be unfair to myself were I to fail to apprise you of the following.

In 1944, less than six months prior to the charge of possession of the knife, previously mentioned herein, I was attacked by a prisoner and stabbed nine times—practically everywhere but the bottom of my feet—while I stood within ten feet of a prison guard, and didn't have so much as a penknife

with which to defend myself. I was carried to the prison hospital, and after
much sewing and patching an emergency abdominal operation was performed upon me; and for days I laid in the hospital in what was said to be
"a critical condition."

The day the doctor, Dr. J. F. McAnally, told me it would be alright for
me to go to the washroom and do a little walking around, the Warden
ordered that I be put in the hole; but the doctor would not allow it. The
Warden then ordered that I be placed and confined in one of the hospital
"rooms." I argued strongly against the move; and the doctor told me that I
was right, that I was not in any condition to be in a "room" but that it was
the Warden's order. He then told me to go on in the "room" and he would
have a talk with the Warden. The next day I was moved back into the hospital ward. After about twenty-five days, when the steel clamps had been
removed from my stomach, and the last stitches had been removed from my
body, that very day the warden had me put in the hole . . . on a bread and
water diet. After five or six days in the hole, the doctor was successful in
prevailing upon the officials to feed me one meal a day.

In due course I was brought before the disciplinary committee, which
was composed of the Warden, the Asso. Warden, and I think the third member was a lieutenant by the name of Buchanon. I was charged with and summarily "found guilty" of possession of a knife. Though no knife was ever
taken from me, nor was one found near me, neither was I ever shown the
knife I was supposed to have had. But I was "found guilty" and sentenced
to 29 days in the hole, on bread and water—even though I was just out of
the hospital.

During my "trial" a gun-guard who was in a gun-tower about 40 or 50
feet away from where I was attacked and stabbed, testified "that he saw the
whole affair from beginning to end." Then he saw my assailant attack me,
that he saw me laying flat upon my back kicking, kicking for my very life
at my assailant, who was standing over me, cutting and stabbing me. He
testified that he saw all of this, yet he did not call out to anyone, he did not
fire a shot, he did not blow his whistle, he did absolutely nothing to stop
my assailant from killing me. And, when a guard did finally come to my
rescue, and disarmed the would be killer, Associate Warden William J. Ryan
questioned the guard, "Why did you stop him!?"

There were no criminal charges ever filed against my assailant, not even
for possession of the knife. He was transferred to San Quentin, and given a
parole shortly thereafter.

That, Sir, is the kind of treatment, the kind of protection, I was accorded
and could expect from and by Folsom officials. Is it any wonder, I respect-
fully ask, that I felt that it was up to me and up to me alone to protect

myself? Is it any wonder that two prison doctors, after lengthy interviews with me, just two days before the unfortunate affair with the guard, is it any wonder that they found that I was suffering from a abnormal fear—years of fear—for my personal safety, is it any wonder? In substantiation of the doctors' findings, I wish to apprise you of one more incident, and then leave it up to you to decide as to whether or not there were any basis for the doctor's findings.

In 1945, Lieutenant Buchanon and several guards came to move me from one cell to another in the back alley. Guard Joe George arrived and told the other guards to leave, that he would, and did, move me to the cell. After I was in the cell, Lieutenant Buchanon then entered and began to jab me in the ribs and stomach with a long, heavy, steel-tipped walking cane. I grabbed a hold of one end of the cane, and with the Lieutenant holding onto the other end, we stood there arguing. Guard Joe George stood just inside of the cell, and listened and watched the argument; guard Joe Nunns stood just outside of the cell and witnessed the whole affair. Guard O. L. Jenson roughly shoved guard Joe George aside and rushed into the cell and, with these words, "You black sonofabitch, you can't talk to my superior officer like that!" he struck me a cruel, vicious blow with his club over my left eye, laying it wide open, requiring several stitches to close. To justify the assault upon me, I was charged with: attempting to assault the lieutenant. When I was "tried" before a disciplinary composed of the Warden, the Associate warden and Lieutenant Buchanon, Guard Joe George testified that he was standing right in the cell doorway, and that he did not see me make any attempt to assault the lieutenant or anyone else. Later that day Dr. P. W. Day, the Chief Medical officer of the prison, questioned Guard Joe George as to just what had happened, and the surrounding circumstances, and was advised, as was the warden, that I had not raised my hands to strike anyone, that the assault upon me was cruel, unwarranted and unjustifiable. As the guard testified Dr. Day made notes. (Guard Joe Nunns testified to the same effect when I was tried in Sacramento for throwing and hitting the guard with the cuspidor.) Notwithstanding guards Nunns and Joe George's testimony, I was "found guilty," and sentenced to 29 days in the hole.

Well, Sir, what do you think? Was there any basis for the doctors findings? Would you say that I had cause to be in fear? I have related only a few of such incidents as above mentioned, there were many more that I would like to tell you of, which my so-called "record" gives no account of. They are recorded, however, in my medical record, a record that you will find very informative, therefore, I urge that you read it. To enable you to better understand and to be able to appreciate somewhat of what I went through in Folsom, the physical and mental suffering, what a "hell-on-earth" my life was, I quote from a couple of letters, one written in October, 1944, to the Adult Authority, and the other one to Mr. Philip C. Wilkins, my attorney, shortly after my arrival here on condemned row, in 1947. First, the Adult Authority letter:

". . . My purpose in writing you this brief of my life is intended to serve you, the members of the Adult Authority, in aiding me, fixing my term and the like; and so I present not as a defense, especially, but at least, as an explanation of the events which have occurred during my time. . . ."

The Telltale Skeletons

After last year's Arkansas prison scandal, with its revelations of physical torture, enforced homosexuality, on-premises prostitution and laissez-faire corruption among trustees and officials, there seemed little that the system could have left to hide. But, as it turned out, there were still skeletons lurking behind the prison walls, and last week they began popping startlingly—and quite literally—into public view. At the week's start workmen dug up the crudely buried remains of three human beings in a cow pasture of east Arkansas's 10,000-acre Cummins Prison Farm. By the weekend, amid charges that the bodies belonged to some of hundreds of "escapees" reported by prison officials over the years, Gov. Winthrop Rockefeller's administration was confronted with a fresh scandal, this one with a grisly medieval flavor. Prisoners began telling of bodies buried all over the lot.

Republican Rockefeller himself, immediately jetting back home from an anti-poverty conference in Washington after the bodies turned up, moved promptly—not to expedite the investigation prison authorities had begun but to slap a damper on all the publicity. Seeing no "need to wash our dirty linen before the nation," Rockefeller ordered a halt to further exhumations, and first suggested that the bodies might turn out to be merely from some forgotten paupers' burying ground. Such was the explanation also advanced by several legislators, including Rep. Joel Y. Ledbetter Jr. Discussing the three newly found skeletons, one of them headless and a second with a crushed skull. Ledbetter told a Little Rock press conference: "Those people all could have died down there without families and were buried there." "Without heads?" a reporter asked.

From *Newsweek*, February 12, 1968, pp. 42-43. Copyright 1968 by Newsweek, Inc. Reprinted by permission.

To Rockefeller's pronounced dismay, the startling new scandal was broken by none other than his handpicked prison superintendent, Thomas O. Murton. Deciding to check out long-circulating rumors that many a Cummins Farm inmate had been murdered by either guards or fellow inmates, Murton was led to one supposed burial site by three different convicts—separately. Murton ordered a convict crew to start digging. In each of three suspected graves they unconvered a skeleton. "We didn't expect to come up with anything, certainly not three out of three," Murton said. One prison official estimated that as many as 300 victims of assorted violence might be illicitly buried on the prison grounds.

Corroboration of brutal and habitual homicide piled up throughout the week. Convict Reuben Johnson, 59, in and out of the Arkansas prison since 1937 for slaying a brother and for robbery, said he personally had seen "quite a few"—perhaps a dozen—men "shot down or beaten to death by guards or wardens" and that he had helped bury several of them. Johnson was among the convicts who told superintendent Murton of the burying ground. Murton spoke favorably about the prisoner's "credibility," and Johnson's allegations were corroborated by many other prisoners.

"I seen many a man killed and buried out there," said thrice-convicted rapist James Wilson, 51. He recalled a prison official fatally beating one recalcitrant prisoner first with a pistol, which broke, and then with a crowbar. Wilson said he saw another guard shoot down a prisoner who refused to submit to a whipping with the 4-inch-wide strap commonly used at the farm. In Houston, an alumnus of Cummins Farm, Edward Redmond, 47, related how in 1940 he saw a horse-mounted guard wrap barbed wire around the neck of an elderly Negro prisoner and drag him to death, Western-style. Redmond also claimed to have seen guards wantonly shoot down two other Negro prisoners.

In the face of all this, Rockefeller backtracked later in the week and announced that further investigation would be conducted. But he insisted on postponing additional exhumations until the state penitentiary board meets this week to consider the affair. "It is important to keep the current investigation . . . in proper perspective," Rockefeller said. "We could be on the brink of uncovering a scandal of untold proportions or, on the other hand, the investigation may reveal no competent evidence of widespread criminal conduct."

Neither Rockefeller nor any one else in Arkansas was eager to point a finger of political blame in the middle of the new disclosures—simply because the sorry prison operation has endured over so many generations that nobody knows whom to blame. But if anything seemed indisputably clear last week, it was that the cleanup still had a long way to go. "This," said prison physician Edwin N. Barron Jr., "is really eighteenth century."

ALAN J. DAVIS

The Sheriff's Vans

The sheriff of Philadelphia County is responsible for transporting prisoners between the courts and the various county and state prisons. For this purpose, there are five sheriff's vans and seven station wagons. Only five inmates can be carried in each station wagon. Some 35 to 40 inmates are crammed into each van. Since hundreds of prisoners must be transported back and forth each day, the vans do most of the work.

Investigators are in complete accord with the following essay written by one articulate inmate who had traveled on the vans some 50 times:

"Prisoners confined in Philadelphia's three prisons commute from their institutions to the courts by way of a prison van. The van is a truck externally resembling the sort of refrigerated delivery truck that delivers meat to food stores. The body of the truck has no windows. At the very top of the truck there is a tiny row of slots purportedly for ventilating purposes.

"Winter—The van is parked overnight in the House of Correction. At eight o'clock in the morning the van driver picks it up and drives it to the Detention Center. There, some 40 prisoners, who have been waiting since six o'clock (packed like sardines in a steel-barred can), are loaded into the van. It has only seating capacity for 15 people. The rest must make themselves 'comfortable' as best they can. There are no handholds. There is no heat. It is freezing with an intensity so great that some prisoners relinquish their seats: The pain of frozen iron pressed against their backsides is unendurable. Packed into the mass of men they may find a little warmth jammed together. The trip from northeast Philadelphia is an hour of grinding stops and bumping halts. The standing men are tossed about inside the van. There is no light in the vehicle and the darkness is punctured by the grunts and groans.

"Summer—The prison van is a sweltering cauldron of red-hot cast iron. The packed bodies of men stink. Prisoners who were arrested in winter are still in their heavy clothes. The sun winks occasionally through the narrow slits on top, but the outside air remains aloof, not wishing to contaminate itself with this Dante's Inferno on wheels.

"Some Interesting Highlights—Riding in the prison van is virtually the

From *Trans*-action, December 1968, p. 12. Copyright © December 1968 by Trans-action, Inc., New Brunswick, New Jersey. Reprinted by permission.

only time in a prisoner's detention that he is completely unsupervised, and some strange things do occur. If anyone is homosexually inclined, and it is summer, a stinking sex orgy may take place in the dim confines of the van. Sometimes this is with mutual consent, sometimes by coercion. All the time it is done with utter disregard for the feelings of the other men in the van, who cannot even avert their faces. Sometimes a prisoner who is going to be a [state] witness is accidentally thrown into the company of the very people he is going to testify against. Threats and even violence break out. The van drivers roll merrily on their way, blissfully unaware of what is taking place.

"The prisoners are alone in their walled-up cage, alone with their dry bologna sandwiches that must serve as sustenance for the next 24 hours. No cooked meal awaits them at the Detention Center when they return from court at night, only the same bologna sandwich. On the return trip from court, the van drops prisoners off at Holmesburg, the Detention Center, and the House of Correction, in that order. At Holmesburg the van drives into a walled-off enclosure that is barred by two massive solid doors and topped by solid concrete and steel. Believe me, it's a very snug fit. It generally takes between 15 to 20 minutes of paperwork until the van is allowed to proceed, and during this time the already high temperature rises sharply, the atmosphere becomes completely stagnant, and the waiting becomes interminable and finally unbearable. The prisoners scream and bang on the sides of the van but there is no relief. The time never gets any shorter, sometimes it gets longer.

"It is difficult to comprehend how the city justifies the van as treatment for untried, unconvicted, unsentenced men, who are the bulk of its passengers.

"I know, as a matter of fact, that the Interstate Commerce Commission requires that certain minimum space be provided for each individual hog shipped in commerce. Couldn't untried prisoners get the same that a pig gets?

"I have written these few words not out of bitterness, but out of the experience of 50 trips.

"I was there, Charlie."

Dennis Cujdik, a 17-year-old charged only with being a runaway from home, describes his ride on the van:

"I was at 1801 Vine in a cell when four Negro boys started bothering me for not having underwear on. Then when we got on the sheriff's van and started moving they told everyone that I didn't have on underwear. As the van was moving they started getting close to me. One of them touched me and I told them to please stop.

"All of a sudden a coat was thrown over my face and when I tried to pull it off I was viciously punched in the face for around ten minutes. I fell to the floor and they kicked me all over my body, including my head and my privates. They ripped my pants from me and five or six of them held me down and took turns fucking me.

"My insides feel sore and my body hurts, my head hurts, and I feel sick in the stomach. Each time they stopped I tried to call for help, but they put their hands over my mouth so that I couldn't make a sound. While they held me, they burned my leg with a cigarette. When the van stopped at the prison, they wiped the blood from me with my shirt. They threatened my life and said they would get me in D1 if I told anyone what happened. They said that if they didn't get me in D1 they'd get me in the van again. When the door opened they pushed me to the back so they could get out first. At first, I told the guard I tripped and fell, but then I thought I'd better tell the truth. I pointed out those who beat me up. A doctor looked at me and said I'd have to go to the hospital. They took pictures of the bruises on my body, and I could just about breathe because my nose and jaw seemed to be broken in many different places. I was asked by the lieutenant to write down what happened, and this is exactly what happened."

Why has this situation been allowed to continue for so long, despite the fact that it was brought to the attention of public officials at least two years ago? The answer is simple: The responsible city officials have blatantly neglected their duty.

GLORIA WADE BISHOP

Four and a Half Days in Atlanta's Jails

On Monday, January 27, at approximately 5 p.m., in Atlanta, Georgia, the city "too busy to hate," I was arrested for taking part in a peaceful demonstration at Leb's Restaurant. Two years ago this popular restaurant refused to serve Harry Belafonte, who had been given the key to the city. Like Belafonte and his group, Atlanta Negroes sought service at Leb's, and when turned away, began a peaceful protest against the restaurant's discriminatory policies. Approximately fifty of us, white and Negro, picketed the block in which Leb's is located, and in line with the city ordinance on picketing, we moved continuously and spaced ourselves thirty-six inches apart. So peaceful was the demonstration that two white parents dared join the picket

From *The Atlantic Monthly,* July 1964, pp. 68-70. Copyright 1964 by The Atlantic Monthly Company, Boston, Mass. Reprinted by permission.

line with their two daughters, Julia, eight, and Giah, twelve. As the picket line passed the front of Leb's for the fourth time, I heard the screams of a young child. When I turned around, I saw eight-year-old Julia and her mother step into a paddy wagon. I was watching this arrest in disbelief when Captain Brooks of the Atlanta Police Department pulled me by the coat sleeve and asked in a very hoarse voice, "Are you with this group?" When I answered in the affirmative, he said to waiting Negro patrolmen, "Take her to the wagon." And so it went, until all demonstrators had been arrested and were en route to the city jail.

Negroes and whites were placed in the same paddy wagons, but not in the same cells. As soon as we reached the city jail, Negro female demonstrators were placed in one section of the second-floor detention ward and whites in another. The usual procedure in the case of arrests is to book criminals at the first-floor desk and then confine them to cells. This procedure was not followed in our case. Upon arrival at the city jail, we were taken immediately to cellblocks without being asked who we were, without being fingerprinted, and without being told why we had been arrested. Not until we had spent three hours in the cellblocks were we asked our names, ages, and addresses. When two Negro patrolmen came into the cell to secure this information, the matron on duty said, "In all my twenty-seven years at this jail, I have never known people to be booked in a cell." Negro police arrested and booked us because the city accepted an editorial suggestion in the Atlanta *Constitution*. The editorial advised that Negro police be used to handle civil rights demonstrators, apparently because the editors believed chances of police brutality would be lessened if Negroes handled Negroes and white sympathizers.

The cellblock in which we were confined was composed of two sections: a front eating area of two benches and four solitary-confinement cells, and a back sleeping area of sixty-two beds. The beds were covered with bug-infested mattresses and filthy blue sheets. In the sleeping area were four seatless, unclean, and tissueless toilets. Tissue is issued only when the prisoner requests it from the matron, who must then go to a supply room, secure the tissue, and bring it to the cellblock.

Meals in the jail corresponded to the physical conditions of the cells. For breakfast we were given strips of salty, shriveled-up, greasy, fried fatback; for lunch, overcooked, unseasoned, souplike beans, and for dinner the same beans. Most of us found the food inedible, but we accepted our share and gave it to other cellmates.

Cellmates who were not demonstrators were mostly drunks or lesbians, many of whom came into the cell without shoes and wearing torn and badly soiled clothes. Most disturbing to us was not the swearing drunks and the strong odor of cheap wines, but the flirting lesbians who fondled some of the teen-agers. One night we saw two highly intoxicated women make love on a back bunk, and numerous times we were told by one lesbian or another, "I'm gonna git you tonight." Such a threat was almost carried out when one of the lesbians pulled a teen-age girl from a top bunk in an attempt to make love to her. Complaints were made against the lesbians, but the jailer made no effort to separate them from the young girls.

After spending three nights with the lesbians, the drunks, the seatless toilets, and the far-from-enticing food, six teen-agers and I were taken from the cellblock to stand trial for disorderly conduct. This charge involves boisterous and disorderly conduct in the form of drunkenness, swearing, kicking, spitting, and fighting. Civil rights attorney Howard Moore, Jr., asked of the city's witness whether we seven demonstrators had been seen committing any of these acts. The witness answered no, but added that he had been noisy and boisterous. When asked who had complained of the alleged noise, the witness answered, "No one." When asked whom, then, had the demonstrators disturbed, the witness, a police officer for the city, replied, "They disturbed me." He further testified that all demonstrators had been asked to disperse or were told that they would be arrested. In spite of the lack of evidence against us, we were found guilty of disorderly conduct. The judge fined us thirty-three dollars and sentenced us to thirty days in the stockade. Upon payment of the fine, the stockade sentence was to be suspended since this was our first offense. Our attorney objected to the fine, the sentence, and the two-hundred-and-fifty-dollar appeal bond. Objection was immediately overruled.

The thirty-three-dollar fine was not paid, however, for civil rights attorneys and leaders were negotiating with Mayor Ivan Allen for release of all demonstrators. Furthermore, to pay the fine would be to accept the judge's verdict of guilty; our innocence merited acquittal, not payment of a fine. We were afraid, therefore, that we would soon be leaving the city jail for the stockade. But our fears were allayed when we returned to the cellblock. The matron told us that prisoners were not "shipped out" to the stockade so late at night and so soon after trial. Either she was mistaken or usual procedures again were not followed; we left the cellblock for the stockade at midnight, only hours after we had been sentenced. A guard took us to the first-floor desk, where we were fingerprinted for the first time. As we walked to the waiting paddy wagon, a desk sergeant pushed a fifteen-year-old girl and threatened to kick her because she was a "smart nigger." His action invited similar action on the part of the driver of the wagon. In a thirty-mile-an-hour speed zone he did fifty and tested his brakes at every stoplight. Each time he hit the brakes we were thrown about the wagon and he was almost overcome with laughter. The joke continued until we arrived at the stockade.

In order to reach the guard's desk we had to pass through a large kitchen where Negro women, wearing white uniforms with blue collars, were cooking over huge stoves. I saw great bins of cooked fatback, sausage, and cornbread, marked "C-F" for colored females, "W-F" for white females, and so on. This food was to be served to prisoners in the stockade and in the city jail. I could not tell whether there was any difference in the food marked "C-F" and that marked "W-F," but I did observe that a bin of sausage was marked "W-M" for white males. During my three days in the city jail, Negroes, male and female, had been given only fatback and no sausage.

As we waved to the working women who smiled expressions of support to us, the guard on duty handed us dirty white uniforms and said, "Put these on and get to work." When we protested starting work at one thirty in the morning, the guard swore and led us immediately to solitary confinement, appropriately called "the hole." Located behind the white men's dressing rooms, the hole is a small windowless, bedless room of approximately four by eight feet and approximately ten feet high. Overhead, a bright light burns constantly, making it difficult to sleep or to distinguish night from day. The feature of the hole that disturbed us most was the lack of toilet facilities; we had to use the concrete floor and had no tissue. Two of us were placed in one hole, two in another, and three in still another. The hole in which sixteen-year-old Patricia and I were confined smelled like a recently used rural outhouse. On the floor were many cigarette butts, two tobacco pouches, fallen plaster, and other trash. Large black roaches crawled around boldly.

Two hours after being in the hole, we were given our first meal: one biscuit and a cup of water. The biscuits were placed on the floor on top of the fallen plaster, cigarette butts, and dried urine.

In spite of the hardness of our bed, we managed to sleep, though only after killing a few roaches. We awoke—how much later I don't know—to the screams of one of the girls. "Diane's sick, Mrs. Bishop," she called to the only adult in the group. "Diane's real sick. She's coughing bad." The mention of Diane's name was enough to upset us, for Diane was only twelve. We called the guards for what seemed like hours, and didn't stop calling until one finally came. The girls promised to do anything if the guard would let Diane out to see a doctor. In a heavy Southern drawl, the guard, who was about fifty years old, said, "Yawl cain't git out cause thar want be work for three weeks. So set tiaght." He left and returned later to take Diane's temperature. She didn't have a temperature; she couldn't be sick: that was his diagnosis. I yelled through a crack in the door that people can be sick without having a high temperature. The guard opened the door to my hole, stared at me hatefully, and said in an angry voice, "You ain't no doctor." Diane remained sick, and all of us remained in our misery. I should give the guard credit for one act of kindness. He placed in each hole an empty three-gallon bean can in which we would relieve ourselves. When we heard hours later that Diane was fast asleep, all of us relaxed, and we, too, slept.

When we awakened, we heard the voices of white male prisoners dressing for the chain gang. Many of them peeped into the hole and said, too jubilantly, "There's some niggers in thar." Of course, we felt duty-bound to serenade them with our freedom songs, and we emphasized one verse of "We Shall Overcome," which simply but powerfully asserts, "We're black and white together." We were sad when the men left the dressing rooms, for once again there was that painful silence, that absence of life that we so dreaded. Luckily, the silence was soon broken by a happy sound. Negro female prisoners brought our second meal, again biscuits and water, but more important, they brought themselves and good news. Two other demonstrators arrested after us sent word that we would be out soon. We cheered and sang again, this time with real gusto. But we were not out soon, and hours later our spirits were no longer high. Breathing was becoming more difficult in the stuffy room as the strong fumes of urine seemed to be inhaled but not exhaled. I tried visualizing the outside, but I could see only the arrest of eight-year-old Julia and the determined movement of the black roaches. Faulkner's novel *The Unvanquished*, which I had stashed in my bra, afforded me some entertainment, though I would have preferred reading another novelist while in a Southern jail. The teen-agers entertained themselves by telling jokes and talking seriously about overcrowded, poorly equipped, double-sessioned Negro schools in Atlanta. We talked or read, but we could not get one question out of our minds: "I wonder if anyone knows we're here?"

Someone did know we were there. At midnight on Friday, January 31, a guard brought a Negro nurse to the holes to administer two green aspirins to each of us. We were informed at that time that we would be released from solitary as soon as we took our medicine. Proudly, we left the hole and walked again through the huge kitchen where Negro women were still working. In the Negro ward we donned white uniforms, but we were not told to work. The Student Nonviolent Coordinating Committee had paid our bonds, and we were going home very soon. We were grateful to rest our tired bodies on a bed, not concrete, and in a room not roach-infested and urine-stenched. An extremely young guard with a boyish face told us that we would be released the next morning and that, for the time being, we should wash up and sleep.

The reward of being released from the hole was the opportunity to talk to other Negro prisoners. They were embarrassingly proud of us and looked at the young girls the way a small boy looks at his favorite hero. On the pretext of using the toilet, one by one the women drifted into the ward where we were dressing. They stood around grinning and asking about the demonstrations. One lady with graying hair squeezed my hand softly, smiled, and walked back into the kitchen.

Our stay in the hole was nothing compared with the plight of other Negro women in the stockade. They work steadily on their feet for twelve hours a day, unloading trucks, cooking, scrubbing floors, washing, and ironing. From twelve to six and from six to twelve they are working like oxen, and as one lady put it, "being treated like dawgs." While Negro women work, white women sleep, lounge, or sew. The Negro nurse at the stockade told me that white women do not work; they sew aprons and sell them to the Negroes.

At two thirty in the morning, we were awakened and told to change our clothes; we were going home. We dressed quickly and walked again through the huge kitchen where Negro women were still working. When I reached the exit, I turned to the guard and said, "Where do the white women work?" Not realizing that I knew the whites did not work, Negro women in the kitchen yelled, "They don't work. Tell the folks outside the white girls don't work." The guard did not answer my question and did not refute the shouts of the women. He just quickly and angrily shut the door.

What a relief that the door was shutting us, not inside as before, but outside where the air was free from the odor of urine and the smell of too obvious inhumanity. And so, twenty-five hours after entering the stockade and four and a half days after being arrested, I was once again free—to the extent that Negroes are in this country and in this city "too busy to hate."

Martin Sostre v. Nelson Rockefeller, Paul McGinnis, Vincent Mancusi, and Harold W. Follette

OPINION OF JUDGE CONSTANCE B. MOTLEY:

This is a civil rights action, 42 U.S.C. § 1983, 28 U.S.C. § 1343(3), brought by plaintiff, Martin Sostre, an "Afro-American citizen of the United States" and resident of Green Haven Prison against the Governor of New York, the Commissioner of Corrections and the Wardens of two New York State prisons.

Mr. Sostre is no stranger to the New York State prison system, having already served twelve years, 1952-1964, four of which were spent in solitary

From opinion of Judge Constance B. Motley, 68 Civ. 4058 U.S. District Court, Southern District, New York, May 1970, pp. 2-12.

confinement at Attica State Prison for Black Muslim activity. He is also no stranger to the federal courts with his civil rights complaints against New York prison officials. He secured for Black Muslim prisoners their rights to certain unrestricted religious liberties during his prior incarceration. . . . His earlier legal activity also resulted in the elimination of some of the more outrageously inhumane aspects of solitary confinement in some of the state's prisons.

Martin Sostre is again in prison. This time he is there pursuant to a sentence of 30-40 years, to be followed by a one year sentence and a sentence of 30 days for contempt of court, imposed upon him by the Supreme Court of New York.

On the day of his sentence, he was immediately taken to Attica Prison where he remained overnight in a cell block which contained no other prisoners. The next morning, he was taken in a "one-man draft" to Green Haven Prison. According to the Deputy Warden in charge of Attica (the warden, a defendant here, being on vacation), he sought Sostre's removal from that prison as soon as possible. He, therefore, called the office of the Commissioner of Corrections of the State of New York and spoke to the Deputy Commissioner who approved the transfer. The Deputy Warden of Attica testified vaguely and without substantiation as follows: "I thought it was best for the interests of the inmate and for the state that this man be transferred to another institution."

Immediately after his arrival at Attica, Sostre began a legal battle for reversal of his conviction. He sought to mail an application for a certificate of reasonable doubt to the state court which he had prepared prior to sentence, but the guard at Attica refused to mail the application.

The next day, Sostre found himself in solitary confinement in Green Haven where he remained for several days. He was then permitted to join the general population and to mail his application for a certificate of reasonable doubt.

However, shortly thereafter, on June 25, 1968, Sostre was back in solitary confinement (now called "punitive segregation" by defendants). He remained in such confinement until July 2, 1969, when he was returned to the general population pursuant to a temporary restraining order issued by this court in the present action, followed by a preliminary injunction. A trial followed upon which were established the facts found herein and upon which the relief granted in this opinion is based.

On June 25, 1968, Sostre placed in the prison mail box for mailing to his attorney a letter with handwritten legal motions and other papers attached. One of these was a motion for change of venue of the trial of his codefendant, Mrs. Geraldine Robinson, who had not yet been tried, from Erie County (Buffalo). He was called to the office of defendant Follette, Warden of Green Haven Prison, who had the papers on his desk. The Warden asked Sostre whether he had a license to practice law, to which he replied in the negative. The Warden admittedly denied Sostre the right to prepare legal papers for his codefendant, since he was not a licensed attorney, and flatly refused to mail out the motion papers.

At the same time, Warden Follette questioned Sostre about a reference in his letter to his attorney about an organization known as R.N.A. (Republic of New Africa) "because defendant Follette was concerned about a statement in plaintiff's May 19, 1968 letter to his sister." This statement reads:

> As for me, there is no doubt in my mind whatsoever that I will be out soon, either by having my appeal reversed in the courts or by being liberated by the Universal Forces of Liberation. The fact that the militarists of this country are being defeated in Viet Nam and are already engaged with an escalating rebellion in this country by the oppressed Afro-American people and their white allies are sure signs that the power structure is on its way out. They are now in their last days and soon they won't be able to oppress anybody because they themselves will be before the People's courts to be punished for their crimes against humanity as were the German war criminals at Nuremberg.

It is undisputed that as a result of plaintiff's refusal to cease and desist from "practicing law" in the institution, and his refusal to answer questions about R.N.A., and because of the statement in plaintiff's letter to his sister that "he would be leaving the institution soon," defendant Follette decided to place plaintiff in the punitive segregation unit.

The proof also established: (1) plaintiff received no prior written notice of the above charges which resulted in his segregation; (2) there was no record made of the discussion with the Warden; (3) defendant McGinnis, the Commissioner of Corrections, was notified of plaintiff's confinement and the reasons therefor but took no action; (4) plaintiff was not charged with violence, attempting to escape, incitement to riot or any similar charge; and (5) plaintiff remained in segregation from June 25, 1968 until released by order of this court, more than a year later, on July 2, 1969.

The parties have stipulated that as a result of solitary confinement for more than a year, Sostre has lost 124⅓ days of "good time" credit, since under the rules a prisoner in solitary cannot earn good time.

There is also no real dispute as to the conditions which obtained in punitive segregation during plaintiff's yearlong stay. There was only one other person incarcerated in the same group of cells as plaintiff (about four out of thirteen months) from August 14, 1968 to December 20, 1968. One prisoner brought to solitary and placed in another group of cells committed suicide the next day. Plaintiff was deprived of second portions of food and all desserts as a punishment for the entire time. He remained in his cell for 24 hours per day. He was allowed one hour per day of recreation in a small, completely enclosed yard. Sostre refused this privilege because it was conditioned upon submission, each day, to a mandatory "strip frisk" (completely naked) which included a rectal examination. He was permitted to shower and shave with *hot* water only once a week. He was not permitted to use the prison library, read newspapers, see movies, or attend school or training programs. He was not allowed to work. Prisoners in the general population who work are able to earn money with which they may purchase items from the prison commissary, or purchase books, or subscribe to newspapers. Prisoners in punitive segregation have access to only a few novels and "shoot-'em ups" selected for them. But, as plaintiff and defendants' counsel put it, the crux of the matter is human isolation—the loss of "group privileges." Release from segregation is wholly within the discretion of the Warden. However, a recommendation from a non-professional, so-called, group therapy counsellor might help.

This court finds that punitive segregation under the conditions to which plaintiff was subjected at Green Haven is physically harsh, destructive of morale, dehumanizing in the sense that it is needlessly degrading, and dangerous to the maintenance of sanity when continued for more than a short period of time which should certainly not exceed 15 days.

After plaintiff was sent to solitary confinement on June 25, 1968, his cell was searched. The Warden alleged in an affidavit filed on July 3, 1969 that the search revealed contraband. This consisted of: (1) a letter from a court belonging to another inmate (which plaintiff was translating into Spanish for that other inmate; and (2) two small pieces of emery paper. A Disciplinary Report dated June 25, 1968 records that plaintiff was reprimanded for possessing the letter. There is no similar report regarding the emery paper, although the Warden alleged both items were found at the same time. The Warden claims that the emery paper was "adaptable for the fashioning of a key or lock picking tool." Plaintiff denied ever having seen the emery paper before trial. The court believes plaintiff's testimony for the following reasons: (1) plaintiff was already in punitive segregation when the emery paper was allegedly found in his cell; (2) the Disciplinary Report of June 25, 1968 does not contain this charge; (3) the first written recordation of any such charge against Sostre does not appear until October 29, 1968, shortly after Sostre filed his *pro se* complaint in this action on October 15, 1968; (4) defendants have not requested this court to make any finding with respect to the emery paper in their proposed findings of fact. On June 25, 1968, search of Sostre's cell also revealed that he was lending his law books to other inmates, after removing therefrom a stamp identifying these books (which turned out to be copies of the *Harvard Law Review*) as belonging to Sostre. This along with the two preceding charges was one of the charges originally put forth by defendants as a reason for Sostre's confinement but dropped upon the trial.

The day after plaintiff's court-ordered release from segregation, July 3, 1969, he was again disciplined. This time he was charged with having dust on his cell bars. The punishment was to confine him to his cell for several days. Again, plaintiff denied this charge, claiming he was so charged and punished in order that he would miss the regular July 4th celebration. This *celebration* would have brought Sostre in contact with prisoners from another part of the prison. Such contact is permitted only once a year on July 4. This court finds that this charge and punishment were imposed upon Sostre in retaliation for his legal success.

On or about August 3, 1969, plaintiff was again disciplined for having "inflammatory racist literature" in his cell. The punishment was deprivation of yard and movie privileges for 60 days. The so-called "inflammatory racist literature" consisted of handwritten political articles by Sostre, some of which contained excerpts from articles printed in newspapers and magazines in general circulation in the prison and lists of officers of the Black Panther Party and the Republic of New Africa, copied from similar articles in *Esquire* and other magazines.

All of plaintiff's letters to and from his attorney, Joan Franklin, were censored by the Warden. He excised therefrom everything which he believed was not directly related to Sostre's immediate case. And a letter to the Postal Inspector of the United States Post Office complaining about plaintiff's failure to receive receipts for certified mail was also not mailed by the Warden.

This court finds from all of the facts and circumstances of this case, as set forth above, that Sostre was sent to punitive segregation and kept there until released by court order not because of any serious infraction of the rules of prison discipline, or even for any minor infraction, but because Sostre was being punished specially by the Warden because of his legal and Black Muslim activities during his 1952-1964 incarceration, because of his threat to file a law suit against the Warden to secure his right to unrestricted correspondence with his attorney and to aid his codefendant and because he is, unquestionably, a black militant who persists in writing and expressing his militant and radical ideas in prison.

IV COURTS

JEROME SKOLNIK

Judicial Response in Crisis

High Bail as Preventive Detention

Another serious problem in the judicial response to riots is found in bail. We have put together a city-by-city survey of bail practices during civil disorder in Detroit, Newark, Washington, D.C., Baltimore, and Chicago. The evidence is clear: the constitutional right to bail was almost invariably replaced by what in effect was a policy of preventive detention. This was particularly unfortunate. Not only did it work great hardships on the individuals involved—such as loss of employment because of absence—it also put these persons through an especially unfavorable experience with the practical workings of "the rule of law," an experience which was unlikely to persuade anyone of the merits of "working within the system for orderly change." In this way, the functioning of the judicial system during disorders may have contributed to the very grievances that lie at the roots of such disorders. Moreover, the implicit justification (if there was one) for these practices—that without preventive detention persons arrested would return to rioting—ignores two most important points. First, no evidence exists that this is true as a general proposition; indeed, it is surely untrue with respect to a great many of riot-related arrests—because of either the circumstances of the area or of the arrest, or the normal lapse of time involved in processing an arrested person. Thus, the "feedback to riot" justification for holding *large* numbers in custody is wholly lacking in evidence; and furthermore, it seems implausible to believe that following a court appearance, an arrestee charged with looting would return to the riot area, especially if his promise not to return was made a condition of his release. Second, the Kerner Commission correctly pointed out that alternatives exist to incarceration and suggested:

> . . . that communities and courts plan for a range of alternative conditions to release, such as supervision by civic organizations or third party custodians outside the riot area, rather than to rely on high money bail to keep defendants off the streets. The courts should set bail on an individual basis and provide for defense counsel at bail hearings. Emergency procedures for fast bail review are needed.

From *The Politics of Protest,* Simon & Schuster, Inc., 1969.

161

In fact, all too often the constitutional right to bail seemed irrelevant. According to Judge Crockett of the Recorder's Court in Detroit:

> . . . hundreds of presumably innocent people, with no previous record whatever, suddenly found themselves separated from their unknowing families and jobs and incarcerated in our maximum security detention facilities . . . ; and all of this without benefit of counsel, without an examination, and without even the semblance of a trial.

Whether this was because the courts were too overcrowded or because the courts intended to aid other public agencies in quelling the disturbances or were expressing distaste and fear of the participants in the disturbances, the effect was the same: punishment was applied before trial.

Detroit: In Detroit the use of bail as preventive detention was explicitly acknowledged by the judiciary. The twelve Recorder's Court judges met on the second day of the riot (Monday, July 27) and agreed to set bonds averaging $10,000; some were set as high as $200,000. The *Detroit Free Press* noted that as a result of the decision, hundreds of persons were "railroaded through Recorder Court Sunday . . . night and Monday, slapped with high bonds and stashed away to await trial." The high bail policy was applied uniformly—ignoring the nature of the charge, family and job status of those arrested, the prior record, and all other factors usually considered in the setting of bail. In response to criticism from black leaders, this policy was defended by one Recorder's Court Judge: "We had no way of knowing whether there was a revolution in progress or whether the city was going to be burned down or what." With the exception of one judge who gave individualized hearings but later said that even he had set bail too high, the judges of Recorder's Court carried out the high bail policy from July 23 to 30.

. . .

According to Judge Crockett, the situation had gotten so "far out of control that there was justifiable fear that if there were no riot then the Recorder Court's actions would surely have started one. We had hundreds of people in buses on Sunday for eighteen hours using a manhole as a latrine. This was prior to arraignment." A week after the start of the riot, judges released hundreds of prisoners. Over 1,000 were released on their own recognizance. Yet, by Monday of the second week, 2,000 people were still confined, and on August 4, the end of the second week, 1,200 remained. Judge Crockett commented later that "even now there is [no real appreciation] of the full extent of the injustices we committed by our refusal to recognize the right to immediate bail and our objection to fixing reasonable bail."

The arbitrariness of Detroit's high bail policy is further supported by a study made of 1,014 arrestees who were being detained awaiting trial in the Michigan State Prison. Forty-four percent of those awaiting trial were married, and 86 percent had resided at the same address for one to five years. Eighty percent were employed, and 41 percent were employed at a major auto company. Moreover, 49 percent of those employed had worked at the same place for one to five years, and 14 percent had had the same employer for five to ten years. There was no consistent prior record. Sixty-seven percent had *no* prior conviction, 19 percent had one prior conviction, and 14 per cent had previously been convicted two or more times. Thus from these statistics, one would have expected *less* stringent bail policies than usual; in fact the contrary was true.

Furthermore, the amount of bond showed little relation to the severity of the crime charged. The study concluded that "arrestees who were married, employed and without prior criminal records were treaty virtually the same as were defendants who were single, unemployed, and had previous convictions and/or arrests." Moreover, there are grounds to believe that future bail policies will have a similar effect. A former judge of Michigan's Supreme Court, for example, feels that the only lesson the Recorder's Court is likely to draw from the events is that "$15,000 to $20,000 bonds were unnecessary—next time bond will be $2000 or so—to accomplish the same objective but to avoid the exposure. $2,000 bonds will keep them off the streets."

Newark: In the summer of 1967, Newark courts employed a similar high bail-preventive detention policy until detention pressures forced a complete reversal. A "Release on Recognizance" program was initiated in the last days of the riot, with half of those arrested being interviewed and 65 to 80 percent of those being released. As in Detroit, public statements by high judicial officials showed a distinct lack of concern for those affected by a high bail policy. At the height of the riot, according to the *Newark Evening News* (July 14, 1967), the Chief Magistrate commented, "If they can't afford it, let them stay in jail."

Chicago: In the April, 1968, disorders following the assassination of Dr. Martin Luther King, Chicago evidently took no notice of the Kerner Report's recommendations that

> Communities and courts plan for a range of alternative conditions to release, such as supervision by civic organizations or third party custodians outside the riot area, rather than to rely on high money bail to keep defendants off the streets. The courts should set bail on an individual basis and provide for defense counsel at bail hearings. Emergency procedures for fast bail review are needed.

No emergency plans were made for release in a mass arrest situation. Rather, the courts continued the use of high bail to keep people off the streets. This policy had results similar to those in Detroit and Newark: detention facilities were overwhelmed and individualized justice was abandoned.

Yet the response of the Chicago courts to the April, 1968, disorders was consistent with plans made *after* Newark and Detroit. Soon after the disorders in those cities, the Chief Judge for the Circuit Court met at the Chicago Bar Association with the State's Attorney, Public Defender, Corporation Counsel, and representatives of the Chicago Bar and Legal Aid Society. They met to discuss "what lessons to draw from Newark and Detroit." At that meeting, the Chief Judge announced a high bail policy that would be followed in Chicago with the explicit intention of keeping those arrested off the streets during a riot.

The April, 1968, riots were not the first time such a policy had been employed. In late January, 1967, Chicago experienced a snowstorm which immobilized the whole city, including the police. During this period, acts of looting and vandalism broke out on the predominantly black West Side. The courts responded to this crisis by imposing high bail on "looters." When the Chief Judge of the Circuit Court, John Boyle, was asked about the constitutionality of using high bond to keep a defendant in jail rather than to guarantee appearance at trial, he replied, "What do you want me to do—cry crocodile tears for people who take advantage of their city? Didn't I read . . . all about President Johnson's 'war on crime'?" The Public Defender, in response to criticism from the ACLU that he was not challenging the courts' bail policies, commented that he was "not going to start fighting with judges because they set some bond that some people think is too high."

According to an ACLU study in Chicago, the average bail for the charge of burglary under "normal" conditions is $4,300. Bail for the winter "looting" cases ranged from $5,000 to $30,000, with an average of $14,000. Bond hearings, as reported in official transcripts, typically took the following form:[1]

> *The Clerk:* Sam B.
> *The Court:* Branch 46. 1-31.
> *The Clerk:* Bond, Mr. State's Attorney?
> *The Court:* Bond for B . . . ?
> *State's Attorney:* On Sam B . . . , your Honor, the State will recommend a bond of $20,000.
> *The Court:* $20,000.

And in another case:

> *The Court:* What do you do for a living, son?
> *Defendant:* Sir, I work for the post office and for . . . two jobs.

1. Illinois Special Legal Project, The Roger Baldwin Foundation of the ACLU: "Preliminary Report and Evaluation on the Bail Procedures in Chicago's Looting Cases —Winter, 1967."

The Court: Can you afford to hire a lawyer?

Defendant: Yes, I could, your Honor.

The Court: All right. You hire yourself a good lawyer, sir. We will continue this case.

Defendant: Your Honor, I have a wife and three kids and I only left them with twelve dollars in the house. Could I possible get . . .

The Court: Twelve dollars.

Defendant: But I get paid from the post office this coming Thursday and I get my check at the other job, your Honor.

The Court: You should have been on the job instead of out on the corner that night.

Defendant: I had to get milk for my baby. I avoided this crowd as far as I could and then I was afraid they would rob me, your Honor; and my baby was crying. He is only 9 months old and I was going to—I was two blocks from my house avoiding these crowds because I am afraid they would rob me, but, your Honor, I got there and the police I saw—I could only see the top of the police car. Then I wasn't afraid any more because I thought the police wouldn't bother me. Then when the police got close the people went out of the store and dropped goods all over the ground.

The Court: Someday you'll learn how order is in Chicago.

Defendant: Sir, may I please have a personal bond?

The Court: No, sir.

State's Attorney: Motion State, February 20, 1967.

The Court: I will not interfere with the bond. February 20, Bailiff.

Counsel was not permitted to represent defendants at the time bail was set, and the preliminary hearings were continued by the court for at least three weeks. This meant that defendants held under unusually high bail were incarcerated for three weeks before the court would even consider if there was probable cause to hold them. Almost all of the arrestees remained in custody unable to make bond. The city's judicial policies with respect to "looting" were well expressed by Magistrate Maurice Lee: "This type of crime during a city-wide emergency is comparable to grave-robbing."

It is perhaps not surprising, then, that the April, 1968, disorders found Chicago courts ready to impose bails which, though actually not "exorbitant," were nevertheless sufficiently high to prevent the immediate release of most prisoners. Moreover, there was no official mechanism for notifying families of the detention or amount of bond required for the release of those arrested. And volunteers were required to put tremendous pressure on the courts even to participate in such matters as notification during the bond hearings.

Problems of actually posting bail were endless. In most cases, the family of an arrested person knew only that he did not return home. The records department of the jail was closed in the evenings and, when open, rarely had information on the location of prisoners. Many prisoners who had money when arrested were initially unable to post bond since no bond clerks were available. At the jail and House of Correction, hundred of concerned relatives were milling around with little idea of how to proceed. Several Sheriff's deputies guarded the jail, pointing their guns at the waiting crowd. Law students and legal aid lawyers performed the tasks that clerks should have performed if they had been assigned to the bond office.

The bail policy was later justified by the Chief Judge of the Municipal Division. "When a man is sitting on the bench and he's looking out the window and he sees the city afire, big blazes here and there and everywhere, and he sees the people who are supposedly involved, it's very difficult for him to make a real considered judgment." This inability to make a "considered judgment" inevitably favored the police over defendants. About 800 defendants were given bonds of $1,000 or over. Release-on-own-recognizance bonds were restricted for the most part to curfew violators, indicating that the gravity of the allegation tended to dictate the amount of bond. In determining bond, the courts paid little attention to such criteria as the background of those accused, despite the fact that over 70 percent of the defendants had never been previously arrested, 83 percent had never been previously convicted, and about 50 percent were arrested within six blocks of their homes. At least 37 percent of the arrestees spent over four days in jail pending the disposition of their cases. Ten days after the riot began, there were still over 200 people in jail who could not make bond.

Baltimore: In Baltimore, according to a local blue-ribbon committee, bail for curfew violations was invariably set at $500 and few, if any, bondsmen were available at the courts. "Very few defendants were released on their own recognizance, and rarely was there time or inclination on the part of the judge to hear a defense plea for a bail geared to the circumstances of the individual defendants."[2] Of 345 curfew defendants who were not tried immediately, only 99 managed to make bail. A significant number of curfew violators stood trial immediately under a stipulated prosecution: many reportedly pleaded guilty because of the "threat of incarceration implicit in the bail systems." Of the 3,500 persons charged with curfew violations, all but 345 had been tried and sentenced during the riot:

> The mass trials of many defendants took place in an atmosphere akin to martial law. The disorders and the administration of the curfew generally made detention of defendants an incommunicado detention. Contact with those who might help in posting bail was problematic at best.

2. Report of the Baltimore Committee on the Administration of Justice Under Emergency Conditions, 1968.

Thus there was considerable pressure on defendants to agree to be tried summarily.[3]

Washington, D.C.: Bail policy in Washington, D.C., varied considerably. Compared with policies in other cities, it was certainly less oppressive and less arbitrary. Nevertheless, some judges set bond during the first two days of the riot with the express purposes of keeping defendants off the streets. Other judges strictly adhered to the provisions of the Bail Reform Act, releasing many prisoners on their own recognizance and cooperating with volunteer lawyers to facilitate immediate release of their clients. Even so, fewer defendants were released on personal recognizance than is usually the case under normal conditions. According to Ronald Goldfarb:

> A check of Bail Agency records, and interviews with Bail Agency personnel, defense lawyers and prosecutors leads to one inescapable conclusion: defendants arraigned during the riot had more stable family ties, better employment records and far less serious criminal records than does the regular criminal defendant in the Court of General Sessions. . . . It is clear that many judges effectively discarded the liberal policies of the Bail Reform Act during the riot.[4]

The Lower Courts as an Agency of Law Enforcement

Although one may liken the functioning of the judicial system during mass disorders to its routine functioning, obviously something more dramatic is occurring. Not only are the problems faced during riots more severe than those confronted in the routine administration of justice; in addition, more varied and intense outside pressures are brought to bear on the courts.

During riots there is fear in the wider community, the courts come under scrutiny by the news media, and judicial authorities are in constant communication with political leaders. Under these circumstances, judicial actions and statements indicate that the courts usually cooperate by employing their judicial authority in the service of riot control, becoming, in effect, an agency engaged in nonjudicial forms of law enforcement.

In Detroit, for example, the Chief Judge of Recorder's Court made it clear in press releases that high bonds would be used to keep "rioters" off the street and that he would not release "thugs who would help to further [a] 'takeover-by-violence' plan." The courts in Detroit refused to release prisoners until they were assured by the Mayor, a federal representative, and

3. Report of the Baltimore Committee.
4. Ronald L. Goldfarb, "The Administration of Justice in Washington, D.C., During the disorder of April, 1968 (unpublished manuscript).

local military commanders that the city was secure. The executive may tend
to perceive judicial action as his responsibility. Regarding the Newark riot,
the Governor proclaimed that "New Jersey will show its abhorrence of these
criminal activities, and society will protect itself by fair, speedy and retribu-
tive justice." The judges and magistrates in Newark were responsive to the
Governor's direction that "the strength of the law . . . be demonstrated."
In Chicago, where the judicial system is routinely under tight political
control, the courts cooperated with the Mayor's office and city prosecutors
in detaining "rioters" until the emergency was declared over. The Chief
Judge of Chicago Municipal Division accurately reflected the political perspective of city hall: "I have seen tremendous progress for this particular
minority group. They have come up so far and are progressing except of
these civil disorders. Civil disorder . . . It is the worst thing for the black
race. It's bad; it's creating a cleavage in our society against them."

In response to, and usually in agreement with, a desire for a quick restora-
tion of order, the courts adopt a law enforcement perspective on riot control.
Such a perspective may be summarized as follows: (1) civil disorders represent a time of extreme and dangerous emergency, requiring extraordinary
measures of control and resistance; (2) the efforts of the police, military,
fire department, and other public agencies must be actively supported to
restore order as quickly as possible; (3) the presumption of guilt of defendants is made necessary by the presence of troops in the city, the sight
of "fires on the horizon," and a common-sense appreciation of the danger
and inherent criminality of a "riot" or "uprising"; (4) high bail is required
to prevent rioters returning to the riot; (5) the nature of the emergency
and the overwhelming number of defendants preclude the possibility of
observing the niceties of due process; (6) due process will be restored as
soon as the emergency has been terminated.[5] Both the courts and the police
seek to prevent growth of the disorder, to distinguish the leaders, and to
control the mob. The courts attempt to control the mob by detaining rioters
until order is restored, by displaying power and resolve in the processing
of defendants, by observing strict security precautions (having troops and
police in court buildings and courtrooms, limiting access to prisoners, and
checking credentials of lawyers), and by coordinating policies with other
public agencies.

We have already suggested that the need for eliminating due process has
not been documented. The evidence suggests that most "rioters" will not
necessarily return to the riot area following a court appearance. Moreover,
when during crisis courts do become an instrument of order, rather than of
law, communities find themselves without a tribunal for impartial judgment.

5. Federal Bureau of Investigation, *Prevention and Control of Mobs and Riots* (1968).

This conclusion has two important consequences. First, as we have already noted, since the guilt of the accused is assumed, the adversary system and its attendant guarantees of due process are further eroded. Second, while there is ordinarily little control over the police and other agencies of government by courts, during riots there is active cooperation.

The criminal courts do more than arraign and try accused persons and sentence the guilty. When they operate properly, the courts insist on lawful standards of operation from other agencies of government. We do not have in mind here suits brought against governmental agencies, but rather what happens in the course of the routine criminal process. The courts have the responsibility to bring legal standards to bear on prosecutors, probation officers, police, lawyers, and other persons and agencies involved in law enforcement. In doing so, the courts are presumed to constrain these persons and agencies to adhere to law.

In order to perform this supervisory task, however, courts must in some degree be independent of other parts of the criminal justice system. The necessity for such independence—for a capacity to be both part of the law enforcement apparatus and in some degree stand apart from it—has long been recognized, for there are strong pressures on the criminal courts to be uncritical of other agencies of law enforcement. Recent Supreme Court decisions concerning the proper use of police power reflect an awareness of this tendency to erode the insulation between the criminal courts and other agencies of law enforcement. Under normal conditions, this tendency is occasionally halted by appellate court decisions and by professional standards of propriety. During periods of civil emergency, however, even stronger pressures are generated for expedient action, and the courts surrender much of what remains of their supervisory function; law enforcement agencies are encouraged, at least implicitly, to exert control by any means necessary. Moreover, the court's own actions—such as preventive detention through high bail—may be in violation of law. By condoning and following such policies, the courts contribute to the "breakdown of law" and to the establishment of an "order" based on force without justice. The implications of this situation are far-reaching. Some have been discussed earlier. To fully appreciate their gravity, however, one must examine the unique role that the courts play in our governmental system and the stresses that our legal system is undergoing in this time of widespread dissatisfaction and protest.

The criminal courts, like all legal institutions, are "political" in the sense that they engage in formulating and administering public policies. The ties and differences between the political and judicial systems, however, are complex, and we must not overlook their distinctive characters.

The judicial system is tied to the political system in several obvious ways. Judicial personnel are sometimes elected; even more often they are appointed by political officeholders. Also, the enforcement of judicial decisions is often left to political officials. Finally, the laws the judiciary is empowered to interpret and apply are created and can be changed through political processes. In general, the closeness of the courts to the political system does much to ensure the flexibility of our legal system, its openness to change.

At the same time the judicial system is relatively insulated from politics. The selection of judicial personnel is guided in some measure by standards developed according to legal rather than political competence, and tenure arrangements have developed to protect judges from political interference. Moreover, judges are expected, and in considerable degree expect themselves, to be constrained by constitutional, statutory, and case law and by general principles of legality, in their assessment of evidence and their decisions. Such constraints are intended both to protect individuals against arbitrary state action and to prevent the courts from usurping powers more properly exercised by legislative and executive agencies.

In a constitutional democracy, then, the judiciary ideally functions as an impartial arbiter of conflict, relatively free from partisan interests—whether they be social, economic, or political. Our society recognizes that departures from that ideal are inevitable. However, it also views them with deep suspicion; for when the judiciary assumes a partisan role, the ideal of legality may seriously be undermined and the resolution of conflict reduced to the distribution and availability of force.

The evidence presented with respect to judicial behavior during the recent urban riots indicates a readiness by courts to lend their support to a system of preventive detention, to become an instrument of political needs relatively unrestrained by considerations of legality. In the process, they undermine their own reputation as impartial arbiters of social disputes. Such actions lead to disaffection among those who have come into contact with a partisan judiciary, or who think they have. The importance of this cannot be underestimated, for the courts are our model for the "rule of law" to which we urge rioters to adhere. And lawlessness is precisely what we condemn in such dissidents.

TOM HAYDEN

Excerpt from *Rebellion in Newark*

. . . The evidence is that most of the prisoners were adults with jobs and families; holding them for several days created serious problems for each.

High bail prevented prisoners from being able to get out of jail. Minimum bond was set at $1,000 for curfew and loitering charges, $2,500 for looting, $5,000 for possession of a gun, $10,000 to $25,000 for other weapons charges. Chief Magistrate James Del Mauro, replying to criticism of the high bail cost, declared in the July 14 Newark *News*: "If they can't afford it, let them stay in jail." As Henry diSuvero of the state American Civil Liberties Union pointed out, this had the effect of detaining people before a judicial proceeding could determine their guilt or innocence. It also kept them out of their homes, and away from their jobs.

During this mass detention no one with the exception of about 150 juveniles, was fed until Saturday and many not until Sunday, even when food was brought to the jails by friends and relatives of the prisoners. As the court pens filled up, prisoners were sent to the Newark Street Jail (condemned as uninhabitable in the 1930s), federal detention facilities, a state prison, and the armory where Hughes and the troops were headquartered. Some of the prisoners were beaten in their cells.

Prisoners were not permitted to receive visitors or make telephone cells for legal assistance, nor were they allowed to notify friends and relatives. The right to preliminary hearings was denied. This right, provided for in New Jersey law, compels the prosecutor to demonstrate to the judge there is "probable cause" to hold the accused; it permits the defendant to discover the state's case against himself as well. Thus, merely the word of the arresting officer became sufficient to hold people without determination of probable cause.

Municipal Court judges started arraigning prisoners at round-the-clock sessions. One prisoner passed through court every three minutes, according to the *Star-Ledger* of July 16. Pleas by attorneys for the reduction of bail were ignored except in rare instances.

Starting Monday two Grand Juries heard felony charges and returned, by week's end, some 500 indictments. With the handing down of an indictment, which itself is a finding of probable cause, the prisoners lost forever their right to preliminary hearing. Thus, by agreeing to rush presentations, the Grand Jury acted more as a rubber stamp for the prosecutors' requests than a body to ensure an objective check on evidence. The ACLU charge that Hughes was using the judiciary as a weapon to restore order is supported by this post-riot statement the Governor gave to *US News & World Report*:

> The full measure of the criminal law should be exacted in these cases. I have insisted on that from the beginning. I went to the extent of arranging with the appropriate courts for the immediate impaneling of grand juries and presentation of cases to them.

But the attitude of the courts was perhaps better indicated on July 21 when Newark's Chief Magistrate Del Mauro rejected the attempt by cabdriver Smith's attorney, Harris David, to file criminal complaints against the two police who arrested Smith. According to the *Times*, Del Mauro's words were:

> In these times of stress, with all the havoc and destruction, a policeman killed, a fireman killed, more than twenty people killed and $15 million of damage, *I am not accepting a complaint against the police.*
> It was this particular man, if I recall from reading the papers, that originally caused the rioting, when he was arrested and rumors swept through the colored community that he had been killed. He has been paroled . . . he is alive and there is nothing wrong with him.

"Mr. Smith," the *Times* reported the next day, "wore a six-inch-wide bandage wrapped tightly around his rib cage" and declined any comment on the advice of his lawyer.

MICHAEL MELTSNER

Southern Appellate Courts: A Dead End

We are still witnessing a struggle for supremacy between state and Federal law a century after the Civil War supposedly settled the matter. Briefly, Federal Constitution and laws secure the Negro against all state-supported and some "private" racial discrimination. While ultimate authority on the meaning of the Constitution and Federal law rests with the United States Supreme Court, it is the duty of state judges, as well as Federal, to give content to Supreme Court decisions. In practice, however, Negroes cannot rely on southern state courts to uphold the supremacy of Federal law. In order to maintain the status quo, state judges have not hesitated to evade or ignore Federal law and to exploit a deeply rooted national tradition of deference to local authority. Or they have been content to see themselves as "a mere way-station on the route to the United States Supreme Court," where Negroes hope "in the light of supposed social and political advances, they may find legal endorsement of their ambitions." Since they see the law-giver's role this passively, delay and equivocation—the cardinal sins against justice—are easily come by.

State judges are nominated or appointed on the basis of party loyalty and service, a scale that weighs ability last and least. But judges in the South are no more creatures of prevailing political cliques than are judges in other sections of the country. The state judiciary in the North, however, is selected from a mixed bag, one filled from a society at least mouthing the rhetoric of equality. The political apparatus as a whole is subject to constant pressure from a constituency that includes articulate Negroes and white allies. In the South, the logic of political survival assures the white Southerner of judges who know and do their duty as far as the Negro is concerned. When a Negro asserts his right to freedom from racial discrimination in the courts of southern states, the decision goes against him and the political system tolerates few exceptions.

As the ranks of southern Negro voters swell, we can expect the attitude of state judges to shift gradually to acceptance of the Negro's legal equality,

and eventually to something approximating impartiality. Whatever the ultimate prospects, however, little change has occurred. At present, civil rights
decisions of the Supreme Court are robbed of practical effect, and settled
rules of state law distorted to justify criminal convictions which would
surely fail if race were not involved. For the unwary civil rights lawyer and
his client, the courts of southern states are traps. Proper procedure is often
indistinct, and the slightest misstep may result in forfeiture of valuable
constitutional rights.

State judges who wish to remain in office and to retain the society of their
fellows (judges, like the rest of us, need someone to lunch with) do not
officially recognize the social consequences to the region and the nation of
maintaining serfdom in place of slavery. They have shown a shocking
eagerness to avoid even the appearance of fariness in areas such as jury
selection, where progress could have been achieved without exposing them
to great political risk. Although exclusion of Negroes from state juries had
been a Federal crime since 1875, and since 1880 sufficient to invalidate a
criminal conviction, the U.S. Civil Rights Commission could report in 1961
that it was still a widespread practice.

It is not surprising, therefore, that the most prominent characteristic of
state courts in the South is that a Negro will not voluntarily bring them a
dispute involving his civil rights. The legal buttress of segregation has
crumbled at the efforts of Federal courts. School boards, voting registrars,
and police have been hailed before Federal judges and ordered to conform
to the Federal Constitution. With Negroes refusing to submit their claims
to state court systems, the primary opportunity for southern courts to deal
with civil rights has occurred in criminal cases. Civil rights workers have
been charged with "trespass" for refusal to leave all-white lunch counters,
"breach of the peace" for sitting in the front of a bus, "parading without a
license" when carrying picket signs, "criminal anarchy" for distribution of
leaflets, and a whole host of other crimes, some petty, others extremely
serious.

Convictions are appealed to courts of statewide jurisdiction from local
courts, in which justice is harsh, speedy, and predictable. Just about the
only thing a civil rights lawyer can accomplish in many of these local courts
is to preserve legal objections for appeal and avoid a contempt citation.
Sometimes the latter is impossible. Negro lawyers moved recently in a
Georgia court to disqualify a judge from presiding at a civil rights trial
because of his reputed bias against Negroes, whereupon the judge gave
substance to the claim by citing them for contempt because they sought his
disqualification.

One expects a degree of impartiality from the state appellate courts.
Because they are elected by a statewide constituency, political pressure is

less concentrated and more easily parried by these judges. They are somewhat removed from the courthouse gang of prosecutors and police who
dominate southern politics in all but the larger cities. Unfortunately, such
expectations of impartiality are not fulfilled. State appellate courts have
shown themselves to be as susceptible as local courts to pressure and prejudice against Negro rights. The major difference is that the local magistrate
may be less prone to legal cant and more likely to call what he is doing by
its right name than does the state appellate court.

On June 25, 1963, Miss Mary Hamilton was held in contempt of the circuit court of Etowah County, Alamaba, and sentenced to five days in jail
and a fine of fifty dollars. She had been testifying in her own behalf on a
petition for a writ of habeas corpus to free her from a Gadsden, Alabama,
jail, where she was held for participating in a civil rights demonstration. The
following exchange took place:
Cross examination by Solicitor Rayburn:

> Q. What is your name, please?
> A. Miss Mary Hamilton.
> Q. Mary, I believe—you were arrested—who were you arrested by?
> A. My name is Miss Hamilton. Please address me correctly.
> Q. Who were you arrested by, Mary?
> A. I will not answer a question—

By Attorney Amaker: The Witness's name is Miss Hamilton.

> A. —your question until I am addressed correctly.
> *The Court:* Answer the question.
> *The Witness:* I will not answer them unless I am addressed correctly.
> *The Court:* You are in contempt of court.
> *Attorney Conley:* Your Honor—your honor—
> *The Court:* You are in contempt of this court, and you are sentenced to
> five days in jail and a fifty dollar fine.

Miss Hamilton's reaction to being called "Mary" by a state prosecutor
in a courtroom where, if white, she would have been called "Miss Hamilton," was not thin-skinned sensitivity. She was responding to one of the
most distinct indicia of the racial caste system, the refusal of whites to
address Negroes with titles of respect such as "Miss," "Mrs." or "Mr.," instead referring to them as "boy" or "girl." The Supreme Court of Alabama
upheld the contempt conviction in such a manner as to suggest the issue
did not exist:

> The record conclusively shows that petitioner's name is Mary Hamilton,
> not Miss Mary Hamilton.

Many witnesses are addressed by various titles, but one's own name is an acceptable appellation at law. This practice is almost universal in the written opinions of courts.

Because use of the first name only in a formal court proceeding is one of the symbolic indignities of the caste system, the U.S. Supreme Court subsequently reversed Miss Hamilton's contempt conviction, finding it as offensive to the Constitution as segregation in the courtroom.

Occasionally, there are shows of prudence and duty from state appellate courts, but they are not frequent enough to rely upon and usually flow from a recognition that a Federal court will ultimately reverse the conviction. Generally, the higher state courts rubber-stamp the outrages of their inferiors. At the worst, state appellate courts throw up obstacles to review of their decisions by the U.S. Supreme Court. The Supreme Court, of course, cannot consider more than a few of the cases which lawyers ask it to decide. As a consequence, it declares guiding principles in significant cases and relies on lower courts—state and Federal—to give them flesh. That some state appellate courts "have openly flouted not only the spirit but also the letter of the Supreme Court's decisions on civil rights," as Jack Greenberg has put it, imposes a policing function to which a national court of last resort, without investigators or police at its disposal, is unsuited.

DANIEL LANG

The Trial of Dr. Spock

A week or so before the conspiracy trial of Dr. Benjamin Spock and four other opponents of the Vietnam war opened in Boston last spring, the sitting judge, Francis J. W. Ford, discussing ground rules in his chambers with government and defense counsel, stipulated that one of the defendants, the Reverend Dr. William Sloane Coffin, Jr., who is the chaplain of Yale University, was to be addressed in court not by his ecclesiastical title but as Defendant Coffin. Judge Ford, an imperious man of eighty-five who early in the proceedings characterized himself as "a slave to regularity," gave no reason for the legalistic unfrocking, but his intent may have been to draw a sharp line of demarcation between considerations of law and those of

From *The New Yorker*, Sept. 7, 1968, p. 38. © 1968 by The New Yorker Magazine, Inc. Reprinted by permission.

conscience and beliefs. This was certainly on his mind throughout the trial itself, for time and again spectators in his courtroom—a small one in the Federal Building—heard him instruct counsel and the jury to guard against the intrusion of extraneous matters and confine their thinking to the letter of the indictment at hand. As the sessions approached their end, after nearly four weeks, it was dazzlingly clear that the elderly magistrate, his hearing strained and his demeanor cantankerous, had set himself a difficult course. The case was simply too palpably entwined with controversial public issues —with the question of dove versus hawk—for its legal form and its social content to be separable. The terms "conscience" and "belief" became stale with use, so often were they uttered, not only by the defense but by the government itself—the author of the indictment that Judge Ford strove so valiantly to keep ever paramount in the minds of all. In fact, it was the government prosecutor—John Wall, a thirty-six-year-old former paratrooper in Korea—who took the initiative in this. He had little choice. Nearly all his evidence was based on public appearances of the alleged conspirators in which (as Wall presented it in court) one defendant or another gave it as his "belief" that the exercise of "conscience" could deflect America from pursuing an "immoral"—as well as an "unconstitutional" and "illegal"—war in Vietnam. To dramatize this evidence, the courtroom was darkened over a period of days while television-news clips, projected on a large screen facing the jury, showed the various defendants holding forth—at an outdoor rally, at a press conference, at a church service in Boston at which young men filed past a flaming taper and some of them incinerated their draft cards. By the time the lawyers offered their summations, things had loosened up to the point where the 1968 Presidential race was being weighed. This occurred when Wall, stoutly denying that the government was conducting a political trial, scoffed at the notion that war protesters like the defendants could have influenced President Johnson's decision to quit the White House. "If Johnson did retire involuntarily," he told the jury, "I submit to you the reason he did, if he did, was because a man named Eugene McCarthy and a man named Robert Kennedy . . . through a regular political process—the ballot box—brought it about."

The case before Judge Ford might not have wandered as far afield as it did—or, at least, might not have done so as often—if it had not been for the catchall nature of the government's indictment. It charged conspiracy, stating that the aims of the plot had been to "counsel, aid, and abet" draftable men to avoid military service and dispense with carrying draft cards and classification notices, and to "hinder and interfere with" the administration of the Military Selective Service Act of 1967. However, it was not these aims that were at issue but, rather, the government's claim that the defendants had formed a conspiracy to achieve them; in short, it wasn't *what* the five

men had done but that they had got together to do it. Unfortunately, the
distinction was not always readily apparent.

Almost from the outset, everyone I met assumed that bad news lay ahead
for the defendants—for all of them except Raskin, that is, who, as the testimony unfolded, was given a chance of acquittal. The evidence adduced in
Boston showed that he had never challenged the government to a legal confrontation or taken part in a sitdown, and that he regarded the turning in
of draft cards as "silly"; his advocacy of a Warren-type commission to look
into the legality of the war was barely controversial; and also going for him
was the fact that several witnesses cast considerable doubt on the government's identification of him as a vociferous protester who had demanded
that a Department of Justice official accept a briefcase filled with turned-in
draft cards. There were a number of reasons for the poor prognosis for the
other defendants. One was a general belief that there must be something
to the charge, since the government had staked its authority on the outcome
of the case. Another was the latitude of the charge, combined with the
difficulty of keeping it separate from "substantive offenses." It was also
conjectured that the jurors might feel they were endorsing civil disobedience
if they returned a verdict of not guilty. A Harvard chemist who attended a
few sessions observed to me, "The defendants are raising difficult questions,
for which they have no clear-cut answers. They're asking the country to
give up old ways for unfamiliar ones." Finally, the defendants had to contend with Judge Ford's management of the trial, which unfortunately, was
not always even-handed.

The official transcript—nineteen mimeographed volumes—includes examples of Judge Ford's style, but its inanimate contents, in the words of the
Washington *Post*'s judicial correspondent, "do not convey the manner in
which 85-year-old Judge Francis J. W. Ford showed his disbelief in the
defense case and his tolerance for the Government's." (The same correspondent, John P. MacKenzie, wrote, "The Judge's display of bias . . . deprived the Nation of a trial that was fundamentally fair.") The official
transcript does not convey the skeptical tone that the Judge employed in
addressing defendants when they denied government allegations. Nor does
anything in its nineteen volumes describe his elaborate shuffling of papers
and ordering about of clerks and marshals when defense attorneys were
scoring points—though the transcript does show that he sometimes capped
such points by admonishing the jury to keep an open mind. In reading the
transcript, one cannot hear his hectoring tone as he urged defense lawyers to
"get on" or "go forward" on numerous occasions—something he rarely did to
the prosecution. When a defense lawyer elicited testimony from Dr. Spock
that many Americans agreed with him, the Judge said, "Strike it out." The

lawyer then asked whether Dr. Spock had met persons who disagreed with him, and Dr. Spock said, "Yes." "Let it stand," the Judge said. ". . . It is obvious. . . . The Court can take judicial notice of that." Upon becoming irritated at a defense counsel, the Judge warned him he might face the type of contempt citation that was once meted out to attorneys representing Communist leaders. (Wall himself made no insinuations of Communist sympathies on anyone's part.) During a colloquy at the bench—not included in the transcript—the Judge was heard to refer to two priests who appeared as witnesses for Ferber as "those so-called Roman Catholic priests." The transcript shows that in another bench conference, this one concerned with the admissibility as a witness of a young war resister described as having long hair, Judge Ford said, "I hope he has long hair." In several instances, he gave the impression of accepting the government's charge as fact, referring to it flatly as "this conspiracy" or "the conspiracy." The day before he gave the jury its instructions, he predicted during a bench conference, 'There will be one verdict, and that will be guilty on [a] conspiracy count."

Judge Ford, in his charge to the jury, said that the flouting of law on the basis of belief "would permit every objector to become a law unto himself." Adhering to the indictment, he endeavored to isolate the charge of conspiracy from its alleged objectives, but as he discoursed on the flexible charge there were moments when it sounded as though the charge of conspiracy were an afterthought—as though the recognition of the crime must be preceded by the attainment of its objectives. Thus, describing conspiracy as "generally a matter of inference," Judge Ford instructed the jurors that "proof of the accomplishment of an objective of a conspiracy is the most persuasive evidence of the conspiracy itself." However, the Judge also said, lack of success was no proof of innocence. Mention was made of the First Amendment's guarantees of freedom of speech and assembly, but there was no exploration of whether the defendants had believed that they were protected by their Constitutional rights in protesting the war. It was ruled "no defense" that some defendants had protested in order to bring about a test case, and in Judge Ford's opinion it was "irrelevant and immaterial" that the accused had made no attempt to conceal their activities from government agencies. The activities were always considered in the light of the strictly criminal; in illustrating the difference between motive and intent ("at times the line . . . is not too easy to draw") he spoke of an automobile thief who steals to improve the efficiency of a benevolent-aid society. Judge Ford invariably referred to the five defendants collectively, leaving their activities undifferentiated. Addressing the jurors as "tryers of fact," he cautioned them not to be misled by "false trails and issues," observing at one point that "we are not trying the United States of America or President

Johnson." And, reiterating what had been his basic view throughout the
trial, the Judge told the twelve men, "There is no freedom to knowingly
conspire to violate a law of the United States with impunity merely because
one believes or doubts that the law is immoral or illegal or un-Constitutional, if the law is within the Constitutional power of Congress to enact,
which [the Military Selective Service Act of 1967] is. The defendants here
have testified that they believed the war in Vietnam was immoral, illegal,
and un-Constitutional."

JASON EPSTEIN

The Trial of Bobby Seale

The United States District Court for the Northern District of Illinois
(Eastern Division) occupies several floors of the new Federal Building in
Chicago's Loop. Of this thirty-story building, designed in steel and glass
by the late Mies van de Rohe, the Chicago Art Institute has said, "The
commitment to order everywhere present is translated into an authoritarian
and heroic presence." Its lobby is designed "without recourse to historical
vocabulary," while the building itself, outside and in, lacks all adornment.
The single exception is an electric carillon on the ground floor which in
normal times plays popular and patriotic tunes, but during the conspiracy
trial which is now in progress the carillon has been silenced. The revolving
doors at each of the four corners of the lobby are each guarded by six
armed marshals and visitors are asked to identify themselves as they enter.
Purses and briefcases are opened and searched. Since the beginning of the
trial pistols have been taken from four visitors.

The courtrooms themselves are to be found along interior corridors on
the upper floors of the building. Judge Hoffman's court, where the conspiracy trial is held, is on the twenty-third floor and, like the other courtrooms, is two stories high. As the visitor enters through swinging doors at
the rear of the room, he finds himself standing in a carpeted aisle between
two rows of wooden benches. Those on his left are for spectators, who are
carefully searched before they are allowed to enter. The benches to the
right are for the press, though the last three rows of this section are reserved

From *The New York Review of Books*, December 4, 1969, pp. 35–50. Copyright © 1969
by The New York Review. Reprinted by permission.

for friends and relatives of the defendants. Because the trial has attracted such attention, the benches on both sides of the aisle are usually filled.

At the end of the aisle is a chain and beyond this chain, in a large open space, sit the defendants around four tables arranged in a large rectangle. At the far end of this rectangle sit the two defense attorneys. Opposite them, seated at a table half the size, are the three government lawyers and an FBI agent who assists them. Behind these lawyers is the jury box with its twelve jurors and two alternates. Of these, all but two are women.

At the front of the room, facing the court, is the judge's bench, elevated to form a kind of stage on several levels. On a low platform to the right sits the court stenographer. Behind her, a foot or so higher, is the witness box. At the opposite end of the stage sits a marshal in a kind of pulpit. Along the wall behind the defendants' table there are folding chairs for additional members of the press and in this wall there are two doors. The one farther from the judge's bench leads to a cloakroom and from there to the corridor, while the one closer to the judge leads to the lockup, one floor above. When this door is opened, the defendants, seven of whom are free on bail, may see the steel grating through which the eighth defendant, Bobby Seale, who is charged with first degree murder in New Haven and is thus without bail, had entered and left the courtroom, before the judge had declared a mistrial in his case. On the wall behind the judge's bench are conventional portraits, which belong to the judge himself, of the founding fathers, as well as one of Abraham Lincoln and three of periwigged English jurists. Above these portraits, on the upper part of the wall, is the Great Seal of the United States. The building is so designed that if this upper wall were transparent one could see directly into the lockup on the twenty-fourth floor.

The proceedings which follow occurred between 2:35 and 4:05 p.m. on Wednesday, November 5, 1969. At eleven that morning Judge Hoffman had recessed the Court until two. That afternoon, when he re-entered the courtroom thirty minutes later than the appointed time, his aspect was even more ominous than usual. The jury had not yet been called in and was not to appear until the end of the day. Twenty-two marshals, each with a pistol concealed beneath his suit coat and a badge on his pocket, guarded the various entrances. Several of them hovered at the defendants' table.

Despite his diminutive size and his curiously dainty manner, the seventy-four-year-old Judge conveys an undeniable authority. Only after one has observed him at length does one discover the source of this authority—not in his juridical wisdom, which is hardly remarkable as the following transcript will perhaps show, but in an unmistakable theatrical gift which, at an earlier time in his life, might have been a contrivance but is now his second nature. Though he stands only five feet four inches tall and weighs hardly more than the smallest of the formidable lady jurors, he makes use of his diminished stature to enter the courtroom from a door behind his bench so that he does not become visible until he has materialized atop the highest of the several stages at the front of the room. His entrance is invariably accomplished in this surprising manner so that even spectators who have become used to the phenomenon and have learned to anticipate it are occasionally startled by what seems to be his magical appearance.

But it is the Judge's formidable gift for impersonation, such as Dickens is said to have revealed when he read from his novels, which completes and enforces the illusion. On the afternoon of November 5 he was able not only to sustain the resonance of his voice through a wide range of modulations for an hour and thirty minutes but to convey an impression of the defendant Seale, as he read his remarks from the transcript, and of himself as he read his own replies, which raised the dialogue to an impressive theatrical level.

The mouth, his most expressive feature, is highly mobile and can be pursed and stretched to considerable effect. The articulation is precise with an occasional British vowel. The pauses, when he so intends, can strike terror. When he utters the name of the defendant Rubin it is as if a chord has been struck on the Wurlitzer of a long forgotten music hall. And when he explodes the middle initial of the defendant Bobby G. Seale, one is made to feel that the innocence of that consonant has been lost forever.

In order to follow Judge Hoffman's statement one must know that the trial began on September 24 and the jury had been chosen by September 26. The events referred to in the transcript thus occurred over a period of five weeks. Throughout these weeks the United States Attorney, Thomas Foran, and his assistant, Richard Schultz, had been presenting their case. Their evidence against the alleged conspirators consisted largely of testimony given by city officials and by undercover agents hired by the FBI, the Chicago police, and, in one case, by a Chicago newspaper columnist who had engaged a young reporter to spy on the organizers of the Chicago protest.

Since Seale had been in Chicago for only two days during the convention and had been invited to come only at the last minute as a substitute for Eldridge Cleaver, the evidence against him was sparse. It consisted of an account by Robert Pierson, an undercover Chicago policeman, of a speech by Seale in Lincoln Park. In this speech, according to Pierson, Seale had urged his audience to "barbecue some pork," and Judge Hoffman, over the objection of the defense, had allowed Pierson to give his opinion to the jury that this meant "to burn some pigs," i.e., policemen.

Normally the First Amendment protects even such provocative language as this, except in the event of a "clear and present danger" that such language will incite the audience unequivocally and immediately to commit the illegal act recommended by the speaker. Since no such acts were committed either at the time or later, Seale's speech would, ordinarily, be innocent. However, in a trial for conspiracy the ordinary constitutional protections don't necessarily apply. A defendant may be found guilty of conspiracy even though the acts of which he is accused are themselves perfectly legal. To most citizens this aspect of the law is puzzling, but in order to understand the case against Seale and his co-defendants, the mystery must be explained, insofar as it can be.

It is no crime to buy gasoline, nor is it a crime for a second person to buy a match or for a third to hold a fire insurance policy on a building which then burns down. But if a prosecutor can convince a jury that the defendant who bought the gasoline had guilty knowledge of the intentions of the defendant who bought the match and that they shared this knowledge with the defendant who collected the insurance on the burnt building, then the jury may find that all three had been guilty of a conspiracy to burn the house down, even though the actual arsonist is never brought before the court. In the Chicago case, the government's plan was to link Seale's statement about pork to acts and statements of the other defendants so as to show that the combination of these acts and statements prove that the defendants as a group conspired to come to Chicago intending to incite a riot.

Under the law, each member of a conspiracy is responsible for the words and actions of all the other defendants, so that if the jury finds that a conspiracy did in fact exist, each defendant who is found to have been part of the conspiracy may then be found guilty of all the acts and statements of the other conspirators. Nor does it matter that Seale did not know most of his fellow defendants at the time of his speech and barely knew the others. A peculiarity of conspiracy law is that the existence of a conspiracy —which is an agreement by two or more people to commit a crime—may be inferred by the jury from the similarity of purpose suggested by the overt acts of the defendants. The defendants need not have met in advance to plan their crime, nor need their arrangements have been made in secret. A conspiracy may be entirely public and may include large numbers of people. Furthermore the government is under no obligation to indict all the members of a conspiracy but can choose as defendants whom it will.

To complicate matters further, the crime which the conspirators are alleged to have committed is hardly as specific as, for example, arson. The statute under which they are being tried, an amendment to the Civil Rights Act of 1968—the so-called Rap Brown Amendment—makes it a crime to cross state lines with the intent to incite to riot. Inciting to riot, under this law, is defined as an act by an individual in a group of three or more which threatens the safety or property of a fourth person. The penalty for such intentions, whether they are carried out or not—so long as a jury perceives them to have existed—is five years in jail. Since the Chicago defendants are indicted not only for having conspired to have such intentions but for actually having them as individuals, each of them faces a prison term of ten years.

As an alleged co-conspirator, Seale is charged in the federal indictment with having come from San Francisco to Chicago with the intention of planning a march on the International Amphitheatre, a sleep-in in Lincoln Park, an attack on the Loop in which, according to the indictment, "large numbers of persons would break windows, set off false alarms, set small fires, disable automobiles," and so on. Together with the other alleged conspirators, he is also charged with a plan to invade the Conrad Hilton Hotel and hold and forcibly occupy all or part of it. The fact that Seale did no more than give two speeches in Chicago, of which only a few lines from the second were admitted in evidence, while in the first speech he urged his listeners not to march on the Amphitheatre because it made no sense for them to do so, is of no account.

Nor is it of account that no march on the Amphitheatre did in fact take place, that no fires were set in the Loop, nor were windows smashed, except in one case by the police, or cars disabled, nor was the Hilton invaded, much less forcibly occupied. The application of conspiracy law to the 1968 anti-riot statute makes it a crime for Seale simply to have revealed, by his single statement concerning "pork" and another urging his listeners to defend themselves with guns against illegal attacks by the police, that he shared a common purpose or "intent"—implying an agreement—with the other defendants, whose own alleged crimes and "overt acts" as they are described in the indictment are no less metaphysically conceived than Seale's own.

Seale, the Chairman of the Black Panther Party, is however in considerably more trouble than his fellow defendants, for under the New Haven murder charge he faces the death penalty. His defiant behavior in Judge Hoffman's court, which led to his being cited for contempt on November 5, may be understood partly in the light of this fact, but it also became apparent, as his outbursts continued, that he was forcing the Judge either to grant him his rights or to appear in a humiliating moral light.

It would be wrong, therefore, to regard Seale's actions as simply those of a desperate man whose difficulties in New Haven put him beyond any punishment Judge Hoffman might inflict. Seale had argued from the day the jury first entered the court on September 26 that he had been unfairly denied the counsel of his choice and was thereafter illegally denied his right to defend himself. The basis of his first charge was that Judge Hoffman had, unreasonably in Seale's opinion, refused to postpone the trial so that Charles Garry, Seale's San Francisco lawyer, who had successfully defended a number of Black Panthers in California, could attend the trial after his recovery from a major operation which was scheduled for September 15. The basis for Seale's second charge was that the judge, having refused the postponement, then refused to permit Seale to defend himself in Garry's absence. These charges were the substance of Seale's several outbursts in the following weeks, which Judge Hoffman was to recite with such eloquence on the afternoon of November 5, and for which he was to charge Seale with sixteen separate counts of contempt and sentence him to jail for four years, an unprecedented punishment for contempt of court.

In late August lawyers for the defense petitioned Judge Hoffman to postpone the trial so that Garry could attend it upon his recovery. On September 9, Garry himself came to Chicago to make the same plea. On both occasions the Judge, perhaps sensing a dilatory tactic, refused. On September 12 Seale was taken from his cell in a San Francisco jail where he was awaiting extradition to Connecticut, placed in a car by federal marshals, chained to two other prisoners, and driven by a circuitous route to Chicago where he was deposited in the Cook County Jail on the eighteenth.

During this period he was out of touch with the defense lawyers who were not only fearful for his safety but eager to consult with him on the preparation of their case. It was in order to see Seale in Cook County Jail that William Kunstler, one of the defense attorneys, filed an appearance on behalf of Seale, that is, agreed formally to serve as his attorney. It is partly on the basis of Kunstler's having filed this appearance that Judge Hoffman denied Seale the right of self defense.

The right of self defense is guaranteed under the Constitution as well as by statute and has often been exercised, especially by defendants who feel that they are on trial for their political views and who want not only to defend themselves but to use the court insofar as rules of procedure allow, as a political forum. Judges are required to grant this right provided it is requested early enough in the trial so as not to interfere with an orderly proceeding. Thus, in two Smith Act cases, Eugene Dennis and Elizabeth Gurley Flynn defended themselves, and earlier this year so did ten of fourteen defendants on trial in Milwaukee for destroying draft records.

On September 26, the jury having been chosen and the trial about to begin, Seale submitted to the Court a motion in his own hand asking that the trial be postponed to permit Garry to attend, but in the event that the Judge denied this motion, he wanted it known that he had "fired" his lawyer of record—William Kunstler—and would defend himself. The Judge ignored this motion. Later on the same day, however, after the lawyers for the gov-

ernment and those for the defense had completed their opening statements
to the jury and the Judge had asked whether there were any other statements by lawyers before the first witness was called, Seale got to his feet
and walked to the lectern which stood before Judge Hoffman's bench. "Just
a minute, sir," the Judge asked, "who is your lawyer?"

"Charles R. Garry," Seale replied. The Judge then asked Kunstler whether
he represented Seale and Kunstler replied, "No, your Honor, as far as Mr.
Seale has indicated, that because of the absence of Charles G. Garry . . ."
whereupon the Judge interrupted to ask Kunstler whether he had filed an
appearance for Seale. Kunstler said that he had and the Judge then said
that he would let Kunstler make an opening statement on Seale's behalf.
Kunstler refused, saying that he "could not compromise Mr. Seale's position
. . . that he was not his full counsel here," at which point the Judge cut him
short and called in the jury.

September 26, the day on which this exchange occurred, was a Friday.
On September 30, the following Tuesday, Kunstler moved formally to withdraw his appearance for Seale but the Judge denied the motion, presumably
because the trial was now in its second full day and the interest of an orderly proceeding outweighed Seale's constitutional right to self defense.
Seale, nevertheless, continued to insist that he had "fired" Kunstler and in
Garry's absence would defend himself.

The Judge repeatedly denied Seale this opportunity and reminded him
that Kunstler, "a very able criminal lawyer from New York," had filed a
written as well as an oral appearance for him. The oral appearance to which
the Judge referred was a statement made by Kunstler on September 24 that
he and Leonard Weinglass, his colleague, would each represent four defendants, thus each lawyer would have a chance to cross-examine government witnesses separately.

It was not only Seale who wanted Garry's services. So did the other seven
defendants. By the end of September it had become apparent to many
observers in the Court that the Judge, in his haste to get on with the trial,
might, by having refused the postponement, have denied all the defendants
their constitutional right to counsel of their choice. In a private conversation
at this time, Thomas Foran, the prosecutor, dismissed the possibility that
the other seven defendants had grounds under the Sixth Amendment to an
argument on appeal, but he admitted that he wasn't so sure that Seale's
rights had not been violated. Accordingly Foran reminded the judge that
not only were the defendants represented by Kunstler and Weinglass as
well as by two local lawyers, but that four other lawyers had filed appearances for the defendants but had never shown up. Foran wanted the record
to show that all the defendants, including Seale, were adequately repre-

sented and that if an error had been made it was the fault of these four absent lawyers.

Kunstler replied that these four lawyers had never intended to participate in the trial but had agreed only to prepare pre-trial motions. Their work in this respect having been completed, their services were no longer needed. Judge Hoffman, however, responded to the government's tactic by issuing bench warrants for the arrest of the four lawyers, one of whom, a professor of law at UCLA, was awakened by a federal marshal, put on a plane to Chicago, and found himself the next morning, having been photographed and fingerprinted in Cook County Jail, in the lockup one floor above Judge Hoffman's courtroom. That morning, as the four lawyers were facing jail sentences for their failure to honor their appearances, Judge Hoffman told Kunstler that the keys to the County Jail were in the pockets of the defense, by which Kunstler assumed the Judge to mean that "if the defendants waived their right to counsel . . . with respect to Garry, then the jailhouse would open for these [four] attorneys." The defendants, who later described Judge Hoffman's tactic as "blackmail," refused to relinquish their claim to Garry's services and the Judge, two of whose warrants had been found invalid by the United States District Court in San Francisco and whose own court was now being picketed by angry lawyers from all over the country, was forced to back down.

Seale's demands, thereafter, increased in vehemence despite Judge Hoffman's warnings that if they continued Seale would be bound and gagged. On the afternoon of October 29, Seale was taken forcibly by two marshals through the door to the lockup and returned, ten minutes later, chained hand and foot to a metal chair. A gag of muslin was in his mouth.

The following morning, since the first gag had proved ineffective and the rattling of the chains against the metal chair had obviously disturbed the jury, Seale was brought to court strapped to a wooden chair. The gag that passed over his mouth and was tied in a knot at the nape of his neck was supplemented by another of the same muslin which passed under his chin and was tied in a sort of bow at the top of his head. Under the gag his mouth was taped. Seale sat quietly throughout most of the day, but as the afternoon session ended he managed to speak in a loud, if muffled voice, once more insisting on his right to defend himself.

The following morning the gag was further strengthened by an elastic bandage and Seale's mouth was stuffed with some kind of cotton which the marshals had managed to insert by holding his nose. This forced him to open his mouth. The arrangement proved effective, but as Seale attempted to breathe the elastic bandage tightened around his head and he choked. Mr. Weinglass, at this point, petitioned the Court to loosen the gag and

Judge Hoffman, having inquired whether the government agreed and upon the affirmative reply of the assistant prosecutor, Mr. Schultz, ordered the gag loosened.

Kunstler and Weinglass then moved to recess the Court for the rest of the day so that one of them could fly to California and consult with Garry about a way out of the impasse. Upon the urging of the government lawyers, the Judge agreed. Mr. Schultz admitted that the gag and straps might damage the government's case in the eyes of the jury.

When the trial resumed on the following Monday, Seale entered the courtroom free of his gag and straps. However he continued to interrupt the proceedings, insisting on his right to defend himself, evidently aware that his demands, and Judge Hoffman's refusal to hear them, had put the Judge and, indeed, the judicial system itself in a most awkward position, a conclusion which the Chicago Bar Association confirmed at a press conference the following day. By Wednesday morning the Judge recessed the Court to prepare the following statement which he read that afternoon.

What follows is the official transcription, taken by the court stenographer, of what the Judge read from his notes on the afternoon of November 5. The text is printed here without changes except for corrections in spelling and punctuation, the deletion of a few redundant passages, and references to the page numbers of earlier parts of the transcript. I have added explanatory notes which appear in brackets.

THE TRANSCRIPT

The following proceedings were had in open court, out of the presence and hearing of the jury:

The Court: There is a matter that I wish to take up, gentlemen, before we proceed further with this trial.

I think, Mr. Witness, you may be excused and go into the witness room.

(*Witness temporarily excused.*)

The Court: As I think everyone who has attended the various sessions of this trial must, if he is fair, understand, the court has done its best to prevent, or to have repeated, efforts to delay and obstruct this trial which I think have been made for the purpose of causing such disorder and confusion as would prevent a verdict by a jury on the issues presented by the indictment and the pleas of not guilty thereto.

I must now, as I perceive my duty and obligation to be, take proper steps to insure that the trial as it continues be conducted in an atmosphere of dignity, an atmosphere that the defendants and each of them are entitled to have prevail in the trial of this case. As we all know, the defendant

Bobby G. Seale has been guilty of conduct in the presence of the court during this trial which is not only contumacious in character but his misconduct was of so grave a character as to continually disrupt the orderly administration of justice.

We have in the federal courts the Federal Rules of Criminal Procedure which together with Title 18 of the United States Code represent the rules that the court must interpret and apply in the trial of criminal cases. In conformity with Rule 42(a) of the Federal Rules of Criminal Procedure and Title 18, United States Code, Section 401, I certify at this time that I saw and overheard the conduct of the defendant Bobby G. Seale to which I shall refer during these observations, which conduct took place in the actual presence of the court during the trial of this case which is entitled United States of America v. David Dellinger and others, the case number being 69 CR 180.

The trial commenced on September 24, 1969, and has continued through this morning. I find not only from seeing and hearing the conduct to which I am about to refer, the conduct of the defendant Seale, but from reading the transcript of the proceedings that the acts, statements and conduct of the defendant Seale which I shall specify here each constitute a separate contempt of this court; that each constituted a deliberate and willful attack upon the administration of justice in an attempt to sabotage the functioning of the federal judicial system.

Mr. Seale: That is a lie. I stood up and spoke in behalf of myself. I stood up and spoke in behalf of myself and made motions and requests.

The Court: I don't permit anybody to speak which I am talking.

Mr. Seale: I stood up and walked to the lectern and demonstrated the fact I wanted to cross-examine the witness. You allowed these men here and Tom Hayden to go all the way to California to see my lawyer, which indicated?, and I tried to persuade you again to recognize it. I was there no more than five minutes. You are talking about disrupting the proceedings of this trial? That's a lie. That's a lie.

The Court: You are making it very difficult for me, Mr. Seale.

Mr. Seale: You are making it difficult for me, Judge Hoffman.

The Court: I tried not to—I have done my best. I have done my best.

Mr. Seale: I have a right to stand up and speak in my own behalf. I do. You know that.

The Court: You know you do not have a right to speak while the Judge is speaking.

Mr. Seale: I have a right to speak and make requests and make arguments to demonstrate the fact I want to cross-examine. When you say I disrupt, I have never tried to strike anybody, I have never tried to hit anybody. I have

never. You know that. And in my arguments and motions I called you a racist
and a fascist and a pig, and that's what I consider you as, and my arguments
and my motions will always carry that as long as my constitutional rights
are being denied. So it is a lie, and you know it.

The Court: I find, I repeat, that the acts, statements and conduct of the
defendant Seale to which I shall refer specifically each constitute a separate
contempt of this Court; that each constituted a deliberate and willful attack
upon the administration of justice in an attempt to sabotage the functioning
of the Federal Judicial System; that this misconduct was of so grave a character as to continually disrupt the orderly administration of justice.

To maintain the dignity of the Court and to preserve order in the courtroom under these circumstances has been a task of utmost difficulty. There
were, accordingly, as the record shows clearly, repeated warnings and ad-
monitions to the defendant Seale to cease this conduct and there were warnings that it would be dealt with accordingly at an appropriate time. However, his continued disruptive conduct made it necessary for the Court for
the first time within the experience of this Court to physically and forcibly
restrain him. Even these measures proved insufficient because of the potential
effect that the continuation of these activities might have had in the future
on the administration of justice.

In this case I find that it is necessary that I deal with his conduct at this
time. I have tried—I have endeavored on many occasions to make it clear to
the defendant that his conduct was contumacious but I was not successful
even right down to a few moments ago in persuading him to so conduct
himself as we expect individuals to conduct themselves in the courts of the
Federal System.

As isolated excerpts from or references to the transcript can give but a
partial view of the acts, statements and conduct to which I refer, I make the
entire record part of these proceedings. The Court also notes that a reading
of this record cannot and does not reflect the true intensity and extent of the
disruption which in some instances were accompanied by a physical violence.

Mr. Seale: That is a lie.

The Court: —which occurred in the presence of the Court.

Mr. Seale: That is a lie. I never attacked anyone, and you know it. I never
struck anyone and you know it.

[On the morning of October 29 a group of perhaps twenty Black Panthers
had taken seats in the spectators' section. Before the morning session began,
and while both the Judge and jury had not yet entered, Mr. Seale addressed
this group. He advised them to remain "cool," but in the event they were
physically attacked by the marshals they were to defend themselves. When
the Judge entered the Court, Assistant US Attorney Schultz accused Seale
of having talked about an "attack." Seale vehemently objected to Schultz's

misrepresentation and repeated before the Court what he had in fact said. The Judge ignored or failed to understand Seale's clarification.]

The Court: Accordingly I adjudge—

Mr. Seale: I will stand up in any court in America and say that.

The Court: Accordingly I adjudge the defendant Bobby Seale guilty of the several criminal contempts to which I shall refer. In citing these specific acts and statements of the defendant Seale as contemptuous, the Court has selected only the most flagrant acts.

On Friday, September 26, 1969, during the motion session prior to the time opening statements were made, the defendant Seale addressed the Court in the following manner:

"If I am consistently denied this right of legal defense counsel of my choice who is effective by the Judge of this Court, then I can only see the Judge as a blatant racist of the United States Court.

"*The Court:* Just a minute. Just a minute.

"*Mr. Seale:* With gross prejudicial error toward all defendants and myself.

"*The Court:* Just a minute. What did you say?

"Read that, Miss Reporter.

"*Mr. Seale:* I said if my constitutional rights are denied as my constitutional rights have been denied in the past in the course of the trial, et cetera, then the tenor is the act of racism and me a black man, there seems to be a form of prejudice against me even to the other defendants on the part of the Judge."

That is Item No. 1.

.   .   .

Item No. 13:

At the beginning of the afternoon session on October 29, 1969, Court and counsel engaged in a lengthy colloquy during which the following occurred:

"*Mr. Kunstler:* Your Honor, I would just like about two minutes to respond.

"*Mr. Seale:* Since he made all of these statements, can I say something to the Court?

"*The Court:* No, thank you.

"*Mr. Seale:* Why not?

"*The Court:* Because you have a lawyer and I am not going to go through that again.

"*Mr. Seale:* He is not my lawyer. How come I can't say nothing? He has distorted everything, and it relates to the fact I have a right to defend myself.

"*The Court:* I ask you to sit down. If there has been any distortion by anybody, I am perfectly capable of understanding it.

"*Mr. Seale:* I don't think you will. See? I don't think you will. Your past actions of denying me the constitutional right to defend myself—

"*The Court:* Did you want to reply, Mr. Kunstler?

"*Mr. Seale:* Yes, I did. I wanted to reply.

"*The Court:* I was talking to Mr. Kunstler, if you don't mind."

The colloquy continued and the Court thereafter sent the jury into the jury room at which time the following occurred:

"*Mr. Kunstler:* Then I have nothing further to say, your Honor.

"*The Court:* Bring in the jury, please.

"*Mr. Seale:* What about Section 1982, Title 42 of the Code where it says the black man cannot be discriminated against in my legal defense in any court in America?

"*The Court:* Mr. Seale, you do know what is going to happen to you—

"*Mr. Seale:* You just got through saying you observed the laws. That law protects my right not to be discriminated against in my legal defense. Why don't you recognize that? Let me defend myself. From the first time when I asked—when I attempted to make an opening statement, and you stopped me and denied me that right—

"*The Court:* I will not hear you now. I am asking you to be silent.

"*Mr. Seale:* I want to know will you—oh, look—it's a form of racism, racism is what stopped my argument.

"*The Court:* Hold the jury, Mr. Marshal.

"*Mr. Seale:* My argument is and I still argue the point that you recognize my constitutional rights to defend myself.

"*The Court:* Mr. Seale, do you want to stop or do you want me to direct the marshal—

"*Mr. Seale:* I want to argue the point about this so you can get an understanding of the facts. I have a right to defend myself.

"*The Court:* We will take a recess. [The Judge addresses the marshals.] Take that defendant into the room in there and deal with him as he should be dealt with in this circumstance.

"*Mr. Seale:* I still want to be represented. I want to represent myself.

"*The Marshal:* Mr. Kunstler, will you instruct the defendants, sir, that it is the order of the Court that they will arise upon the recess?

"*Mr. Kunstler:* If that is a direction of the Court, I certainly will pass it on.

"*The Court:* Let the record show none of the defendants have stood at this recess in response to the Marshal's request. The Court will be in recess for a few minutes.

"*Mr. Seale:* Let the record show that—

"*The Marshal:* This Court will take a brief recess.

"*Mr. Seale:* Let the record show—"

In an attempt to maintain order in the courtroom, the Court thereupon ordered the defendant Seale removed from the courtroom at which time he was forcibly restrained by binding and gagging.

The defendant Seale was then returned to the courtroom but continued to shout through the gag. The Court then order the Marshal to reinforce the gag. The gag was then reinforced and the defendant Seale was returned to the courtroom. Eventually the jury was allowed in the courtroom for the afternoon session.

Item No. 14:[1]

On October 30, 1969, at the opening of the morning session the Court ordered the marshal to adjust the restraint on the defendant Seale after he had complained of discomfort. Thereupon the following occurred in open court:

"*The Court:* If the marshal has concluded that he needs assistance, of course.

[Upon the request of Mr. Weinglass and with the agreement of Mr. Schultz, Judge Hoffman orders the marshal to loosen the elastic bandage which has begun to choke Mr. Seale.]

"I will excuse you, ladies and gentlemen of the jury, with my usual orders.

(The following proceedings were had in open court, out of the presence and hearing of the jury:)

"*Mr. Kunstler:* Your Honor, are we going to stop this medieval torture that is going on in this courtroom? I think this is a disgrace.

"*Mr. Rubin:* This guy is putting his elbow in Bobby's mouth and it wasn't necessary at all. [Mr. Rubin is a defendant. He refers to a very large Negro marshal who has attempted to silence Mr. Seale.]

"*Mr. Kunstler:* This is no longer a court of order, your Honor; this is a medieval torture chamber. It is a disgrace. They are assaulting the other defendants also.

"*Mr. Rubin:* Don't hit me in my balls, mother fucker. [The Judge declined to read these obscenities and the one that follows into the record, asking the reporter to add them later. He explained his reluctance on the ground that there were women and young people in the courtroom.]

"*Mr. Seale:* This mother fucker is tight and it is stopping my blood.

"*Mr. Kunstler:* Your Honor, this is an unholy disgrace to the law that is going on in this courtroom and I as an American lawyer feel a disgrace.

"*Mr. Foran:* Created by Mr. Kunstler.

"*Mr. Kunstler:* Created by nothing other than what you have done to this man.

"*Mr. Hoffman:* You come down here and watch it, Judge. [Mr. Hoffman is a defendant.]

"*Mr. Foran:* May the record show that the outbursts are by the defendant Rubin.

"*Mr. Seale:* You fascist dogs, you rotten, low-life son-of-a-bitch."

[Mr. Seale is addressing the Negro marshals.]

Mr. Seale: [Interrupts the Judge's reading from the transcript] That was right after I got hit in the testes by your marshals who attacked me.

The Court: [After Mr. Seale's interruption, Judge Hoffman continues to quote Seale from the transcript.] "I am glad I said it about Washington used to have slaves, the first President—

"*Mr. Dellinger:* Somebody go to protect him.

"*Mr. Foran:* Your Honor, may the record show that that is Mr. Dellinger saying someone go to protect him and the other comment is by Mr. Rubin.

"*Mr. Rubin:* And my statement, too.

"*The Court:* Everything you say will be taken down.

"*Mr. Kunstler:* Your Honor, we would like the names of the marshals. We are going to ask for a judicial investigation of the entire condition and the entire treatment of Bobby Seale.

"*The Court:* You ask for anything that you want. When you begin to keep your word around here that you gave the Court, perhaps things can be done . . .

"*Mr. Kunstler:* I just feel so utterly ashamed to be an American lawyer at this time.

"*The Court:* You should be ashamed of your conduct in this case, sir."

Thereafter, because of the chaos in the courtroom, the morning session of court recessed.

Item No. 15:

During the afternoon session on Thursday, October 30th, 1969, the following occurred:

"*Mr. Seale:* I never intruded until it was the proper time for me to ask and request and demand that I have a right to defend myself and I have a right to cross-examine the witness. I sit through other cross-examinations and after the cross-examinations were over, I request, demanded by right to cross-examine the witness, and in turn demanded my right to defend myself, since you cannot sit up here—you cannot sit up here and continue to deny me my constitutional rights to cross-examine the witness, my constitutional right to defend myself. I sit throughout other cross-examinations, I never said anything, and I am not attempting to disrupt this trial. I am attempting to get my rights to defend myself recognized by you.

"*The Court:* You have employed one of the most competent criminal lawyers I have ever seen. . . .

"*The Court:* Gentlemen, we will recess until two o'clock."

Accordingly, it is therefore ordered that pursuant to the authority vested in this Court by Rule 42(a) of the Federal Rules of Criminal Procedure and by Title 18, United States Code, Section 401, the defendant Bobby Seale be punished for contempt.

I will hear from you, Mr. Kunstler.

Mr. Kunstler: Your Honor, I have already indicated that because I have been discharged I can say nothing for Mr. Seale. He wants to be his own attorney, as your Honor has read at least thirty or forty times from your own opinion, and I think that I would be derelict in my duty to my understanding of my right and liability as an attorney were I to speak for him now.

The Court: Mr. Seale, you have a right to speak now. I will hear you.

Mr. Seale: For myself?

The Court: In your own behalf, yes.

Mr. Seale: How come I couldn't speak before?

The Court: This is a special occasion.

Mr. Seale: Wait a minute. Now are you going to try to—you going to attempt to punish me for attempting to speak for myself before? Now after you punish me, you sit up and say something about you can speak? What kind of jive is that? I don't understand it. What kind of court is this? Is this a court? It must be a fascist operation like I see it in my mind, you know,—I don't understand you.

The Court: I am calling on you—

Mr. Seale: You just read a complete record of me trying to persuade you, trying to show you, demonstrating my right, demonstrating to you the need, showing you all this stuff about my right to defend myself, my right to defend myself, history, slavery, et cetera; and you going to sit there and say something about, "OK, now you can speak"?

What am I supposed to speak about? I still haven't got the right to defend myself. I would like to speak about that. I would like to—since you let me stand up and speak, can I speak about in behalf of—can I defend myself?

The Court: You may speak to the matters I have discussed here today, matters dealing with your contemptuous conduct. The law obligates me to call on you to speak at this time.

Mr. Seale: About what? About the fact that I want a right to defend myself? That's all I am speaking about.

The Court: No, about possible punishment for contempt of court.

Mr. Seale: Punishment? You've punished black people all your life. I mean, you, they even say you own a factory that produces raw materials to kill people in Viet Nam [the family of Judge Hoffman's wife is involved in the Brunswick Corporation which produces war materials, among other things], you know, so it's nothing, death is nothing, I mean, if that is what you're talking about, or putting me in jail, or prison, or hanging people, and all that stuff. I have nothing to say about that. I have something to say about the fact that I want to defend myself still. I want my rights, to be able to stand up and cross-examine the witnesses. I want that, so I don't know what you're talking about.

The Court: I have tried to make it clear.

Mr. Seale: All you make clear to me is that you don't want me, you refuse to let me, you will not go by my persuasion, or my arguments, my motions, my requests to be, to the extent of even having to shout loud enough to get on that record for that record so that they can hear me half the time. You don't want to listen to me. You don't want to let a man stand up, contend to you that that man is not my lawyer, show you and point out that fact, in fact, made motions and told you that I fired the man.

And to stand up here and say, "Look, I have the right to defend myself," continuously over and over, even to the point just recently on Friday you recognized that I did have only one lawyer by letting this man and Thomas Hayden to go and to talk to Charles R. Garry to see about coming out here for me, which begin to show me that I was beginning to persuade you to do something, at least allow somebody to investigate my situation. Now what are you talking about? Now all of a sudden on the record?

The Court: I want to make it clear. I don't want to be questioned any further. The law gives you the right to speak out now in respect to possible punishment for contempt of court, sir.

Mr. Seale: Well, the first thing, I'm not in no contempt of court. I know that. I know that I as a person and a human being have the right to stand up in a court and use his constitutional right to speak in behalf of his constitutional rights. That is very clear, I hope. That's all I have to say. I still want to cross-examine the witnesses, I make those requests. I make my motions, and I make those requests, and I will continue to make those requests, hoping that once in one way along this trial, you will recognize my rights as a human being, a black man living under the scope and influence of a racist decadent America where the Government of the United States does not recognize the black people's constitutional rights, and have never recognized them from 1867 to the Dred Scott case situation, in a period of slaves you never recognized them, and here you are, and all I can say is that you're probably acting in the same manner as Benjamin Franklin and George Washington. We are hep to that kind of business.

. . .

The Court: In conformity with the provision of Rule 42(a) of the Federal Rules of Criminal Procedure, I shall certify that the series of criminal contempts committed as described by the Court in its oral observations and specifications 1 to and including 16 were committed in actual presence of the Court, and were seen or heard by the Court during the trial of the case of United States of America vs. David T. Dellinger and others, 69 CR 180.

I find that the acts, statements, and conduct of the defendant Bobby Seale constituted a deliberate and wilful attack upon the administration of justice, an attempt to sabotage the functioning of the Federal Judiciary System, and misconduct of so grave a character as to make the mere imposition of a fine a futile gesture and a wholly insignificant punishment. Accordingly, I adjudge Bobby G. Seale guilty of each and every specification referred to in my oral observations, and the Court will impose—strike that—and the defendant Seale will be committed to the custody of the Attorney General of the United States or his authorized representative for imprisonment for a term of three months on each and every specification, the sentences to run consecutively.

[According to a recent Appeals Court ruling, a defendant in a contempt proceeding is entitled to a jury trial if the possible penalty exceeds six months. By sentencing Mr. Seale to sixteen terms of three months each Judge Hoffman presumably meant to circumvent this ruling.]

ART GOLDBERG AND GENE MARINE

Officer O'Brien: "I want to kill a nigger so goddamned bad I can taste it! He killed George Baskett"

THE SCENE: *San Francisco. Its climate is moderate; tempers do not flare; passions are not abraded by the heat. It is renowned for an easy-going, live-and-let-live attitude. It prides itself on its cultural diversity.*

Michael O'Brien was returning with some friends from a Sunday outing at Lake Berryessa. The double date had not gone well: O'Brien had been drinking and was in an unpleasant mood. At one point, he made his date get out of the car with him and told her to "be a little more affectionate" or walk home. She calmed him down a little, though, and they got back into the car.

On the way across the San Francisco-Oakland Bay Bridge, he suddenly brandished a .38 revolver. After a minute he put the gun away, and a few minutes later they were at Brush Place.

From *Ramparts,* July 1969, pp. 9-16. *Copyright* 1969 by Ramparts Magazine, Inc. Reprinted by permission of the editors.

You'd have to be a pretty determined San Franciscan to know where Brush Place is. About two and a half blocks from the ugly new Hall of Justice, there's a little dead-end alley off Folsom Street called Hallam Street. Off that alley there's an even smaller alley, also a dead end. That's Brush Place. O'Brien kept his boat in one of the garages in Brush Place that are rented out for that purpose.

Carl Hawkins, a mild-mannered black street car motorman, seems to have scraped O'Brien boat trailer with his car. Hawkins immediately stopped and got out.

This is how all the witnesses who were not police described what happened next:

One thing quickly led to another. O'Brien yelled at Hawkins, "If you scrape my car, I'll shoot you!" People in the neighborhood, many of them black, came out or looked out their windows to see what was happening. Suddenly O'Brien pulled out his .38 and shouted, "Get your heads back in, niggers, or I'll kill all of you. I'll blow your heads off." Hawkins' wife went inside to phone the police; Mike's companion, Willis Garriott, went out toward Folsom Street on the same errand.

As Garriott returned with Special Patrol Officer Raymond Adkins (a private policeman, but one with a uniform and a gun), there was the sound of a shot and confusion in the street; O'Brien had three black men at gunpoint, their hands against the wall at the end of the alley. O'Brien was getting nastier by the minute; according to witnesses, he said, "I want to kill a nigger—I want to kill a nigger so goddamned bad I can taste it!"

A black truck driver and neighbor of Hawkins, George Baskett—five inches shorter than O'Brien and 75 pounds lighter—picked up a slat out of a chair back, a thin piece of wood about 23 inches long and about an inch and a half wide, and tried to knock the gun away from O'Brien. Garriott and the special cop had their guns out by now and watched as O'Brien growled, "Drop the stick, drop it, goddammit." He counted in a rapid cadence, "One . . . two . . . three. . . ." There was a sharp crack. The bullet ripped through Baskett's chest, severing a major artery As Baskett lay moaning and dying in the street, O'Brien approached him. "Shut up, dammit," he growled, "shut up." He kicked at Baskett's side, turning his victim over on his back. Baskett's pregnant wife ran out toward her husband. "Get out of here, you black bitch," O'Brien shouted, forcing her down the street. Then he looked up at the black faces peering down from the windows above him. "Get your heads back in niggers," he shouted, "before I blow them off." Within minutes, Baskett, twenty-eight years old and the father of five children, was dead. Michael O'Brien had killed his nigger.

The police came, including San Francisco's head-cracking Tactical Squad. They immediately began questioning "suspects." They arrested Mr. and

Mrs. Carl Hawkins, Mrs. Hawkins' son Richard Dickerson, and Otis Baskett, on charges of conspiracy, assault to commit murder, and assault with a deadly weapon. Then they helped the dazed O'Brien out of the alley and away from the angry crowd.

. . .

THE JUDGE

Superior Court Judge Joseph Karesh grew up in South Carolina, but that does not make him a bigot. In fact, he is proud of the fact that his father, a rabbi, taught Hebrew to the local black ministers. Like Jake Ehrlich and Mayor Joseph Alioto, Karesh is a liberal. When a probation officer was fired for having a beard, Karesh ordered him rehired with back pay. He ruled that the city could have topless joints and ordered the police to allow performances of Michael McClure's play, "The Beard."

He has, however, a couple of minor hang-ups. He doesn't like student dissidents, he loves cops, and he appears to have a somewhat racist way of not being a bigot.

One local attorney recalls, "In many previous dealings I had with Karesh, he seemed to have a very strong block against perceiving that any policeman could be guilty of any misconduct. One sure way to arouse his anger would be to suggest that the police were guilty of any impropriety. It would sort of destroy his world if he thought O'Brien really called those people 'niggers' or shot to kill."

And a local reporter notes that, ". . . in his chambers he'd cut up prosecution witnesses, and talk about how the blacks are getting away with everything, how juries are afraid to convict them, how they are arrested one day and walk away free the next day."

THE BLACK-WHITE ENTANGLEMENT

On January 13, 1969, in the Superior Court of California, Joseph Karesh presiding, Michael O'Brien went on trial for manslaughter in the death of George Baskett.

Two days later George Baskett's sixth child was born.

It took only one day to choose a jury. Ehrlich used two peremptory challenges; one eliminated airlines supervisor George A. Buckner Jr., the only black called. No "personal reflection," said Ehrlich.

Similarly, *any* lawyer can insure an all white jury by use of his allotment of peremptory challenges, which the judge cannot review.

Ehrlich made it quite clear, when questioning jurors, what the trial was going to be about. A key issue, he said, would be "this black-white entanglement." Judge Karesh found nothing to criticize in that formulation.

Attention on the second day focused on Elizabeth Hawkins, a tall, striking woman who said flatly that she had watched Michael O'Brien deliberately murder George Baskett. The next day, Ehrlich moved in, contempt dripping from his tiny frame. He accused Mrs. Hawkins of having lied outright on three occasions.

But she refused to be Ehrlich's pigeon. After she insisted again that she had seen O'Brien kick the dying Baskett:

Ehrlich: "What kind of shoes did O'Brien have on?"

Mrs. Hawkins: "Sneakers, I think."

Ehrlich: "Then he couldn't have hurt Baskett much if he kicked him, could he?"

Mrs. Hawkins: "I have no idea—I have never been shot and then kicked."

Carl Hawkins followed his wife to the stand and corroborated her story, with additional details. During the early part of the incident, he said, his stepson, Richard Dickerson, had arrived and asked a neighbor, Mrs. Anne Thomas, what was going on.

"Your father's having trouble with the white man," she replied.

That, she testified, angered O'Brien further. "Shut up, you goddamn nigger bitch!" he yelled.

Mrs. Thomas promptly yelled back, "Ask God why he made me a nigger bitch and made you a honky."

Baskett had picked up a stick and tried to use it to knock the pistol from O'Brien's hand, but O'Brien ordered him to drop it and began to count.

"O'Brien," Hawkins testified, "extended his arm, braced his right arm with his left hand to steady the pistol, and fired one shot. I saw the flash of the gun."

Otis Baskett, the dead man's brother, appeared and told the same story.

Ehrlich tore into him, shouting that he was a "professional liar." Assistant District Attorney Walter Giubbini, who prosecuted the case, called the use of the phrase "disgusting." Karesh, however, let Ehrlich rant.

But the next witness—Special Officer Adkins—had seen none of this at all. What *he* had seen was a silent confrontation, no words at all, in which Baskett was beating O'Brien on the head. "O'Brien stumbled backwards, kind of shaking his head. Mr. Baskett was preparing to strike him again when the gun discharged." Later he said that O'Brien was "tensing up, trying to regain his balance," but that he was off balance and "back-pedaling," leaning backward with his gun "straight out in his hand," when it went off.

On redirect examination Adkins admitted to consulting with Ehrlich about a week after the shooting. The police department had been "harassing" him to talk to the district attorney, he explained. Ehrlich interrupted to say that he had advised Adkins only to tell the truth.

Dickerson's turn came next, and his story varied from that of the other black witnesses only in the quotation from O'Brien, which he remembered as, "Drop it—drop it, goddamn it, nigger, I'll kill you." Then the count.

The score, by witness, was: four who matched each other almost exactly, one who differed. Up to this point memory divided along racial lines.

THE TRAITOR TO HIS RACE

David Anderson, the eighteen-year-old son of an elementary school principal, testified that he was listening to a rock record "when I heard shots and a big commotion." He went up on his roof, which commanded an excellent view of Brush Place, to see what was going on, and he told the court what he saw.

David Anderson is not only white, he's "clean": his father's professional job is in San Leandro, just south of Oakland across the bay, and the family lives in the pristine suburb of Castro Valley. Anderson had taken this apartment while going to college.

From the roof, he said, he saw three black men spread-eagled against the wall and a white man with a gun; he identified the white man as O'Brien. Then, Anderson went on, a fourth black picked up a stick and swung it, hitting O'Brien either in the left side or on the left elbow. As Baskett backed away, crouching, O'Brien deliberately shot him.

Shortly thereafter, he went on, O'Brien held his gun on one of the men leaning against the wall, and deliberately kicked him in the seat of the pants. "Just give me an excuse—just give me a reason and I'll shoot you!" O'Brien was quoted as shouting. Then O'Brien moved back and yelled at the people looking out of the apartments to get their heads back in.

Ehrlich was faced with a calm and believable young witness, and one who was white—apparently beyond the reach of simple racism. But he knew his judge, and he knew his jurors. The key lay in Anderson's attendance at San Francisco State College, and the possibility of making the young man appear a traitor to his race.

Ehrlich immediately asked whether Anderson was participating in the strike there; Anderson answered that he was. There followed a barrage of questions about Black Panthers, hair, SDS, prejudice, and a number of other subjects, none of which were particularly relevant, though they seemed to fascinate the judge, and Giubbini gave up trying to stem the flow.

What Anderson actually said was fairly mild. He is not a member of Students for a Democratic Society, though he is in sympathy with some of its aims (which no one asked about). He thinks students and teachers have a right to strike. He hopes the strike will help to end institutional racism.

But this alone doesn't convey the effect. Ehrlich met Giubbini's objection to the whole line of questioning by saying that he was trying to prove bias, because "these people who are part of SDS think every white policeman is a pig." He asked Anderson: "If there is any feeling between white man and black man, you are standing against the white man?"

Ehrlich kept Anderson on the stand for two more days, hammering at left-wing associations that weren't there and ideas that Anderson refused to agree with. He demanded that Anderson show his draft card and pretended surprise when Anderson produced one.

Having raised the specter of SDS, the bombastic attorney made another try, this time with the Black Panthers. He asked whether Anderson knew Richard E. Brown, a Panther who had given a lower apartment in the same building as his address when arrested five times between March and November, 1968. Anderson said he didn't know Brown, but that he had moved into the building in September and that no blacks lived there.

Finally, Ehrlich said that he "had been informed" that a police report, dated the night after the shooting, involved Anderson's apartment, and that the report said a black youth was living with Anderson and his white roommate, David Dixon, and that the apartment was decorated with "Free Huey," "Black Revolution" and Che Guevara posters. Anderson merely noted that his apartment is decorated with travel posters, not revolutionary posters, and that he and Dixon have no other roommate.

At one point during the testimony, Ehrlich found reason to thunder an accusation which, in its wording, effectively let the jury know which side Anderson was supposed to be on. "This is a white and black fight," Ehrlich shouted. "This man Anderson is an unmitigated liar. Any man who would sit there and lie a man's life away is not entitled to a fair trial—he should be taken out and shot."

For this bit of legal theory from the city's foremost criminal attorney, the judge had not a word of rebuke.

But that wasn't Ehrlich's most extravagant shot for the day. He made his position, his tactics and his opinion of the judge all very clear just a short time later, when a Tac Squad officer said that he believed Richard Brown was in the courtroom.

Ehrlich strode to the railing separating the spectators from the front of the court, leaned over, and bellowed, "What's your name? Stand up, *boy!*"

There were some audible gasps in the courtroom, but Ehrlich ignored them. The black youth, after a brief but obvious struggle for control, said quietly, "My name is not 'boy.' My name is Richard Brown."

Ehrlich walked back to the counsel table, threw himself into the chair, and said, "Why don't you lock him up?" That's a little obscure, but that's what he said.

Judge Karesh leaned solicitously forward and said, "I'm sure you didn't mean to offend anybody, Mr. Ehrlich."

Jake took the cue and leaped up again. Facing the jury, he thundered, "Some black people seem to think it disgraceful to be called 'boy.' My grandfather and father called me that. What's wrong with it? I don't understand this childish, infantile feeling. I have defended these people many times without fee. I have no hatred for these people, no feeling for them at all. But I won't take any backtalk out of them, either!"

Karesh finally decided that maybe it was time for the jury to leave. When they were gone, he repeated to Ehrlich, "I did not mean to imply earlier that you meant any offense to anyone."

O'BRIEN'S TESTIMONY

Michael O'Brien told his own story earnestly and well. He'd had a few nips of the Red Mountain burgundy, it was true, but he wasn't drunk at all. He would never do a thing like threatening a girl with a long walk home—he was only a little put out because she had turned moody and was spoiling his "fun day."

When Baskett attacked him with a stick, he said, he tried to shoot him "between the knee and the thigh, but the gun clicked and didn't go off," so he thought it was empty.

"Here's this man with a club," O'Brien explained. "He made a real lunge at me. I backed away but he caught me across the right side of the head. I fell backward and hit the ground. As I'm falling backward the gun discharged."

The stick, he said, looked bigger in the alley.

And, when they told him in the police station that Baskett was dead, he said, "I couldn't talk any more. I was crying."

He also said that his "Gas Huey" tie clip (which he wore in the Hunter's Point ghetto during Huey Newton's trial) was only a gag. It didn't have anything to do with gassing Huey.

O'Brien was convincing, and the jury probably didn't pay all that much attention to the one serious use of physical evidence by Giubbini, who asked O'Brien to demonstrate what had happened.

When he demonstrated, his gun arm—inevitably—moved upward. Giubbini quietly pointed out that (1) the bullet that killed Baskett traveled *downward*, and (2) there were no powder burns on Baskett's clothes, as there would have had to have been according to O'Brien reenaction. (A .38 police revolver will spray powder into clothing three feet away. It's hard to hit a guy over the head with a 23-inch stick from more than three feet away.)

Giubbini got in a description of another episode in O'Brien's life—when on a drinking spree at a Broadway topless joint called Pierre's, he took off after a topless waitress and chased her into her dressing room, waving his

.38 all the way. O'Brien tried to say that it was a water pistol, then back-tracked when Giubbini seemed to know what he was talking about. But after hearing it all, Karesh decided it was irrelevant and ruled the whole thing inadmissible.

The rest of the witnesses all supported the prosecution in one way or another, and several demonstrated that there was a conscious attempt to alter evidence in O'Brien's favor. But by then the jury had the message: black people lie; white people tell the truth, unless they're traitors to their race and belong to SDS and fraternize with Black Panthers, in which case they lie about that too.

Finally, nobody listened when Giubbini—who had started out in mild-mannered enough fashion, but who got increasingly incensed as he watched the Ehrlich-Karesh racism tandem—blasted the police department for the errors and omissions in its reports and investigations, and said that the original report (written without any black witnesses having been questioned) showed "some effort to . . . reflect what the lieutenant thought it should reflect, not what the facts were. . . . We're talking," he told the jury, "about credibility in this case. We have to keep our eyes open."

But he was the only one talking about credibility. The others were talking about niggers.

HYENAS

Jake Ehrlich spent six days on his summation. Not preparing it—*giving* it. It was the longest defense summation in the history of San Francisco criminal law. It was also the most vicious, bigoted, nauseating, low and piggish performance any local courtroom has ever seen. Contrary to press suggestions, it was not racist; it was nothing that subtle. It is a disgrace to the Bar that the Bar Association did not meet the next day with censure and possible disbarment in mind; it is a disgrace to the bench that Joseph Karesh was not hounded out of his robes—and out of town as well—for letting it happen. Any Mississippi backwoods judge in the past ten years would have told an attorney making the same speech to tone it down.

Ehrlich started things off by referring to Brush Place as "a hellhole, with 200 hyenas in there."

He slashed at Alioto for "ordering" the trial because the mayor is "looking for the minority vote."

Banging on a lectern with the stick used by Baskett, he shouted, "Mike didn't do what I would have done. I would have shot him then and there. But he backed away, remembering his policeman's training."

Mrs. Hawkins, he shouted, "should be in jail for perjury. The blood of Baskett is on her hands. I don't know how she can sleep at night."

He repeatedly returned to racism, and told the jury that the residents of Brush Place had manufactured "a false facade of lies, chicanery and trickery," and that Giubbini had "patched up all these stories to make them fit one mold." The "litany of lies" was to be expected, however: "You must realize we're dealing here with people of little or no moral honesty or integrity."

Carl Hawkins, in Ehrlich's peroration, became "Mr. Holier than Thou," "Old Mr. Prayer Meeting" and, most often, "The Deacon," after Ehrlich said that Hawkins reminded him of "the old prayer meetings down home." Hawkins "manufactured" the story of O'Brien kicking Baskett, Ehrlich said, and was in any case "a sanctimonious little liar."

In the middle of the attack on Hawkins, Ehrlich suddenly said, "I'd better stick to the record; otherwise, I'll be accused . . . of being a racist or something."

"These people," Ehrlich told the jury, apparently relishing the hated phrase, "would have killed . . . O'Brien, and they would have killed you, too, if you'd been there. They have absolutely no respect for an oath, the truth or for common decency. They would just as soon sacrifice you as they did this boy here."

Otis Baskett, whom Ehrlich accused of "bobbing, weaving and double-talking," because "that big phony." And what David Anderson became was something else again.

"This boy is a member of SDS and hates police as sure as I'm standing here. He hates them and would shoot them if he had a chance. . . . [He] is a vicious young punk who wants to destroy our government . . . our homes, our children, 200 years of American democracy and the flag and all that stands for."

But it wasn't America that Ehrlich wanted the jury to see Anderson as betraying; that was incidental.

"I can realize our black brethren sticking together," the tiny lawyer intoned. "They do things I don't approve of, but I can understand. What I can't understand is Anderson coming apparently from a good home and selling his soul to prove his hatred for a policeman, what he calls a pig." (Anderson testified that he never uses the term "pig.")

Ehrlich called one or another witness "liar," "punk," "knucklehead," "little fool," "perjurer," "killer." He charged that Giubbini had deliberately implied that all 19 policemen who testified were liars and had "manufactured evidence," and he added, "This breaks my heart when I see it."

Finally, he wound up with an almost tearful plea for poor victimized Mike O'Brien, begging, "Don't sacrifice this boy on the altar of chicanery to get a few lousy, dirty votes. If you don't find O'Brien not guilty, there is only one answer—the Golden Gate Bridge." He didn't say for whom.

Unaccountably, Ehrlich and Giubbini seem to have made an agreement in advance not to interrupt each other's closing statements—and Giubbini is a gentleman, though it must have taken considerable effort.

For Judge Karesh, there is not even that excuse. He sought to interrupt Ehrlich only when Ehrlich launched into a tirade against the *Chronicle,* and then only on the grounds that the jury had been instructed to avoid or ignore all mention of communications media during the trial!

One lawyer who was there put his opinion graphically: "Any judge with any balls would have cut Ehrlich off right away. A member of the Bar is not allowed to make racist remarks." A reporter who was at many of the trial sessions said that Karesh's role in the entire trial was vital: "The judge practically turned into a defense attorney" (the same reporter also called Ehrlich "a racist of the Bilbo type" and said that "at times, the word 'nigger' slipped out of his mouth accidentally").

The jury reported itself deadlocked, ten to two (for acquittal, it turned out), but the judge sent them back. The jury asked for instruction as to whether they should give weight to O'Brien's police training—whether, in effect, they should expect more restraint from him than from an ordinary twenty-seven-year-old kid with a gun and a jug of Red Mountain. The judge refused to give such an instruction (Giubbini wanted it, Ehrlich didn't); shortly thereafter the jury acquitted Michael O'Brien.

KENNETH DOLBEARE AND JOEL GROSSMAN

The Arrest and Trial of LeRoi Jones

At the height of the riot, 2:30 a.m. on July 14, 1967, LeRoi Jones drove his Volkswagen camper bus down one of the main streets of the riot area.[1] With him were Charles McCray, a 33 year old accountant, and Barry Wynn, 24, an actor. Practically all of the rest of the facts of the case are in dispute: it is clear that Jones was arrested, taken to jail, and booked for illegal possession of two loaded revolvers and some ammunition, but the accuracy of the

From *Political Trials* edited by Theodore Becker, pp. 230-34. Copyright © 1971 by The Bobbs-Merrill Company, Inc. Reprinted by permission.
1. Sources for our description of the trial of LeRoi Jones include the trial record, newspaper and magazine accounts, and our interviews with the prosecuting and defense attorneys. Judge Kapp declined to be interviewed, but kindly supplied us with a verbatim copy of his sentencing speech.

charge and the behavior of the police are both the real and the controverted aspects of the case. Jones denied possession of the guns, claiming that they were planted by the police to create a basis for prosecution after they had beaten him up; the police insisted that they had stopped his car because it resembled one from which shots had previously been fired at policemen, and that they had found the guns after subduing Jones' assault upon them. Jones emerged with a head wound requiring stitches, which police alleged had occurred when a thrown bottle ("from somewhere") had hit Jones during their arresting process. Jones' attorney, who saw him in jail several hours after the arrest, reports that he was bloody and battered and needed hospital attention. Even the prosecutor conceded in his summation to the jury that Jones suffered some injuries, but dismissed them as occurring during the melee which followed arrest, when "all hell broke loose." In any event, Jones was finally freed on $25,000 bail pending trial for illegal possession of the guns.

Jones' defense attorney was Irvin Booker, a flamboyant Negro lawyer from Newark. His understandable request for a change of venue out of Newark was granted, but the trial was set in Morris County, a middle class suburb. To Booker's chagrin, both the prosecutor, Andrew Zazzali, and County Judge Leon Kapp followed the case to the County Courthouse in Morristown. The jury panel consisted exclusively of middle class whites, although upon exhaustion of the first group of available members, the sheriff included three Negroes among those he rounded up from the streets; all were excused, however, and the jury ultimately was composed entirely of whites.

At the trial in November, 1967, five policemen testified that they had stopped Jones' car because of the previous reports of gunfire from a similar automobile, and that he had then assaulted them. They declared that the guns, pearl-handled revolvers, had been found in the back of the bus. Other testimony identified a different car as the one from which the previous shots had been fired, so that the entire issue before the jury was that of Jones' illegal possession of the guns. (No records were produced to link the guns to Jones, but under New Jersey law the unlawful act was complete if the guns were carried in his car, with or without Jones' ownership or knowledge.) Jones' version of the facts was completely at odds with that of the police. As he told his attorney in a statement:

> After midnight on July 14th, 1967, I and my companions were driving in my station wagon, talking and listening to the radio. As we reached the corner of South Orange Avenue, which was on our direct route home, we were stopped by at least two carloads of white-helmeted police with shotguns and several detectives.
>
> We were told to come out of the car. When I opened the door and stepped down, one detective, whom I recognized as having once at-

tended Barringer High School while I was there, preached to me, screaming that "we were the bastards" who'd been shooting at them. "Yes," he
said, "a blue panel truck." (My station wagon is an olive green camper
bus.) I said that we had not been shooting at anyone. I told the officer
that I thought I remembered him from high school—whereupon he hit
me in the face and threw me up against the side of the truck. (The others
had also been taken from the truck.)

The detective then began to jab me as hard as he could with his pistol
in my stomach, asking, "Where are the guns?" I told him that there were
no guns. Suddenly it seemed that five or six officers surrounded me and
began to beat me. I was hit perhaps five times on top of my head by
night sticks, and when I fell, some of the officers went about methodically
trying to break my hands, elbows and shoulders. One officer tried to kick
me in the groin—and there were many punches thrown. As they beat me
they kept calling me "animal" and asking me,"Where are the guns?"
Inside the wagon, the beating continued. They took us from the wagon,
and as I was pushed up the stairs at Police Headquarters, an officer called
out, "Wait a minute" and then punched me in the pit of the stomach. I
fell to the ground clutching my stomach.

Inside the station, Mr. Spina (the police director) was standing behind
the desk. I asked him had he ordered me beaten. He replied, "They got
you, didn't they?"—smiling. . . .

We were then taken to City Hospital; I was dragged in and handcuffed in a wheelchair. The "doctors" put in eight or nine stitches, and
one doctor shouted at me, "You're a poet, huh? Well, you won't be
writing any poems for a long time now."

We were then taken to police headquarters on Franklin Street, fingerprinted and brought into the courtroom and arraigned. The prosecutor
asked for $25,000 bail for me, which the judge allowed. I was taken to
the Essex County jail and put into solitary confinement, where I remained until I was released. (All motions for lowering the bail were
denied.)

County Judge Kapp made his own position clear through repeated intervention in the trial. He frequently took over the questioning of witnesses
hostile to Jones, directing them to repeat damaging testimony in a loud
voice for the benefit of the jury. At the end of the trial he charged the jury
so as to leave no doubt of his belief that Jones was a liar and a scoundrel
and the arresting officers were model policemen who had simply been doing
their patriotic duty in difficult circumstances. Booker was convinced that
the Judge was prejudiced against Jones, and Negroes in general. Jones himself did nothing to ease the tension. Garbed in African robes, he ignored the
proceedings when he was not shouting at the Judge, and ultimately received
a 30-day contempt-of-court sentence. Zazzali, an Italian with long-term ties
to Newark, played the role of the abrasive, hands-in-pockets District Attor-

ney to the hilt. Between his summation and Judge Kapp's charge to the jury, little was left unsaid about Jones' guilt and responsibility for escalating the riot. The jury did not fail them, convicting all three men as charged.

But the sentencing stage of LeRoi Jones' trial is the point for which it has becoming most celebrated. The sentence was announced on January 5, 1968, in the old courthouse in Newark. Judge Kapp began his address by harking back to his days in the Navy and intoning "Now hear this . . ." in stentorian boatswain's mate style; his demeanor and tone were perceived by many of the Negroes in the packed courtroom as thoroughly racist and deliberately provocative. The two codefendants were sentenced respectively to 12 months in the county jail, six months' probation, and a fine of $500, and nine months in jail, nine months on probation, and a fine of $250. But the Judge found that Jones was not a fit subject for probation, sentencing him to 2½ to 3 years in the New Jersey State Penitentiary and a fine of $1,000—virtually the maximum possible penalty (3 years would have been maximum) and denying entitlement to probation. The basis for the Judge's action was one of a group of three poems by Jones which had been published in the *Evergreen Review* in December, 1967, between the trial and the sentencing. Kapp read the poem aloud in the courtroom, substituting the word "blank" for certain "obscenities." The poem was as follows:

Black People!
    What about that bad short you saw last week on Frelinghuysen or those stoves and refrigerators, record players, shotguns, in Sears, Bamberger's, Klein's, Hahnes', Chase, and the smaller joosh enterprises? What about that bad jewelry, on Washington Street, and those couple of shops on Springfield? You know how to get it, you can get it, no money down, no money never, money dont grow on trees no way, only whitey's got it, makes it with a machine, to control you you cant steal nothin from a white man, he's already stole it he owes you anything you want, even his life. All the stores will open if you will say the magic words. The magic words are: Up against the wall mother fucker this is a stick up! Or: Smash the window at night (these are magic actions) smash the windows daytime, anytime, together, lets smash the window drag the shit from in there. No money down. No time to pay. Just take what you want. The magic dance in the street. Run up and down Broad Street niggers, take the shit you want. Take their lives if need be, but get what you want what you need. Dance up and down the streets, turn all the music up, run through the streets with music, beautiful radios on Market Street, they are brought here especially for you. Our brothers are moving all over, smashing at jellywhite faces. We must make our own World, man, our own world, and we can not do this unless the white man is dead. Let's get together and kill him my man, lets get to gather the fruit of the sun, let's make a world we want black children to grow and learn

in do not let your children when they grow look in your face and curse
you by pitying your tomish ways.[2]

Jones contributed to the tumult in the courtroom by laughing frequently
during the Judge's rendition. Again dressed in flowing African robes, he was
the rhetorical equal of Kapp. When Kapp noted his failure to appear for
presentencing examination by the county psychiatrist, Jones filled in his
sentence ". . . who needs treatment himself." When the Judge then declared,
"You are sick and require medical attention," Jones shot back, "Not as sick
as you are!" He and Kapp then performed a duet:

". . . you are in the vanguard of a group of extreme radicals who advocate
the destruction—"

"The destruction of unrighteousness!"

"—of our democratic way of life. . . . If the philosopher can make his own
law, so can the fool."

"We see that."

"The sentence of this court, on the basis of your conviction for the unlawful possession of two revolvers . . ."

"—and two poems!"

After the sentencing, protests arose from some in the crowd, and two
people, including Jones's wife, were led out of the courtroom by bailiffs.
Booker sought mitigation of the sentence but was rejected. Jones began his
authorized statement, "You are not a righteous person, and you don't represent Almighty God. You represent a crumbling structure. . . ." According to
The New York Times, the Judge then shouted at him to sit down;
as Jones was led from the courtroom, he called back at Kapp, "The black
people will judge me!"

2. *Evergreen Review,* December 1967.

The American Way of Justice???

On Friday, May 16th at 10:30 a.m., members and friends of the Jersey City Chapter of the Black Panther Party appeared in Newark Municipal Court before the Hitler-fascist Judge James Del Mauro.

While awaiting to hear the verdict and ransom to be imposed upon Bro. Ralph (Buddha) Cobb, we had the opportunity to watch PIG JUSTICE in operation. The entire court as usual was filled with poor oppressed Black, Brown, and White people, with the Blacks being in the majority and receiving the harshest sentences and highest ransoms. Of all the cases we sat and watched appear before pig judge Del Mauro only 3 received suspended sentences, two victims were white and the other a black youth accused of taking $1.98 worth of merchandise. All others felt the whip! In many cases even those who sat in the courtroom let out sighs of surprise as they watched the many innocent victims being railroaded through "due process (PIG INJUSTICE) of the law."

At about 12:20 p.m., Bro. Ralph (Buddha) Cobb appeared before the dishonorable racist judge Del Mauro, (Bro. Cobb was still wearing the same clothing that the pigs had kidnapped him in, because each time his family attempted to bring him clothes he had been moved to a different jail.) The Star Liar took the stand and oath of hypocrisy . . . during the entire questioning his eyes were held down. All Party members and friends were shocked when we first saw the accuser. He appeared to be a cross-breed of "Stepping Fletcher," "Uncle Remus" and "Rochester" . . . Yes he was a negro, of the house nigger breed. . . . He was a plain ordinary janitor, who appeared underpaid as most working class people are . . . yet . . . this fool sat there and pointed the finger at an innocent man.

As he was questioned the contradictions in this buffoon's tales were extremely high. (1) the incident occurred Friday morning, May 9th, he went to the pig pen the same day and filed a complaint, yet he did not make a statement until Monday morning May 12th; (2) during the entire time he rode the 2 men around, the one who sat in the front seat with a shot gun and the lying nigger identified as Bro. Cobb, he only looked at approximately 2 times; (3) the 2 men identified themselves as belonging to the black Brothers and/or Black Panthers; and (4) the only thing the 2 men

From *Black Panther* newspaper, 1969. Reprinted by permission of Charles H. Garry, National Counsel Black Panther Party.

wanted who he said kidnapped him, was the telephone number and address of the rabbi, which anyone with an ounce of sense knows you should look for in the telephone book. Dishonorable judge Del Mauro sat and listened to all this bulls--t and imposed ransom on Bro. Cobb at $5,000

All of us present in pig court noticed while watching this racist corrupt appendage of injustice in session was (1) pig judge Del Mauro's total disregard for the rights of the oppressed people who appeared for the most part without lawyers. Their right to an attorney was not explained to them and (2) the hog prosecutor's attempt to deny Bro. Cobb's attorney the rights to see and challenge the statement of the crazy, funky nigger accuser, by some stupid statement about he the prosecutor would agree to allow Bro. Cobb's attorney to see the statement only if he could see any statement that Brother Cobb's attorney might have . . . By their own actions once more the pigs within the racist, capitalist judicial system have shown that this is a "GOVERNMENT OF THE PIGS, BY THE PIGS, AND FOR THE PIGS."

V THE BUREAUCRACY

OMAR GARRISON

How Private Is Our Mail?

It is shocking to the conscience to think that the Government, after an indictment is filed, may put a mail watch on the attorney for the defendant. . . .

Judge Archie O. Dawson

On February 5, 1964, as Marie Bolan was about to leave her home in Cambria Heights, New York, the mailman arrived. He was not the regular letter carrier, Charlie, but a stranger substituting for him.

As he handed Mrs. Bolan the day's mail, he asked her if she had been living very long at that address. She replied that she had. He then handed her a slip of paper saying, "I don't know what this is, but perhaps you should have it."

Mrs. Bolan, the wife of an attorney, did not know what to make of the notice handed her by the substitute mailman either. It appeared to be an official memorandum of some kind, and it was plainly marked *Confidential*. On the paper were both her name and that of her husband, together with their address, and the following statement:

"Submit all first-class mail to supervisor. Do not reveal this to addressee or other unauthorized persons."

It also said, across the top, *Indefinite until cancelled*.

Mrs. Bolan took the paper back into the house with the rest of the mail. She was certain her husband would know what it meant when he returned that evening.

It is not surprising that the Cambria Heights housewife could not identify the mysterious communication. She had in her possession a document rarely, if ever, seen outside a narrow official circle—an order to postal employees to monitor a citizen's private mail. Although thousands of such interceptions are carried out year after year, it is only by rare accident that Americans ever learn of it.

Even the power of Congress was not sufficient to pry loose information about the practice from the Post Office Department. A Senate subcommittee

From *Spy Government*, by Omar Garrison, Chapter 5, pp. 107-119. Reprinted by permission of Lyle Stuart, Inc.

looking into snooping techniques of federal agencies asked then Postmaster General John A. Gronouski for a list of persons—twenty-four thousand of them by official estimate—whose mail had been scrutinized during the past two years. Gronouski refused.

Among reasons given by the postmaster for his refusal were: (a) such disclosure would violate the civil liberties of many innocent persons; (b) it would jeopardize national security; (c) it would cripple any criminal investigations.

In reply, the committee wryly observed:

"There is no indication that you feel that the civil liberties of the same persons might have been violated by the placement of mail covers without their permission or knowledge, and without any statutory authority. You also emphasized that a large percentage of the list would consist of the names of persons 'innocent of any crimes.'"

As to the question of security, said the committee spokesman, every committee staff member had been given a full FBI investigation. Furthermore, the committee chairman intended to keep the list locked in his personal office safe when it was not being used by him or a member of the staff.

The letter also pointed out that, when a mail cover is placed on an individual on behalf of a sensitive agency, several members of the postal establishment know of the cover. These employees are not cleared for security information.

Noting that the postmaster had invited the senators to submit reports they had received of alleged abuses, the committee said, "It must have occurred to you that reports of such abuses are rare indeed. How can anyone know of an abuse when mail covers are supersecret, when no central files are kept, when most records are destroyed instantly, and when *all* records are destroyed within two years? Abuses come to light only when a postal employee makes a serious mistake."

When Mrs. Bolan gave her husband, Thomas A. Bolan, an experienced New York attorney, the notice that had been left by the substitute mailman, he instantly recognized it as an order placing a watch on the Bolans' private correspondence. The temporary letter carrier had blundered in turning it over to Mrs. Bolan.

When he explained its import, his wife was gravely concerned. After all, they were not criminals, tax evaders or fugitives from justice. Why should a mail cover be put on them?

Bolan thought he knew why. He was defense counsel for Roy Cohn, the late Senator Joe McCarthy's former investigator, then under indictment for perjury and conspiracy to obstruct justice.

Lawyer Bolan told his wife that getting possession of the mail-watch order

How Private Is Our Mail?

might mean a tremendous break for him in his defense of Cohn. He said he had heard about such mail interceptions, but had never before been in possession of documentary proof.

The evidence provided by an erring postal employee would enable him to go into court and bring the whole procedure out into the light of day.

The attorney immediately filed an affidavit with Federal Judge Archie Dawson, requesting a hearing. To the affidavit, he attached the order for the mail cover, together with a statement that he had information and believed that all mail coming into his law office was being intercepted by the government.

The U.S. attorney submitted an affidavit opposing the hearing and asserting that the federal prosecutor's office had nothing to do with placing a watch on Bolan's mail.

Later, in response to a direct query from Judge Dawson, the U.S. attorney admitted that, yes, it was he who had requested a mail watch. He then swore under oath that, when he got the information from the mail cover, he put it away in a locked file cabinet, and did not make any use of it.

After the hearing was concluded, according to Attorney Bolan, the government lawyers sent a letter to Judge Dawson, saying that he had forgotten something. "What he had forgotten," said Bolan, "was that when he got from the Post Office the names of certain banks which Mr. Gottesman (Cohn's co-defendant) had been communicating with, he immediately sent the FBI out to those banks to interview them with respect to Mr. Gottesman. So his testimony there was erroneous also."

Bolan said it was disclosed later that the U.S. attorney had not even given the postal authorities a written request for the mail cover. He had orally asked a postal inspector whom he encountered in the corridor of the U.S. courthouse to do it. It was that easy.

There was the added advantage that, if no written records existed, it would be extremely difficult for the person being spied upon to prove his case.

Chief Postal Inspector Henry B. Montague defined mail covers as the recording from a piece of mail the name and address of the sender, the place and date of postmarking, and the class of mail. The notation is made by a postal employee, but the information is then passed on to the agency or official requesting it.

Inspector Montague insisted that a mail cover is authorized only when there is good reason to believe that it may be instrumental in the solution of a crime.

The truth is, as Postmaster General Gronouski stated in his letter to the Senate committee, thousands and thousands of innocent persons are among those each year whose personal correspondence is scrutinized. In one case in Kansas City, the Internal Revenue Service even ordered a watch on the mail of a ten-year-old boy.

Information brought to light during Senate hearings indicated that mail covers could also be placed on an individual's doctor, priest, minister or attorney.

On February 26, 1965, the *Washington Post* noted that the post office department seemed to have embraced snooping as a universal policy. "Instead of hurrying domestic mail to its destination, it apparently goes sniffing about for smut and feeling envelopes for fraud, peering at postmarks and generally conducting itself like a collection of professional Peeping Toms."

There are indications that not all postal employees are enthusiastic about that kind of work. Jerome Keating, president of the National Association of Letter Carriers, said that members of his organization, when required to cooperate in conducting a mail cover, "feel sullied and besmirched by what they have to do."

Keating added that while the postal inspection service avers that letters subject to a mail check are never opened—not even "steamed open by mistake"—it would be hard to convince the average American that the professional curiosity of the postal inspector is fully appeased by merely noting the information on the outside of the envelope.

The union official said his organization regarded use of the mail cover for any purpose other than national security cases or to insure safety of the mail itself as "both reprehensible and unjustifiable."

A retired postmaster of Poplar Bluff, Missouri, recalled that during his tenure, a federal agent disguised himself in a letter carrier's uniform and went to a home, claiming he had a registered letter that required the addressee's signature. His plan was frustrated because the individual under surveillance was not at home.

Testimony of post office officials at Senate hearings in 1965 disclosed that all federal agencies, as well as any law-enforcement officer from J. Edgar Hoover to a village constable, can order a mail cover.

Various requisition forms, both printed and improvised, are used by different agencies to order a mail watch. The most commonly used, apparently, is POD Form 2008. It caries the official designation: Request For Information Concerning Mail Matter. A space is provided for the date, and one to identify the official or agency requesting the cover. The text of the requisition is worded as follows:

"For a period of ——— days, please furnish me daily on Form 2009, copies enclosed, information concerning ——— class mail received for delivery to the person(s) or addressee(s) listed below. If no mail is received, please so advise at end of period specified.

"Under no circumstances should the addressee or any unauthorized person be permitted to become aware of this action. Do not delay delivery of mail to obtain this information. Destroy this form at end of period specified. Do not retain any copies of Form 2009."

Records of the U.S. government printing office show that in the four-year period between March, 1961, and January, 1964, a total of 835,000 copies of this form were printed for the Post Office Department.

The extensive need for Form 2008, reflected in these figures, makes the official post office estimate of one thousand mail covers a month nationwide seem overly modest, even granting that several forms might be used for a single cover.

Postal authorities have said that normally mail covers are limited to no more than thirty days, and that agencies are encouraged to keep the watch to a maximum of fifteen days. They conceded, however, that it is possible to put a cover on an individual's mail for an indefinite period, as was done in the case of the Bolan cover cited earlier.

Until March, 1964, all postal inspectors (there are 1,028 of them) were permitted to authorize mail covers. But after that date, and no doubt because a Senate investigation of the practice was under way, the regulations were changed.

Today, except for requests involving fugitives from justice, that authority is limited to the chief postal inspector and inspectors in charge of the department's fifteen geographical divisions.

Although the practice of monitoring mail sent or received by citizens has been going on since 1893, postal authorities admit they have no statutory authority for doing it. It is purely an administrative procedure.

They defend the practice by citing custom and usage. Chief Postal Inspector Montague also pointed to paragraphs (1) and (5), Section 501, Title 39 of the U.S. Code as conferring upon the postmaster general authority to issue regulations permitting mail covers.

Actually, the portion of the Code recited does not refer to mail covers, even by implication. It merely empowers the postmaster general to prescribe rules and regulations he deems necessary to accomplish the objectives of Title 39, namely, "to issue regulations to implement the acts of Congress." No act of Congress ever authorized a mail watch.

The U. S. Supreme Court has never ruled upon the legality of mail covers, which many constitutional lawyers hold to be a clear violation of the Fourth Amendment.

Certainly the practice imposes a restraint on the freedom of communication, so necessary to an open society. The citizen who fears that the letter he writes to another may be examined, and the names of both sender and recipient noted down in a secret record, will be hampered in his freedom of expression. He may be afraid to write the letter at all, lest it put him under surveillance as well, or bring to his door some federal agent or law officer to question him about the addressee.

Whatever value such a practice may have as an aid to law enforcement is far outweighed by the general loss of freedom and public confidence.

No group of men in government has ever been more keenly aware of this truth than our country's first lawmakers. In 1789, members of the first Congress passed a law declaring the privacy of personal letters to be inviolate. Still smarting from the injustices that had resulted when the king of England had instructed postmasters in the American colonies to intercept and read correspondence, the founders of the new nation wanted to put an end to the reprehensible practice once for all.

Then as now, however, bureaucratic snoopers apparently regarded themselves beyond the reach of the law; or thought that their flouting the law in secret would never be discovered. Ten years after the Continental Congress had prohibited the scrutinizing of private letters, Thomas Jefferson evidently had reason to believe that his own correspondence was being opened and read. In a private letter to a friend, he wrote: "I pray you always to examine the seals of mine to you, and the strength of the impression. The suspicions against the Government on this subject are strong."

Jefferson had been accused by some of his political enemies of being a "French agent," and the mail cover was probably placed on his correspondence in the hope of uncovering information that would lead to his ruin politically.

That controversial public men, including U.S. senators, may still be subject to mail watch was revealed in the case of the late (and by many, unlamented) Senator Joe McCarthy.

In December, 1954, the Senate appointed a committee, headed by Senators Homer Ferguson of Michigan and Walter George of Georgia, to investigate the use of mail covers on Senator Joseph R. McCarthy "or any other senator."

In their subsequent report to their colleagues of the upper house, the committee disclosed that the private correspondence of McCarthy and certain of his associates had indeed been intercepted and examined.

The mail cover had been imposed, not by the executive branch of the government, but by a subcommittee of the Senate itself: the subcommittee on Privileges and Elections. This was the body which was investigating charges against Senator McCarthy that were to lead to a later vote of censure by his fellow senators.

In the course of their inquiry, the Ferguson-George investigators learned that a mail watch had been placed on all first-class mail incoming to Senator McCarthy at his home address for the period from October 24, 1952, to November 16, 1952. The post office in Washington, D.C., was asked during that period to furnish the names of addressees, the postmarks and the names and addresses of the senders, and to forward that information daily to the Hennings subcommittee, marked for the attention of Paul J. Cotter, chief counsel.

A similar cover was placed on mail addressed to 3032-24th Street N.E., residence of Miss Jean Kerr, a close friend of Senator McCarthy.

Covers were likewise imposed upon mail addressed to Donald A. Surine at 9606 Garland Avenue, Takoma Park, Maryland.

Senators Ferguson and George, obviously embarrassed at finding their own confreres engaged in such scandalous undertaking, stoutly insisted in their report that Senator Thomas C. Hennings, Jr., who chaired the group investigating McCarthy, was never aware that the mail check was put into effect.

It was initiated, they said, by Chief Counsel Cotter and carried out by staff investigators Francis X. Plant and Robert Shortley without the knowledge or consent of Senator Hennings or any other member of his committee.

Letters requesting postmasters in Washington and in Kinsington, Maryland, to place the covers had been written on Senate stationery, it was true; but both original and file copies carried a facsimile signature of Senator Hennings, made by a rubber stamp.

"Your committee is convinced," says the report, "that the representation of Senator Hennings' signature was affixed to the letters without his knowledge or consent."

As to whether mail covers had ever been maintained against other members of the Senate, the committee found it impossible to make an exhaustive or conclusive finding.

The report noted that evidential determination of such a broad question could be made only after examining the records of every post office in the nation.

The committee left little doubt, however, about their own attitude towards using mail covers to aid congressional probes: "Your committee desires in strong language to condemn the use of mail covers by a Senate committee or its staff."

The senators fully understood the implications of permitting mail interception for any purpose. They realized that if surveillance could be exercised over the correspondence of even an unpopular figure like McCarthy, it could likewise be imposed upon their own.

If they have not expressed their concern in terms of legislation that would outlaw mail checks altogether, except in cases of national security and fugitives from justice, perhaps it is because they have not been pressed to do so by their constituents.

On the other hand, as in the case of so many other government intrusions into our private affairs, the general public has remained, for the most part, unaware of the scope and nature of postal snooping. At the present time, it is doubtful that more than a small fraction of the nation's citizens have any idea what a mail cover is.

This is hardly surprising, considering the strict secrecy under which the surveillance has been carried out. Post office employees have been close-lipped (to save their jobs); and records have been destroyed. As late as April 27, 1964, a memorandum from a federal agency's division of regulatory management, addressed to its district directors, quoted the chief postal inspector as saying:

"The source of information obtained from mail covers should never be disclosed under any circumstances. I am sure that you can appreciate that a careless word or misuse of information obtained from a mail cover could prove most embarrassing."

The memorandum went on to point out that a few years previously, legislation had been introduced in Congress providing severe penalties for the supplying of information concerning mail covers to any person, including law-enforcement agents. That legislation, warned the inspector, was deferred only "with some difficulty."

About this time, the mail interceptors were also beginning to feel the heat of the Long committee's inquiry into their procedures. When brought into the arena of public hearings on the issue, postal authorities not only stoutly defended the practices, but were considerably less than candid in answering the senators' questions about the extent to which postal espionage had been pushed.

Appearing before the Long subcommittee on February 23, 1965, Chief Postal Inspector H. B. Montague piously intoned:

"The seal on a first-class piece of mail is sacred. When a person puts first-class postage on a piece of mail and seals it, he can be sure that the contents of that piece of mail are secure against illegal search and seizure. *The only time first-class mail may be opened in the postal service is when it can neither be delivered as addressed nor returned to the sender.* [Italics mine.] Then, it is treated by trusted employees in the dead letter office to determine whether it contains any information to establish ownership. A court may issue a search and seizure warrant for a particular letter or letters, but such instances are rare because of the time element involved. Mail cannot be deliberately delayed in the postal service."

Less than two months later, senate investigators had turned up irrefutable evidence, later acknowledged by the Post Office Department itself, that since as far back as 1942, post offices across the country had been turning over to the Internal Revenue Service first-class mail addressed to businesses seized for tax delinquency.

In late 1962, this practice was extended to private, nonbusiness mail.

Revenue officials opened and read the correspondence and, said Senator Long, in one instance even answered one of the intercepted letters.

In making these seizures, IRS agents were empowered by nothing more than an administrative form and the arrogance of office.

The piece of paper which IRS said it regarded as a warrant—"or equal to a warrant"—was simply a form the agency itself had dreamed up. It was not issued upon probable cause supported by oath or affirmation. It was not signed by a judge. It did not specifically describe the things to be seized; rather, it was used to lay hold of *all* mail matter meant for the addressee.

An assistant to the Post Office Department's General Counsel reported that, in a number of cases, the IRS merely wrote "a letter saying, would you please deliver, because this guy owes us some money."

That such seizures were flagrant violations of the Fourth Amendment, there can be no doubt.

As long ago as 1877, the U.S. Supreme Court made it clear (in *Ex Parte Jackson*) that mail enjoys the same constitutional protection as papers in our own homes. To search and seize first-class mail, law enforcement agents must go before a court of competent jurisdiction and obtain a warrant. Said the court:

"Letters and sealed packages of this kind in the mail are as fully guarded in examination and inspection, except as to their outward form and weight, as if they were retained by the parties forwarding them, in their own domiciles. The constitutional guarantee of the right of people to be secure in their papers against unreasonable searches and seizures extends to their papers, thus closed against inspection wherever they may be. Whilst in the mail, they can only be examined under like warrant, issued upon similar oath affirmation particularly describing the thing to be seized, as is required when papers are subjected to search in one's own household.

"No law of Congress can place in the hands of officials connected with the Postal Service any authority to invade the secrecy of letters in such sealed packages in the mail. And all regulations adopted as to mail matter of this kind must be in subordination to the great principle embodied in the fourth amendment to the Constitution."

When publicly confronted with the question of having violated the Fourth Amendment by unlawful seizure of citizens' private papers, the Post Office Department passed the buck. Their argument was that there was no opening of the mail by postal employees themselves. They had done nothing more than deliver unopened mail to the Internal Revenue Service in compliance with their levy. It was the IRS agents who had really opened the mail and confiscated its contents.

As mentioned earlier, the 89th Congress put an end to this travesty of due process by enactment of Public Law 89-44, which went into effect June 21, 1965. Section 812 of that act specifically prohibits seizure and opening of first-class mail by agents of the Internal Revenue Service, or anybody else.

The question of mail covers, however, remains unresolved. When Senator Edward V. Long announced that he might seek passage of his bill (S.973) outlawing mail covers, Internal Revenue Commissioner Sheldon S. Cohen opposed the move. Revenue agents had found the mail watch a valuable investigative technique, he said, in solving tax crimes and determining integrity.

Enactment of the bill, he asserted, would seriously hamper the Service in investigating and enforcing the criminal provisions of the federal tax laws.

Passage of the legislation would also hamper the IRS (and other agencies of the government that engage in the same practice) in their postal surveillance of thousands of innocent persons, in the hope of apprehending a few of the guilty.

STEVEN ARTHUR WALDHORN

Pathological Bureaucracies

Distorted by conflicting political pressures, allocated inadequate resources, and often operating under low visibility, public-serving bureaucracies, such as welfare, schools, police, urban renewal, and public housing, have, in case after case, adapted themselves by radically reorienting their missions. Richard Cloward and Francis Fox Piven, Professors of Social Work at Columbia University, have described how this reorientation has occurred in many welfare agencies:

> Public welfare systems are under the constant stress of conflict and opposition made only sharper by the rising costs to localities of public aid. And, to accommodate this pressure, welfare practice everywhere has become more restrictive than welfare statute; much of the time it verges on lawlessness. Thus, public welfare systems try to keep their budgets down and their rolls low by failing to inform people of the rights avail-

From a paper delivered at the 65th Annual Meeting of the American Political Science Association, September 4, 1969, New York, pp. 2-8. Reprinted by permission of the author.

able to them; by intimidating and shaming them to the degree that they are reluctant either to apply or to press claims, and by arbitrarily denying benefits to those who are eligible.[1]

So thoroughly do welfare bureaucracies adapt themselves to their hostile environment, that they end up taking punitive actions against their clients, in violation of both welfare law provisions and established Constitutional rights. A flagrant example of this was the midnight raid in which welfare authorities make unannounced inspections of welfare recipients' homes to check on their eligibility for public assistance. What this usually amounted to was a search—almost always without a warrant—of a welfare mother's home for evidence of a "man in the house" supposedly capable of supporting the family, thus rendering the woman ineligible for continued assistance. The welfare worker's demand for entry into the home was usually accompanied by the threat—explicit or implied—that a refusal to let him in would result in automatic termination of welfare benefits. As a result of recent court action this practice has now been largely curbed.

Police practices in city after city have also been revealed as often arbitrary and sometimes in clear violation of the law. Members of minority groups are almost routinely subject to unnecessary force by the police. The investigations of both the Crime Commission task force and the National Commission on Civil Disorders reported that while the extent of police brutality could not be precisely determined, it was clear that such practices did exist in many American cities. On the other hand, police protection in the ghetto is often totally inadequate. Calls for help are not promptly answered; few policemen patrol the street; and complaints are sometimes not fully investigated. Thus the poor simultaneously demand more and less police protection.

In virtually every major urban center it has also been clearly demonstrated that slum schools have replaced the ideal of educating poor children with something more akin to a custodial ethic. Teachers have low expectations for ghetto children and consequently discourage creativity and initiative. A recent study of New York City school system pointed out that even when faced with devastating educational failures, the local school bureaucracy moved only to thwart all attempts at innovation and change.

Public housing has also been pointed up as a vivid example of a pathological bureaucracy. Restrictive admission requirements keeping out potentially troublesome tenants are imposed, often arbitrarily, to shield administrators from possible criticism and to simplify their jobs, rather than to advance *bona fide* social goals of projects. Until only recently, New York City was typical in this regard:

1. "Poverty, Injustice, and the Welfare State," *The Nation*, Feb. 28, 1966.

The basis for turning down a family's application may be based on a
report of "anti-social" behavior from past landlords, neighbors, or social
agencies. Information may be received from any source without verifica-
tion. . . . No provision is made for informing the applicant of adverse
information or of the criteria used by the Authority.[2]

Evictions have often been made on similar arbitrary grounds and often for
participating in political activities such as civil rights and tenant organizing.[3]
These abuses and other general problems in project management have combined to transform public housing from a program designed to alleviate
social problems to one which has resulted in the establishment of pathological bureaucracies that often impose severe inequities on the persons they
are supposed to serve.

Pathological bureaucracies can be defined as bureaucracies which have
displaced a major part of the goals originally assigned to them by the
broader society. In their place, new purposes have been covertly adopted
which can be achieved more easily from the bureaucrats' point of view, but
which do not serve legitimate social aims. Because of the constant interplay
between organizational goals and structure, this redefinition of aims causes
a corresponding change in the internal functioning of pathological bureaucracies. These institutions often become so completely transformed that they
pursue courses of action which would not be supported even by those least
sympathetic to their social goals. The pathological nature of many public-
serving institutions must be understood in order to comprehend how dys-
functional these organizations have become, and to appreciate the potentials
and problems of intervention in them by citizens and courts.

Typically, the goals of pathological public-serving institutions are ambiguous and often look in different directions. Thus, a major underlying
premise of the urban renewal program as set forth in the Housing Act of
1949 was directed toward encouraging the rejuvenation of downtown business districts. As the Douglas Commission has pointed out, urban renewal
was seen by many of its proponents as a program quite distinct from public
housing and meant "to encourage rebuilding of slums and blighted areas
in non-housing and upper income housing uses."[4] However, other aspects
of the statute, particularly the goal of providing "a decent home and suit-

2. Michael B. Rosen, "Tenants' Rights in Public Housing," Housing for the Poor: Rights
and Remedies, Project on Social Welfare Law, New York University Law School,
Supplement No. 1 (1967), p. 168.
3. Holt v. Richmond Development and Housing Authority, 266 F. Supp. 39F (E.D.
Va., 1966).
4. Building the American City, Report of the National Commission on Urban Problems
(Washington, D.C.: U.S. Government Printing Office, 1968), 152.

able living environment for every American family"[5] and the explicit requirement that decent, safe, and sanitary homes be provided for all displacees, simultaneously directed urban renewal toward the construction of low-income housing. Local redevelopment agencies are required to fulfill detailed requirements relating to both these opposing goals. Similarly, the public housing program looks both toward providing shelter for the poor and at the same time making tenants sufficiently uncomfortable so as to penalize them for having to live in publicly-subsidized housing. While the announced goal of the public housing program is "to remedy the unsafe and unsanitary housing conditions and the acute shortage of decent, safe, and sanitary dwellings for families of low income,"[6] regulations insisted on by Congress have until recently provided that public housing must look cheap as well as be cheap, and harsh management policies, such as those cited above, have not only been allowed to continue, but encouraged.

This paradox of mixed goals is not an accident. It is a typical manifestation of the schizophrenia of liberal society, torn between the values of property and egalitarianism. Since Hobbes, there has been a tension in Western liberal thought between the conservative notion of liberty, centering on the protection of property, and the revolutionary maxim of equality, emphasizing the equal distribution of wealth. Ameliorative institutions designed to redress the balance of a competitive society, such as welfare and public housing, must necessarily be founded on compromise between these values and thus vacillate between one and the other. Commonly, institutions resolve this tension by being rhetorically committed to one set of principles and operationally to another.

Because the amounts of money provided public-serving institutions are almost invariably inadequate for them to accomplish the tasks assigned to them, these institutions are often forced to substitute less costly goals for their official ones. This occurs because decisions regarding the allocation of resources to these institutions are usually subject to the same kinds of compromises that were involved in their initial establishment. Thus, as pointed out above, public welfare departments are forced to deny assistance to many persons on arbitrary grounds simply because there is not enough money for all those persons legally eligible to receive it.

The ambiguity of goals characteristic of public-service institutions is further affected by changes which take place regarding the problems with which they must deal and in the political climate in which they must function. The failure to adapt bureaucratic programs to changing social reality

5. Sec. 2 of the Housing Act of 1949.
6. Sec. 1 of the United States Housing Act of 1937.

is often a major factor in the displacement of goals so characteristic of these institutions. The federal program of Aid for Dependent Children, for instance, was originally conceived as an honorable form of assistance to needy persons such as widowed mothers. Through time, however, the typical AFDC recipient increasingly became the minority group unwed mother. Although the original goal of the program was retained—to maintain the dignity of the poor and unfortunate—this transformation in the clientele of the program was not accompanied by corresponding changes in the way the program was administered. As it became increasingly apparent that the existing program was inadequate—and in fact detrimental—to the new clientele, the professional bureaucrats responsible for welfare not only failed to adapt themselves to the new reality but also to apprise the wider public of the growing problems. This was done both out of fear that the public would reject the reforms needed to aid the minority urban poor and that needed reforms would rob them of an institution that had become well established in the bureaucratic system.

The autonomy which bureaucracies must have in order to develop their special competences also allows them to distort their officially-assigned goals. Moreover, many public-serving institutions in American cities are not only bureaucratically autonomous but also politically unaccountable to any clearly designated constituency. As part of the general reform movement of the early 1900's, many public agencies were established apart from the mainstream of political activity and still maintain this independence even today. In addition, because the clients of these institutions are the poor, there are few outside interests concerned with maintaining the integrity of their social goals, even though there are often groups such as taxpayers which protest their rising costs. In addition, public-serving agencies have often been caught up in a romance with "scientific" principles of program operation which supposedly make it appropriate for them to operate in an atmosphere of neutrality and detachment. For all these reasons, most public-serving bureaucracies are not directly responsible to the electorate or even locally elected officials, even though their policies and action are major determinants of the allocation of resources within a locality. Redevelopment agencies, for instance, are usually governed by an independent board of commissioners, even though they may control the allocations of millions of dollars in federal subsidies coming into the city. Instead of accountability, they forge informal alliances of convenience with coalitions of real estate and banking interests. Similarly, police have traditionally been deemed to operate outside the normal political realm, although as the custodian of the state's legitimate use of force, they are clearly an integral, if not major, factor in the allocations of political resources.

Problems caused by the excessive neutrality and autonomy of these institutions are exacerbated by the low visibility of their decision-making processes. Without any formally-designated constituency to which they must answer and protected by a cloak of professional jargon and technical details, many public-serving bureaucracies have been—and continue to be—reluctant to open up their decisions to public scrutiny or tolerate the intrusion of outside participants. These problems are especially acute when low-income clients are involved. For the poor lack the informal resources available to more powerful interests in the city with which to inform and protect themselves against harmful—and often arbitrary—action.

Internal features of public-serving bureaucracies also distort their goal orientations. The penalty and reward structures in most of these bureaucracies are skewed so that they do not support the legitimate goals which the bureaucracies should seek. One cause of this is that the ambivalence in the goals of social institutions is often reflected in a division between economically-oriented, concrete factors which can be measured, such as cost per unit, tickets issued, or acres cleared, and more intangible concerns, such as human dignity, neighborhood attachments, or respect for Constitutional rights. Because decisions in our property-oriented society are often made solely on economic grounds, economic indicators have been developed more fully than social indicators, thus making property concerns more amenable to measurement than egalitarian ones. In addition, the difficulty of achieving egalitarian objectives, such as relocations, particularly with inadequate resources, encourages administrators not to measure them, but rather to define success using available—although inadequate—empirical indices. Finally, the infatuation of American society with technology rather than the quality of life leads to a greater concern for those aspects of social programs most easily associated with efficiency and computer programming, even if this results in disregarding the human needs for which the programs were initially established.

The inherent nature of rule governance in bureaucracies also works against the ability of public-serving institutions to take a creative and sensitive approach to complex social problems and thus leads them away from their intended goals. One of the most important characteristics of bureaucracy as a form of social organization is the attempt to encapsulate reality in voluminous handbooks and manuals of detailed rules. Management practices in bureaucracies typically emphasize rule-following over goal-following. The very nature of reality ensures that this will be an unsuccessful undertaking, for the swiftly changing and complex problems of the urban scene cannot be captured or dealt with in this way. The failure of administrative leadership to imbue lower echelons with the goals of the organization exacerbates this tension between rules and reality. On the one hand, when faced with non-self-applying rules, low level administrators are often incapable of fitting the rule to reality or do not know what to do with special cases for which there are no rules. In these situations, non-goal-oriented administrative discretion results in the arbitrary application of rules more on the basis of personal standards than with reference to the purpose of the rules. On the other hand, rules are often followed for their own sake, regardless of their consequences, especially when goals are only dimly understood and difficult to achieve. For example,

> A welfare worker may fear the risk of making a decision on his own; he plays it safe by observing mutely the organization's rules and policies with the result that more important treatment considerations are underplayed. This is illustrated for example, when a social worker in violation of his own judgment as to what would be beneficial to the client, recommends that a mentally disturbed child remain with his family, because the agency has a policy of not breaking up family units, even though the child's presence at home may disrupt the adjustment of the other children in the family. Instead of making procedures means to the organization's goals, he makes them ends in themselves. The policy becomes the prevailing criterion for decision, the worker bends the client's needs to fit the policy. Adherence to the organization's policy (instead of its goals) has become the organizational goal of the bureaucrat.[7]

Abuses of this nature have become a special problem when dealing with low-income clients who are often unaware of bureaucrats' discretion in applying rules and are hesitant to challenge decisions even when they feel such decisions are unjust.

Finally, the hierarchical organization of public-serving bureaucracies—made inflexible by the plethora of rules—makes it difficult, if not impossible, for clients to seek redress when they feel they have been wronged. Not only is it unclear to an aggrieved client who has responsibility for his problem, but the authority structure makes it exceedingly difficult to secure a hearing. As Jean and Edgar Cahn have pointed out:

> Most typically, (these situations) will involve relationships where the person responsible for grievance is accountable (only) to his superiors. His duties and responsibilities will not be considered as vesting a basis for formal complaint in the person injured. The chain of duty usually extends up in the line of authority leaving the "consumer" of these services in a state of helpless dependency.[8]

Perplexed by all these problems, public-serving institutions lose the ability to gather information they would need if they were seeking to realize their

7. Amitai Etzioni, *Modern Organizations*, p. 12.
8. "The War on Poverty: A Civilian Perspective," 73 *Yale Law Journal* 1317.

legitimate goals. Similarly, the technical competence which is supposed to be the cornerstone of their legitimacy erodes because they are no longer trying to perform the talks originally assigned to them. As a result of both these factors, public-serving bureaucracies which have become pathological lose any abilities they may have had to carry out their official functions.

All of these bureaucratic pathologies revolve around the central problem of displacement of goals. Institutions set up to solve various social problems have not only failed to achieve their purposes but actually exacerbated situations they were supposed to ameliorate. This has become increasingly intolerable as the rising expectations of minority groups and the poor during the 1960's and the whole thrust of community action have generated more and more strident demands for reform. Unable to achieve a national consensus for total change, these groups have adopted citizen participation and legal intervention as strategies for curbing the most blatant abuses in these institutions.

Each of these two strategies tries to commit bureaucracies to the most egalitarian and often most rhetorical parts of their recognized goals. This is, at once, the strength and weakness of each. Holding institutions to their commitments is both a way to get them to do the best possible job and to demonstrate to the wider society the inadequacy of present solutions for solving social problems. At the same time, inasmuch as society's commitment to deal with these problems is lacking, any successes these strategies win are subject to reversal in the political arena.

ADAM WALINSKY *et al.*

Excerpts from *Official Lawlessness in New York State*

... The worst single offender is the State of New York itself. The state government (with its constituent agencies and authorities) now carries out 25 percent of all contract construction in New York; and the state's commitment is rising further still, both absolutely and as a percentage of the whole. Because of the state offices at the Albany Mall (a $1 billion project), the expansion of the State University system ($3.8 billion in the next six years),

From *Official Lawlessness in New York State: Construction Employment, Government Inaction, and the $275 Million Annual Cost*, 1969, pp. 1-12. This is the first of several reports on the government of New York State sponsored by the Committee for Efficiency in Government.

and similar programs for new roads, mental health facilities, etc., New York State awarded $3.9 billion in construction contracts in the single year of 1967; actual expenditures during the last fiscal year were over $1 billion, with new additional appropriations of $1.8 billion. Yet it is precisely on these vast state projects, particularly in Albany and Buffalo, that employment discrimination—against black residents of New York, in favor of white craftsmen from other states and Canada—has been most serious. The population of Buffalo is roughly 20 percent black: blacks are 2 percent of the skilled construction labor there, and head counts have shown as little as 1 percent black labor at specific state construction sites.

This anomalous situation is directly contrary to the laws of New York State. At least five separate Departments and Agencies of the State are charged with enforcement of various laws, regulations and constitutional provisions. These are the State Division of Human Rights; the Department of Law under the Attorney General; the Department of Labor; the Industrial Commissioner; and the Office of General Services. These officials and agencies are equipped with the most complete and far-reaching laws prohibiting discrimination in employment of any state, far more rigorous than comparable Federal laws. These State laws include, among others:

The Human Rights Law, prohibiting employment discrimination, making uninhibited access to employment a civil right, and granting to the State Division of Human Rights (SDHR) the authority to hold hearings, compel testimony and the production of documents, and issue cease-and-desist orders where any unlawful practice is found.

The Labor Law, prohibiting discrimination by any labor organization, requiring that standards and procedures for all apprentice programs be fair and objective, and further making mandatory that an apprentice program be de-registered if its standards and procedures do not comply with law.

The Executive Law, giving the Attorney General the power to bring and prosecute civil actions on behalf of the Industrial Commissioner, the SDHR, or victims of discrimination in employment either individually or as groups.

Far more powerful still are the state's plenary powers over its own contracts and contracting procedures. These are the absolute power to control hiring on that one-quarter of all contract construction carried out by the State itself; and the mandatory duty, under State law, to ensure that employment on State projects is free of any taint of discrimination. As regards state contracts:

The State can void any construction contract where discriminatory practices are found:

The hiring process *must* give preference to New York State citizens, and a contract must be voided for failure to give such preference.

Every contractor and subcontractor must maintain a list of his employees, stating whether they are citizens of New York State. The Industrial Commissioner must present evidence of noncompliance or evasion to the officer, department, board, agency or authority having charge of the work; this governing body, in turn, is charged with the enforcement of the "affirmative action" clause, required in all State contracts, placing on all parties to the contract the responsibility to enforce the fair hiring provisions of State Law. . . .

Without exception, the Agencies and Departments of New York State have failed and continue to fail to enforce the mandatory provisions of State law. Despite massive and repeated evidence of discrimination in hiring in the construction trades, no agency or department of the State has taken any significant corrective action. *The State Division of Human Rights,* since acquiring in 1965 the power to initiate complaints on the basis of its own investigations and findings, has initiated only one study of the construction trades; meanwhile, it has refused to hold hearings in 92 percent of the construction industry cases brought before it. An official of the United States Equal Employment Opportunity Commission, which has referred many cases to the SDHR for action, states to us that many of the SDHR investigations were "rinky dink," with often no investigator even sent to the employer or the job site. In the single case in which the SDHR has conducted an investigation of the construction industry in an area, massive evidence was found, that discrimination exists in all trades throughout the Buffalo area in clear violation of State law. Despite this evidence the Division has initiated no action in the Buffalo area, although it did grant relief to three individuals who initiated complaints on their own behalf. The Annual Report of the SDHR predicted a "banner year" for 1969. We asked what that meant. A staff attorney at the SDHR replied that the Report was "a lot of pulp."

The State Department of Labor and the Industrial Commissioner are, if anything, less active in enforcing the law than is the SDHR. Despite his legal duty to do so, the Industrial Commissioner has not reviewed the selection standards for apprenticeship programs in the state. The Apprenticeship Bureau explains this inaction by the large load of paperwork involved. We observed, however, an occasion on which an official of the Department was playing cards with three colleagues at 3:00 P.M. of a normal workday. We were unable to ascertain whether this was a regular practice. It is a regular practice not to de-register any apprenticeship program, despite the law's command that this be done when objective standards for admission are not maintained. Both the Attorney General's Office and the SDHR have success-fully initiated at least some complaints against discriminatory apprentice-ship programs in the last few years; the findings in these proceedings con-stituted more than sufficient evidence to support de-registration. In fact, however, no apprenticeship program has ever been de-registered by the Industrial Commissioner.

Neither has the Industrial Commissioner ever enforced those sections of the Labor Law requiring contractors with the State to maintain records of their employees' citizenship. This failure alone makes the legal preference for hiring of New York citizens a nullity. No contractor with whom we spoke had ever been contacted by the Commissioner with reference to these laws; most were unaware of their existence. Furthermore, the State Department of Labor, before any alien workers may be admitted to the United States or to the State of New York, must certify to immigration authorities that their entry will not prevent the employment of any United States citizen. Yet the Department's Buffalo office, in the face of massive black unemploy-ment in Buffalo, continues to certify that Canadian workers will not displace Americans. The Albany area office claims to keep no records of any certi-fications whatever.

Worst of all, the Industrial Commissioner has acted to prevent freer access to construction employment, even when a labor union took the initia-tive in seeking it. Many union officials have stated that apprentice pro-grams are unnecessarily long (length of apprenticeship often discourages black applicants), but when Frank Schoenfeld of Painters' District Council 9 sought to shorten their apprenticeship program to 18 months the Depart-ment's Bureau of Apprenticeship Training refused to certify the proposed new program.

The Office of General Services, which is responsible for much of the State's vast construction activity, nevertheless refuses any responsibility for enforcement of the anti-discrimination clauses in its own contracts. OGS has conducted no surveys of hiring on its own projects; it has never can-celled a contract even when other agencies found conclusive evidence of discrimination. Contrary to the plain wording of statute, an OGS official told us that "OGS can't tell (the contractors) who to hire, that's their business." Yet even when contractors themselves have sought OGS assistance in open-ing up hiring on state projects—as they have at the Albany Mall—OGS, like other state agencies, has refused to act. The same is true of the State University Construction Fund.

In all these areas, there is another state official with power to act: *the Attorney General,* who is charged not only with the responsibility for the general enforcement of the Civil Rights laws, but also with the power and duty to investigate and make findings in any case affecting the "health, safety or welfare" of the people of the State of New York. As the State's lawyers, the Attorney General might be expected to remind other state officials of their legal duties. This he has not done. But neither, we add, has he been noticeably diligent about his own. The Attorney General's Civil Rights Bureau has focussed on the enforcement of a single section of the Civil Rights Law, which prohibits admission of apprentices on other than objective criteria. The Attorney General's Annual Report for 1967 states that the Bureau dealt with two cases in that year; one had begun in 1964. The second 1967 case succeeded in reducing the requirement for admission into the New York City Steamfitters' Union from three years' residency to one. The 1968 Report showed activity in two cases: one of these was the carry-forward of the second 1967 case. The second, which resulted in a conciliation order being filed in 1969, provided for the entry of two black applicants into the Westchester County Electricians' Apprenticeship Program. When we spoke to them, the Civil Rights Bureau could not think of a single complaint being issued in 1969. With regard to employment in the construction trades, the record of the Attorney General's Office was crudely, if accurately described by an attorney in the Civil Rights Bureau itself: the Office, he told us, "does (obscenity) nowadays."

The meager efforts thus far taken by the State have been in the area of apprenticeship programs: seeking (where action is taken at all) to increase the proportion of admission standards, and increasing the proportion of black and Puerto Rican apprentices. These efforts can only be described, at present, as token; where they are more substantial, credit belongs not to the state agencies, but to the unions themselves. Even if all apprenticeship programs were to be fully integrated, however, there would be little significant change in the overall employment picture. Apprenticeship programs, as the New York State Advisory Commission to the United States Civil Rights Commission says, currently "provide from one-half to one-third of the skilled workers needed simply to replace craftsmen who retire, die or leave the trade" in New York. As Secretary of Labor George Schultz has made clear, "only a minority of journeymen acquire their skills through apprenticeship." Most skills are learned and most journeymen trained on the job; most construction workers are admitted to unions on the sponsorship of a current union member. Black enrollment in present apprenticeship programs, in fact, is barely keeping pace with attrition of current black union members. That is why, in the words of one state official, what was once the "total absence of non-whites" in the construction unions, decades after the passage of elaborate Civil Rights laws, is now "near-total absence."

·   ·   ·

State inaction results in more than abstract discrimination against black workers. It costs the State of New York nearly $300 million a year. By violating its own laws and allowing—by conservative estimate—over 30,000 out-of-state workers to take construction jobs that could otherwise go to unemployed black workers in New York, the State is in effect exporting 30,000 jobs. At the same time, of course, the State must maintain the unemployed and their families on the welfare rolls. There are now 1.2 million people, 285,000 families on welfare in New York State. Most of these, of course, are families where the father has left home, often because he cannot find work, and his family cannot receive welfare if he remains. Each welfare recipient in these families—man, woman or child—costs the state over $1,000 a year. Let us assume, again very conservatively, that out of these 285,000 families 30,000 could be removed from the welfare rolls by providing the father with a job in the construction industry. *The State would be saving over $125 million a year. By not enforcing the state laws regarding employment since 1964 (when the sharp increase in State welfare rolls began), the authorities of New York State have cost the taxpayers well over $250 million. If the State authorities continue their policy of nonenforcement for the next six years, given the number of new construction jobs that will be created by presently-planned construction, the cost of the state will be well in excess of $250 million a year, $1.5 billion for the six-year period. Even a moderate effort to gradually substitute unemployed New York residents for out-of-state workers would save, over the next six years, over $800 million.*

Even these vast sums are not the full measure of the monetary loss accruing to New York by virtue of the state government's inaction. Our estimate, which we believe to be conservative, is that these out-of-state workers who leave their families at home, remit to these families over $150 million each year: a direct and substantial loss to the state's economy. As construction wages rise, this yearly loss, in the further absence of any state initiative, will continue to rise as well.

That, in brief, is a summary of our report. But no summary can do full justice to the results of our investigations. No summary can do justice to the many state officials, particularly at lower levels, whom we found impeded and frustrated in their work, unable, because of the attitudes and policies of their superiors, to enforce the laws of the state. No summary can convey the tones of bitterness and despair in which they told us of the state's non-enforcement efforts; but neither can a summary convey the eagerness with which they spoke, hoping that our report in some small way could help to reverse the state's present policy. It was not one of us, but an official of the State Division of Human Rights, who told us flatly that "nothing is being done" about employment in the construction trades. It was another SDHR official who told us that "I won't say if we're really meeting the problem because if I answered that I'd lose my job." It was no black militant, but still another official of the SDHR, who said that only the political power of the construction trade unions, or fear of it, prevented action. It was a young attorney in the office of the Attorney General who told us that nothing is being done because of "the political climate," that his superior is "a politician" and that action against discrimination would be unpopular because the electorate is composed of what he called "Procaccino's people." It was an official of the State Department of Labor who stated that the Department did not "tangle" with the labor unions because if it did "its appropriation would be cut off."

Nor can any summary do justice to the open cynicism of the responsible officials, those entrusted with the high responsibility of enforcing the laws of New York State. An executive of the State Division of Human Rights told us that discrimination in the construction industry is "not a substantial issue," that it is more important "to get construction going." An official in the Office of Anthony Adonolfi, head of the State University Construction Fund, replied to our inquiry of how many blacks were employed at the Albany Mall project with a flip suggestion that we "go out and count them." (With the help of thirty students from the Albany area, we did; and found that the Office of General Services had told us that there were three times as many as there actually were.) Finally, however, responsibility rests not even with these high officials but with the chief law enforcement officers of the state: with the Attorney General and the Governor himself. These are the men, and theirs are the policies that have doomed tens of thousands of New York residents to unemployment while the jobs that should be theirs are given to residents of other states. The consistent pattern we found: nonenforcement of state laws, disregard of powerful weapons to eliminate discrimination and half-hearted efforts in areas of little importance, these patterns lead us to conclude that not only are the highest officers of the state administration aware of the discrimination against non-whites, but that those men have made it a conscious and deliberate policy to condone and even support its continuation. These are the men, and theirs are the policies that cost the taxpayers of New York hundreds of millions of dollars each year, and if it is true, as so many of those we talked to asserted, that politics are at the heart of this situation, then these are the men who have made and benefitted from whatever political calculations have been made.

Finally, no summary can and almost no report can do justice to the full cost of these policies for New York State. Thus far, the only progress that has been made in the hiring of blacks in the construction trades has been as the result of confrontation and nearly open conflict. Not until students at the State University at Buffalo picketed the campus was construction there halted, and an effort to achieve improvement begun. Now, even as confrontation has eased, the State has begun to delay and hamstring local efforts to hire the unemployed for state-financed construction there. A high

official of the State Division of Human Rights put it to us succinctly: "The
only time the Division can act," he said, "is when pressure is brought from
outside." Thus the entire policy of the state is directed at inviting confrontation by not acting in its absence; and further, encouraging confrontation
by responding to the pressure it brings. The result is to invite in New York
and Buffalo, in Albany and elsewhere across the state precisely that kind
of racial confrontation which has so severely divided this country and this
state already. It is a prescription for disaster.

And there is, of course, something more. It is the young men, fellow New
Yorkers all, standing on street corners because there is nothing else to do:
sentenced to a life of idleness, scorned as unproductive burdens on the rest
of society. It's in the deep cynicism they must feel, as attempt after attempt
to secure useful work is denied them, as the liberal rhetoric of this progressive state is flouted time and time again by its elected public officials. A
government that practices cynicism in its public life can expect to produce
cynicism in its young. That may be the most severe statement we can make
about the policies examined in this report.

STUART S. NAGEL

The Poor, Too, Want Law and Order

It is unfortunate that cries for law and order have acquired a connotation
of suppression of Negro militancy and lessened concern for poverty and
discrimination as causes of crime in the streets. It is particularly unfortunate to imply that law and order is a goal of the middle class and an
anti-goal of the poor. The truth of the matter seems to be that the poor,
too, want law and order; but the law and orderliness they especially want
to see enforced is not necessarily the same law and order on which the
middle class places such a high priority.

In his capacity as the Director of an OEO Legal Services Program in a
middle-sized city, this writer has heard numerous complaints from the poor
with regard to how the law is administered. The poor are primarily concerned with the law as it relates to their legal rights and obligations as
tenants and arrested persons and to a lesser extent as welfare recipients,
consumers, employees, and general citizens.

From *Chicago Daily Law Bulletin*, Law Day Edition, April 26, 1968, pp. 1-11. Reprinted by permission.

As tenants they frequently complain bitterly of the lack of enforcement of housing codes and the lack of objectivity in public housing operations. Numerous studies have revealed the callousness of housing inspectors, city attorneys, and judges toward a meaningful enforcement of minimum housing standards.[1] Both the city of Champaign and the city of Urbana, for example, provide for fines of up to $200 a day for each day that each violation continues. In spite of this power, however, it seems that almost never has any fine of any amount been levied for a housing code violation in Champaign County. This cannot be interpreted to mean that there are no violations in view of the fact that approximately 60% of the houses in the Champaign urban renweal area were found to have serious housing code violations, and 30% were so bad they were beyond feasible rehabilitation.

What needs to be done within the law to get these laws enforced are such things as encouraging tenants to call the police and file criminal complaints with regard to serious housing code violations. The police should be as willing to make arrests in these cases as they are in other ordinance violations. A second powerful but seldom-used tool in the state of Illinois is the legal right of Illinois Public Aid to withhold rent from landlords who violate the housing codes. Unfortunately in Champaign County, for example, the Illinois Public Aid people are overly cautious in recognizing their obligation to help improve the housing conditions of their welfare recipients, and there has thus far been only one such rent withholding case in the almost three years that the statute has existed. A recent case in the District of Columbia[2] has now declared that housing code violations make voidable the contractual relationships between any tenant and his landlord.

As for public housing, this area of governmental activity has been far more a matter of government by subjective men than government by objective laws. It would not be hard to develop a rational published point system based on things like income, family size, and current housing for determining the order of admission of applicants to public housing subject to justifiable exceptions for extenuating circumstances. For 30 years until the last few months, nothing approaching such an objective system existed in Champaign County public housing. There was also a lack of impersonal rule-following in eviction matters to say nothing of the lack of procedural due process. In addition (contrary to the equal protection clause of the Constitution, congressional statutes, and federal regulations), three of the six public housing projects are all black and the other three are virtually all white due to discriminatory site selection and the appeasement of discriminatory attitudes held by tenant applicants.

1. E.g., Gribitz and Grad, "Housing Code Enforcement," 66 *Columbia L. Rev.* 1254, 1966.
2. *Brown v. Southall Realty Co.*, D.C. App. 238 A.2d, 1968.

As tenants, the Negro poor particularly complain about the lack of enforcement or lack of existence of open occupancy ordinances. Being confined in the Negro ghetto when one is financially able to get out, but is not racially able to do so, is certainly depressing to one's ambitions to advance himself. It also leads to an artificial housing shortage causing many Negroes to accept expensive, sub-standard housing.

Next to housing, the poor are greatly concerned with lack of lawfulness and objectivity in the administration of criminal justice. A frequently-heard complaint in Champaign County and undoubtedly elsewhere is that the setting of bail too often bears no rational relationship to the likelihood that arrested persons will fail to show up for trial. The Illinois system of allowing release on payment of ten percent of the bond has reduced the problem, but what is needed is an objective point system (like that developed by the Vera Foundation in New York City) based on items like employment, family status, length of residence, and criminal record. If the probability is high that the defendant will show up for trial, then he should be released without a cash bond no matter how poor he is. If the probability is low, then he should be detained in jail pending a speedy trial no matter how rich he is.

Right to counsel may be the most important criminal procedure right because without it the other rights are not very meaningful. Illinois wisely provides for appointing a public defender or assigned counsel to indigents where a jail sentence is possible. Unfortunately, neither the statutes nor the reported precedents provide any objective financial eligibility guidelines for determining indigency. Numerous complaints have been heard at the Champaign County Legal Services Agency that the public defender has been denied to deserving indigents and granted to undeserving non-indigents. Since Legal Services programs use financial guidelines to determine who is entitled to their free help, there is no reason why arraignment magistrates cannot do likewise with regard to the public defender.

It is particularly disturbing to hear so many complaints relating to the lack of the most elementary courtesy on the part of certain judges and certain assistant state's attorneys. Such behavior clearly brings disrespect for law and order among both the black and white poor. More well-known and more flagrant discourtesies by the police and deputy sheriffs have been documented in chapter 11 of the Kerner Commission's report although only a minority of the law enforcement personnel may be involved.

In the realm of welfare law, there is a notorious lack of objective published standards to guide the township supervisors in determining who is eligible for emergency relief. In some communities, although not so much in Champaign County, studies have revealed blatant disregard for relevant regulations, by case workers who are more interested in getting welfare recipients off the relief rolls by finding them guilty of wrongdoing than by rehabilitating them.[3] In reality, the public aid system encourages sloth or dishonesty in reporting outside income by providing for a dollar-for-dollar reduction in welfare benefits for outside earnings rather than providing for a sliding scale like $1 deducted for every $3 earned.

Consumers also complain of dishonest merchants who are not adequately pursued by the Chamber of Commerce or the state's attorney, although in a middle-sized city like Champaign, merchants operate in more of a goldfish bowl atmosphere and possibly tend to be more law-abiding than in larger cities. Potential Negro employees complain of racial discrimination by business firms and especially by unions, although better enforcement of the Illinois FEPC statute would decrease these complaints.

As general citizens the poor, both white and black, are bothered by mal-apportioned legislative districting. The 50-man Champaign County Board of Supervisors, for instance, only allocates 13 seats to the cities of Champaign, Urbana, and Rantoul in spite of the fact that those cities constitute practically all of the county's population. The city of Champaign provides no districts at all for its City Council, thereby depriving the poor white neighborhoods and the Negro ghetto from any representation on the Council. Both the poor whites and blacks also complain of their inferior school environments, but that will be partially remedied next year by a one-way busing program.

In conclusion, there is indeed a need for greater law and order, especially with regard to (1) stricter enforcement of housing ordinances and various anti-discrimination legislation and (2) more objective standards in the operations of public housing, the setting of bail, the appointing of the public defender, and the relief work of the township supervisors. The poor cannot fully respect the law if they feel that it is twisted to favor those who are not poor or who are not black. The poor, too, want law and order.

---

3. E.g., Reich, "Individual Rights and Social Welfare," 74 *Yale L. J.* 1245, 1965.

Karst *vs.* Regents of the University of California

The operative facts in this action, as the Court views the facts would not appear to be in dispute as the Regents have passed the resolutions with which plaintiffs take issue. Miss Davis has stated that she is a member of the Communist Party and the Regents have directed the President of the University to take such action as will comport with its previously announced policies.

I believe there is no triable issue of fact raised by the parties. The Regents urge the notion vigorously that the nature of the Communist Party is in issue in this case. The Court disagrees.

The nature of the beliefs and positions of the Communist Party (simple membership in which is protected by the First and probably the Fourteenth Amendment of the United States Constitution) is not litigable in the opinion of this Court. We are not concerned here with the wisdom of hiring Professor Davis but with the question of whether or not the Regents can by resolution rule out the employment of members of the Communist Party solely because of such membership. Miss Davis is not charged here with misconduct or lack of qualifications.

We believe that the question has long since been settled by the higher courts of the United States as well as the courts of California, particularly having reference to Keyishian versus The Board of Regents of New York and Elfbrandt versus Russell and Vogel against the County of Los Angeles. These are cases to which the Court has referred during argument and they hold that the University cannot deny an individual employment simply because or by virtue of membership in the Communist Party or any other party or organization, and one cannot be denied employment or penalized by criminal proceedings on the basis of membership alone.

It seems to me that the reasoning of these cases is applicable here and that they dispose of the claims and arguments made by the defendants here. I believe that the Keyishian case particularly on the facts presents almost identical problems to those presented here. The Court has not lost sight of the defendants' argument that it wishes to be permitted to introduce evidence which it states could demonstrate that membership in the Communist Party alone renders a prospective applicant for a teaching position aca-

From transcript of Judge Jerry Pacht, Superior Court of the State of California for the County of Los Angeles, 1969.

demically unqualified because of the nature of the affiliation with the Communist Party and the requirements of that affiliation which have all been urged as cogently as I think is available to counsel, and have been urged upon the Court.

The Court believes that litigating those alleged facts would place the Court in the position of determining that the Regents had a right to place a political test upon employment. We understand that the Regents contend that it is not a political test they wish to apply. The Court believes that it can only be characterized as a political test when the membership alone in a legally recognized political party is the basis for academic disqualification.

The Regents themselves have, I believe, wisely declared in their standing order number 102.1 that "no political test shall ever be considered in the appointment and promotion of any faculty member or employee." Any other approach, including the position taken by the Regents in this action, I believe would constitute the Regents as a kind of political elite empowered to decide whose views were dangerous or palatable; anathema to the concept of a free university and a free people.

The Court believes it would be both unlawful and dangerous to allow the Regents to dip political litmus paper into the volatile cauldron of political controversy in order to determine the academic qualifications of faculty members.

As counsel was arguing, I sent Mr. Phillips, our law clerk, out to get a case, a quotation from Mr. Justice Jackson in Barnett versus West Virginia in which he says "if there is any fixed star in our constellation, constitutional constellation, it is that no government official or party can prescribe what shall be orthodox in politics, religion or other matters of opinion or information which he contends by word or act to confess their faith therein, and he says elsewhere in that opinion, "compulsory unification of opinion achieves only the unanimity of the graveyard."

The courts have consistently ruled that the Constitution forbids the erection of barricades around the thought processes of citizens. The viability of our constitutional system rests upon the idea that the people must have the right and the capacity to choose between contending points of view, ideologies and systems. The United States Supreme Court has held consistently that the options of the people must be kept open and their access to the information on which they will have their choices may not be foreclosed, either by private list or by overzealous government.

The United States Constitution, this Court believes, permits neither the dictation of orthodoxy nor the suppression of unorthodoxy by the instrumentalities of the State. This proscription was directly applied to the Regents of a State University in the Keyishian case. When the New York Legislature enacted and the State Board of Regents of New York attempted to enforce a political test for University employment, the United States Supreme Court struck down that test.

We are aware that counsel argues that the situations are not analogous. We believe the distinction, if any, must be characterized as a distinction without a difference.

DAVID ROE

U.S. Agencies Violate Information Act—Nader

The private citizen gets less information than lobbyists and special interest groups from the government agencies which are supposed to protect his health and safety, consumer advocate Ralph Nader charged Tuesday.

Nader released a 20-page report at a news conference alleging violations of the 1967 Freedom of Information Act under which government agencies are supposed to disclose information, as a general rule, to everyone on an equal basis. The act also calls on them to justify withhholding any document, and provides that improper denials of information may be taken to court.

The list of alleged violations cited by Nader was the first hint of the results of his summer-long, 105-man investigation of federal regulatory agencies.

Under his guidance, a team of students, mostly graduate students in law, medicine, and science, has been concentrating on air and water pollution, food standards, highway and airline safety and occupational health and safety. It is also studying the Interstate Commerce Commission and the Washington law firm of Covington Burling.

To work for Nader, the students in Washington make do with low salaries and meager living conditions. They are receiving at most $500 for the summer.

Nader accused the Federal Highway Administration of not revealing violations of automobile safety standards although "these violations are relayed quickly to the manufacturer involved."

The Department of Agriculture refused his investigators information on the fat content of hot dogs, Nader said, although the department conducted extensive negotiations with manufacturers to ensure their approval for its proposed fat content standards.

The Nader investigation was financed by funds from the New World Foundation, the New York Foundation and the Taconic Foundation.

Nader said that despite the problems confronting his student investigators, they, along with reporters and lobbyists, were told more than individual private citizens.

Project leader James Turner cited a Food and Drug Administration document listing the cyclamate content of soft drinks whose existence the FDA denied when a Nader student requested it as a private citizen.

Turner said he watched the same officials who made the denial read figures from the list to reporters who called his office. When the student identified himself as a Nader worker the official gave him a copy of the list, Turner said.

"The most systematic close-out" of his investigators, Nader said, was attempted by the Federal Water Pollution Control Agency, an arm of the Interior Department.

Asst. Secretary of the Interior Carl Klein ordered all interviews with agency officials monitored and "repeatedly denied information by cancellation or delay of scheduled meetings," Nader said.

After three weeks, Nader said he appealed to White House Communications Director Herbert Klein and Carl Klein "withdrew his edicts promptly."

Nader said his group, known in Washington as "Nader's Raiders," had discovered that the same type of information one agency provided them was refused by another. He listed routine audits and minutes of advisory council meetings as examples.

He also accused the news media of shirking its responsibility as "prime public guardians" of freedom of information. He said the media has never taken a government agency to court for withholding information.

The Freedom of Information Act "will remain putty in the hands of narrowminded government personnel unless its provisions are given authoritative and concrete interpretation by the courts," Nader said.

Currently, he noted, the Defense Department refuses to disclose the amount of pollution its plants pour into rivers on grounds of "national security."

EDWARD F. COX, ROBERT C. FELLMUTH, AND
JOHN E. SCHULZ

The Nader Report on The Federal Trade Commission

Confidential Information

The Commission's rules specify certain rather broad categories of matters
that it deems specifically confidential. These categories are roughly those
defined as exemptions in the Freedom of Information Act. The three categories used by the FTC are trade secrets, "internal communications," and
matters under "investigation."

We found that in practice the Commission appeals broadly and woodenly
to these categories to support non-disclosure of various kinds of documentary
information, and that it uses other tactics to avoid disclosure of agency
records.

Trade Secrets

FTC policy here is illustrated by attempts made over the last few years by
Professor Kenneth Culp Davis of the University of Chicago, author of a
four-volume treatise on administrative law, to secure Commission disclosure
of samples of pre-merger clearances issued by the FTC.

Professor Davis's ordeal began in August, 1966, when he visited Chairman
Dixon and requested to examine Commission files showing clearances for
mergers. Mr. Dixon refused, suggesting a request by letter, which Professor
Davis obligingly made in November. In December, he made a revised request, limited to the files of *"the three latest cases* in which the Commission
has granted clearance for merger." On January 13, 1967, Chairman Dixon
responded, agreeing to make public only *digests* of pre-merger matters, on
the specific analogy of advisory opinions. Professor Davis wrote back immediately expressing his dissatisfaction as a scholar:

> . . . [publication of digests] does not meet my need to examine the files.
> You are quite right in saying that I want to know the law and policy of

the Commission with respect to such clearances, but such digests clearly will not suffice.

He then repeated his request, stressing the nature of his interest:

> My purpose is wholly scholarly. I have absolutely no interest in the kind of business facts a corporation wants kept confidential . . . ; such facts can be taken out of the files I examine. My lifetime project is to try to understand the administrative process. . . .

This letter was apparently ignored, and Professor Davis sent two follow-up letters in October and one in November, 1967, requesting "permission to examine Commission files showing interpretations made in pre-merger clearances during 1966 and 1967." Finally, on November 27, 1967, came the Commission's singlespaced three-page response—denying Professor Davis's request. In this letter, pre-merger clearances have been fully conceptualized as advisory opinions, and the agency goes on record as exceptionally protective of information handed over to it by parties who approach it voluntarily, thus:

> . . . parties who approach the agency in this posture [voluntarily] are entitled to an even greater degree of protection than those against whom it has been necessary to invoke mandatory procedures for no law compels them to come in and make the disclosures they make. Instead they do so of their own free will in order to avail themselves of the services which the agency affords, secure in the knowledge that the secrets which they voluntarily unfold will be held in strictest confidence by the public agency. . . .

But Commissioner Elman disagreed, convincingly, in a separate statement:

> In my view, there is no substantial interest which would be harmed by letting Professor Davis examine these materials. Professor Davis is not asking to see any correspondence or records which the Commission secured under a pledge they would be kept secret.

Professor Davis answered on November 29, 1967, citing relevant provisions of the Freedom of Information Act and commenting that he intended to bring the matter to the attention of various other governmental agencies if not satisfied with the Commission's handling of the matter. This produced a bristling Commission response dated December 15, 1967, in which Professor Davis's view of the Freedom of Information Act was hotly rejected and the following statement appeared:

In closing, the Commission wishes to add one or two other observations. While it feels that there must somewhere be an end to this dialogue, you may be assured that it is also our desire to have you work with us rather than against us and that the Commission has here evidenced a wish to cooperate with you in every way it properly can. A great number of our top level personnel has spent a great deal of time in making available to you all the information which could be released and the Commission itself has spent an unusual amount of time in considering this individual request because it considered the matter to be important and because it wished to cooperate with you in the work you are doing. But it is evident that cooperation involves considerable give and take on both sides and not the complete capitulation of one side to the other. Certainly, this Commission will not be forced into that sort of cooperation by undisguised threats that request will be made for Congressional action, which are not to be expected from one of your outstanding reputation and which the Commission cannot believe were intended in the manner stated.

Once again, Commissioner Elman disagreed, stating that he

does not regard Professor Davis's letter . . . as carrying any "threats." A citizen has the right to bring matters of public concern to the attention of interested committees of Congress. No government agency should feel threatened by such a proposed course of action.

Not yet discouraged, Professor Davis sent another letter on January 2, 1968, focusing on merger files containing no confidential information, and making a new, more limited request:

I request access to the Commission's pre-merger files to the extent of examining the names of corporations involved in applications for pre-merger clearances, and only to that extent.

The Chairman's response, January 18, 1968, was another denial, stating, among other things:

Certainly, the question of disclosure of the names of corporations involved . . . is undoubtedly the most confidential information of all and would be the very last thing the Commission would make public.

On February 20, 1968, Professor Davis wrote again, this time appealing to the whole Commission with regard to the Chairman's letter of January 18, 1968, arguing his case on the basis of the Freedom of Information Act, and requesting only "those papers in the clearance files that are not within one of the nine exemptions to the Information Act."

This approach was equally unsuccessful—on April 30, 1968, the Commission informed the professor that it had once more denied his request (Commissioner Elman dissenting), emphasizing once again the need to extend confidential treatment of voluntary submissions by businessmen.

At this point, Professor Davis gave up, at least for now, sadder but wiser about the realities of the administrative process.

JOINT ECONOMICS COMMITTEE

Economics of Military Procurement

Chairman Proxmire. Thank you very much, Mr. Fisher.

I will begin my questioning with Mr. Fitzgerald.

Air Force Directs Witness Not To Prepare Written Statement

Mr. Fitzgerald, I wrote you on October 18, and asked that you prepare a statement in advance, and that you submit 100 copies of your statement at least one day before your appearance.

You have told us this morning you did not prepare a statement for the record. Why not?

Mr. Fitzgerald. Mr. Chairman, I was directed not to prepare a statement.

Chairman Proxmire. Who told you not to prepare the statement?

Mr. Fitzgerald. Directly my immediate superior, Mr. Nielsen, the Assistant Secretary of the Air Force for Financial Management, but it is my understanding that he was, in turn, acting on the direction of our legislative liaison people. Mr. Stempler, I believe, signed the response to the letter which you wrote me.

We have with us this morning Commander Dauchess, who, I think, represents Mr. Stempler's office, and if I may, I should like to refer this question to him.

Chairman Proxmire. All right, let me ask Commander Dauchess. Commander Dauchess, who told Mr. Fitzgerald not to prepare a written statement for this committee?

Commander Dauchess. I don't know.

Chairman Proxmire. You don't know. Would it come with the authority of Secretary Morris or would Secretary Brown have anything to do with it?

Commander Dauchess. I don't know if it would come within their authority. Secretary Brown would probably be more knowledgeable.

From the Joint Economics Committee Congressional Hearings (November 1968–December 1969), pp. 199, 280–91.

Chairman Proxmire. He would be more knowledgeable. Would he take responsibility for it?

Commander Dauchess. I wouldn't know that, Mr. Chairman.

Chairman Proxmire. Well, this is very troublesome to this committee, very disturbing. We ask witnesses to appear and prepare a statement. Here is a man who is well qualified, has information of importance to the Congress, nothing classified in it. He is directed by the Air Force not to prepare a statement for the committee. We have the right to know who told him not to prepare it. Did Secretary Clifford provide instructions to muzzle this witness?

Commander Dauchess. I am not aware of any.

Chairman Proxmire. Has there been any effort by the Pentagon to restrict witnesses who appear before other committees, to your knowledge?

Commander Dauchess. No, sir; none that I know of.

Witness Free To Answer Questions

Chairman Proxmire. So far as you know, is Mr. Fitzgerald free to discuss issues before this committee if we ask him questions; provided, of course, the questions do not deal with any classified information?

Commander Dauchess. Definitely.

Chairman Proxmire. He is free to answer?

Commander Dauchess. Yes, sir.

STATEMENT OF HON. ROBERT H. CHARLES, ASSISTANT SECRETARY OF THE AIR FORCE (INSTALLATIONS AND LOGISTICS); ACCOMPANIED BY THOMAS W. NELSON, OFFICE SECRETARY OF THE AIR FORCE

Mr. Charles. After this hearing I hope you will agree with Senator Symington.

Chairman Proxmire. Well, I must say we have set up a nice adversary situation. If anybody can knock it down, I am sure you can.

Suppression of Written Testimony of A. E. Fitzgerald

Before you begin your statement though I would like to ask you a few questions concerning or surrounding, the testimony before this committee last November of Mr. A. E. Fitzgerald, an Air Force official. Mr. Fitzgerald was instructed not to provide a written statement for the subcommittee in November even though we requested one.

Did you have anything to do with the decision to instruct the witness not to give a written statement?

Mr. Charles. Not directly.

I should say this: I personally was concerned about Mr. Fitzgerald's appearance before your committee in November. This concern did not at that time pertain to any misstatement he might make concerning his own area of responsibility. My concern was this: He is not responsible for procurement nor has he so indicated. Nevertheless, when you start discussing a program like the C–5A, even though that discussion is intended to deal with those financial aspects for which he does have responsibility, the implication therefrom naturally impinge on the entire procurement process for which he does not have responsibility. The C–5A, as you well know, is a very complex matter. I feared that an isolated discussion of only one of its elements would not be placed in perspective. My fear turned out to be justified.

The public now has the impression that the C–5A is a bad program, and that the manner in which we are procuring it is equally bad. For example, the responsible *Washington Post* in an editorial on last November 17 stated, and I quote:

> The first 58 C5A Galaxy aircraft . . . may now cost $2 billion more than the original estimate. Since the original estimate was about $3 billion it makes a total of $5 billion. This $5 billion . . . for 58 airplanes.

Again, in "The Nation" of December 23 appears this statement:

> Between 1965 and 1967 Lockheed Aircraft's net income dropped 21 percent. . . . so to help Lockheed along, the company was allowed to pad its costs for building the monster freight airship, the C–5A.

Chairman Proxmire. If I can just interrupt, Mr. Charles, and you proceed in any way you want, but it might be more orderly if you understood what I am trying to get at.

What I would like to do, if possible, is to develop your thoughts and your response and the Air Force position on Mr. Fitzgerald first.

Mr. Charles. I am trying to do that.

Chairman Proxmire. Under the C–5A.

Mr. Charles. I am trying to do that.

Chairman Proxmire. Fine.

Mr. Charles. I am still quoting from this article:

> The job of padding has been so accomplished that it now appears costs will run at least 100 percent ahead of estimates—an extra $2 billion.

In assessing the merits and demerits of the C–5A program and of Total Package contracting, no one who has publicly discussed this matter so far has asked the most critical question of all; namely, "Compared to what?"

When the question "Compared to what?" is asked, then we get an entirely different conclusion.

Comparing this airplane's actual performance with the contractor's proposed performance and with his contractual commitments, both of which it is expected to exceed, the results are far better on the C–5A than any other system ever procured by the Air Force.

Comparing the C–5A cost growth—25 percent above our original estimate excluding inflation, and 10 percent including it—with the much greater increases on other systems, again the results are far better on the C–5A program; and the method of procurement used on the C–5A has effected great improvement in the cost area.

Now, the reason I was concerned, of course, is that I think the public has gotten the wrong impression, and this was my concern at the time.

Chairman Proxmire. But, Mr. Charles, what we did was to invite Mr. Fitzgerald, and we invited other representatives of the Air Force to appear.

Mr. Fitzgerald simply answered our questions and said there were overruns, and the overruns he told us about, so far as we could determine, were precisely accurate. If the public got the wrong impression, the Air Force was not only in the position at the hearings but any other time to correct that impression.

Mr. Charles. We are going to correct it today.

Chairman Proxmire. So it would seem to me Mr. Fitzgerald performed a most useful function in letting Congress know what it had every right to know. We have the responsibility for it.

Mr. Charles. I think I have the facts, and we will get over them today.

Chairman Proxmire. Do you know whether the fear Mr. Fitzgerald would tell us about C–5A overruns had anything to do with instructing him not to give a written statement?

Mr. Charles. Would you ask that question again?

Chairman Proxmire. Do you know whether the fear Mr. Fitzgerald would tell us about C–5A overruns had anything to do with instructing him not to give a written statement?

Mr. Charles. Not that I know of. As I understand it, he was to be a backup witness. Backup witnesses normally do not have statements. On the other hand, he was perfectly free to come over here, and he did.

Chairman Proxmire. We invited him to make a statement, we invited him in writing to make it. Under those circumstances when a congressional committee invites a responsible official in the Air Force to make a statement, isn't he normally permitted to do so?

Mr. Charles. I do not know whether he is normally permitted to do so or not. He did come over here and he did answer your questions.

Chairman Proxmire. Well, there was also some effort made in the Defense

Department to prevent Mr. Fitzgerald from testifying at all. Do you know anything about that, trying to prevent him from testifying at all?

Mr. Charles. No; I do not. He was to be a backup witness.

Chairman Proxmire. Was the effort made to keep him away from the committee related to the C–5A overruns or other overruns, the cost control problems?

Mr. Charles. No. As I said, my only concern was that the matter would not be presented in its entirety and, therefore, the perspective would be lost.

Civil Service Status of A. E. Fitzgerald

Chairman Proxmire. Now, this is the most puzzling and distressing case because, you know perhaps what happened. As I recall, in September Mr. Fitzgerald was given a memorandum which indicated that his position was going to be given civil service status and civil service tenure.

Then on November 13 he testified before this subcommittee, and on November 25 he was notified that this September notice was a mistake.

I discussed this with the Secretary of the Air Force not very long ago, in this year, and he indicated to me that this was a computer error.

When I related this in a statement to the press, saying how unhappy I was that there was the coincidence of a computer error—and the computer, after all, cannot sign the memorandum, cannot deliver the memorandum, it has to be done by a human being—that this coincidence, and it seems to me one in 10,000 prospect, that the computers go wrong, I hope it is not more than that or we are going to be in real danger, in view of the computer's powers in the Defense Establishment, that this should happen to one of the very rare people who come before us and tell us that there are mistakes or in this case that there was an overrun.

So I pointed this coincidence out. Then, on January 9, Secretary Brown said he was shocked at my statement, objecting to the treatment of the witness following his testimony.

As I had done earlier, I invited Secretary Brown to discuss publicly this extremely disturbing matter at today's hearings. Unfortunately, Secretary Brown has declined my invitation, although he was shocked enough to release his letter to me to the press. The shock apparently was not sufficient to bring him to this hearing to openly discuss it, and to make any comments about the actions taken against Mr. Fitzgerald after his November testimony.

Mr. Charles. I know of no action taken against him.

Chairman Proxmire. Well, the action taken against him was a memorandum indicating that he had tenure, that he was protected, that he would not be discharged from a position of this kind, that this was apparently revoked.

Mr. Charles. Mr. Chairman, no one regrets more than I the coincidence that did occur. I am not qualified to answer all of your questions on this matter, but Mr. Nelson, who is here with me, may be responsive to these questions.

Chairman Proxmire. Fine. Will you identify your position and your first name, sir?

Mr. Nelson. Yes, sir.

Mr. Chairman, Thomas W. Nelson. I work in the Office of the Secretary of the Air Force, for the Administrative Assistant to the Secretary.

My job is in the field of administration, including responsibilities in the personnel area.

What I would like to do is give you a short——

Chairman Proxmire. Do you work for John Lang?

Mr. Nelson. Yes, sir; I do.

Chairman Proxmire. Thank you.

Mr. Nelson. I would like to give you just a little chronology, if I can, of what happened and shed some light.

On the 6th—well, I should start back.

In June of last year, in Headquarters, Air Force, for the Office of the Secretary and the rest of the people in the headquarters, we placed our personnel records in a computer. Our personnel actions are now prepared by machine, so it is a thoroughly new process as little over a year old, and we do have problems with it, as in any new program. We do make errors, and we have made an error.

On the 6th of September a Standard Form 50, which is a notification——

Chairman Proxmire. You used the plural on errors. Have you made other errors?

Mr. Nelson. Yes, sir; we have.

Chairman Proxmire. With this computer?

Mr. Nelson. Yes, sir.

Chairman Proxmire. Can you tell us how many?

Mr. Nelson. Yes, sir; I can.

Chairman Proxmire. How many?

Mr. Nelson. We have 55 people in the headquarters in the excepted service, as with Mr. Fitzgerald. There were eight errors made since June of 1967.

Chairman Proxmire. How many people are affected by this computer, how many?

Mr. Nelson. Approximately 4,300.

Chairman Proxmire. 4,300?

Mr. Nelson. Yes, sir.

Chairman Proxmire. It has made—would it be an accurate statement to say that it had made 4,300, I cannot call them decisions, I do not know what you call what a computer does, 4,300 memoranda had come as a result of this computer?

Mr. Nelson. It is many more than that.

Chairman Proxmire. How many more?

Mr. Nelson. It is at least—I do not know the exact number, sir; I can provide it.

Chairman Proxmire. Would you say it is 50,000?

Mr. Nelson. Let me just do a little thinking just a minute. Perhaps I can give an estimate.

Chairman Proxmire. Sure.

Mr. Nelson. I am afraid I cannot give you—there are approximately 4,300 people, approximately 225 actions per week that come out.

Chairman Proxmire. Two hundred twenty-five actions per week over a period of what, 6 months?

Mr. Nelson. No, sir; no, sir. This is the normal production, 225 per week come out of the computer.

Chairman Proxmire. How long has this computer been in operation?

Mr. Nelson. Since June 1967, a little over a year and a half, since June 1967.

Chairman Proxmire. A year and a half?

Mr. Nelson. Yes.

Chairman Proxmire. That is 18 months times 4 times 225, and we have it; is that correct?

Mr. Nelson. That is correct.

Chairman Proxmire. I don't blame you for taking a little while to figure that out.

At any rate, it would be maybe 20,000 or 30,000. Maybe you can figure that out back there and let us know what it is, and just eight mistakes made?

Mr. Nelson. No, sir. This was for the 55 people in the excepted service, not the full 4,300. I did not make this point clear, I am sure.

Chairman Proxmire. So it has made eight mistakes on the 55 people?

Mr. Nelson. Yes, sir.

Chairman Proxmire. How about the 4,300?

Mr. Nelson. I do not have the number of errors made on that. I assume it must be proportionate. I do not know.

Chairman Proxmire. It must be proportionate.

Mr. Nelson. In the same proportion. I do not know what the situation is.

Chairman Proxmire. I should think that computer ought to be fired. [Laughter.]

Mr. Nelson. There are a great many—I think there are 90-some separate programs on the computer.

Chairman Proxmire. Were these mistakes made both in favor of the employee——

Mr. Nelson. Yes, sir. As a matter of fact, of the eight errors that I pointed out, six of them were in favor of the employees. Two of them might be——

Chairman Proxmire. Only two were against the employee?

Mr. Nelson. Yes.

Chairman Proxmire. And this was one of the two?

Mr. Nelson. Yes, sir.

Chairman Proxmire. Was the other just a matter of paying him too much, or something of that kind?

Mr. Nelson. No, none of these affected pay. This is just terminology on this document. None of them have affected pay.

Chairman Proxmire. So in a year and a half this computer made only two errors against an employee, and Mr. Fitzgerald was one of the two?

Mr. Nelson. Of the people in the excepted service.

Chairman Proxmire. Of the 55 people?

Mr. Nelson. That is correct.

Chairman Proxmire. All right. Go ahead.

Mr. Nelson. If I may go on.

This was on the 6th of September with an effective date of the 20th of September 1968.

The reason for this is Mr. Fitzgerald would have been or was on the—in this position for 3 years as of the 20th of September 1968.

This position that he occupies has existed since 1962. It has been in the excepted service, as opposed to the competitive civil service, that full time. It has never been changed. It is not being changed now. There is no intention of changing it.

Therefore, this error that was made and Mr. Fitzgerald pointed out, in essence, gave him tenure that the Air Force does not have the authority to bestow on him in the first place.

Chairman Proxmire. You have the authority if the Civil Service Commission approves.

Mr. Nelson. Yes, sir. But we have to request it from the Civil Service Commission, which we have not done.

Chairman Proxmire. So the authority depends—you have the authority to request it?

Mr. Nelson. Yes, sir; we do.

Chairman Proxmire. And it has been done in the past, that you have requested positions to be covered under civil service?

Mr. Nelson. I am sure it has been done: yes, sir.

At this point, since we did not have the authority to bestow this career status—

Chairman Proxmire. Without civil service approval.

Mr. Nelson. That is correct. Since we took no action we have still taken no action, nor is any action contemplated, it was not possible for us to give Mr. Fitzgerald what we told him we had given him on this document.

Chairman Proxmire. Well, you could have done it. He had every reason to expect that he was getting it. After all, he got this memorandum. If I received a memorandum like that I would have assumed you would have consent from the Civil Service Commission, and getting approval from the Civil Service Commission is simply notifying them with a carbon copy and if there is no adverse action on their part.

Mr. Nelson. No, sir.

Chairman Proxmire. This has to be affirmative?

Mr. Nelson. Yes, sir. It has to be published in the Federal Register before we can change a position from the excepted service to the competitive. It is quite an elaborate procedure here and quite time consuming.

Then, if I may proceed, during—since this is a new computer program, we conduct—and when I say "we" I should identify this a little closer, the clerical staff of the Headquarters, Air Force Personnel Office that services the Office of the Secretary—the clerical staff conducts a 100-percent postaudit of these actions primarily, of course, to catch mistakes. But until in this computer all the bugs are worked out of this program, it also points out where the errors are so corrective action can be taken.

Mr. Fitzgerald's conversion at the end of this 3-year period was the first of these schedule A excepted service appointments that we have had since the computer has been in operation.

What it boiled down to is we had not properly programed the computer to cover this type of an exception. As soon as it was discovered a corrected copy of this Standard Form 50, a corrected copy of this Standard Form 50 was provided Mr. Fitzgerald, and that is where the impression came—and I can understand how we would get this impression, it is two pieces of paper —naturally, the impression was created that we had given him something and taken it away.

Chairman Proxmire. Once again, perhaps I missed it, did you say why this was programed into the computer to begin with, why Fitzgerald's name got in there?

Mr. Nelson. No, I did not, sir. I can. It gets a little complicated here.

All employees, whether in the competitive service or in the excepted service, as Mr. Fitzgerald is, are in a conditional type of employment, whether it is career conditional or excepted conditional, for a 3-year period in the Air Force.

So the computer was programed for when the 3 years are up you automatically convert them into career. There are 55 people in the excepted category, most of whom had had their excepted—they had been out of the conditional status for years. This was just overlooked. It has been corrected now.

Chairman Proxmire. This means Mr. Fitzgerald's name was put in in error; that was the mistake?

Mr. Nelson. No. All the employees' names are in the computer, all the records are in the computer.

But what happened was when he had 3 years' service it automatically cut an action giving him career tenure. It should have given him tenure in the excepted service.

Chairman Proxmire. He is the only one, however, the only one who received tenure who should not have had tenure?

Mr. Nelson. That is correct.

Chairman Proxmire. That is the only time this computer has made this mistake?

Mr. Nelson. Yes, sir; that is correct.

Chairman Proxmire. Any further observations?

Mr. Nelson. There is one other thing that I should point out. On the face of the document Mr. Fitzgerald received there is a basic inconsistency between two blocks. In one place at the top of the form it says that he acquired career tenure. Then down in the center of the form it shows him being in the excepted service, which is a basic inconsistency on the form itself.

The form was in error, and it still is when you look at it. The two are inconsistent with each other. Rather than go through the rest of this, I would —I do have a statement. We have gone through some discussion, with some correspondence and Mr. Fitzgerald did visit the Civil Service Commission to discuss the case with them. I was asked to accompany him and did.

He was given an explanation by an official of the Civil Service Commission, and we have received a document which I would like to read today and have entered in the record, if I could.

Chairman Proxmire. Go right ahead.

Letter from Civil Service Commission

Mr. Nelson. Dated the 16th of January 1969, from the Honorable Robert Hampton, U.S. Civil Service Commission:

> By telephone conversation with the Administrative Assistant to Air Force Secretary this date the following statement on the case of A. Ernest Fitzgerald.
>
> Mr. A. Ernest Fitzgerald was appointed in 1965 as a GS-17, Schedule A, as Deputy for Management Systems in the Office of the Assistant Secretary of the Air Force (Financial Management). At no time has the

Commission been requested to take any action to convert this status. The Air Force does not have the authority to convert Schedule A appointment to Career Appointment or Career Conditional. Those actions can be taken only by the Commission. If queried by Congress on this subject, the above would be the response of the Civil Service Commission.

Chairman Proxmire. That completes your statement?

Mr. Nelson. Yes, sir; it does.

Further Actions Against A. E. Fitzgerald

Chairman Proxmire. Now, Mr. Charles, I would like to ask you, do you know whether any further action is planned or contemplated against Mr. Fitzgerald?

Mr. Charles. I not only know of no further action that is planned against him, I know of none that has been taken against him.

Transmittal of Fitzgerald Supplemental Testimony

Chairman Proxmire. All right.

I want to get into that in a minute. In the November hearings I asked Mr. Fitzgerald to provide us with certain cost data on the C–5A and other information. That was at the November hearing, November 13.

I received nothing from him or from the Air Force until December 24. The delay in transmitting this supplemental testimony has held up publication of the November hearings.

Can you tell us why the Fitzgerald inserts were not sent to the committee until December 24?

Mr. Charles. I am not an expert in that, but I will say this: it is my understanding that something was sent over around the latter part of December, about the 20th of December, something like that, which those who sent it over were under the impression it was in accordance with your wishes.

We understood later, I think from Mr. Fitzgerald, that more was wanted, and therefore, it was sent over several days ago.

Chairman Proxmire. It was not just more that was wanted. The Christmas Eve package that was received on December 24 was labeled, and I quote in full, "Insert for the record, testimony of A. E. Fitzgerald."

Now, do you know whether this accurately reflected Mr. Fitzgerald's testimony?

Mr. Charles. I do not.

Chairman Proxmire. Do you know the C–5A cost figures in the package had been changed from the ones submitted to this office by Mr. Fitzgerald?

Mr. Charles. I did not.

Chairman Proxmire. Well, they were.

Yesterday we received another package from the Air Force labeled, "Insert for the record, testimony of A. E. Fitzgerald."

Can you explain to the committee why it took so long to transmit these materials?

Mr. Charles. I think this is the same answer I just gave.

Chairman Proxmire. Well, what happened? All right, the explanation to our staff was that the first—when we asked them, as a matter of fact, when we got this testimony, it did not square with what we had heard from Mr. Fitzgerald. The cost figures were quite different. Mr. Fitzgerald said that that was not his testimony. So we went back to the Air Force and we asked them why they did not send us Mr. Fitzgerald's testimony, and they said, "Well, we felt that we should give you the Air Force position, total Air Force position, including what Mr. Fitzgerald thought and what we thought," and so on.

Well, this would have been useful and interesting provided it had been properly labeled, but it was labeled "Testimony of A. E. Fitzgerald." That was all we got, and it was not Mr. Fitzgerald's testimony.

The testimony we got after that was quite different, and it was Mr. Fitzgerald's testimony, and he has told us that it is.

Mr. Charles. I cannot respond to that because I am not familiar with it. If you will give me the details on the discrepancies, I can look into them and provide them for the record.

Chairman Proxmire. We will come to that.

Lang Memorandum

Before we do that, I have a memorandum for Dr. Brown dated January 6, 1969, called "Background Information Relating to Fitzgerald Case."

Now, this fascinating memorandum, what it does, it suggests what can be done to Mr. Fitzgerald, how he can be handled. It goes on to explain the civil service position. I will read part of it:

"In the civil service, all positions are either in the competitive or excepted service. The latter simply means that employees may be selected without the normal competition by examination which is required," and so forth.

It also goes into details to explain Mr. Fitzgerald's position is excepted under schedule A, and so on.

Then it says this:

"As an employee in the excepted service under schedule A, with veterans preference, Mr. Fitzgerald has certain rights, which can be grouped in two categories": And it indicates the three alternative ways in which Mr. Fitzgerald can be handled.

One is "Adverse Actions. Chapter 752 of the Federal Personnel Manual applies to discharges, suspensions, furloughs without pay, and reductions in rank or compensation taken by agencies against employees of the U.S. Government. Mr. Fitzgerald's rights are": And they are listed (a) through (f), and I will make that available for the record, and I am going to have that available to the press. I won't go into detail now in the interest of time.

"Reduction in Force." This is the second way Fitzgerald can be handled:

> In the event his job is abolished, Mr. Fitzgerald is in Tenure Group I in the Excepted Service and has the right of full application of all reduction-in-force procedures insofar as "bumping" and "retreat" rights within his competitive level grouping. However, since he is the only employee in his competitive level grouping and since he did not progress to this position from other lower grade positions, the net result is that he is in competition only with himself. He could neither "bump" nor displace anyone.

So all that has to be done is reduction in force by one, and Mr. Fitzgerald is out on that, and that might seem the best available.

Now, the third alternative which, incidentally, is not recommended by Mr. Lang, is most fascinating. Mr. Lang says in this memorandum the following:

> There is a third possibility, which could result in Mr. Fitzgerald's departure. This action is not recommended since it is rather underhanded and would probably not be approved by the Civil Service Commission, even though it is legally and procedurally possible. The Air Force could request conversion of this position to the career service, utilizing competitive procedures, and consider all the eligibles from the Executive Inventory and an outside search. Using this competitive procedure, Mr. Fitzgerald might not be selected. If not, displacement action would follow.

Now, this memorandum by John Lang, I presume, was prepared because the Air Force was contemplating disciplinary action or dismissal of Mr. Fitzgerald. Once again it seems to me this contributes, in my mind, to a conclusion that this man who testified before us, who only answered a question put to him by this committee, and who had no apparent adverse action against him until he did appear before this committee, is being disciplined; perhaps being dismissed, or they contemplate dismissing him. The Air Force does this simply because he came up here and did what public officials are told to do—and we are assured by every Cabinet officer especially the Secretary of Defense, he is going to encourage this—simply told the truth when we asked him.

Mr. Charles. I would have to disagree with your conclusion.

Chairman Proxmire. All right, sir.

(The memorandum, quoted in part above, follows:)

January 6, 1969.

Memorandum for Dr. Brown.

Subject: Background Information Relating to Fitzgerald Case.

In the Civil Service, all positions are either in the competitive or excepted service. The latter simply means that employees may be selected without the normal competition by examination which is required in the competitive service. The vast majority of positions are in the competitive service, however, there are three categories of positions excepted: Schedule A (positions other than those of a confidential or policy-determining character for which it is not practical to examine); Schedule B (The same type of positions where it is not practical to hold a *competitive* examination); and Schedule C (positions of a confidential or policy-determining character).

Mr. Fitzgerald's position is excepted under Schedule A. In the Air Force, there are several types of positions excepted under Schedule A: all attorney positions; civilian chaplain positions; part-time and intermittent positions; summer trainee positions under the Youth Opportunity Campaign; cadet hostesses, physical education and music instructors at the Academy; positions on the AF cable ship operated by the AF Communications Service; and the *specific authority which covers Mr. Fitzgerald's position;* "213.3109(a). *Office of the Secretary.* Three special assistants in the Office of the Secretary of the *Air Force.* These positions have advisory rather than operating duties except as operating or administrative responsibilities may be exercised in connection with the pilot studies." It is important to note that positions are excepted from the competitive service only after being recommended by the agency, approved by the Civil Service Commission and published in the Federal Register. The other two positions excepted by this specific authority are: Deputy for Personnel Policy, GS–17, SAFMR, occupied by James P. Goode; and Deputy for Transportation and Communications, GS–17, SAFIL, occupied by John W. Perry.

As an employee in the excepted service under Schedule A, with Veterans Preference, Mr. Fitzgerald has certain rights, which can be grouped in two categories:

(1) *Adverse Actions.* Chapter 752 of the Federal Personnel Manual applies to discharges, suspensions, furloughs without pay, and reductions in rank or compensation taken by agencies against employees of the United States Government. Mr. Fitzgerald's rights are:

(*a*) Adverse action may not be taken except for such cause as will promote the efficiency of the service;

(*b*) He must be given at least 30 full days advance written notice, identifying the specific proposed action, stating the reasons supporting the proposed action, including names, times and places;

(*c*) The notice must tell the employee that he has the right to reply both personally and in writing and to submit affidavits in support of his answer;

(*d*) Normally he must be retained in an active duty status during the notice period;

(*e*) Full consideration must be given to his reply and if the decision is to effect the action originally proposed, or some action less severe, he must be given a dated and written notice of the decision promptly after it is reached;

(*f*) The notice of decision must inform him of the effective date of the action, of his right to appeal the adverse action within the agency and to the Civil Service Commission and of the time limits and procedures for making the appeals.

(2) *Reduction in Force.* In the event his job is abolished, Mr. Fitzgerald is in Tenure Group I in the Excepted Service and has the right of full application of all reduction-in-force procedures insofar as "bumping" and "retreat" rights *within his competitive level grouping*. However, since he is the only employee in his competitive level grouping and since he did not progress to his position from other lower grade positions, the net result is that he is in competition only with himself. He could neither "bump" nor displace anyone.

These are the rights involved should charges be preferred or should his position be abolished. There is a third possibility, which could result in Mr. Fitzgerald's departure. This action is not recommended since it is rather underhanded and would probably not be approved by the Civil Service Commission, even though it is legally and procedurally possible. The Air Force could request conversion of this position to the career service, utilizing competitive procedures, and consider all the eligibles from the Executive Inventory and an outside search. Using this competitive procedure, Mr. Fitzgerald might or might not be selected. If not, displacement action would follow.

When Mr. Fitzgerald was appointed in September 1965 by Assistant Secretary Marks to fill the vacancy created by the departure of Mr. J. Ronald Fox, it was with a mutual understanding that this was to be a Schedule A appointment of *two or three years duration*. There is nothing in official records to support this understanding. Dr. Flax contacted Mr. Marks by telephone on January 2, 1969, and verified this understanding and reflected the conversation in his memorandum to the Secretary of Defense, a copy of which is attached. We have carefully screened all files and records and can find no formalized confirmation of this understanding.

If you desire additional information or more detailed specifics, I have the complete files available.

John A. Lang, Jr.,
The Administrative Assistant.

Mr. Charles. As I indicated earlier, I am not thoroughly familiar with this aspect of the case. But your reading of that simply indicates to me that Mr. Lang was outlining various things that could happen under certain conditions. It does not sound like an invitation to dismissal to me.

Chairman Proxmire. If I were working for anybody and a memorandum like this was written on how you could handle me and get rid of me, and each one of these alternative suggestions as a way of ending the career in the Air Force of Mr. Fitzgerald, I would figure that they were not exactly contemplating a promotion or giving me a medal. [Laughter.]

Mr. Charles. The wording may have been unfortunate; I do not know.

Chairman Proxmire. It sure it.

Mr. Charles. I do not know who drafted the memorandum.

Mr. Nelson. If I may answer that: this was an answer to a question, "What are Mr. Fitzgerald's rights?," and from a subordinate standpoint I can tell you if the boss wants to know what his rights are he wants to know what they are all the way across. There is nothing in that that said, does not say, nor was in intended to say, that he is going to be dismissed. It is a question of what are the alternatives that the boss is entitled to know, sir.

Chairman Proxmire. Well, all I want to say is that it is very, very difficult for Congress ever to determine whether there has been disciplinary action against people who come up here and are frank. It is very difficult for us to determine whether action is taken or not. In the 11 years I have been in the U.S. Senate, this is by far the most conspicuous example of direct retribution against a man who spoke out, and spoke the truth.

I have never seen anything as shocking as this, even though you make the defense that the language was unfortunate; or that the timing is bad; or that computers make mistakes, and so on.

It seems to me it is impossible to give a stronger case that the Air Force is disciplining a man who had the courage and the conviction to tell Congress the truth when he was asked a question.

Now, let us get into the C–5A. You have a very fine statement, and you may proceed any way you want to. This involves as you have said, a complicated and very important procurement.

It is an extremely long statement.

Mr. Charles. Yes, it is.

Chairman Proxmire. It is available to the press, I take it. We can put it in the record and you can either read the entire statement—I am willing to stay here as late as you want—or you can summarize it and then respond to questions. It is 34 pages long and that is the reason I raise that point.

Total Package Procurement

Mr. Charles. Yes.

Before I even get into the statement, let me say this: I am responsible for Total Package procurement; I am responsible for its being applied to the C–5A, and I accept that responsibility.

Now, with respect to the statement itself, it is a long statement. I can summarize it in one-third of the time it would take to read the statement.

Represenative Griffiths. Let me ask a question before you start, please, because I cannot stay that long.

May I ask you: What, in your judgment, is the effect of permitting the research and development costs to be applied against the production costs, other than fooling the Appropriations Committee?

Mr. Charles. Would you repeat that question?

Representative Griffiths. What, in your judgment, is the effect, good or bad, or the desirability of permitting research and development costs to be allocated over on the production costs?

Mr. Charles. They are not allocated to production costs.

Representative Griffiths. Well, you show me how they are not.

Mr. Charles. They simply are not.

JAMES D. BARNETT

Prosecution or Persecution?

In an address before a conference of United States district attorneys in 1940 Attorney General Jackson declared: "Nothing better can come out of this meeting of law enforcement officers than a rededication to the spirit of fair play and decency that should animate the federal prosecutor. Your positions are of such independence and importance that while you are being diligent, strict, and vigorous in law enforcement you can also afford to be just. Although the government technically loses its case, it has really won if justice has been done." And this is ancient doctrine in the courts. Thus the prosecuting attorney is said to occupy a "quasi-judicial," or "semi-judicial" position, and so is "presumed to act impartially in the interest only of justice." He is "an officer of the court, whose duty to see that the defendant in a criminal case shall have a fair trial is not less than that of the presiding judge." He is thus not, properly, an advocate of *either party* in a criminal action. Said an English court over a hundred years ago:

From the *Oregon Law Review*, Vol. 30, June 1951, pp. 322-29. Reprinted by permission. Professor Emeritus of Political Science, University of Oregon. To Professor Charles G. Howard, Editor in Chief of the REVIEW, and Mr. J. E. Bailey, Assistant University Editor, thanks are due for suggestions and corrections.

> The learned counsel for the prosecution has most accurately conceived his duty, which is to be assistant to the Court in the furtherance of justice, and not to act as counsel for any particular person or party.[1]

And American courts have been quite as emphatic.

> The United States Attorney is the representative not of an ordinary party to a controversy, but of a sovereignty whose obligation to govern impartially is as compelling as its obligation to govern at all; and whose interest, therefore, in a criminal prosecution is not that it shall win a case, but that justice shall be done. As such, he is in a peculiar and very definite sense the servant of the law, the twofold aim of which is that guilt shall not escape or innocence suffer. . . . It is as much his duty to refrain from improper methods calculated to produce a wrongful conviction as it is to use every legitimate means to bring about a just one.[2]
>
> The state's attorney is the representative of all the people, including a defendant.[3]

All this is summed up in the brief statement that "the duty of the prosecuting attorney is not to persecute but to prosecute."

And, when the defendant cannot be convicted in accordance with these just principles, "the state has no interest to have him convicted."

There have been some prosecuting attorney who have, more or less, mostly less, conformed to the ideals that courts have laid down for their conduct. But alas, generally, for the ideals! The sad truth clearly appears in this classic statement by the Supreme Court of Oregon in the case of *State* v. *Osborne:*

> It is as much the duty of prosecuting attorneys to see that a person on trial is not deprived of any of his statutory or constitutional rights as it is to prosecute him for the crime with which he may be charged, but it is a matter of common knowledge, and every practitioner at the bar will bear witness that the district attorney who fully appreciates and practices this self-evident duty is a rare exception rather than the rule. In practice he is usually as enthusiastic to add one more conviction to his string of legal conquests as the counsel for defense may be to clear his client; and equally in such instances, in the extremes followed, do we, as a rule, observe no difference between the methods adopted by the prosecution and those of counsel defending.[4]

And the reports of courts of other jurisdictions furnish abundant illustrations of the prevailing abuses. And conditions must be much worse than they

1. Regina v. Thursfield, 8 C. & P. 269, 173 Eng. Rep. 490-491 (1838).
2. Berger v. United States, 295, U.S. 78, 88 (1935).
3. People v. Sweetin, 325 Ill. 245, 156 N. E. 354, 356 (1927).
4. 54 Or. 289, 296, 103 Pac. 62, 65 (1909).

appear in the reports of the higher courts because multitudes of defendants are too poor to appeal.

The continued repetition of such abuses, in spite of much severe criticism by the courts, is due, at least to some extent, to the frequent failure of both trial and appellate courts to enforce well conformity to the ideals that they preach. Many of the judges have themselves been prosecutors, and all of them have probably been affected by the adverse environment of the courtroom.

Some of the "realists" among the judges practically repudiate the ideals. "The public prosecutor is necessarily a partisan in the case. If he were compelled to proceed with the same circumspection as the judge and jury, there would be an end to the conviction of criminals."

Under the circumstances, it is perhaps almost useless to suggest that the particular concrete rules (not here considered) developed by the courts in the application of the ideals do not, in various instances, conform to the ideals.

There are some matters that should be especially considered in this connection since they have been little discussed so far by either courts or jurists.

In the exposition of the ideals of justice, the courts have insisted, broadly, that *all* the defendant's legal rights, constitutional and other, must be protected by the prosecuting attorney. This, of course, cannot be fully accomplished unless the prosecutor's "impartiality" is extended to questions of the interpretation or the validity of the laws involved. But, apparently, this self-evident truth has not often been recognized, either in theory or in practice.

> Although this may be the law, the counsel for the people may in some cases find it consistent with his duty to argue in support of that interpretation of the law that will sustain the theory of the prosecution, regardless of how his own private judgment may be.[5]

This statement would probably better accord with practice if "almost all cases" were substituted for "some cases." Attorney General Cummings, in spite of his unusually enlightened views of the functions of his office in prosecutions, was not heretic in this particular, as appears in his statement pointing out the embarrassment that would ensue upon his rendering an opinion questioning the validity of a statute and then later defending that same statute before the courts. The incongruity apparent in the orthodox practice is well illustrated where a city attorney in Oregon, having won a decision on an important point of constitutional law in the Supreme Court, declared emphatically, out of court, that the decision was wholly wrong.

The heretical view has been followed at times by both courts and prosecutors. In a very old state case the court said:

5. McKean, *Functions of a Prosecuting Officer*, 17 Am. L. Rev. 529, 539 (1883).

> The Attorney General entertaining doubt as to the correctness of these convictions [in the lower court], if supported by the Act of '69 alone, has, with candor highly creditable to him as a public officer, signified the same to the Court, thereby strengthening the judicious arguments of the counsel for the defendants in support of this objection.[6]

And this principle has been applied by courts in some modern decisions.

> The reason given by the respondent [state's attorney] that it was contrary to his duty to challenge in any way the validity of an act of the Legislature was entirely insufficient. His oath of office requires him to support the Constitution of the state, and if an act of the Legislature violates that Constitution he is under no duty to refrain from challenging it and submitting to a court the question of its constitutionality.[7]

Moreover, in the *Lovett Case*[8] attorneys from the Department of Justice appeared in both the Court of Claims and the Supreme Court to maintain the unconstitutionality of a rider attached to an appropriation act in spite of the protest of the President and the opinion of the Attorney General that the rider was unconstitutional. Congress was represented by special counsel in both courts. The litigation had been initiated by the individuals concerned, and the Department of Justice was not involved until the question of constitutionality came before the courts. There was then a conflict between one department of the government and another. But if the precedent of the *Lovett Case* should be followed in the litigation concerned with the Internal Security Act of 1950, there will appear not only a conflict between the Department of Justice and Congress, but also a conflict of action in the department itself. Upon the advice of the Attorney General that the bill was unconstitutional, the President vetoed it; but it was repassed by Congress. The Attorney General has begun the enforcement of the act in spite of his own opinion that it is invalid. If he contests the validity of the act in the courts, as in the *Lovett Case*, the department will be in the position of attacking its own previous action in the matter.

Where the attorney general of Oregon had rendered an official opinion that a certain constitutional amendment was not self-executing, he maintained this position before the court in a proceeding instituted by an individual for a mandamus against the state officer who, in accordance with this opinion, had refused to recognize the amendment.

The apparently orthodox view is induced, probably chiefly, by the prevail-

6. State v. Sanford, 1 Nott & McC. 512 (S.C. 1819).
7. People ex. rel. Miller v. Fullenwidder, 329 Ill. 65, 160 N. E. 175, 178 (1928).
8. Lovett v. United States, 104 Ct. Cl. 557, 66 F. Supp. 142 (1945), *aff'd* United States v. Lovett, 328 U.S. 303 (1946).

ing principle that, "as a general rule, subject to certain exceptions, officers must obey a law found on the statute books until in a proper proceeding its constitutionality is judicially passed upon.[9] But there is a very great difference, in this connection, between the function of a ministerial officer and that of the (presumably) quasi-judicial prosecuting officer before a court. Surely there is no "public interest" (which it is the duty of the prosecutor to protect) in having the statutes upheld as such; the public interest would seem to require that they be upheld only so far as they conform to the provisions of the Constitution, which has been established by the public. And there is no public interest in having the constitutional law, the common law, or the statute law distorted by the prosecutor for the purpose of convicting a defendant in a particular case.

One of the most serious abuses in prosecution is involved in the multiplication of the number of prosecutors, but this has seldom aroused any discussion. Not uncommonly two or more prosecutors appear for the state (sometimes loaned from the attorney general's office to the county) when the defendant has but a single attorney to represent him; and the outrageous disparity is increased when the attorney, appointed by the court because the defendant is poor and unable to employ one, is, as is often the case, young, inexperienced, and inadequately compensated.

> Cases frequently arise where the administration of public justice requires that the state's attorney should have assistance. There are cases where the state's attorney is clearly outclassed and overmatched by counsel for the defendant. . . .[10] It might be a wrong and oppression to a defendant to permit able and experienced counsel employed by private parties to assist a competent state's attorney in a contest with inexperienced or inefficient counsel for the defense.[11]

In the latter case it is certainly *always* a wrong, whether the attorney is public or private. But the evil practice goes on with little objection by the courts. "It is the duty of the court to prevent oppression of the accused, and to permit such assistance, only, as justice and fairness may require."[12] Two to one, three to one, four to one! However, the practice is so widely spread and, apparently, so generally accepted as proper that protests even by defendants' counsel seldom appears in the reports. Of course, where the assistance of private counsel is permitted, all pretense of impartiality is abandoned.

A court has said that "the people of the state desire merely to ascertain

9. 43 Am. Jur. 79 (1942).
10. J. Rutledge, (Douglas Black, J. J. Murphy, joining), dissenting in Foster v. Illinois, 332 U.S. 134, 141, 142 (1947).
11. Hayner v. People, 213 Ill. 143, 72 N. E. 792, 794 (1904).
12. People v. Gray, 251 Ill. 431, 437, 96 N. E. 268, 271 (1911).

beyond a reasonable doubt that the accused is guilty of the crime charged, and do not countenance any unfairness upon the part of their representatives in court."[13] But what evidence is there for this bald assertion?

Abuses committed by prosecutors are doubtless at times provoked or increased partly by those committed by counsel for defense. The conduct of each tends to demoralize the conduct of the other. But the final responsibility for this situation rests upon the judges. They could change it if they would.

The unsatisfactory conditions present might, slowly, be improved if the offices of both judge and prosecutor were wholly removed from the contaminating influence of politics. "In our jurisprudence," said a justice of the Court of Appeals of Ontario,

> a criminal prosecution is not a fight between the Crown, doing all possible to secure a conviction and an individual doing all possible to prevent it, it is a solemn investigation by the state into the question whether the accused has been guilty of the offense against the state charged. It is the duty of the prosecuting counsel to bring out all the facts, as well those favoring the accused as those tending to convict him.[14]

The matter here discussed cannot be re-emphasized too often, for the benefit of the prosecutors, the judges, and the general public.

Miller v. Pate

Mr. Justice STEWART delivered the opinion of the Court.

On November 26, 1955, in Canton, Illinois, an eight-year-old girl died as the result of a brutal sexual attack. The petitioner was charged with her murder.

(1) Prior to his trial in an Illinois court, his counsel filed a motion for an order permitting a scientific inspection of the physical evidence the prosecution intended to introduce. The motion was resisted by the prosecution and denied by the court. The jury trial ended in a verdict of guilty and a

13. Lickliter v. Commonwealth, 249 Ky. 95, 60 S. W. 2d 355, 357 (1933).
14. Justice Riddell, *Criminal Law Administration in Ontario*, 23 Am Jud. Soc., J. 67, 68 (1939).

386 U. S. 1 (1967).

sentence of death. On appeal the judgment was affirmed by the Supreme Court of Illinois. On the basis of leads developed at a subsequent unsuccessful state clemency hearing, the petitioner applied to a federal district court for a writ of habeas corpus. After a hearing, the court granted the writ and ordered the petitioner's release or prompt retrial. The Court of Appeals reversed, and we granted certiorari to consider whether the trial that led to the petitioner's conviction was constitutionally valid. We have concluded that it was not.

There were no eyewitnesses to the brutal crime which the petitioner was charged with perpetrating. A vital component of the case against him was a pair of men's underwear shorts covered with large, dark, reddish-brown stains—People's Exhibit in the trial record. These shorts had been found by a Canton policeman in a place known as the Van Buren Flats three days after the murder. The Van Buren Flats were about a mile from the scene of the crime. It was prosecution's theory that the petitioner had been wearing these shorts when he committed the murder, and that he had afterwards removed and discarded them at the Van Buren Flats.

During the presentation of the prosecution's case, People's Exihibit 3 was variously described by witnesses in such terms as the "bloody shorts" and "a pair of jockey shorts stained with blood." Early in the trial the victim's mother testified that her daughter "had type 'A' positive blood." Evidence was later introduced to show that the petitioner's blood "was of group 'O.'"

Against this background the jury heard the testimony of a chemist for the State Bureau of Crime Identification. The prosecution established his qualifications as an expert, whose "duties include blood identification, grouping and typing both dry and fresh stains," and who had "made approximately one thousand blood typing analyses while at the State Bureau." His crucial testimony was as follows:

> I examined and tested "People's Exhibit 3" to determine the nature of the staining material upon it. The result of the first test was that this material upon the shorts is blood. I made a second examination which disclosed that the blood is of human origin. I made a further examination which disclosed that the blood is of group "A."

The petitioner, testifying in his own behalf, denied that he had ever owned or worn the shorts in evidence as People's Exhibit 3. He himself referred to the shorts as having "dried blood on them."

In argument to the jury the prosecutor made the most of People's Exhibit 3:

> Those shorts were found in the Van Buren Flats, with blood. What type blood? Not "O" blood as the defendant has, but "A"—type "A."

And later in his argument he said to the jury:

> And, if you will recall, it has never been contradicted the blood type of
> Janice May was blood type "A" positive. Blood type "A." Blood type "A"
> on these shorts. It wasn't "O" type as the defendant has. It is "A" type,
> what the little girl had.

Such was the state of the evidence with respect to People's Exhibit 3 as
the case went to the jury. And such was the state of the record as the judgment of conviction was reviewed by the Supreme Court of Illinois. The
"blood-stained shorts" clearly played a vital part in the case for the prosecution. They were an important link in the chain of circumstantial evidence
against the petitioner, and, in the context of the revolting crime with which
he was charged, their gruesomely emotional impact upon the jury was
incalculable.

So matters stood with respect to People's Exhibit 3, until the present
habeas corpus proceeding in the Federal District Court. In this proceeding
the state was ordered to produce the stained shorts, and they were admitted
in evidence. It was established that their appearance was the same as when
they had been introduced at the trial as People's Exhibit 3. The petitioner
was permitted to have the shorts examined by a chemical microanalyst.
What the microanalyst found cast an extraordinary new light on People's
Exhibit 3. The reddish-brown stains on the shorts were not blood, but paint.

The witness said that he had tested threads from each of the 10 reddish-
brown stained areas on the shorts, and that he had found that all of them
were incrusted with mineral pigments "which one commonly uses in the
preparation of paints." He found "no traces of human blood." The State
did not dispute this testimony, its counsel contenting himself with prevailing upon the witness to concede on cross-examination that he could not
swear that there had never been any blood on the shorts.

It was further established that counsel for the prosecution had known at
the time of the trial that the shorts were stained with paint. The prosecutor
even admitted that the Canton police had prepared a memorandum attempting to explain "how this exhibit contains all the paint on it."

(2) In argument at the close of the habeas corpus hearing counsel for the
State contended that "[e]verybody" at the trial had known that the shorts
were stained with paint. That contention is totally belied by the record.
The microanalyst correctly described the appearance of the shorts when he
said, "I assumed I was dealing . . . with a pair of shorts which was heavily
stained with blood. . . . [I]t would appear to a layman . . . that what I see
before me is a garment heavily stained with blood." The record of the
petitioner's trial reflects the prosecution's consistent and repeated misrepresentation that People's Exhibit 3 was, indeed, "a garment heavily stained

with blood." The prosecution's whole theory with respect to the exhibit depended upon that misrepresentation. For the theory was that the victim's assailant had discarded the shorts *because* they were stained with blood. A pair of paint-stained shorts, found in an abandoned building a mile away from the scene of the crime, was virtually valueless as evidence against the petitioner. The prosecution deliberately misrepresented the truth.

(3) More than 30 years ago this Court held that the Fourteenth Amendment cannot tolerate a state criminal conviction obtained by the knowing use of false evidence. Mooney v. Holohan, 294 U.S. 103, 55 S.Ct. 340, 79 L.Ed. 791. There has been no deviation from that established principle. . . .

Giles v. Maryland

Mr. Justice BRENNAN announced the judgment of the Court and an opinion in which THE CHIEF JUSTICE and Mr. Justice DOUGLAS join.

In December 1961, petitioners, who are brothers, were convicted of rape of a 16-year-old girl after trial by jury in the Circuit Court for Montgomery County, Maryland. In May 1964, petitioners brought this proceeding under Maryland's Post-Conviction Procedure Act, Md. Laws, 3 Md.Ann. Code art. 27 § 645A et seq. (1966 Supp.). Their petition alleged that the prosecution denied them due process of law in violation of the Fourteenth Amendment by suppressing evidence favorable to them, and by the knowing use of perjured testimony against them. An evidentiary hearing was had before Montgomery Circuit Judge Moorman who, in an unreported opinion, ruled that the proofs did not sustain the allegation of bad faith or knowing use of perjured testimony by the prosecution, but did establish the suppression of evidence which, although not in bad faith, constituted a denial of due process. He therefore ordered a new trial. The Court of Appeals of Maryland, sitting en banc, reversed, two judges dissenting. State v. Giles, 239 Md. 458, 212 A.2d 101. We granted certiorari. 383 U.S. 941, 86 S.Ct. 1194, 16 L.Ed.2d 205. We would vacate the judgment of the Maryland Court of Appeals and remand to that court for further proceedings.

The rape allegedly occurred about midnight, July 20, 1961, near Rocky Gorge, a swimming and fishing spot on the Patauxent River, in a secluded, wooded area of Montgomery County. The petitioners swam and fished there from early evening with Joseph Johnson and John Bowie. The prosecutrix came there by automobile shortly before midnight with her date, Stewart Foster, and two other young men. Their car ran out of gasoline near Bowie's parked car. The girl and Foster remained in the car while the other young men went for gasoline.

The girl and Foster were the State's principal witnesses. They testified that they had been sitting in the back seat of the car for some 15 minutes after the two young men left when a noise near Bowie's car attracted their attention. They saw petitioners and their companions loading something into Bowie's car. Bowie drove away and the petitioners and Johnson approached the stranded car. Foster rolled up the windows and locked the doors. The girl and Foster testified that the three demanded his money and his girl and smashed the car windows with rocks to open the car doors. Foster unlocked the door on his side and told the girl to get out. . . . The girl ran into the woods followed by John Giles who caught up with her when she tripped and fell. Petitioner James Giles and Johnson joined them a few minutes later. She testified that, when one of the trio attempted to remove her clothes, she disrobed herself below the waist and submitted to all three youths without resistance because of fear.

Both petitioners testified in their own defense. Their version of the events was that the three young men approached the car and asked Foster for a cigarette, that Foster responded with epithets and reached down as if to pick up a gun or other weapon, and that they broke the windows to prevent his getting it. They said that they did not know it was a girl who fled into the woods. Petitioner John Giles testified that when he caught up with her, she offered to submit to him if he would help her escape from the others but that he declined. Petitioner James Giles testified that when he and Johnson joined the couple, the girl told the three that she had had relations with 16 or 17 boys that week and two or three more wouldn't make any difference, that she disrobed herself and invited all three of them to have relations with her, and that he and Johnson, but not petitioner John Giles, had relations with her. Both petitioners testified that the girl said that if they were caught in the woods she would have to say she had been raped because "she was on a year's probation" and "was in trouble."

The credibility of the witnesses was thus important to the outcome of the case. The Court of Appeals recognized this in affirming the convictions on direct review: "There was some evidence tending to indicate consent on the part of the prosecuting witness, which, if believed by the trier of facts, would have been a complete defense to the charge of rape." Giles v. State, 229 Md. at 381, 183 A.2d. at 364. Credibility was also critical on the issue whether, in any event, petitioner John Giles had relations with her, as she testified, or had not, as the petitioners testified.

The evidence allegedly suppressed consisted first, of the fact that in a proceeding pending on June 20 in the Juvenile Court of Prince Georges County, a caseworker had recommended probation for the girl because she was beyond parental control. Also allegedly suppressed were the facts concerning an occurrence in Prince Georges County at a party on the night of August 26, 1961, five weeks after the alleged rape, and over three months before the trial. The girl had sexual relations with two men at the party, and later that night took an overdose of pills and was hospitalized in a psychiatric ward of Prince Georges General Hospital for nine days as an attempted suicide. She told a friend who visited her at the hospital that the two men had raped her. The friend told her parents who reported this to Montgomery County Police Lieutenant Whalen, head of the investigation for the State's Attorney into the charge against petitioners. Lieutenant Whalen advised the mother that he had no jurisdiction of Prince Georges County offenses, after which the girl's father filed a formal charge of rape against the two men with the Prince Georges County authorities. A Prince Georges County police officer, Sergeant Wheeler, interviewed the girl at the hospital. She refused to say she had been raped. She told the officer she had previously had relations with one of the men and also that in the previous two years she had had sexual relations with numerous boys and men, some of whom she did not know.

Finally, the prosecution allegedly suppressed facts concerning a hearing conducted in the Montgomery County Juvenile Court on September 5, 1961, apparently the day after the girl's release from her nine-day confinement in the psychiatric ward at Prince Georges General Hospital, and three months before the trial. The hearing resulted in the commitment of the girl to the Montrose School for Girls where she remained for some time. Lieutenant Whalen testified that he had arranged this hearing with the Montgomery County Juvenile Court authorities, although the girl was a resident of Prince Georges County. He testified that the girl's mother had complained to him that "the boys in Prince Georges County were harassing the girl, driving back and forth past the house all hours," and that he arranged the proceeding "to place the girl in some place for protective custody." The Montgomery Juvenile Court record discloses, however, that the hearing also inquired into the necessity for the girl's confinement as a juvenile "out of parental control and living in circumstances endangering her well being." The girl testified at the hearing that she had taken pills because she felt that "she wanted to die and there was nothing to live for."

The petitioners' contention was that all of this evidence tended to support their testimony and discredit that of the girl and Foster and might, therefore, have produced an acquittal or, at least, a reduction of penalty. They also argued that knowledge of it by the defense would have provided valuable leads to evidence supporting a conclusion that the girl testified falsely in denying that she consented to relations.

The petitioners were represented at the trial by appointed counsel. He testified at the post-conviction proceeding that he knew nothing before the trial of the incidents of August 26, the girl's suicide attempt, her confinement in the hospital, the psychiatrist's diagnosis of her mental illness, or of her commitment to the Montrose School for Girls. He testified that he had tried, before August 26, to interview the girl at her home but that her mother told him "she had talked to Lieutenant Whalen and he told her not to discuss the case with us." He also testified that, based on petitioners' story to him that the girl had told them she was on probation, he inquired of the Juvenile Courts of both Prince Georges County and Montgomery County whether there were any proceedings in those courts concerning the girl and was told records of such proceedings were not released.

Judge Moorman found "that the State withheld from the defense and suppressed both evidence concerning the second rape complaint of the prosecutrix and the evidence relative to her attempted suicide and emotional disturbance." He ordered a new trial, despite the absence of a pretrial request by defense counsel for disclosure of the evidence suppressed. Brady v. State of Maryland, 373 U.S. 83, 87, 83 S.Ct. 1194, 1196, 10 L.Ed.2d. 215.

The Court of Appeals read Judge Moorman's opinion to hold that nondisclosure of evidence by the prosecution denies the accused due process if the evidence could reasonably be considered admissible and useful to the defense. The Court of Appeals viewed that formulation to be incomplete, holding that "for the nondisclosure of evidence to amount to a denial of due process it must be such as is material and capable of clearing or tending to clear the accused of guilt or of substantially affecting the punishment to be imposed in addition to being such as could reasonably be considered admissible and useful to the defense." 239 Md., at 469-470, 212 A.2d. at 108. The court found the evidence allegedly suppressed did not meet that test and held that in any event "the failure of the prosecution to disclose the information relating to the alleged rape of August 26th and the subsequent suicidal attempt was not prejudicial to . . . [petitioners] and did not therefore warrant the granting of a new trial on the basis of the denial of due process." 239 Md., at 471, 212 A.2d. at 109.

The facts found by Judge Moorman do not include elements present in earlier decisions which determined that the suppression of evidence constituted the denial of due process of law. . . . Thus the case presents the broad questions whether the prosecution's constitutional duty to disclose extends to all evidence admissable and useful to the defense, and the degree of prejudice which must be shown to make necessary a new trial. We find, however, that it is unnecessary, and therefore inappropriate, to examine those questions. In Napue v. People of State of Illinois, supra, 360 U.S., at 269, 79 S.Ct., at 1177, we held that a conviction must fall under the Fourteenth Amendment when the prosecution "although not soliciting false evidence, allows it to go uncorrected when it appears," even though the testimony may be relevant only to the credibility of a witness. We now have evidence before us, which neither Judge Moorman nor the Court of Appeals considered, which in our view justifies a remand to the Court of Appeals for its consideration whether that court should order an inquiry to determine whether such a situation arose at petitioners' trial. The evidence consists of two police reports, not part of the record, which came to our attention when the State at our request supplied the material considered by the trial judge in imposing sentence.

On the morning after the alleged rape, July 21, 1961, Montgomery County Police officers, including Lieutenant Whalen and Detective Collins, conducted interviews with the girl and Foster. The interviews were written up in one of the police reports. In an effort to prove the allegations of the petition, defense counsel moved during the post-conviction proceedings that Lieutenant Whalen be directed to produce the report for inspection. The motion was denied; Judge Moorman ruled the report was a police "work product" and therefore not producible under Maryland's Rules of Civil Procedure.

There can be little doubt that the defense might have made effective use of the report at the trial or in obtaining further evidence. In the first place, the report attributes statements to the girl and Foster that appear inconsistent with their trial testimony. The report quotes both as stating they were engaged in sexual relations when they were distracted by the noise at Bowie's car, and that the girl dressed before petitioners and Johnson approached. They testified at trial, however, that they were merely "sitting" in the back seat of the car from the time their companions left until their attention was drawn to the presence of the four men at Bowie's car, and Foster buttressed this testimony on cross-examination by answering "No" to the question whether he "didn't take her out three to have sexual relations with her yourself . . . ?" Finally, neither Lieutenant Whalen nor Detective Collins mentioned, in their summaries at trial of what each person involved in the incident had told them, the fact that the girl and Foster had stated they were engaged in sexual relations when they heard the three men.

The testimony of the girl and Foster is open to the construction that these key witnesses deliberately concealed from the judge, jury, and defense counsel evidence of the girl's promiscuity. While under the law of Maryland specific acts of misconduct are inadmissible to impeach a witness' credibility, Rau v. State, 133 Md. 613, 105 A. 867, and specific acts of intercourse are inadmissible to establish the prosecutrix's consent, Humphreys v. State, 227 Md. 115, 175 A.2d 777, prior inconsistent statements and evidence of general reputation for unchastity are admissible to impeach a witness' credibility, Giles v. State, 229 Md. 370, 183 A.2d 359. And to the extent credibility could have been effectively attacked in this case, resolution of the issue of consent necessarily would have been affected since it turned wholly on credibility.

The report could also have been used in connection with an issue which has been in this case from its inception. At the original trial, counsel sought in numerous ways to establish that John Giles had not had intercourse with the victim. At the trial the girl said all three had raped her. She admitted, however, that she had testified at the preliminary hearing and had told the police immediately after being attacked that only two of the three had intercourse with her. Detective Collins testified, on the other hand, that he "questioned the girl at the station and she said all three of the boys had intercourse with her." With specific reference to John Giles, Collins stated that the girl "was asked if she knew anybody in this line-up and she walked over and pointed to the defendant, John Giles, and stated to us, in his presence, that he was the first . . . that had intercourse with her. . . ." Lieutenant Whalen, too, denied that the girl had told him "that only two of these boys had intercourse with her on that evening. . . ."

Counsel at the post-conviction proceedings continued to attempt to prove John Giles was innocent of rape. He introduced newspaper articles from the Washington Evening Star and the Washington Post attributing to Lieutenant Whalen a story that the girl had said only two men had raped her. When Whalen said these stories were incorrect, counsel asked: "would your interview report of this interview show what . . . [she] said about the number of men who had attacked her?" Whalen answered that it would. Counsel thereupon moved for the production of the report, but the court refused to allow him to see it because of the work-product rule. Counsel also asked the girl how many men she originally claimed had raped her and, unlike her testimony at trial, she said she had told the police all three had raped her.

In contrast to much of this testimony the police report states that, both when interviewed and at a police line-up later that day, the girl had identified petitioner John Giles not as the first to have intercourse with her, as Detective Collins testified, but as "the one that tried to have intercourse with her but was unable to do so," "the man that tried to rape her. . . ." The contents of the report thus go, not only to the credibility of the State's witnesses, but also to the issue at trial whether John Giles had raped the girl.

Yet nothing appears in the trial transcript to show what, if any, action was taken by the prosecution to correct or explain the inconsistencies between the testimony of the state witnesses and the report.

Only the most strained reading of the materials before us can explain away the questions raised by the report without the aid of further inquiry.

JUDGE GEORGE CROCKETT

Statement

The distortions of fact and the confusion over this Court's actions in the recent events at New Bethel Church compel me to make certain facts clear. I am personally deeply affronted by reports and stories which have clearly and deliberately twisted the truth and the law in this matter.

More serious than any harm to me personally is the profound damage being done to this Court and to our entire community by those who would use this tragic affair to intensify community hostilities which are already so deep and divisive.

The actions taken by me in my capacity as presiding judge, following the New Bethel Church shootings and the mass arrests, were legal, proper and moral. Indeed, it is precisely because I followed the law, equally and without partiality, that questions and accusations are being raised. If I were to have reacted otherwise, if I were to have ignored my judicial and constitutional responsibilities and followed the often accepted practices of condoning long police detentions, of ignoring prisoners' rights to counsel and of delaying the hearing on writs of habeas corpus, possibly the adverse publicity about Judge Crockett may have been averted. But in doing so, justice would have been denied.

I deplore the senseless shooting of the policemen. I also deplore the armed assault on a church, particularly a church occupied by men, women and children, whom we must presume to be innocent until and unless evidence to the contrary is presented. I deplore, too, that so many innocent people were rounded up by the police, incarcerated for many hours in violation of their rights as citizens, and that some officials who are sworn to enforce equal justice have complained because I have done so.

From a press conference held in Recorder's Court, March 29-April 3, 1969, Detroit, Michigan. Excerpts of this statement have also appeared in *Judicature*, Vol. 53, No. 9, April-May 1969. Reprinted by permission of Judge Crockett.

Michigan law requires—does not suggest, but requires—that "any judge who willfully or corruptly refuses to consider an application action, or motion for habeas corpus, is guilty of malfeasance in office."

Moreover, "any justice of the Supreme Court and any judge of a Circuit Court may issue a writ of habeas corpus . . . upon his own motion whenever he learns that any person within his jurisdiction is illegally restrained of his liberty." By statute, Circuit Court, as used in this rule, includes Recorder's Court.

Justice last Sunday demanded a prompt judicial examination and processing of the persons arrested. If there was any sound legal basis for their detention, they were detained; otherwise they were entitled to be released and they were released upon reasonable bond.

Let us review the sequence of events following the shooting of the officers and the storming of the church by police, which occurred some time before midnight Saturday.

At 5 a.m. I was called—not by the police but by Representative Del Rio and Reverend C. L. Franklin, the church's pastor, who came to my home and wakened me. As presiding judge of this Court for the day, I went immediately to the police station. I requested a list of the prisoners and was told—about six hours after they were taken into custody—that police didn't know whom they were holding.

I then talked with Commissioner Spreen who agreed to furnish a list. He also agreed to set up a courtroom on the first floor of the police station. I requested that the Prosecutor be called, and Assistant Prosecutor Jay Nolan arrived. The press was present. Mr. Nolan, the police and I agreed on the processing of the prisoners. They were to be brought immediately outside the temporary courtroom in groups of 10, beginning with the women. But they appeared before me individually and each was interviewed separately by me in open court.

The cases of 39 arrestees were then heard and determined as follows:

15 Detroit residents were released on $100 personal bond to reappear at noon.

1 man (the church janitor) was discharged with consent of the Prosecutor.

1 man from Ohio was released on $100 personal bond and ordered to reappear at noon.

22 persons from out-of-town were remanded to custody until noon. All persons released on personal bond appeared at noon as directed.

Further hearings were terminated by the entrance of the Wayne County Prosecutor who, in the presence of the Court, issued verbal orders to the police countermanding a court order. The Prosecutor, in the presence of the

Court, prevented the police from producing any further arrestees for the hearing.

I have condemned the Prosecutor's action as not only contemptuous, but also as having racial overtones.

Subsequently, in a letter to presiding Judge Robert E. DeMascio dated April 1, I declined to press the formal contempt charge. To pursue the contempt proceeding, I felt, would aggravate the already tense community confrontation.

Moreover, the Prosecutor himself, after the contempt incident, and before the Court reconvened at noon and after the Court reconvened, himself released or requested the release of some 130 arrestees.

It is essential to emphasize that the vast majority of those released, approximately 130 persons, were released with the Prosecutor's concurrence. Despite this fact, the press has several times referred to my actions in terms of "unwarranted leniency." There was no unwarranted leniency.

By noon, the number of prisoners whose disposition was under question had been reduced sharply. Out of approximately 142 persons arrested, only 12 remained to be processed. Two of these prisoners I ordered held without bond because there was evidence to do so. Another I released on $1,000 bond after his attorney said he would vouch for him.

The other 9 prisoners were those who, police said, had positive nitrate tests. On this question, I hold that such tests are unconstitutional when taken without the presence of counsel or at least upon advice to the prisoner that he is entitled to counsel at this critical step in his interrogation. For me to have held those nine men, without objective evidence and under those circumstances, would have been improper. The police had many hours to identify those nine men. They should know who they are. If those men committed a crime, the police must gather evidence to make a case that will hold up in court. They still can do so if their investigation warrants it.

I am most anxious that criminals be apprehended, tried and brought to justice. But I will not lend my office to practices which subvert legal processes and deny justice to some because they are poor or black.

I understand, of course, why the hue and cry arose. An angry Prosecutor, lacking police evidence or testimony which might produce a probable suspect, and resentful that ordinary and undemocratic police practices were challenged, chose to divert public attention to Judge Crockett. And some of the media, particularly the Detroit News, picked up that lead and began their campaign to help the police and the Prosecutor's office continue their efforts to dominate and control the courts and legal processes. The judiciary cannot allow its independence to be threatened in this fashion.

Finally, and regretfully, let me repeat that this whole case does have racial overtones.

Can any of you imagine the Detroit Police invading an all-white church and rounding up everyone in sight to be bussed to a wholesale lockup in a police garage? Can any of you imagine a church group from, let us say, Rosedale Park, being held incommunicado for seven hours, without being allowed to telephone relatives and without their constitutional rights to counsel? Can any of you justify the jailing of 32 women all night long when there was admittedly not the slightest evidence of their involvement in any crime? Can anyone explain in other than racist terms the shooting by police into a closed and surrounded church?

If the killing had occurred in a white neighborhood, I believe the sequence of events would have been far different. Because a terrible crime was committed, it does not follow that other wrongs be permitted or condoned. Indeed, constitutional safeguards are needed even more urgently in times of tension than in ordinary times.

The best guarantee to avert the kind of social disaster that occurred in Detroit in 1967 is prompt judicial action with strict observance of constitutional rights.

I intend to continue to maintain law and order in my court by dispensing justice equally and fairly, by protecting each individual's rights, and most importantly, by upholding the independence of the judiciary and the dignity of this court.

If the real dangers to our community are to be uprooted, let the news media and all other forces of truth and justice concentrate on the underlying causes of crime and social disorder as described by the Kerner Commission and as identified by virtually every responsible commentator in America. The causes are steeped in racism . . . racism in our courts, in our jails, in our streets and in our hearts.

EDWARD RANZAL

U.S. Judge Scores Draft Unit Again: Accuses Mt. Vernon Board of "Lawless Acts"

For the second time in six weeks, a Federal judge severely criticized a Mount Vernon, N. Y., draft board yesterday for what he called "blatantly lawless" acts.

Six weeks ago, Judge Lloyd F. MacMahon ordered the board to drop an induction order and grant a deferment to Thomas J. Walsh, a 24-year-old University of Bridgeport student from Eastchester.

At the time, Judge MacMahon denounced what he described as the board's high-handed and erroneous handling of Mr. Walsh's application for a student deferment.

The draft board had originally reclassified the student because he had fallen behind in his classwork.

Judge MacMahon said the board reluctantly followed his edict and granted Mr. Walsh a student deferment, but reclassified the student retroactively for one year beginning Sept. 23, 1968. The effect of the board's action was to make Mr. Walsh liable for induction as of last Sept. 23.

"This retroactive reclassification," Judge MacMahon said, "occurred during the period of time our decision had allowed for submission of proposed judgments, and, therefore, the determination of its validity is properly within our jurisdiction."

Judge MacMahon ruled that retroactive reclassification is "wholly unauthorized either by statute or regulation." He said that every registrant must be classified in one of the 18 classifications based on the facts existing at the time of classification.

The judge said it appeared that the board was trying to circumvent his decision, "but worse, to accelerate petitioner's eventual induction without due process, as punishment for his temerity in resorting to the courts for vindication and protection of his legal rights."

"We find," he said, "that the draft board's totally unauthorized action is 'blatantly lawless' and prejudices petitioner because it denied him the right to a 1-S (C) classification for the upcoming year."

Judge MacMahon permanently enjoined the board from inducting Mr. Walsh under its June 10, 1969, order and invalidated the board's retroactive reclassification of Mr. Walsh.

The Sparling Report: *Dissent in a Free Society*

NEGOTIATIONS

1. *Coalition for an Open Convention*

The Coalition for an Open Convention proclaims its slogan on its leaderhead, quoting Emerson: "If a single man plant himself on his convictions and there abide, the huge world will come round to him." But "convictions" were not enough to overcome the position of the city.

During negotiations for permits to use Chicago Park District facilities, COC was usually represented by Martin Slate, its "On to Chicago" program coordinator. The Park District spokesman was Thomas Barry, Acting Superintendent. Slate began his requests on July 12, 1968, with a call to Barry at the Park District. A chronology, supplied by COC, indicates that on the next day Slate directed a special delivery letter to Barry advising him in detail of the COC plans and requesting use of Park District facilities:

> As rally co-ordinator for the "ON TO CHICAGO" project of the Coalition for an Open Convention, I would like to request the use of a park facility for a series of rallies to be held during the period of August 25 to August 28.
>
> We plan to hold lectures, speeches, and entertainment during these rallies that will illustrate and communicate our support for an open and representative convention of the Democratic Party.
>
> From our preliminary estimates, we are confident that 100,000 people will be coming to Chicago during this week in August to voice their support for an open convention. We feel quite strongly that the city of Chicago in its interest in maintaining freedom of speech and assembly— and at the same time, law and order—could serve these ends by providing public park facilities for the series of rallies.
>
> Given the size of crowds expected, we feel that one of Chicago's largest parks, such as Grant or Washington, or Soldier Field, could best accommodate our rallies.

From *Dissent in a Free Society,* a report by the Chicago Citizens Commission to Study the Disorder of Convention Week, 1969, pp. 27-37. Reprinted by permission.

Since we are anxious to cooperate with the city and to begin our preparations for these events so that they can be planned as carefully as
possible, we hope that our request will be considered and acted upon as
soon as possible.

From July 13, the date of the letter, until July 25, Slate made repeated
calls to Barry with no response. He then transmitted his request again in a
registered letter. The same day, Slate wrote to Governor Samuel Shapiro,
who responded two weeks later, suggesting that COC contact the mayor's
office. And Lanny Davis, National Staff Coordinator for COC, requested
help from Vice President Humphrey, his campaign manager Senator Fred
Harris, and Terry Sanford, former Governor of North Carolina. On July 26,
the Coalition leadership held a press conference:

> The Coalition for an Open Convention announced plans on July 26 to
> hold a mass rally in Chicago on the eve of the Democratic National Con-
> vention. Allard K. Lowenstein told a press conference that the rally will
> be "peaceful and orderly." He charged that Mayor Daley and the
> Democratic National Committee had "blocked our efforts to hold a peace-
> ful rally" by making Soldier Field, Auditorium Theatre and the city parks
> unavailable for the rally. "If we receive no response to the letter we sent
> to Vice-President Humphrey asking him to intercede with party leader-
> ship to allow a site for the rally we will find ways to protest this denial
> of peaceable assembly outside of the Convention." Lowenstein sought to
> distinguish the Coalition plans from those being made by the National
> Mobilization Committee. "We are good Americans and good Democrats,"
> he said, adding that plans for a march at the Convention had been called
> off because of the danger of an incident touching off some kind of vio-
> lence.
>
> *Chicago Sun-Times,* July 27, 1968

On July 29, after two weeks of silence, Barry finally called Slate and agreed
to meet with COC representatives on Wednesday, July 31, at 2:00 P.M. The
meeting was held and lasted 30 minutes. Below is a COC record of the
meeting:

> Slate reported that the meeting had been cordial and that Barry had
> pledged to bring the Coalition's request for facilities before the Park Dis-
> trict Commission on Friday, August 2. Barry promised at least a tentative
> decision on a specific site would be reached at that time and that he
> would call Slate at 2 P.M. on Friday with that decision, Slate said.
> August 2 Barry failed to call Slate at 2 P.M. as promised. At 2:15 Slate
> called Barry's office and was told that Barry was "too busy" to talk to
> Slate then but would return his call. At 3:15 Slate called Barry's office
> again and was informed that Barry was "too busy." Barry's secretary said

he would return Slate's call. At 4:45 Slate called Barry's office and was told that Barry was gone for the day, to attend the All-Star Packers game.

On August 7 Slate met with David Stahl, a deputy mayor who was central to negotiations with Yippie and MOBE. He was noncommittal. The next day Slate again wrote to Barry complaining that without a decision by the ninth, the Coalition would be unable to plan a program. Barry called on August 13 to tell Slate that the Park District Board had met that day and had taken no action on the COC requests.

The Coalition announced at a press conference on August 14 that it was filing suit in U.S. District Court to force the city to authorize use of Soldier Field for a rally on the twenty-fifth. At the press conference, COC warned:

> "If trouble breaks out next week during the Democratic Convention, it is perfectly clear whose fault it will be; Chicago's Mayor Daley and National Chairman Bailey," said Martin Slate, Rally Coordinator. "Mayor Daley should be very embarrassed. He has overplayed his hand and proven to the world that he is so unresponsive and unreceptive that he won't let a group of decent kids hold a simple rally in the park. It should be perfectly clear now that coming to Chicago is going to be a risk. But some kids have a confrontation philosophy—they will come anyway."

Although the Coalition for an Open Convention presented no threat to either the city or the Democratic Convention, the Chicago Park District and other city officials refused to issue permits, offer alternatives, or even negotiate. No one can accurately appraise the extent to which denial of peaceful expression resulted in violent confrontation. But there is no doubt that the Coalition for an Open Convention was denied basic First Amendment freedoms.

2. *Yippie*

The Youth International Party (Yippie) began planning its Chicago activities late in 1967.

> Their intention to bring thousands of young people to Chicago during the DNC (Democratic National Convention) to groove on rock banks and smoke grass and then to put them up against bayonets—viewing that as radicalizing experience—seems manipulative at best.
> Bulletin, Students for a Democratic Society, March 4, 1968

Yippie's rhetoric no doubt had an adverse effect upon the facility with which they secured permits for their public gatherings:

A Yippie is what happens to a hippie when a cop hits him over the head. They said that they would come to Chicago where perhaps one night 100,000 people may burn draft cards with the fires spelling "beat army." They said that they would nominate and eat a pig because it's better to eat the candidate than to have the candidate eat you. We are demanding the politics of the toe freaks and kisses as opposed to the politics of the worm farm suicidal hysteria slums, baby broil and natal drool cancer. We are going to Chicago not to drop out of society but to claim what is rightfully ours.

Washington Post, March 20, 1968

We ain't playing your phoney games America. Your nationalism game —burn the flag. Your war game—burn the American military uniform and root for Charlie. Your money game—burn the dollar bill. And we ain't falling for your election. We are going to disrupt the election. We are going to call for disruptive International demonstrations on election day against the American election. We are going to make it impossible for Hubert Horatio or Richard Millhouse Nixon or Wallace or Rockefeller or Reagan or Ted Kennedy or McCarthy or any other comedian to appear anywhere in America without a demonstration. We are going to make it clear to the people of the world that the streets belong to the people— not to cops and not to cars—and that the people in the streets don't want any of those fools representing us.

New York Free Press, August 1, 1968

Yip writer Abbie Hoffman gave this account in the publication, the *Realist,* of how the Chicago gathering was planned:

We had four main objectives: 1. the blending of pot and politics into a political grass leaves movement—a cross fertilization of the Yippie and New Left philosophy; 2. a connecting link that would tie as much of the underground together as was willing into some gigantic national get-together; 3. the development of a model for an alternative society; 4. the need to make a statement, especially in revolutionary terms, about LBJ, the Democratic Party, electoral politics and the state of the nation.

Sun-Times, August 15, 1968

Yippie in March, had demonstrated that their rhetoric could be coupled with action:

Police using night sticks broke up a milling shouting crowd of 3,000 Hippies in Grand Central Station today for a "Yip-In"—a combination salute to spring and antiwar demonstration. More than fifty persons were arrested, and several were injured. Singing and chanting "hell, hell, we

want to go!," they marched back and forth bouncing balloons into the
air and climbing at the top of the circular information booth in the center
of the main rotunda. A police spokesman said police entered into action
after the demonstrators climbed on the information booth canopy and
ripped the hands off the clock.

Chicago's American, March 23, 1968

This was the group seeking Chicago's parks for a "Festival of Life" during
Convention Week. The protagonists in these "negotiations" would be Dennis
Gaston, a VISTA worker, Abbie Hoffman, and Abe Peck, Editor of "Chicago
Seed" and the late William McFetridge, the President of the Chicago Park
District, Albert Baugher, an official of the Chicago Commission on Youth
Welfare, and David Stahl, the "Deputy Mayor."

Although the Yippies began their Chicago planning late in 1967, no formal
permit procedure was undertaken until March 26, 1968. On March 24, the
Yippies made rather an informal request to the Park District:

> Park District officials, when met by the Yippie delegation dressed in
> long hair, togas, beads, white makeup and such, told the Yippies, "You
> know there's a law against sleeping in the park all night." Responded the
> Yippies, "We don't plan to sleep all night. We plan to make love all
> night." Park officials, after calling attention to the need for formal re-
> quests and provision for insurance, referred the Yippies to City Hall. At
> City Hall, they were referred to David Stahl, Deputy Mayor. They
> handed him their letter of request.
>
> Afterwards, when asked what they expected to accomplish by their
> celebration, one replied, "We're not going to accomplish a ————
> thing."

Chicago Daily News, March 26, 1968

Because the Park District had no permit application form, a written request for Grant Park was made on March 26 for a Convention Week "Festival of Life" to be attended by 500,000 people. No response was ever made
to this request. The City did, however, assign Albert Baugher to work with
the Yippies' Chicago branch. Over the next five months, Baugher showed
the Yippies several sites (e.g., Soldier Field, Lincoln Park Zoo, Navy Pier)
and suggested that permits might be forthcoming.

April passed with no word on permits, but during this month the Chicago
Yippie group formed its own "Free City Survival Committee" to seek a
"Festival" site. On a visit to Chicago on May 10, Abbie Hoffman, the
national Yippie leader, had no success in discovering Park District intentions.
But the day following Hoffman's departure, Deputy Mayor Stahl's office
arranged a meeting for the week of May 20. At a meeting in the offices of an
"underground" newspaper, "The Chicago Seed," Stahl ruled out Grant Park

as a site for the Festival and demanded a list of specific requests. Later the "Free City" Yippie group switched its festival plans to Lincoln Park because Stahl indicated that "there would be greater likelihood" of getting a permit for that park. On the basis of an understanding reached at a meeting on June 14 attended by Stahl, Abe Peck and George Sells, the "Free City" group was under the impression that they would receive a permit for the "Festival" by June 26. June passed without a permit.

Early in June several meetings were held with city negotiators and a formal application for the use of Lincoln Park was filed on the fifteenth by the "Free City Survival Committee." Soldier Field was also requested for a "concluding rally" on August 30. The Park District schedule of events showed Soldier Field open for that date. No reply to the request was made until July 31, when Barry wrote Abe Peck, "Free City" spokesman, to request a meeting. After four months of negotiations, the Park District was ready to discuss the matter.

Police Commander James R. Rochford told "Free City" representatives on August 1 that the 11:00 P.M. curfew would be strictly enforced. At the meeting with the Park District, Barry said that he had no knowledge of plans to sleep in the park, though several Yippie representatives present claim to have discussed such plans with him on more than one previous occasion. Barry said that plans to sleep in the parks necessitated renegotiating the entire request. This was the last Yippie meeting with representatives of the Park District. A meeting with Stahl August 7 was inconclusive, and negotiations came to a halt. By August 19, Yippie, like COC and MOBE, saw no alternative to action in court.

3. *MOBE*

Of the three groups seeking Convention Week permits in Chicago, the most persistent was the National Mobilization Committee to End the War in Vietnam (MOBE). Leaders involved in the attempt to secure permits included Rennie Davis, Chicago coordinator, and Tom Hayden and David Dellinger, national leaders whose trips to Hanoi, Paris and Cuba were called to the attention of city officials. Negotiators also included Gene Cerruti and Mark Simons, law students, and Dennis Cunningham, Chicago attorney. Principal city representatives were Stahl for the mayor's office and Baugher of the Commission on Youth Welfare.

One year before the Democratic Convention, MOBE announced plans for a march to the Pentagon opposing the war in Vietnam:

> A coalition of anti-Viet Nam war groups announced Monday it planned a massive demonstration in Washington on October 21st in an attempt to shut down the Pentagon. Thousands of people will disrupt the center

of the American war machine, read a statement issued by MOBE. The statement continued that the action was planned to move from simple protest to collective resistance. The demonstrators will try to fill the hallways and block the entrance to the Pentagon.

Chicago Daily News, August 29, 1967

Violence did erupt, and MOBE leadership interpreted this as a portent for the future:

The Pentagon siege can be treated as a tactical event and criticized as one possible model for future physical confrontations. This is a necessary process: there will be more occasions for physical confrontations and they ought to be better planned than the Pentagon was. Can we do better at the Democratic National Convention in Chicago?

Liberation, November 1967

When the Democratic Party announced, on October 8, 1967, the choice of Chicago as its convention site, MOBE planning began in earnest. Though MOBE was to assault Chicago with its own style of preconvention rhetoric, all mentions of possible violence were subdued and stated defensively:

"Details of the protest have not yet been drafted, but every effort will be made to stage nonviolent and nondisruptive demonstrations," Mr. Rennie Davis said.

"But a lot depends on how we are treated," he said.

"If we are unable to get public space for our meetings or sufficient housing, and if we are maced and arrested by the Chicago police, we can't be responsible for what happens." Mr. Davis said that several peace demonstrations in Chicago this spring had been broken up by policemen who told the marchers, "If you think this is bad, wait until August."

New York Times, June 26, 1968

Davis also said the anti-war group plans next week to meet Mayor Daley's aides to work out details for parade permits and camp sites for the protests.

Daley agreed to such a meeting. "We are always willing to talk," said the mayor, reached at City Hall.

"There will be no violence in this city if the mayor cooperates," Davis said. "We don't want police protection," he continued. "Police are more a source of violence than of protection."

Chicago Sun-Times, June 30, 1968

The City prepared for violence, and negotiations were begun in this spirit.

MOBE's permit requests were the most extensive and complex of the three discussed. The organization originally requested permits from the

Park District for several widely separated parks which would serve both as sleeping and small group meeting areas throughout convention week. Also requested were permits for two large rallies at the Grant Park bandshell on August 28 and 29. From the Bureau of Streets and Sanitation permits were requested for an afternoon march to a Grant Park rally and an evening march to the International Amphitheatre.

Attempts to negotiate with the city for these permits began with a meeting between Davis and Baugher on June 16. Davis presented MOBE's plans for the parades, rallies, and sleeping areas. He indicated a desire to meet with appropriate officials. Baugher attempted to arrange a meeting.

Among the sleeping areas sought were Washington and Garfield Parks, in predominantly black neighborhoods. Baugher said that permits for these parks presented special problems for the city. At later meetings other city representatives, particularly Elrod, emphasized potential dangers which MOBE's plans presented. MOBE leaders, aware of these apprehensions, suggested alternative routes of march which avoided both black neighborhoods and those white neighborhoods which might be especially hostile to peace marchers.

At the same time officials of the U.S. Justice Department's Community Relations Service attempted to establish direct communication between MOBE and Mayor Daley. Davis accepted their offer to serve as mediator; the mayor did not. Justice Department officials concluded that the mayor was not interested in negotiating a compromise. They inferred that the failure to agree beforehand might result in violent confrontation, and according to some sources, apparently briefed newsmen in Washington along these lines before they came to Chicago.

Officials of the Community Relations Service conveyed the same conclusion to MOBE in early August. They did not believe that the city would grant permits for sleeping in the parks. MOBE was nevertheless confident that permits would be forthcoming, perhaps at the last possible moment, though some officers of the group were less hopeful and urged litigation. Simons had arranged follow-up meetings with city officials. Preliminary efforts to meet with Baugher and Stahl were frustrated. Finally a meeting was arranged for August 2, to include Cunningham, Davis, Simons, Cerruti and Stahl. Davis reiterated the group's needs and proposals without eliciting affirmative response.

Two subsequent meetings also proved inconclusive. At a meeting on August 10, Stahl emphasized that he had no authority, but could only transmit information. He said that the Park District and the Department of Streets granted permits, not Mayor Daley.

The National Mobilization made its final attempt to contact appropriate officials on August 12. Telegrams were sent to the Park District, Department of Streets and Sanitation and Police Department inviting officials to meet on that date at City Hall with MOBE's national leaders, then arriving in Chicago to discuss final plans. The invited officials failed to appear. Present were 15 members of MOBE's National Administrative Committee, Stahl, Baugher, Baugher and Assistant Corporation Counsel Elrod. A city spokesman wanted to know whether MOBE would still march if they did not receive a permit.

The Park District Board met on August 13. It did not consider MOBE's application. The Democratic National Committee was asked to intervene. Mayor Daley was asked by telegram to attend an emergency meeting. His office did not reply. The national steering committee met on August 18, and finding no other resource, filed suit in U.S. District Court.

4. Summary

Negotiations were separately conducted by the three organizations with representatives of city departments. The earliest application for use of city facilities was filed in March. City officials were assigned to work with each group. After many delays it became apparent to each group that permits would not be issued. Between August 14 and 19 the three groups independently suit in the U.S. District Court.

HAL DRAPER

Excerpt from *Berkeley: The New Student Revolt*

That day, the argumentation swirling in knots around the car and the campus had naturally tended to shift away from the "free speech" issues to the derivative issue of "Law and Order." Assuming that the administration was wrong in imposing the new restrictions, as an overwhelming majority of the campus agreed, was this the way to fight it? asked anxious students, turning over the crisis in their minds.

There were undigested rhetorical platitudes on both sides. On the one hand, what would society be without Law and Order? On the other hand, one could read, in a local guidebook to the East Bay area, that President Kerr was a great civil-libertarian who had loftily proclaimed:

> I would urge each individual . . . to teach children, in the home and in
> the school, "To be laws to themselves and to depend on themselves," as
> Walt Whitman urged us . . . for that is the well-source of the inde-
> pendent spirit.

"Laws to themselves!" This Whitmanesque anarchism went far beyond what
the students were demanding. It appeared that, in his character as a Liberal
Philosopher, Kerr called on students to be Independent Spirits, but in his
character as Responsible Administrator he had to punish them if they took
him seriously.

Although "Law and Order" seemed to be an indivisible phrase like "hue
and cry," the events of this day and subsequent days suggested a cleavage.
Whatever indignities the law was suffering, the mass of students went
through the entire three months of sharp conflict with a regard for order,
orderliness and individual self-discipline that was phenomenal. The scuffle
that day around the Sproul Hall doors was a minor exception, but even such
an incident did not recur. On the night of October 1, it had been the touters
of Law who were the flouters of Order.

The CIO sitdown strikes of the thirties had been clear violations of law
too. As a result they had brought a measure of democracy and human
dignity to the shops and assembly lines. Many who denounced the students'
sit-ins seemed to think the students had invented the tactic. Nor did they ask
themselves how "criminal" it could be if the Berkeley halls of learning suddenly produced such a multitude of criminals. If several thousands of the
brightest scholars in California had been driven to measures so heinous,
didn't this suggest there might be something dreadfully wrong with what
the administration was doing, that it had pushed them to desperate courses?[1]

The students that day heard many abstract appeals to the sanctity of law,
but the "law" itself did not seem to behave so abstractly. It was certainly not
blind. Instead of impartially punishing all "lawbreakers," the administration
was openly and "gratuitously" singling out leaders for punishment ("almost

1. The same point has been made about the American colonists of 1776. In this connection, interestingly enough, Governor Brown has revealed that he isn't at all sure but
that Sam Adams & Co. were a bunch of troublemakers like the FSM. Here is his discussion of civil disobedience in a radio interview (KPFA, March 28, 1965): "I spoke
to Mario Savio on the telephone and he said, 'Would you have opposed the Boston Tea
Party?' and I said, 'Well, I don't know whether I'd have opposed the Boston Tea Party
or not. But I do know that the colonial government sent representatives to the court of
King James in order to achieve—or King George—I forget who it was—King George,
that's right—to achieve their proper objective, and they only resorted to that as a last
resort. Now I wouldn't be prepared to say that under circumstances where rights are
denied an individual that he might not feel he can achieve it is by revolt [*sic*], but if
he does revolt then he'd better be prepared to either win or suffer the civil consequences
of what he does.'—Or in better-known terms: the Patriots are the side that wins."

as hostages," as the Heyman Committee put it). It was acting as if interested not in enforcing blind law but rather in beheading a mass protest.

The issue was put most provocatively from the top of the police car as dusk was falling. We have mentioned that a number of professors had been trying to act as mediators between the demonstrators and President Kerr. One of them climbed on top of the car to tell the crowd of students not only that it was useless to expect concessions from Kerr but also that the police-car blockade was antidemocratic and immoral.

This was Seymour Martin Lipset, one of the most upwardly mobile of the sociology professors, who had recently been honored by Kerr with the directorship of the Institute of International Studies, an academic entrepreneur of notable talent in channeling government and foundation grant money, who was himself then engaged in research on foreign student movements for the Air Force (which was presumably interested in a bird's-eye view of the question).

Lipset charged that the students were acting "like the Ku Klux Klan," for did not the Southern segregationists also believe in violating the law when they didn't like it, instead of obeying decisions adopted in a democracy? (Kerr was going to echo this line later.)

An impromptu debate broke out as students called out rebuttals. The most obvious answer was that the university community was not even theoretically a democracy, even though it existed *within* a democracy (just as any factory is an authoritarian regime within the larger society). Kerr openly wrote of the Multiversity's government as a "benevolent bureaucracy." Although one of the easy platitudes of the day was the advice that the students should "exhaust all channels" before restorting to drastic protest, there were in fact no "channels" open to the students that had not been available to the sans-culottes under Louis XVI, such as the right of petition. Prescisely when the students had sought to appeal to the larger democracy in which the university was embedded—"to precipitate a test of the (constitutional) validity of the regulations *in some arena outside the university*," as the Heyman Committee said—the Benevolent Bureaucracy inside the university had reacted violently with the *coup de force* of the summary suspensions.

Others stressed that "democracy" in the situation meant acting only through the so-called student government, ASUC.[2]

This argument assumed that ASUC was indeed "student government." But as we have mentioned, the most advanced one-third of the students were excluded from it, and the simulacrum of government which did exist was firmly circumscribed by the administration itself. No one, including the administration, too ASUC seriously as a government, especially since the

2. Cf. Lewis Feuer, "Rebellion at Berkeley—II," *New Leader*, January 4, 1965.

1959 disfranchisement of the graduate students. "Acting through ASUC" usually had the operational meaning of waiting while Charles Powell and his "sandbox" colleagues sparred with the administration, or else of waiting for the next election—but in any case doing nothing *now*. (But when the next election took place, the rebel students did "act through ASUC to the extent of winning the most smashing group victory in the history of the student government.)[3]

But fundamentally the students' demands did not merely depend on proving that a majority supported them. The number of students themselves interested in "mounting social and political action" was admittedly a minority, but the majority (it was contended) does not have the right to exclude this minority from the possibility of acting. Democracy, of course, does not mean "majority decision" without the maintenance of the rights of minorities. If a majority passes a law to gag you, you have the moral and political duty of fighting back with every means left. Thus went the students' case.

So much for the context of democracy. The Lipset analogy with the KKK went further. The Klan do not like the Supreme Court's directives and wish to violate them; and so, skulking in the dead of night with hooded visages, they terrorize—not the Supreme Court itself (which would take some courage) but defenseless Negroes, by beating them, burning churches, murdering civil-rights workers. And this even though as citizens they have full rights (denied to their victims) in helping to determine the law.

The case of the students was just the reverse. In the microcosm of the university community, the students were informed—by an administration in which they had no say, by a Power Structure in which they had no vote—that *they* (not their "victims") were being deprived of some basic freedoms of campus life. They were also informed that the issue was "not negotiable," that they had no further recourse. They responded, in the open light of day, with civil disobedience. They did not beat up their "victims," the administration; on the contrary, it is they who were eventually roughed up. Yet they were told that they were "just like the Ku Klux Klan."

3. Later, the ASUC vice-president, not an FSM'er, "explained the actions of the [ASUC] Senate are frequently ignored by the faculty and administration on the grounds the government is not respected by the students. The students, he stated, do not respect the government because its actions are not honored by the faculty and administration." (*Daily Cal*, Feb. 4, 1965.) The usual number of students voting in an ASUC election was less than one of the smaller FSM demonstrations. On October 1, ASUC President Powell issued a formal statement jettisoning the ASUC position of September 22. He now informed the students that nothing could be done about the ban on recruitment and fund-raising because "the prohibition . . . is not a ruling of the chancellor or of President Clark Kerr. It is, in fact, a State law." (This, of course, was untrue.) "I ask," he concluded, "that you not oppose the administration—the administration can do nothing to meet the demands being made."

What is the meaning of civil disobedience? It deliberately violates a law, with as great an insistence on open publicity as the Ku Klux Klan and other criminals insist on clandestine evasion, because the act has meaning only as an appeal to the public conscience. Its aim is to put the *authorities* on the spot. It says: We hereby put our bodies on the line publicly and openly, and challenge you to enforce your Law and Order. *We wish to compel you to take the consequences of arresting us. . . .*

All this is the exact opposite of criminal violations of law, even if these are politically motivated violations like the Klan's. "The consequences of arresting us" concentrate public attention on the concrete evil which is under attack. "We" do not meekly collapse under arrest; we vigorously protest the step. A strange argument is frequently made: if you challenge arrest and do in fact get arrested, "you have no right to complain." On the contrary: "complaining" (protest) is the whole point of civil disobedience.

Lipset was finally pushed by the give-and-take to admit that civil disobedience might be all right in the South because of the lack of democracy there; yet, in terms of his own analogy, he did not conclude that Ku Klux Klan lynchings were all right in the South (or anywhere else) because of the special circumstances. The new Berkeley chancellor, Martin Meyerson, was later to concede, also, that civil disobedience might be legitimate "as a last resort"; but presumably Lipset would not agree that Ku Klux Klanism could be legitimate in any resort. By fathering the "Ku Klux Klan" charge against the student protest, Lipset became known as one of the prominent adversaries of the movement among the faculty.

VI   ELECTED OFFICIALS

G. MENNEN WILLIAMS

Little Rock: Challenge to the Democratic Party

Although the dust has far from settled in the Little Rock crisis, it is certain that the political issues involved must concern the Democratic Party in terms of its tradition and spiritual integrity, rather than in counting votes in the next election. The issues of Little Rock affect the very reason for the party's being. They have to do with whether the United States can maintain its free way of life, and indeed, even survive in the world of the twentieth century.

There are those in the South who may see Little Rock only as the picture of a white adult bleeding at the feet of a federal soldier standing with bayonet unsheathed. But responsible opinion throughout the United States, and the entire world I believe, sees the picture of armed soldiers preventing a handful of bright-eyed, spotlessly clad, book-laden children from attending school simply because they happened to be Negroes.

At this writing, at least, the facts seem clear. The armed force of a state was violently interposed against the lawful fulfillment of a lawful order of a federal court; an order pursuant to a recent and clear mandate of the Supreme Court interpreting the Constitution. At the last minute, to uphold the ultimate law of the sovereign people, the President of the United States exercised his undoubted Constitutional powers to maintain law and order.

Behind these unfortunate events there are many historic reasons, in the making of which none of us now living had any part. There was slavery, then a long and bitter Civil War, then an often brutal policy of reconstruction, followed by the reassertion of white supremacy in the South. These things left a bitterness which, even today, has not entirely vanished.

But if some historical factors may be adduced in extenuation or at least explanation of the viewpoint of the South, the future response of the Democratic Party to this issue must also be viewed in the light of the party's history.

The Democratic Party from Jefferson and Jackson to Wilson, Roosevelt, Truman and Stevenson, has recognized the preservation and elevation of the dignity of the individual as the reason for its existence. The expressions of this philosophy have been as varied as the facets and needs of human

From *The Nation*, October 12, 1957, pp. 235-37. Reprinted by permission.

nature. But their direction has been clear—to uphold the doctrine of the Declaration of Independence that all men are created equal.

As in most groups of men, there has not been unanimity. There has been debate and battle as to the development of this philosophy into program and action. The last Democratic National Convention at Chicago debated the point while the entire nation looked and listened. While there were some of us who felt that we could have given clearer and more direct expression of our policy, the platform we did adopt clearly bespoke our opposition to the interposition of state armed forces to prevent integration.

Here are the pertinent words of the Democratic Party, speaking—almost unanimously, as I recall—in convention assembled:

> We reject all proposals for the use of force to interfere with the orderly determination of these matters [integration efforts] by the courts.

So much for the past. What of the future?

The ugly facts of the civil-rights issue must be faced. It is a fact that we have, in one degree or another, and in every part of the country, the problem of racial prejudice. It is a fact that the principles of the Democratic Party require that Democrats everywhere should work to the end that every citizen shall have equal rights of citizenship. It is a fact that resistance to those principles, and to the law of the land as laid down by the Supreme Court, is coming mainly from Democratic Party leaders in the Southern states. It is a fact that the interference of a Democratic Governor with the order of a federal court left the President of the United States with no alternative but to uphold the Constitution and the courts with federal troops. (I must temper this statement with the fact that two Southern Democratic Governors have called out their state militias to enforce the Supreme Court's decision, namely Governor Frank Clement of Tennessee and Governor A. B. Chandler of Kentucky.) Although the President might have avoided this whole situation altogether by firm and prompt action, it is a fact that in the circumstances which prevailed at the time, he acted rightly, and it is a fact that they who now assail him for his action are wrong.

Whether we like it or not, that is the situation.

What can the Democratic Party do in these circumstances? In my opinion, it can do but one thing: hew vigorously and forthrightly to its own principles of the dignity of the individual and the supremacy of the Constitution, and let the chips fall where they may.

We do not want to drive anyone out of the Democratic Party. We desire party unity for obvious partisan reasons, of course. Then, too, no one wants to see the leaders of almost a third of the American people wrap themselves, as Governor Collins of Florida said, in a Confederate blanket and constitute themselves a lost-cause Third Party of Segregation. That would be a national tragedy, destructive to the interest of the South, disruptive of the two-party system, and stultifying to the millions of good citizens of the South who, with admirable courage, and frequently against their own personal convictions, are trying to achieve a gradual and orderly effectuation of the Supreme Court decision.

No, we do not want to drive out the South, but the Democratic Party— the majority of the party—simply must stand on its own principles, whether the stand results in political gain or political disaster.

It has been the Democratic Party which, at least in our generation, has led the fight for civil rights. It has been the Republican Party, in our times, which has withheld the support which would have resulted in progress, thwarting liberal Democrats in every effort to enact civil-rights legislation. Whatever we may think of the motives behind the relatively sudden conversion of the Republican leadership, and regardless of the fact that the President did not march but was driven by a constitutional challenge, into the role of champion of integration—nevertheless, we hope and pray that Republican professions of concern for equality of citizenship are genuine and lasting. The test we face is not one for Democrats alone but for all men of good will, regardless of party or geography.

Mr. Eisenhower has the opportunity for leadership. A civil rights act, not the strongest law we might have desired, but the first such Congressional act in generations, has been adopted by a Democratic Congress. Specifically, the President can show his intentions by appointing persons to the Civil Rights Commission, under the new law, who will carry out its intent—rather than the kind of appointments he has made to federal commissions in other areas. I have recommended to him the name of a former Senator Herbert Lehman of New York, whose stature and reputation in this and other fields would do much to reassure the nation and the world. Whether he appoints men of this caliber will be an index of the President's approach to the problem.

It is unquestionably true that much of Southern resistance to integration is pure and simple demagoguery. But much of it also is the manifestation of a sincere, if woefully misguided, belief, bred into the bone of many Southerners, in the moral rightness of segregation. Leadership dedicated to the ideal of the Declaration of Independence is the only kind of leadership that can provide the moral strength necessary to alter Southern convictions about this question. If we are to see a solution of this problem in our lifetime or in the lifetime of our children, it will not be enough to confine ourselves to legal and constitutional judgments. Political leaders at every level must deliver their own affirmations of American principles. The President— whether he be Mr. Eisenhower or his Democratic or Republican successor—

must lead the nation; but if he is failed by the leadership below, his best efforts will be futile.

It is the duty, I feel of all of us to reply to the reckless cries of "storm troopers" and "Hitler tactics" which have been leveled against the President's unavoidable action. It is the voice of the liberal Democrat which will be most effective in countering the invective and cries for impeachment which have been heard in the South.

One of the cardinal tasks for Northern leaders is to work constantly to put and keep their own houses in order. Intolerance is not peculiar to the South. The problem is a Southern problem only in the narrow sense that some Southern leaders deny there is a problem, and refuse to work for its solution. In all sections, we can pride ourselves on the progress of the past only if we pledge ourselves to continued progress in the future.

The Democratic Party must lead, as it has in the past, in efforts to strengthen federal and state laws designed to guarantee equality of citizenship, regardless of race, creed or color. We must seek to move with understanding, as well as with speed, *but we must move.*

In all our decisions, we must bear constantly in mind that we render judgment not only on today and tomorrow, but on the fate of generations to come. In a world where our safety depends upon the outcome of a struggle for men's minds—and the great majority of them the minds of colored men— we can ill afford to stand before the world as a nation which cannot or will not carry out its own principles. The explosive aspects of Little Rock may well be more important to the lives of men and women yet unborn than the conference on atomic weapons, the latest crisis in the Middle East or the race for the intercontinental ballistic missile.

When these consequences are clearly understood, I have every confidence that the American people will rise to the challenge and find a moral solution to this difficult problem.

Crisis in Civil Rights

On a bus traveling through the Deep South, a youthful Negro said calmly: "We can take anything the white man can dish out, but we want our rights. We know what they are—and we want them now." In the midst of a sleepless night in his Justice Department office in Washington, U.S. Attorney General Robert Kennedy, 36, hung up his telephone and said wearily: "It's like play-

From *Time*, June 2, 1961, p. 14. Copyright Time Inc. 1961. Reprinted by permission of *Time*, The Weekly Newsmagazine.

ing Russian roulette." And in Montgomery, the capital of Alabama and the birthplace of the Confederacy, Governor John Patterson, 39, wearing a pure white carnation in his lapel, complained bitterly: "I'm getting tired of being called up in the middle of the night and being *ordered* to do this and *ordered* to do that."

The young Negro, the young Attorney General and the young Southern Governor were central figures last week in a national drama. It was a drama of conflict and violence. It saw U.S. marshals and martial law in Alabama. It saw cops with police dogs on patrol in Mississippi. It was the drama of the Freedom Riders, and it represented a new and massive assault against segregation in the U.S. South.

The assault was launched late last month when a band of six whites and seven Negroes set out to ride by bus from Washington to New Orleans. The integrated trip was sponsored by the Congress of Racial Equality, a Manhattan-based organization. Its purpose was to prove, by provoking trouble, that Southern interstate travel is still segregated in fact, although integrated by law. The original Freedom Riders passed with little incident through Virginia, North Carolina, South Carolina and Georgia. Then they came to Alabama—whether they found the trouble they wanted.

For that, they could in part thank Governor John Patterson. A militant segregationist who solicited Ku Klux Klan support in his election campaign. Patterson once said that integration would come to Alabama only "over my dead body." In his inaugural address Patterson declared: "I will oppose with every ounce of energy I possess and will use every power at my command to prevent any mixing of white and Negro races in the classrooms of this state." Said he as the Freedom Riders approached: "The people of Alabama are so enraged that I cannot guarantee protection for this bunch of rabble-rousers."

Thus confident that state authority would not stand in their way. Alabama mobs attacked the Freedom Riders in Anniston and Birmingham. Battered and bruised, the original Freedom Riders decided to discontinue their bus trip and fly from Birmingham to New Orleans.

But what they had started was far from ended. Until then, little active support had been given the Freedom Riders by the Negro students who last year fought and won the sit-in battles against segregated Southern lunch counters (*Time*, Feb. 22, 1960 *et seq.*). When the first Freedom Riders gave up, these students took over. They vowed that they would travel all the way to New Orleans by bus—or, literally, die trying. They were tactical disciples of Martin Luther King, Jr., the Negro minister whose Gandhian methods of nonviolence won municipal bus integration in Montgomery in 1956. Willing to suffer beatings and endure jail, the students last week jumped onto regularly scheduled buses and headed south.

In Montgomery, the new Freedom Riders were mauled by another mob. Again Governor Patterson failed to act—and at that point Attorney General Bobby Kennedy reluctantly sent in 400 U.S. marshals, a force that was later increased to 666. The marshals (mostly deputized Treasury agents) were led by Deputy Attorney General Byron ("Whizzer") White, who met with Patterson in a long and angry conference. White carefully explained that the U.S. was not sponsoring the Freedom Riders' movement, but that the Government was determined to protect the riders' legal rights. John Patterson was having no part of such explanations. Alabama, he cried, could maintain its own law and order, and the marshals were therefore unnecessary. He even threatened to arrest the marshals if they violated any local law.

Even as White and Patterson talked Montgomery's radio stations broadcast the news that Negroes would hold a mass meeting that night at the First Baptist Church. All day long, carloads of grim-faced whites converged on Montgomery.

That night the church was packed with 1,200 Negroes. In the basement a group of young men and women clustered together and clasped hands like a football team about to take the field. They were the Freedom Riders. "Everybody say 'Freedom.'" ordered one of the leaders. "Freedom," said the group. "Say it again," said the leader. "Freedom!" shouted the group. "Are we together?" asked the leader. "Yes, we are together," came the reply. With that, the young Negroes filed upstairs and reappeared behind the pulpit. "Ladies and gentlemen," cried the Rev. Ralph Abernathy as the crowd screamed to its feet, "the Freedom Riders."

"Give Them a Grenade"

Slowly, in twos and threes, the mob started to form outside the church. Men with shirts unbuttoned to the waist sauntered down North Ripley Street, soon were almost at the steep front steps of the church. "We want to integrate too," yelled a voice. Cried another: "We'll get those niggers." A barrage of bottles burst at the feet of some curious Negroes who peered out the church door. The worst racial battle in Montgomery's history was about to begin.

Despite the long and obvious buildup toward trouble, only a handful of Montgomery cops were present—and they looked the other way. Into the breach moved a squad of U.S. marshals—the men Patterson had said were not needed. Contrary to Justice Department statements, the hastily deputized marshals had no riot training. They moved uncertainly to their task until a mild-looking alcohol tax unit supervisor from Florida named William D. Behen took command. "If we're going to do it, let's do it!" he yelled. "What say, shall we give them a grenade?" Whereupon Behen lobbed a tear-gas grenade into the crowd.

The crowd retreated temporarily, but kept up a fusillade of bottles, rocks and paving stones. Inside, Martin Luther King took the pulpit to say: "The ultimate responsibility for the hideous action in Alabama last week must be placed at the doorstep of the Governor of the state. We hear the familiar cry that morals cannot be legislated. This may be true, but behavior can be regulated. The law may not be able to make a man love me, but it can keep him from lynching me."

"Have Him Call Me"

Back at the white mansion on South Perry Street, John Patterson and his family had finished an informal dinner of charcoal-broiled steaks on the terrace. The Governor was following the progress of the riot by telephone. When Public Safety Director Floyd Mann phoned that the mob was growing, Patterson declared martial law, ordered Adjutant General Henry Graham, a National Guard major general, to lead his troops to the church. Then Patterson called Bobby Kennedy to report that the Guard had gone into action, but that the general could not guarantee the protection of Martin Luther King.

Kennedy exploded. Earlier he had seriously considered sending in federal troops, had reassured King by phone that he was safe in the church. Kennedy's voice rose as he worked over Patterson: "Have the general call me. I want him to say it to me. I want to hear a general of the U.S. Army say he can't protect Martin Luther King." Patterson backed won, admitted that it was he, not the general, who felt that King could not be protected. As it turned out, General Graham was capable of protecting King and everyone else. He kept the Negroes in the stifling hot church until the mob was dispersed, then escorted them home early in the morning.

Yale's Revenge

After the church riot, Bobby Kennedy urged the Freedom Riders to go slowly. But the Freedom Riders in Montgomery were determined to push on to New Orleans by way of Mississippi, a state ruled by Governor Ross Barnett, who had once declared: "The Negro is different because God made him different to punish him." Barnett, noting well what had happened in Alabama, assured Attorney General Kennedy that Mississippi would protect the students from violence. Kennedy was deciding to trust Barnett and withhold federal forces from Mississippi when he got word that still another integrated bus contingent, led by Yale University Chaplain William Sloane Coffin, Jr., was starting out for the South. Cracked Harvardman Kennedy: "Those people at Yale are sore at Harvard for taking over the country, and now they're trying to get back at us."

On Wednesday morning the student Freedom Riders appeared at Montgomery's Trailways bus terminal—ready to head for Mississippi. Alabama National Guardsmen lined both sides of the street in front of the terminal, surveyed the area from the second level of a garage across the street. At 7:15 the first bus pulled out for Jackson carrying twelve Freedom Riders, six National Guardsmen and 16 newsmen. Once out in the countryside, the bus was convoyed by three planes, two helicopters and 17 highway patrol cars. Bobby Kennedy followed the progress of the convoy by a special telephone rig that let him monitor police radio messages.

Aboard the bus, Freedom Rider Jim Lawson held a workshop on tactics for the riot that might come: "If we get knocked down, I think the best bet is to stand where we are if we can—or kneel where we are." But the only man in Alabama who lifted a finger at the Freedom Riders was a farmer, who thumbed his nose. At a rest stop, while Guardsmen glared a empty fields, Lawson disavowed the armed guard: "We appreciate the Government's concern, but protection does not solve the problem of segregation."

Polite Police

At the Mississippi line a similar escort, but the fixed bayonets, picked up the caravan for the trip to Jackson. Someone hurled a rock at the bus, but most of the spectators just stared, took pictures, or waved derisively.

At the Jackson terminal the crowds were hanging out of the windows of nearby buildings. "Get your team ready," said Lawson. In pairs, the Freedom Riders walked into the "white" waiting room. A Jackson policeman politely asked two Negro girls to move on, and when they refused, arrested them for causing a disturbance. In similar fashion the remaining Freedom Riders —one white and eleven black—were arrested, including eight who actually entered the white rest room before being led away.

Several hours later, the second contingent of Freedom Riders, including CORE National Director James Farmer, planted themselves in the waiting room. "You all have to move," said a police captain. No one stirred. "You all going to move?" asked the captain. "No," came the reply. "You all are under arrest." said the Captain.

Spreading Action

Back in Washington Bobby Kennedy issued a statement outlining the Government's position of impartial enforcement of the law. Later in the day Kennedy publicly requested a "cooling-off period." But the very next morning Coffin, three other whites and three Negroes defiantly sat down at the Montgomery Trailways bus terminal and were arrested for breach of the peace.

As the Freedom Riders were taken to Alabama and Mississippi jails, others headed south to take up the crusade. Action was spreading fast on other fronts in John Patterson's home state. Birmingham businessmen, who had been trying to attract outside industry to their fading city, sent Patterson a sharp wire complaining that the riots had torpedoed their campaign. The Justice Department brought suit against four local Alabama police officials, including Birmingham's Commissioner Eugene ("Bull") Connor to enjoin them from interfering with interstate bus traffic. Justice's charges: the cops had not only failed to respond quickly to the riots but had actually withdrawn from some trouble spots to give the mobs a free hand.

Declared the Montgomery *Advertiser*—one of the many Southern papers roasting the Governor: "Patterson is not the exclusive author of Montgomery's troubles by any means, but he is the chief author because his is the supreme responsibility as chief guardan against disorder."

Latter-Day Crusader

Ironically, John Patterson built his political career in large part on a reputation for enforcing the law. He was raised in wide-open Phenix City, where the gamblers and madams catered to soldiers from nearby Fort Benning. Patterson played the slot machines as a kid, drank his share of "wildcat" whisky and, with time out for Army service during World War II and in Korea, turned into just another easygoing Alabama lawyer. But in 1954 his father, Albert Patterson, was murdered by racketeers 17 days after winning the Democratic nomination for state attorney general on the promise to clean out Phenix City. Says John Patterson: "I was practicing law and going fishing and enjoying my days off, but when they shot down my daddy, I became a crusader."

At 33, Patterson was elected to his dead father's job, led the fight to mop up the mob in Phenix City. More important, became a hero to many an Alabama voter by putting the N.A.A.C.P. out of business in the state for refusing to disclose membership lists. He fought Negro boycotts of stores in Tuskegee, and of buses in Montgomery.

O.K. for the K.K.K.

In 1958 Patterson started out way back in the pack in the race among the Democrats for the Governor's mansion. He gained ground fast. With no program of his own to speak of, Patterson made himself the chief critic of the clownish reign of James ("Kissin' Jim") Folsom, the outgoing Governor. Using his attorney general's stationery, Patterson sent out a letter to the Ku Klux Klan mailing list, which declared: "A mutual friend, Mr. R. N. Shelton, of ours, in Tuscaloosa, has suggested that I ask for your support." When it turned out that Shelton was the Grand Dragon of the state Ku Klux Klan, Patterson professed astonishment. Said the *Advertiser:* "If this innocent, this Fearless Fosdick, is so dense that he doesn't know that he is riding around with a Klan chief, how in the world can such a man investigate and bring to book the Folsom gang and the gangsters he talks about?"

A Favor Rewarded

John Patterson was elected Governor of Alabama, and he set right out to make a segregationist record. He expelled students from Alabama State College for Negroes who took part in sit-ins, promised to close down the University of Alabama if it accepted a Negro. If anyone pushed for school integration, Patterson said flatly, "I will be one of the ones leading the trouble."

In 1959 Patterson dropped by Jack Kennedy's Georgetown home for breakfast and emerged so impressed that 13 months before the convention he became the first Southern Governor to back the young Senator for President. Alabama still went for Lyndon Johnson in Los Angeles, but Patterson got his reward this spring when Charles M. Meriwether, his old campaign manager, was nominated by Kennedy as a director of the Export-Import Bank. Meriwether was eventually confirmed by the Senate despite reports of connection with the Klan.

Vagabond Toad

One morning last week, Governor Patterson strode briskly down the cherry-red carpeted staircase in the Governor's mansion and out into the marble terrace for breakfast. Already at the table were his wife Mary Jo (called "Tuti"), their twelve-year-old son Albert L. and their eight-year-old daughter Barbara Louise. Cardinals flitted through the gigantic water oaks and pecan trees on the mansion lawn, and a squad of six Negro trusty prisoners in white uniforms trimmed the grass while the Governor attacked a plate of muffins and bacon. Suddenly a furor arose in the yard. "They've found the horned toad," cried Tuti. "I hope they don't kill it."

The chief executive of the state of Alabama whirled into action. "Hey," he yelled. "Hey, don't you kill that toad!" Patterson jumped up from the table and sprinted across the lawn to save a horned toad, a family pet that is consigned by Tuti to a vagabond's life in the garden.

Worst Insult

Back at the table, Patterson told a visitor that he had no apologies to make for any of his actions during the weeks of crisis. The Kennedy Administration was to blame, particularly Bobby Kennedy. "He has no idea of conditions here." said Patterson. "God Almighty, what he's trying to do is provoke a civil war. They try and get you to admit you can't or won't guarantee law enforcement, and then they twist your words because the marshals are on the way anyway. That Bobby Kennedy is just treacherous, that's what he is.

I don't trust him and he don't trust me." A hurt tone crept into Patterson's voice. "To say that I couldn't enforce the law is the worst insult they could have thrown at me. The Kennedy's couldn't get enough votes in Alabama this morning to wad buckshot.

"I'm a segregationist, and I tell you 98% of the people down here feel the way I do. There shouldn't be any battles over rights. There shouldn't even be court fights. We have to give the colored people pride in themselves and pride in their communities. A fellow who's making money, he doesn't worry about things like riding buses."

Blunt Warning

On a tour of the mansion, Patterson later pointed out a deer head on the wall, paused at a picture of the 1868 Alabama legislature, which had ratified the 14th Amendment guaranteeing citizens "due process" of law. Nearly one-third of the men in the picture were Negroes. "I keep it as a historical curiosity," said Patterson. He gestured toward a picture of Confederate General Joseph ("Fighting Joe") Wheeler. "I'm related to Wheeler. My mother's mother's mother was a Wheeler."

Before leaving for his office, Governor Patterson fired a parting shot: "If they attempt to integrate the schools, it will be just like last Sunday night was."

It was just that sort of talk that had helped land John Patterson in his present mess and had brought federal forces into his state. If he had kept his mouth shut and accepted his responsibility to maintain law and order, the Freedom Riders would probably have passed through Alabama with little incident—just as they had passed through Virginia, North Carolina, South Carolina and Georgia. As the Freedom Riders themselves admit, segregation would have returned to Alabama before their bus was out of sight. Says a CORE lawyer: "A trip like this is like hacking your way through the jungle with a machete. After you've gone, the jungle grows right back."

Instead, Patterson helped set off integrationist movements that last week were spreading throughout the South. In Florida, the N.A.A.C.P. ordered a segregation test of all rail and bus facilities. In New York, CORE headquarters announced that it was sending field secretaries to New Orleans, Jackson and Montgomery. In Nashville, more students were ready to go to Jackson, where the 27 arrested Freedom Riders were fined $200 each and given suspended sentences of 60 days. At week's end, 22 of the 27 were still in jail because they refused to ante up any money.

The boldness and bravery of the Freedom Riders won over most of the old-line, conservative Negros leaders, leaving only a few doubters, who were shrugged off by the students as "Uncle Toms." "These kids are serving notice on us that we're moving too slow," said Thurgood Marshall, the N.A.A.C.P.

lawyer who won the school segregation case. "They're not content with all this talking." Said Martin Luther King: "I think all of this is unfortunate, but I think it is a psychological turning point in our whole struggle, just as Little Rock was a turning point in our legal struggle. The people themselves have said we can take it no longer. If we can through this, I think it will mean breaking the backbone of massive resistance and discrimination."

None Too Soon

Over the Voice of America, Bobby Kennedy last week reminded the world that the U.S. has an Irish Catholic for President, and added "There is no question about it. In the next 40 years a Negro can achieve the same position that my brother has." And at Columbia, S.C., Howard University President James Madison Nabrit, Jr., told the graduating class of Negro Benedict College: "Swifter than you can imagine you will have all the rights and privileges of every other citizen in the U.S." That time cannot come too swiftly for the young Negroes of 1961—and the John Pattersons of the South can do little to stop them.

JAMES W. SILVER

Mississippi: The Closed Society

APPENDIX: ON READING THE CONSTITUTION IN THE CLOSED SOCIETY

Printed below are the views of a well-known professor of constitutional law, born in the South and a long-time resident of Mississippi, on the constitutional questions raised in the Junior Chamber of Commerce pamphlet, *Oxford: A Warning for Americans.*

In October, 1962, the Mississippi Junior Chamber of Commerce distributed a 24-page pamphlet entitled *Oxford: A Warning for Americans,* which put the blame for the insurrection on the University campus squarely upon John and Robert Kennedy. In November, John Satterfield, past president of the American Bar Association, Citizens Council leader and intimate counselor of Barnett, delivered an address to the Jackson Rotary Club which was later

From *Mississippi: The Closed Society* by James W. Silver, pp. 134-140. © 1963, 1964 by James W. Silver. Reprinted by permission of Harcourt Brace Jovanovich, Inc., and Victor Gollancz, Ltd.

published and circulated in pamphlet form under the title *Due Process of Law or Government by Intimidation*. Both pamphlets advanced legal arguments that cast a mantle of respectability on Barnett's unlawful conduct and challenged the validity of the federal government's action throughout the Meredith affair. These legal arguments, however plausible to credulous Mississippians, are specious and untenable. The most important legal distortions and misrepresentations are as follows:

1. *Interposition*. After Meredith was ordered admitted to the University, Barnett issued a so-called declaration of state sovereignty in which he "interposed" the rights of the state of Mississippi between the people of Mississippi and the federal government. The pamphlets assert that this declaration raised legal issues not previously decided. This is false. Interposition is but another name for defiance of federal law. It is not a new doctrine. As long ago as 1809 (in *United States* v *Peters*) and as recently as 1960 (in *Busch* v *Orleans Parish*) the Supreme Court expressly repudiated interposition as a valid constitutional doctrine. Interposition is squarely in conflict with the Supremacy Clause of the Constitution (Article VI). Obviously, if each state were free to determine to its own satisfaction and with finality what the Constitution means in any given instance, the decision of each state, rather than the Constitution itself, would be the "supreme law of the land."

2. *The Tenth Amendment*. Barnett maintained that operation of the public school system is not one of the powers delegated to the United States by the Constitution, and therefore is one of the powers reserved to the states by the Tenth Amendment. The pamphlets assert that this postion raised legal issues not previously decided. This is false. The Tenth Amendment on its face states that certain powers are prohibited to the states and are therefore not reserved. One of these is the power of a state to deny to persons within its jurisdiction the equal protection of the law, which is prohibited by the Fourteenth Amendment. It is a denial of equal protection to deny admission of a qualified Negro to a public school solely because of his race, which is the very thing Mississippi was seeking to do to James Meredith. Thus, by its own terms, the Tenth Amendment affords no basis upon which Meredith could have been barred from admission.

3. *The Fourteenth Amendment*. The pamphlets also suggest that the Fourteenth Amendment, on which the desegregation decisions were based, was never validly ratified. The circumstances surrounding the adoption of the Amendment are discussed by the Supreme Court in considerable detail in the 1939 decision of *Coleman* v *Miller*. These circumstances afford no sound basis for concluding that the Amendment is not a valid part of the Constitution. Furthermore, since its adoption in 1868, the Amendment has been accepted as an integral part of the Constitution by every President,

every Congress, and every state. It has been applied by the Supreme Court, the lower federal courts, and the state courts in thousands of cases. The assertion of its invalidity does not raise a debatable question.

4. *The "Law of the Land."* The court order to admit Meredith to the University was based on the 1954 landmark case of *Brown* v *Board of Education*, which in turn was based on earlier cases prohibiting discrimination against Negroes in state-supported institutions of higher learning. The pamphlets attack the decision in *Brown v Board of Education* on the ground that it is not "the law of the land" but merely the "law of the case" binding only upon the parties in that lawsuit. This is false. Because our basic law, the Constitution, is necessarily couched in general terms, some persons or some institution must have the task of authoritatively interpreting its meaning and applying its provisions to contemporary society. The founding fathers delegated this task to the federal courts, of which the Supreme Court is the final arbiter. Thus, the rulings of the Supreme Court interpreting and applying the Constitution are, unless they are later overruled by that same tribunal, the law of the land. This is true of the decisions of the Supreme Court in the field of school desegregation, involving the interpretation and application of the Fourteenth Amendment. Mr. Satterfield's "law of the case" theory completely disregards the doctrine of precedent, under which the rule of law declared in one case is applicable to all other like cases arising thereafter, unless and until the law is changed. Thus, if the Supreme Court should decide in a given case that a certain kind of income is not taxable, presumably Mr. Satterfield would countenance the federal government's regarding the decision as being only the law of the case, taxing all citizens on such income notwithstanding the decision, and thus forcing every taxpayer in the country to litigate the matter all over again. Subsequent Supreme Court decisions since 1954 have reiterated the ruling in *Brown* and applied it in other areas of racial discrimination. There is absolutely no doubt that *Brown* is what the Court expressly declared it to be in the 1957 decision in *Cooper* v *Aaron*—the law of the land.

5. *Justice Black's Order.* Judge Ben Cameron of Meridian, Mississippi, was not a member of the Fifth Circuit panel of three judges that issued the order to admit Meredith to the University. Nevertheless, he promptly issued a stay of the order. The panel which decided the Meredith case then set aside Judge Cameron's stay, thus putting the admission order back into effect. Again Judge Cameron issued a stay. Three times this happened, until finally Supreme Court Justice Black issued an order vacating Judge Cameron's stays. The pamphlets maintain that there was procedural irregularity in Justice Black's action. This is completely erroneous. In the first place, stays are normally issued by the same panel of judges who issued the original order. It was most unusual for a single judge of the court of appeals, who

had not even participated in the case, to attempt to render inoperative the order of the other judges of the court who had heard the case and ordered Meredith admitted. After Judge Cameron's three attempts to thwart the order of his colleagues, Justice Black simply restored the status quo by setting aside Judge Cameron's stays. Although it is clearly within the proper prerogative of a single Supreme Court Justice to issue such an order, Justice Black nevertheless consulted all of his colleagues on the Court and they unanimously concurred in his action. If anyone was guilty of procedural irregularity, it was Judge Cameron and not Justice Black.

Furthermore, it must be realized that stays are not normally issued pending an appeal. They are issued only upon a showing that, if the stay is not issued, the party against whom the original order runs will suffer irreparable damage and also that issuance of the stay will not cause irreparable damage to the beneficiary of the original order. There must also be a showing that the appeal raises such questions of substance that there is some possibility that the case may be reversed. No such showings could possibly be made in the Meredith case, as the Fifth Circuit pointed out. First, there was no possibility that the Court would reverse (or even review the case) since the petition for certiorari raised no arguable questions of fact or law. The Court on October 9 did refuse to review the case. Thus, issuance of the stay would have done Meredith irreparable injury, since it would have kept him out of classes for several weeks after school commenced. Second, even on the assumption that the Court would review the case and reverse the decision, not issuing the stay would not cause the University any irreparable damage, since it would only have matriculated for a few weeks an ineligible student.

6. *Conviction in absentia.* Barnett and Johnson were found guilty of civil contempt by the Fifth Circuit on September 28 for violating a court order restraining them from interfering with Meredith's admission. The pamphlets suggest that the contempt proceedings were improper because neither Barnett nor Johnson was present. This is false. Barnett and Johnson were absent from the proceedings by their own choice. They had ample notice and opportunity to appear and defend themselves. For reasons of their own, they refused to do so. Mr. Satterfield seems to be saying that Barnett and Johnson had a right to defeat the court's jurisdiction by refusing to appear. But, of course, court proceedings are not annulled simply because the defendant refuses to show up.

7. *Completion of Judicial Process.* The pamphlets charge that the government did not await the completion of judicial processes before using military force to enforce the court order to admit Meredith. Federal marshals and troops were sent to the University campus on September 30–October 1, 1962, to quell the civil disorders that arose because of Barnett's defiance of the federal court order. But well before this date Meredith's right to enter the

University had been definitely established. After more than a year of litigation the Fifth Circuit Court of Appeals in June, 1962, had ordered that Meredith be admitted. On September 10, 1962, Justice Black had ordered Meredith's admission in September by setting aside the stays which would have delayed his right to enter pending disposition of the state's petition for Supreme Court review. After this action, Meredith had an absolute legal right to enter the University, and no further judicial proceedings were necessary to perfect that right. The only legal proceedings which were uncompleted on September 30 were the contempt proceedings against Barnett and Johnson, who had on September 25 been restrained by a Fifth Circuit order from blocking Meredith's admission, and who had thereafter violated that order. But these contempt actions had no bearing whatever on Meredith's right to enter the Univerity. The validity of the earlier order to admit Meredith was not in issue in the contempt proceedings, and therefore the outcome of that proceeding could in no way affect his right to enter. That right had already been finally established.

8. *Use of Troops.* The pamphlets charge that President Kennedy's use of troops was contrary to the Second Amendment of the Constitution and also to Article IV, Section 4. The Second Amendment provides that the right of the states to maintain a militia shall not be infringed. But Article I, Section 8 of the Constitution confers upon Congress the power "to provide for organizing, arming, and disciplining the militia" and also "to provide for calling forth the militia to execute the laws of the Union," and to "suppress insurrections." Article II, Section 2, of the Constitution imposes upon the President the duty to "take care that the laws be faithfully executed." This includes the "law of the land" as set forth in the decisions of the Supreme Court. Sections 332 and 333 of Title 10 of the United States Code expressly authorize the President to use both the militia of any state (National Guard) and the armed forces of the United States in certain described situations, such as obstruction of the authority of the federal government. This was exactuly the situation at the University of Mississippi on September 30, 1962. The basic statute authorizing the President to call out the militia was enacted in 1795 and was upheld by the Supreme Court as early as 1827.

Nor was there any violation of Article IV, section 4 of the Constitution, which requires the United States to protect the states, upon application of the legislature or governor, against domestic violence. Clearly, this provision must contemplate domestic violence against a state which the state by itself is unable to quell. It is equally clear that the provision does not apply when the domestic violence is against the federal government and is precipitated by state officials. This was the situation at the University on September 30. Mr. Satterfield's position is that, under these conditions, the federal government has not right to protect itself unless it is requested to do so by the very officials who are responsible for the obstruction of federal authority. Obviously, this is nonsense.

In 1895, in the case of *In re Debs*, the Supeme Court upheld the use of the Army by President Cleveland to enforce a federal court injunction against a strike by railway workers which interfered with interstate commerce and the transportation of U.S. mail. The Court stated in that case: "The entire strength of the nation may be used to enforce in any part of the land the full and free exercise of all national powers and the security of all rights entrusted by the Constitution to its care. . . . If the emergency arises, the army of the Nation, and all its militia, are at the service of the Nation to compel obedience to its laws." In the Debs case, the violence and the riots were not directed at the federal government as such, nor were the state officials engaged in the obstruction of federal law. The Mississippi situation was therefore a much stronger case for the use of troops than was *Debs*.

PAUL CHEVIGNY

A Busy Spring in the Magnolia State

The State Capitol in Jackson, where the Mississippi House and Senate sit, is a monument to the Mississippi legislative mind. A handsome building, finished in 1903 at what was then the terrific cost of a million dollars, it is a delicious combination of the humbug of the back-country politician and the pomposity of the Victorian swell. The floors and walls contain sixteen different kinds of marble, and the archways under the rotunda are set with thousands of light bulbs (which cause the temperature to go up above the point of endurability in the summer). If one goes in the doorway at ground level, one faces a bronze statue of the late Theodore Bilbo in a double-breasted suit, striking an oratorical stance. If one walks up the broad marble steps and through the main entrance, on the other hand, one is flanked on either side by an immense color transparency of one of the two Miss Americas who have come from Mississippi.

The legislative activities of the Mississippi House and Senate have been in keeping with their decorative instincts. They have always tried to protect

From *Southern Justice,* edited by Leon Friedman, pp. 13-16. Copyright © 1965 by Random House, Inc. Reprinted by permission of Pantheon Books, a Division of Random House, Inc.

southern womanhood and the southern way of life, though they have devoted increasing energy to the job since 1954. After the House and Senate
were convened in January, 1964, they passed the spring in prodigies of legislation designed to terrify Negroes and civil rights workers and to give law
enforcement agencies the power to prevent demonstrations. Much of this
activity had been completed by the time the summer volunteers arrived
late in June of that year. Newspaper reporters were unable to resist the
temptation to speak of the Council of Federated Organizations and its
efforts to register voters in terms of a military operation. But the fact is
that, aside from the lack of firearms, the COFO campaign failed in its
resemblance to a military attack in one signal respect: surprise. The COFO
operation was one of the major news stories of the year, and Mississippi had
heard much about each step in the invasion, beginning with the initial dispute among the civil rights groups as to whether Mississippi really was the
best target for the movement and including the details of the training of
the summer volunteers. Furthermore, a group of SNCC, CORE and NAACP
workers had been there all year, and some of them for years before, quietly
trying to organize Negroes to register. White Mississippians knew a great
deal more than they cared to know about field secretaries, Freedom Houses,
Freedom Schools, and Negro voter registration. Their elected representatives, most of whom obtained office by being more rabid race-baiters than
any of their opponents, not to speak of their constituents, undertook to
throw up a wall against the foreign invasion.

As the bills were proposed and passed, the COFO office at 1017 Lynch
Street in Jackson kept a running record of them, together with newspaper
clippings. Law students went around to the legislative sessions, then quietly
requested or filched copies of the bills.

These were no Black Codes; they were a good deal more subtle than that.
Though there are still a few segregation statutes scattered through the
volumes of the Mississippi Code, the legislature has learned that raw segregation by state action will be declared unconstitutional by the Federal
courts, even in Mississippi. The Mississippi legislators have shifted from
trying to limit civil rights to trying to limit what are loosely denoted civil
liberties, although their real purpose was never in doubt. Instead of perpetuating the system of segregation directly, the legislature passes bills of
attainder and impairs contracts; it interferes with the liberties preserved in
the Bill of Rights, including the rights to freedom of speech, press and
assembly, as well as the prohibitions against excessive fines and bail, and
cruel and unusual punishment. In short, the legislature sets out to maintain
segregation indirectly by controlling the protest against it. This raises the
question why, if they know that segregation laws are unconstitutional, the
legislators do not know that laws which infringe civil liberties are uncon-

stitutional as well. Part of the answer lies in the fact that the purpose of the statute is often hidden, sometimes artfully and sometimes not, under a thicket of pious verbiage intended to show that the law is a health measure or a police reform. Those cases where the unconstitutional intent of the statute is obvious must be explained by the fact that the legislators in Mississippi have not had as much practice with the rest of the Constitution as they have had with the equal protection clause. Part of the civil rights lawyers' job is to give them a little more experience with the rest of the Constitution.

In a few cases the legislators do in fact think that a statute is unconstitutional, but they pass it anyhow. For example, in June, 1964, a statute was passed penalizing persons located outside the state who foment crimes to be perpetrated inside the state and later come into the state. The chairman of the Senate Judiciary Committee, Senator Collins, was quoted in the *Greenwood Commonwealth* of May 12, 1964, as saying, "The bill may be unconstitutional, but it can't do us any harm." Why anyone who entertains this attitude should stop at a segregation statute is a mystery. It is probably because he expects that not even Mississippi judges will any longer uphold a segregation statute. But a law infringing civil liberties may survive the Mississippi courts until it is struck down by the Supreme Court. The longer the law is on the books the longer it can be used as a tool against civil rights.

DONALD S. STRONG

The Struggle for the Records

Only a minority of the total number of suits have arisen under a claim of coercion or intimidation. The greater number of suits have involved section 1971(a) which prohibits racial discrimination in voting. The section reads:

> All citizens of the United States who are otherwise qualified by law to vote at any election . . . shall be entitled to vote at all such elections without distinction of race, color, . . . ; any constitution, law, custom, usage, or regulation of any state . . . to the contrary notwithstanding.

In many areas of the Deep South it is common knowledge that Negroes were prevented from voting or certainly discouraged from registering and

From *Negroes, Ballots, and Judges* by Donald S. Strong, pp. 20-24. Copyright © 1968 by The University of Alabama Press. Reprinted by permission.

voting. However, this "common knowledge" is not enough to persuade a federal judge. The first step in proving discrimination is to secure a county's registration records. Without the records one cannot demonstrate even so basic a fact as that 98 per cent of whites of voting age in the county are registered whereas the corresponding figure for Negroes is 2 per cent. The demonstration of this disproportion is not necessarily persuasive; it might be coincidental. In addition, the records may often be used to demonstrate that the registration imbalance is due to the rigorous standards required of Negroes and the very indulgent standards applied to whites. Both federal and state officials are aware of the importance of access to the records. It will be recalled that the 1960 act requires that all election and registration records be preserved, in effect, indefinitely, and that any record or paper thus preserved must be made available by the person having custody of it for inspection or reproduction by a representative of the Attorney General. Earthy incidents recounted in cases attest to the importance that registrars attach to these records. In *U.S. v. Cartwright* two members of the Elmore County, Alabama, Board of Registrars, learning of a forthcomnig FBI investigation of their records, quietly carried a large supply of records to the city dump and set them on fire. Both Alabama and Mississippi legislatures passed laws permitting (not requiring) registrars to dispose of these records. While these state laws are in conflict with the federal law and therefore unconstitutional, their passage indicates the general agreement on the importance of access to records.

One may reasonably infer that a person who has nothing to conceal will voluntarily permit inspection of his records. Contrariwise, tenacious litigation to prevent inspection of the records suggests that a registrar has something to hide. By January, 1964, the Justice Department had asked to inspect the records of 100 counties. In 38 instances, court action had to be brought to secure access. It is a tribute to the ingenuity of defense attorneys that the Department should have to resort to the courts in 38 instances. It would seem that the third section of Title III of 1960 Civil Rights Act is plain enough. It provides:

> Any record or paper required by section 301 to be retained and preserved shall, upon demand in writing by the Attorney General or his representative directed to the person having custody, possession, or control of such record or paper, be made available for inspection, reproduction, and copying at the principal office of such custodian by the Attorney General or his representative. This demand shall contain a statement of the basis or purpose therefor.

Yet great ingenuity may be exercised here. The question may be raised over who has actual physical custody of the records at a given time since the

government must address its demand to "the person having custody. . . ."
What happens if the registrar has temporarily given custody of the records
to the county solicitor or the county grand jury? In *U.S. v. Majors* the Attorney General made a formal request on April 13, 1961, that the records be
made available for photographing. Upon refusal, the case was taken to
court, and a trial held on October 30, 1961. The defendant held that the
records were in the hands of the grand jury and not in the custody of the
board of registrars. On February 19, 1962, the district court finally ruled in
favor of the Government, holding that all records were in daily use by the
defendant. This technicality delayed the Attorney General nearly a year. A
monumentally absurd legal issue arises when a voting registrar holds another
job and title. In the case of *Kennedy v. Owen* the Government had asked
the district judge for an inspection order directing the circuit clerks of seven
Mississippi counties to make their records available for inspection. Under
Mississippi law a registrar is also the circuit clerk. U.S. District Judge Cox
granted an inspection order as to the records each defendant possessed in
his capacity as circuit clerk but not as registrar. The Court of Appeals
would have none of this quibble and ruled that the records be made available.

The most fertile source of delaying action was the defense effort to con-
strue this section as a criminal prosecution in which the defendant could
not have his papers searched unless there were a precise description of the
records that were wanted. This reading of the act also raised the question
whether a registrar must make available the records of his predecessor. It
was necessary to try a series of cases to clarify the meaning of Title III. The
struggle to inspect the records of Wilcox County, Alabama, took two years.
Eventually several cases stated with considerable clarity the meaning of this
part of the law—namely Title III. In *Kennedy v. Lynd* the circuit court was
at pains to emphasize that there was here no question of the relevancy of
the documents, that is, the Government need not demonstrate that a document is relevant to the case before examining it. Nor is there any question
of time limit; establishing a pattern or practice of discrimination may require a study of documents that goes back many years. In other respects,
Title III is unlike a traditional criminal action. Title III requires that "every
officer of election shall retain and preserve . . . all records and papers which
come into his possession relating to any application, registration. . . ." Congress has specified what papers must be preserved. Hence, there can be no
room for a quibble about what papers are to be made available to the Attorney General. The law governing preservation and examining of papers applies to *all* papers, not merely those that some applicant thinks would demonstrate discrimination against him. Nor does it make any difference whether
there has been a change of registrars. Records of earlier registrars cannot be

denied on the theory that an office-holder cannot be held accountable for the acts of his predecessor. The registrar is not accused of having violated constitutional rights. He is a party to the suit because he has custody of records. The Court of Appeals emphasized that there was no hidden meaning in the final sentence of Title III which states that the Attorney General's demand "contain a statement of the basis and purpose thereof." In another case when counsel representing a Mississippi registrar attempted to read much into this statement, the court went into the legislative history of the act. It quoted Senator Keating as stating to his colleagues, "Clearly a sufficient statement would be assertion that the demand was made for the purpose of investigating possible violations of a federal statute." No showing even of a *prima facie* case of violation of federal law need be made. Mississippi continued to fight on this issue by taking the case to the Supreme Court where certiorari was denied.

Securing the records is the first step in a laborious process, which may or may not justify the filing of a suit which may or may not result in a court order enfranchising some Negroes. From the standpoint of the determined enemy of Negro voting, all litigation on the get-the-records issue has been a strategy of defense-in-depth. You fight at the outposts to stave off the day when you will have to defend the inner citadel. Yet the Justice Department has had to spend a great part of its energies trying to lay hands on the raw materials out of which a case may possibly be made. While the Government has eventually won all these get-the-records cases, the defense tactics have compelled tedious litigation over technicalities and postponed consideration by the courts of substantive issues, thereby lessening the effectiveness of civil rights legislation.

ROBERT H. BIRKBY

The Supreme Court and the Bible Belt: Tennessee Reaction to the "Schempp" Decision

If the *Schempp* decision had any effect in Tennessee it should be noticeable in the policies adopted and enforced at the school district level. The State Commissioner of Education was reported as saying that it was permissible to read the Bible in public schools despite *Schempp* but he left the final

From the *Midwest Journal of Political Science*, Vol. 10, August 1966, pp. 304-315. Reprinted by permission of the Wayne State University Press and the author.

decision to local school officials.[1] The school boards were left free to continue the practice required by state law or to comply with the Court's ruling. This study was undertaken to determine what the school boards did and, if possible, why. Even though it was expected that, in Gordon Patric's words, the "decision was put into effect in diverse ways and 'obeyed' to varying degrees,"[2] board action in response to *Schempp* was classified as changing or not changing policy. All districts reporting a departure from the pre-*Schempp* provisions of state law were considered changing districts. It was believed that one of several factors could be used to explain the differences between changing and non-changing districts. These were degree of urbanization, extent of religious pluralism, articulate opposition within the district to devotional exercises, or differences in the socio-economic composition of the school boards.[3]

To test these suppositions three questionnaires were prepared and sent out in late 1964 and early 1965. One was mailed to each of the 152 superintendents of schools in the state. The second was mailed to the chairman and two other randomly selected members of each school board. The third was sent to the remaining school board members in those districts from which responses were obtained to either or both of the first two questionnaires. The superintendents were asked what the policy on Bible reading and devotional exercises had been in their district before June, 1963, and what it currently was. They were asked to identify any factors inducing change and to describe, in each time period, the policy-making role of the board, superintendent, principals, teachers, parents, religious groups, and any other participants. The first group of board members was asked about current (post 1963) policy, how it differed from that of the past, what groups or persons made policy suggestions to the board, and what groups or persons were consulted by the board. The second group of board members was simply asked to supply information on age, occupation, education, income, religious affiliation, length of service on the board, and length of residence in the school district of its members. Response to the first and third questionnaires was good. . . .

Of the 121 districts, 70 were reported to be still following the requirements of state law. The other 51 districts were reported to have made some

---

1. *Nashville Tennessean,* August 23, 1963, p. 1. In an interview October 16, 1964, the Commissioner confirmed that he had left the decision to local officials. He said at that time that he had taken no official position on the issue.
2. Gordon Patric, "The Impact of a Court Decision: Aftermath of the McCollum Case," 6 *Journal of Public Law,* 455 (1957).
3. Daniel F. Boles, *The Bible, Religion and the Public Schools,* 3rd ed. (Ames: Iowa State University Press, 1965). The author suggests (p. 340) the urbanization and religious pluralism explanations.

changes in their policy but only one of these completely eliminated all Bible reading and devotional exercises. The other 50 merely made student participation voluntary and left the decision whether to have devotional exercises to the discretion of the classroom teacher. Thus 42 percent of the reporting school districts no longer adhere strictly to the provisions of state law even though all but one could have some form of classroom devotional exercise.

The most reasonable explanation for these differences in response to *Schempp* seemed to lie in the extent of urbanization. Table 1 shows the distribution of changing and non-changing districts according to this factor.

Table 1

RELATIONSHIP OF URBANIZATION AND SCHOOL RELIGIOUS EXERCISE
POLICY CHANGE

% of District Population Urbanized*	Number of Districts	
	Changing	Not Changing
90–100	17	19
80–89	1	0
70–79	0	0
60–69	0	0
50–59	1	0
40–49	3	1
30–39	2	0
20–29	5	9
10–19	3	4
0–9	19	37
Totals	51	70

* On the basis of 1960 census data.

Using the point bi-serial correlation[4] the relationship between urbanization and tendency toward partial compliance with *Schempp* was found to be practically non-existent ($r_{pb} = -0.08$). Thus, on the basis of questionnaire responses, school boards and superintendents in urban areas showed no greater tendency to change Bible reading and devotional exercise policy than the respondents from rural areas.

The possibility that increasing religious pluralism may account for objections to religion in the schools must remain largely in the realm of speculation since accurate figures on denominational membership by school dis-

4. Allen L. Edwards, *Statistical Methods for the Behavioral Sciences* (New York: Rinehart & Company, 1954), pp. 182-85.

trict or even county do not exist. The National Council of Churches has issued a rough compilation by counties and in lieu of anything else these figures were used to test this possibility. Only those counties with a single area-wide school district (no city districts) and those counties in which the county district and the city district took the same position could be used. This distorts the results somewhat but was made necessary by the impossibility of breaking county religious affiliation figures down into smaller units. On this rough test there is only slight correlation between religious pluralism and tendency to change ($r_{pb} = 0.02$). The pattern of change classified by total population of the district was also checked on the theory that heavily populated districts would be more likely to be religiously heterogeneous; again only a slight correlation was found ($r_{pb} = 0.24$).

The other two possibilities advanced above are equally ineffective in explaining the pattern of change. From only one of the eighty-four districts represented by responses from the first group of board members was there a report that the board had been approached by an individual who objected to a continuation of the Bible reading and devotional exercises. In this instance the protester's efforts were in vain since that district still complies with state law. Either there was no significant opposition to devotional exercise or else no board member wanted to admit that there had been any.

Using the chi square test and rejecting the null hypothesis at the 0.01 level of significance, tabulation of the responses of the second group of board members produced no significant differences in socio-economic characteristics between changing and non-changing boards. . . .

In each instance the null hypothesis must be accepted.

Thus far this paper has presented only negative results. Partial compliance with *Schempp* is not explained by degree of urbanization. There are no significant differences in the socio-economic characteristics of changing and non-changing board members. In the changing districts the board members did not report any overt pressure for compliance. And, by a rough test, the extent of religious pluralism in the district had no effect. These findings are significant and justify reporting. It may well be that the population of the State of Tennessee is too homogeneous—socially, religiously, and economically—for any of these tests to be significant. In some other state with greater diversity, urbanization and religious pluralism might be more important. Even so, Tennessee reaction would remain unexplained.

The reported response by Tennessee school districts to *Schempp* might be explained by one other hypothesis. There is in the questionnaires some support for it but not enough to make it possible to assert that it is correct. What follows then is largely speculative. The line of reasoning starts with a distinction between procedural and substantive change in policy. Policy change in any situation may take the form of (1) altering procedure without altering the policy goal, (2) changing procedure to reach a new policy goal without, however, making the new goal explicit, or (3) changing the policy goal with or without a change in procedure. Although we cannot be sure, it seems fairly safe to say that in the fifty school districts which overtly changed their policy on Bible reading and delegated the decision to the teachers there has been little change in fact. That is, it is suspected that the classroom teachers are "voluntarily" conducting Bible reading and devotional exercises just as they did before *Schempp*.[5] One might go a step further and assert, without being able to prove it, that the school boards were aware that this would probably happen. I am suggesting that the board members acted consciously either to save the substance of the program or to avoid upsetting the community status quo by making slight procedural changes. In the language of Sayre and Kaufman, the contestants who had the prizes of the game were able to keep them by responding to a rules change with a rules change of their own.[6] A comment by a lawyer on the board of a changing district indicates the compromise nature of the policy adopted:

> My personal conviction is that the Supreme Court decisions are correct, and I so told the Board and Superintendent; but I saw no reason to create controversy. If the Board had made public a decision abolishing devotional exercises, there would have been public outcry. I believe all staff members understand that the continuance of devotional exercises in their schools and in their rooms is entirely voluntary and subject to discontinuance upon objection of any individual or minority group.

There are other reasons that a board might adopt this strategy of procedural change. It could be used to reduce disagreement within the board itself. It could be suggested by an individual as a means of reducing his own tensions between a desire to comply with the Court's decision and a desire to retain perceived advantages of devotional exercises. Finally, change in procedure without change in substance might be made to forestall demands for even greater change. There is nothing in the questionnaire responses to indicate which of these alternatives is correct and it is possible that all were present to some extent. If any or all of these suppositions are correct, a desire to retain the program rather than religious pluralism and urbanization would be responsible for the formal change. To this point the

5. This suspicion is based on unsystematic conversations with classroom teachers from two or three districts which made this formal change and on the questionnaire responses of a few superintendents who indicated doubt that any actual change had occurred.
6. Wallace S. Sayre and Herbert Kaufman, *Governing New York City* (New York: Russell Sage Foundation, 1960).

hypothesis does not provide an answer to the question of why the form was changed in some districts and not in others. It does emphasize that the answer must be sought in psychological rather than in demographic or socio-economic factors.

The question being asked in any impact study is why the Court's decision is not self-executing. In a different context Richard Neustadt has concluded that a self-executing order must have five characteristics: (1) the issuer of the order must be unambiguously involved in making the decision, (2) the order must be unambiguously worded, (3) the order must receive wide publicity, (4) those receiving the order must have control of the means of implementation, and (5) there must be no doubt of the individual's authority to issue the order.[7] Neustadt was speaking of orders issued by the President but there is no reason that the same analysis cannot be applied to Court decisions. In this instance, there was no doubt that the Court did in fact make the decision though one school board member suggested that the Court was "controlled by small pressure groups." When applied to the Tennessee statute the wording of the order, although negative in content, was clear enough.[8] There was wide publicity. The members of the boards of education had control of the means of implementation. However, the fifth factor was not so obviously present.

There was some confusion about the Court's decision. It was clear enough that required devotional exercises were forbidden but the Court did not commit itself on the status of voluntary programs such as those adopted by the fifty changing districts in Tennessee. This ambiguity caused one super-intendent to assert confidently "we believe our policy [voluntary participation] is in accordance with the ruling of the Supreme Court and in accord with the desires of the people in this community."

More important is the question of the Court's authority to issue the order. The policy maker's reaction to a judicial decision will be conditioned by his perception of the Court's role in general, his beliefs concerning the importance of the challenged activity or program, his perception of the attitudes of his reference groups and constituents on the issue, and his perception of his role. The differences in policy position may be the result of a general

---

7. Richard E. Neustadt, *Presidential Power* (New York: John Wiley and Sons, 1960), p. 19.
8. In some instances this criterion will not be met by a decision. The best examples are the confusion resulting from the "with all deliberate speed" formula in school desegregation and general ambiguity in the majority opinion in *Zorach v. Clauson,* 343 U.S. 306 (1952). See Jack W. Peltason, *Fifty-Eight Lonely Men* (New York: Harcourt, Brace & World, 1961), and Frank J. Sorauf, "*Zorach v. Clauson:* The Impact of a Supreme Court Decision," 53 *American Political Science Review,* 777 (1959).

attitude toward the Court and its role in the American system of government.[9] The following comments are typical in content and intensity.

Changing Districts

A Surgeon: We must conform with Federal law. If we are to teach our children to obey laws we must set an example.

A Farmer: We did not want to violate any federal law.

A Superintendent: I think the Supreme Court is correct. Very few people understand the religious issue, less seem to understand what is meant by religious freedom, and relatively few seem to understand the Supreme Court's role in our government.

A Farmer: We are commanded by the Bible to be subject to civil powers as long as their laws do not conflict with laws of God.

Non-Changing Districts

A Superintendent: Impeach Earl Warren.

A Housewife: The decision of the Supreme Court seemed senseless and I could see no advantage in making changes.

A College Professor: The Supreme Court decision didn't mean a damn.

A Banker: The general public in this country do not have the respect for the U. S. Supreme Court as they once did. They think it is packed, so to speak, and doubt very much if all are qualified and unbiased and listen to the whims of the President that gave them the appointment. The standards are on a lower level than back several years ago.

A Superintendent: I am at a loss to understand the necessity for this survey. I am of the opinion that 99% of the people in the United States feel as I do about the Supreme Court's decision—that it was an outrage and that Congress should have it amended. The remaining 1% do not belong in this free world.

A Lawyer: We felt that in the absence of some good specific objection, there was no compelling reason to change previous policy.

If one had these comments without information on the policy adopted, it would not be too difficult to predict the position taken by each of these school boards.

The Court-attitude is only one of the variables affecting the impact of a

9. Speaking to the American Philosophical Society in 1952, Justice Felix Frankfurter observed that "broadly speaking, the chief reliance of law in a democracy is the habit of popular respect for law. Especially true is it that law as promulgated by the Supreme Court ultimately depends upon confidence of the people in the Supreme Court as an institution." Frankfurter, *Of Law and Men* (New York: Harcourt, Brace & Co., 1956), p. 31. Brehm and Cohen report an experiment demonstrating that the more credible the source of a communication the greater the change in the recipient's attitude even when there was wide discrepancy between the recipient's initial attitude and the content of the communication. Jack W. Brehm and Arthur R. Cohen, *Explorations in Cognitive Dissonance* (New York: John Wiley and Sons, 1962), pp. 247-48.

judicial decision. The other major variable is the policy maker's assessment of and commitment to the challenged program or activity.

. . .

Perceptions of the attitudes of constituents or clientele are important but seem to be secondary. They play the role of reinforcing or modifying the Court-attitude and/or the program-attitude. A dentist on the board of a changing district observed that "we thought public opinion would want us to comply with Federal Law," while a chairman of a non-changing board (who did not indicate his occupation) said that the most important factor influencing him was that "we would have had complaints if we did not have Bible reading." Both of these board members were reacting to their perception of constituent attitude. . . .

Kirk Has Youth Arrested as Florida Rock Fete Opens

Gov. Claude R. Kirk Jr. paid a call today on thousands of youths massed for a weekend rock festival near West Palm Beach and ordered one of them arrested. The Governor said that he would not let Florida become a playground for hippies.

The Governor ordered the youth's arrest following a brief conversation in which he asked the long-haired youngster how he felt. The teen-ager responded, "pretty good," but refused to tell Mr. Kirk where he was from.

"Take him," Governor Kirk said, gesturing to Sheriff William Heidtman. Two deputies grabbed the boy, dragged him to a squad car and drove him away as a group of more than 200 youths shouted profanities at the Governor.

The deputies refused to say what charges would be lodged against the boy, who looked to be about 15 years old.

"These kids think they can play in Florida," Governor Kirk told newsmen. "Well, they are wrong. You can't play anywhere in this state or in Palm Beach County."

Hunger Crusader Jailed in a Carolina Drug Case

Dr. Donald Gatch went to jail today.

Dr. Gatch, a soft-spoken crusader against hunger, refused to post $10,000 bond because he said any other doctor would be released on his personal recognizance in similar circumstances.

He was indicted earlier this month on four charges involving drug law violations, and his trial has been set for Jan. 5. Dr. Gatch has been out of the state and was under treatment for anemia and malnutrition in a North Carolina hospital before returning to South Carolina last night.

Dr. Gatch is accused of illegal use of drugs, failure to keep proper records, and dispensing drugs without a prescription.

Dr. Gatch, who maintains he is being persecuted by the state, said before going to jail, "I don't think they're treating me like they would treat any other doctor under the circumstances."

On the advice of his lawyer, Dr. Gatch declined to talk to newsmen after going to jail.

He was denounced by other doctors when he first brought to public attention severe malnutrition and intestinal parasites among Negro children in Beaufort County two years ago .

He says he became the subject of harassment and economic reprisals.

Early this year he helped to guide Senator Ernest F. Hollings, Democratic of South Carolina, on a tour of hunger areas. Mr. Hollings returned to Washington after three other tours and urged Congress to commit the country to the elimination of hunger and malnutrition.

Accompanied this morning by his wife, Anita, Dr. Gatch walked into the office of the court clerk, T. Legare Rogers and asked if he could be released on his personal recognizance.

Mr. Rogers told him he could not be released without court authorization. When Dr. Gatch asked what he should do, Mr. Rogers suggested that he contact Sheriff L. W. Wallace.

Dr. Gatch asked if he should call or go in person to see Sheriff Wallace, whose office is a block away at the county jail. Mr. Rogers suggested he go in person, and Dr. Gatch then drove to Mr. Wallace's office.

From there, he called a lawyer, John Bolt Culbertson of Greenville, who agreed to handle the case.

Sheriff Wallace said he had no authority to release Dr. Gatch without the cash bond, but he told Mr. Culbertson he could release the doctor if approval was given by Randolph Murdaugh Jr., the state prosecutor.

Mr. Culbertson called Mr. Murdaugh, who said he would discuss the matter with Circuit Judge William L. Rhodes. Mr. Murdaugh said he would make no recommendation in the matter but would not oppose the release.

BEN A. FRANKLIN

Post Town Upset By Antiwar G.I.'s

When they signed the one-year lease last July, H. H. Basham, the 81-year-old Kentucky land owner who is reputed to hold title to most of this one-square-mile civilian enclave in the middle of Fort Knox, said he thought he was renting an old clapboard house on main street to a bunch of clean-cut kids for a G.I. "ice cream parlor."

It would be a nice place for the troops to gather after hours. Besides, the tenants were paying $250 a month. But that was before the posters of Mao-Tse-tung went up on the walls, along with the upside-down American flag, in what turned out to be an antiwar G.I. coffee house.

By September, Mr. Basham was in Meade County Quarterly Court, testifying that he did not like "the goings on" at his property and threatening the young tenants' lawyer—a "Communist like the rest of them," he testified —with his walking stick.

Without warning, Muldraugh, a sleepy, run-down country town 25 miles south of Louisville, had been propelled into its first major ideological controversy since this part of Kentucky decided to join the Confederate States in 1861.

By refusing the September rent check, Mr. Basham and his lawyer, J. R. Watts, who is the Meade County attorney, quickly persuaded county Judge Bert Allen that the young dissenters were delinquent in payment and got an eviction notice.

When Stuart Lyon, a young lawyer from Louisville, attempted to appeal the eviction, Judge Allen set an unusually high "traverse bond" of $3,000. Under Kentucky law, such a bond is supposed to guarantee a landlord three months' rent should the eviction appeal fail, defense lawyers said. Judge Allen set the bond at the equivalent of 12 months' protection for Mr. Basham.

Before the coffee house sponsor could post the bond, the judge announced that he had "looked more thoroughly" into the bond matter and had raised the bond to $10,000. To the surprise of many, the coffee house group posted that amount in cash.

The Muldraugh Town Council then adopted a new business license ordinance and the Kentucky Health Department objected to sanitary conditions in the coffee house. Denied both business and health permits, not a drop of coffee has yet been poured there. But Police Chief David C. Ridenour of Muldraugh ordered the place closed contending that it was a nuisance.

Mr. Lyon and two other lawyers, Robert E. Delahanty of Louisville and William Allison of Lexington, Ky., overcame that with a temporary restraining order obtained from Judge James F. Gordon of United States District Court and the antiwar, anti-Army "rap sessions" have continued.

The mood of the G.I. dissenters is probably best embodied in an under ground newspaper published at Fort Knox that Muldraugh regards as subversive.

"Communistic people have got hold of that place and are agitating against the capitalistic system," Mr. Watts said in an interview yesterday.

Some here say that the "Communists" have infiltrated the Fort Knox command. This belief stems from the decision of Maj. Gen. James W. Sutherland Jr., the base commander, to follow as far as possible a "hands-off" policy toward the dissenters under recent Army guidelines designed to avoid embarrassing military confrontations in the courts with uniformed militants. Such incidents occurred earlier this year at Fort Jackson, S. C.

Officers at Fort Jackson seem delighted, however, that Muldraugh's civilians are fighting the coffee house. There has been "some Army cooperation" with local authorities, a base spokesman said, but Chief Ridenour maintains that it has been "not enough."

Then came the arrests. The Meade County Grand Jury subpoenaed and questioned six of the coffee house organizers a week ago and indicted them under the public nuisance and sanitation laws.

Circuit Judge A. Murray Beard set bond at $1,500 each and the five of the six organizers went to jail Oct. 30 in lieu of bail. District Judge Gordon lowered the bail to $500 last Tuesday and the five were released on bail.

Having witnessed the arrests on Oct. 31, four more coffee house witnesses invoked the Fifth Amendment against self-incrimination in their grand jury appearances but went to jail—this time without the possibility of posting bond—under Judge Beard's ruling that they were in contempt of court. Yesterday the Kentucky Court of Appeals ordered them released under $500 bond while it considers their contention that they have a right to "peaceable dissent."

ED SALZMAN

Stiff Terms Urged in Campus Riots

Bold and unusual steps are being taken by key Republican legislators to convince judges that stiff penalties must be handed out to agitators convicted of offenses at San Francisco State College and other California campuses.

Assemblyman Don Mulford, of Oakland, chairman of the Assembly GOP caucus, said the public is furious because some judges are issuing "slap-on-the-wrist sentences" instead of six months in jail to hard-core troublemakers.

At Mulford's instigation, judges from throughout the state were brought to Sacramento for a meeting on the problem with Mulford and Assemblyman Frank Murphy of Santa Cruz, chairman of the criminal procedure committee.

Mulford said that if the situation does not change, lenient judges will find themselves with heavily financed opposition the next time they face the voters.

Murphy emphasized that he wants to know whether the judges feel that additional laws are needed to help them stiffen their backs.

He explained that "social pressure" in a community frequently prevents a judge from handing out a tough penalty even where it is clearly indicated.

Murphy said one solution might be to make a jail sentence mandatory for second offenders involved in a campus altercation.

Mulford said he is eager to introduce any legislation that will help authorities restore order to San Francisco State and other campuses.

"But the cold truth is that the laws on the books are not implemented in the courtroom," he declared. "The public wants to know why these agitators are allowed to go back on campus instead of going to jail for six months."

One problem, Mulford added, is the current practice of releasing suspects on their own recognizance while they are awaiting trial.

From the *Oakland Tribune*, February 2, 1969, p. 3. Reprinted by permission.

Mulford wants the judges to make the suspects raise a reasonable amount of bail in order to be released.

The assemblyman said the Berkeley Municipal Court has set an excellent example for the rest of the state in handling those arrested on the University of California's Berkeley campus.

He said the late Judge Rupert Crittenden and Judge George Brunn have not allowed agitators to get away with a mere slap on the wrist.

The problem, according to Mulford, is not restricted to campus disturbances.

The meeting with judges came after Mulford conferred with two of Gov. Ronald Reagan's top aides, executive secretary Edwin Meese III and education adviser Alex Sheriffs.

Murphy cited two cases where organized campaigns for stiffer sentences have been successful—the mandatory jail terms for Bay Bridge speeders and for second-offense drunk drivers.

The Mulford Gap

From the depths of an abysmal generation gap, Assemblyman Don Mulford of Oakland has not only called for draconian punishment of student demonstrators but has now overstepped the bounds by threatening judges who decline to hustle them into jail for six months or such other terms as the law allows.

At his behest, judges from all sections of the State were recently summoned to Sacramento for a meeting with him and Assemblyman Frank Murphy, chairman of the criminal procedure committee. They were informed, by Mulford himself, that those who are guilty of leniency in such cases will find themselves up against "heavily financed opposition" when they next file for re-election.

Some judges describe his remarks as overt intimidation and a near-miss on blackmail. We find them a flagrant attempt by a legislator to interfere with the judiciary and frighten some of its members out of their constitutionally endowed independence. They represent a cynical violation of the separation-of-powers principle and fly directly in the face of efforts by the State Bar and Governor Reagan (through his widely advertised "merit plan") to remove the bench from political pressures.

From the *San Francisco Chronicle*, February 6, 1969, p. 40. Reprinted by permission.

In this connection, it is highly disquieting to learn that Mulford issued his invitation to the judges and threatened them with dire retaliation after conferring with two members of the Governor's close official family—Edwin Meese III, his executive secretary, and Alex Sheriffs, his education adviser.

In this performance, Assemblyman Mulford presents an amazing figure when, posing as a champion of law and order, he tries to bully the assembled judges into repudiating the established, orderly processes of trial courts.

VII   IN PURSUIT OF A REMEDY

DAVID WALLEY

Arms and the Man: The ACLU *vs.* The NYPD

Pretty soon, demonstration time will be rolling around and everyone will get out their gas masks, baseball bats, football helmets and Vaseline from storage for the Spring Offensive. People will be preparing to demonstrate their constitutional rights to peacefully assemble and protest. The police will be there to meet them, probably reeling from the latest excoriating and well-documented report by the New York American Civil Liberties Union called *December 9, 1969—A Report.* It is the latest in a long series of papers concerned with police violence to demonstrators. *December 9* accounts one of the bloodiest outbursts of police violence which, according to Peggy Kerry's scholarship, was ". . . more extensive and more serious than any demonstration since the police raids at Columbia University in May of 1968."

Those who were there are quite familiar with the terrorist tactics of wholesale arrests and detention of innocent bystanders, unprovoked attacks by uniformed and plainclothes cops, and station house antics of New York's finest. All details are amply elaborated upon in this twenty-one page booklet which you can get by writing the New York Civil Liberties Union at 156 Fifth Avenue, NYC 10010. I'm not going to rehash the details. More enlightening is the foreword to the report which sets up the circumstances of the report and gives the Union's suggestions for the policing of future demonstrations. It is interesting because it gives an insight into civil libertarian thinking which is relevant to the Movement on both a personal and a mass level.

The American Civil Liberties Union is a guild of lawyers who believe in giving all people access to their Constitutional rights. Recently, they have been fighting various state and local loyalty oath provisions, mandatory prayers in the school, and helping the Conspiracy obliquely. As far as I can determine, they look on the police as necessary, but note that police have a habit of overstepping their functions by dispensing crude instant justice instead of making arrests and having the courts determine guilt or innocence. The ACLU believes in the ideals of law enforcement, and the ideal of participation in the democratic process. Ideals are not what make this country run, though lip service is always being paid to "the American way" of jurisprudence (meaning a quiet necktie party for unruly blacks or tar and feathering of perfidious radical sympathizers or longhairs) and the Bill of Rights. Idealists are needed in this society to keep everyone at least paying lip service to the law. The ACLU stands as a good watchdog to protect against the deterioration of these vital rights for all of us. Idealism in police matters is something else to consider.

The Union listed in *December 9* eight suggestions for police in handling future demonstrations. Rather than comment on them separately, I will list them first and comment later:

1. Discontinue dragnet procedures and prosecute officers responsible for such practices.

2. Eliminate flying wedge tactics because it leads to unnecessary injuries.

3. Eliminate the use of nightsticks and blackjacks at demonstrations.

4. Eliminate plainclothesmen at demonstrations for they cannot be adequately supervised.

5. Use nametags in addition to shields to aid in police identification.

6. Bring departmental charges against those commanders of units responsible for abuses.

7. Maintain a substantial number of senior police observers and high ranking civilian observers at demonstrations.

8. Establish a centralized booking procedure for demonstration arrests.

If you read between the lines, you can easily see that most of the suggestions deal with the immediate problems arising from police violence. They neither attempt to locate nor effectively deal with the reasons why there is police violence at all in demonstrations. As I said before, the ACLU is concerned with legality, not morality. Morals cannot be legislated anyway. The basic premise of any lawyer is that this is a country of laws and not men. So be it, but the reasons why people do things are equally important as the precautions one takes against them recurring. This the NYACLU takes no responsibility for, at least in this document. (You can pick up on a perceptive book by Paul Chevigny called *Police Power* (Vintage V-551), *Police Abuses in New York City* which does.)

The tale told in *December 9, 1969* is chock full of accounts of aimless violence by uniformed and plainclothes police, but why violence at all? Well, that is another question entirely which the book makes no attempt to expose. Perhaps the reason for violence on the part of the police is that they are confronted with a paradox. They are servants of the law, and in a way, try to become the epitome of THE LAW. They metamorphose themselves into THE AUTHORITY, the final arbiter. They are paid to support the system which feeds them and accordingly, they strongly identify with all that American society holds prominent. In this specific demonstration, the President represents America which the police swear to uphold. Anyone who demonstrates or disparages the country, even if there is no law on the books, is violating everything the country, and those boys in blue stand for. The result is predictable: overzealous police tactics, flying wedge tactics to take down a red flag over the Bankers Trust building even though, according to the writer, "The violation is exactly the same as that which takes place every time someone puts a political sticker or poster on the side of a building without the permission of the owner . . . the charge through the crowd to secure the flagpole on December 9 can be most generously considered as asinine." (p. 4) All right, so there was an unnecessary charge to secure a flagpole from the red menace of revolution. The booklet doesn't even speculate why there was such a charge in the first place. (It's not really supposed to since this is about abuses. Nevertheless, *December* 9 could have offered some reason, and the act itself is certainly no explanation by itself.)

All eight suggestions for better policing do not concern themselves with reasons behind an action, but rather with base legal caveats (prohibitions against continued abuses). Dragnet procedures are abortions of justice besides being excessive. Flying wedge tactics are an inefficient way to stop an illegal (sic!) action in a crowd and besides is a rather outmoded and inefficient police tactic. Nightsticks and blackjacks are defensive weapons only, while in a crowd they can be used as offensive tools, and, as it seems in the case of December 9, implements of vengeance for some unspecified ideal.

Plainclothesmen cannot be recognized, and are not present to help people. Nametags are for identification in case of violence, but if the policeman is doing his rightful job of keeping the peace, there should be no reason to have his name on call. Bringing departmental charges against offending police captains do not lessen the threat of violence on the part of the captain's men—it is the men themselves who must see that they are doing illegal acts. The trials are nothing but a coverup which is normally used as a public relations gimmick anyway. Maintaining a number of "official observers" is exactly like having a monitor in a classroom, violence is not abated because it is bad *per se*, but because there is a threat of superior recriminations, and cat will get busted from his job. (One could make the whole thing into a game, and if you get caught kicking ass, you're out, otherwise everything's cool.)

If policemen didn't take the law into their own heads, and were trained not to do so, "official observers" would never be necessary. Finally, the centralization of booking procedures just makes the mills of justice grind a little faster initially. There's still the problem of justice being the most expensive commodity in the country, and if you're poor, that's tough—you rot in the can just the same whether you get in there speedily or after a few hours. (The real villains are bail procedures, unconstitutional stop-and-frisk laws and a system of justice which favors property.)

I am not attacking the work that the ACLU or the New York chapter of that organization does—it has not been my intention to do that with a criticism of this fine report. The ACLU is a lawyers' guild, lawyers are servants and interpreters of the law. What I am attacking is the conception of the law itself in the American society. Lawyers know the ropes, they know how to play the legal game. A good radical lawyer knows that the System he traffics in is corrupt, the most he can do for his client is to keep him free to continue his radical work. So it goes. The *December 9* booklet deals quite adequately with the illegal acts of the police and gives suggestions how they can be stopped. *December 9* does not even come close to the root of the problem for the problem is in the very nature, concept, and function of police. There is quite a distinction to be made between an officer of the peace and a policeman (and quite a difference in feeling between peace and order).

There will be many more studies of police brutality. Many good minds will churn out these reports, Presidential platitudes will be wafted in the political air while the violence will continue until people find a way to deal with the violence within themselves. The police who beat and kicked demonstrators on December 9 will never be legally nor morally convinced that they erred. The problem is with the institutions and not the men who staff them.

The suggestions put forth by the NYACLU do no more than attempt to see that the same violations of personal liberty don't recur (but only through childish threat of recrimination), while failing to make suggestions about how to educate these officers of the peace. *December 9* did bring forth one important caveat which is known to any Movement veteran: there will be people who will come to demonstrations to get their personal grudges against authority off their chests. When they do, they involve other people, and bring down the wrath of the police on everyone's head. "If the actions of such persons are allowed to justify police violence, their joint actions (i.e. violence-prone people and violence-prone police) will serve as an effective veto upon people who seek to exercise their constitutional right of peaceful assembly. That is the danger to which this report is addressed."

The problem is much larger than the scope of this small mimeographed paper. Read it yourself, show it to your parents, your old lady, tell it to the Judge—they will agree with its contents. The suggestions for the police do no more than attempt to mitigate the circumstances of police violence, they will never alter its presence. Those eight suggestions are the Establishment way of fighting its own excesses. Perhaps there is no better way to educate but through the use of threats. Certainly the police know better, but the System which they serve does not, and the Conspiracy trials grind on.

ALFONSO A. NARVAEZ

New Police Patrol a Hit in the Slums

It was after 11 p.m., following the glistening light rain, streets were almost deserted. A cruising police car turned quickly off Lenox Avenue, then slowed and stopped near three black youths huddled at the corner of 120th Street and Mount Morris Park.

"Hiya, Babe," a policeman called out. "Howarya. Howyadoin."

"Fine, brother, just fine."

"Here it is Friday night and you guys don't have girls."

The three youths laughed, then turned and walked slowly toward Lenox Avenue.

"We're going to a party," the youth called out.

"Good, good. Seeyaround."

This sort of exchange between strangers on the streets of Central Harlem is rare. Between a police sergeant and black teen-aged youths, it is even rarer.

Yet this is the kind of banter that goes on continuously between members of the Preventive Enforcement Patrol (PEP), a new and special squad of black and Puerto Rican policemen, and the people who live in Harlem communities.

"It's the kind of thing we encourage," said Assistant Chief Inspector Eldridge Waith, who commands the 23-man unit.

'We want the men to talk to people, to talk to the kids in their own language," Chief Waith continued. "We want them to meet people and talk up what we're trying to do. We're not a goon squad or a cooling squad. We are visible policemen, riding in patrol cars and making arrests.

"But," he added, "we want to show the people that we're sensitive to their problems and that we understand the community."

From *The New York Times*, November 19, 1969, p. L57. © 1969 by The New York Times Company. Reprinted by permission.

For years, slum residents have complained that they are the victims not only of most of the city's crimes but also of a seeming apathy on the part of the police to track down criminals.

PEP, a hand-picked experimental unit consisting of 23 men—a lieutenant, two sergeants and 20 patrolmen—all volunteers, is an attempt to answer these complaints.

Today, after only a month of operation, Chief Waith says that community leaders are enthusiastic about the unit and have asked that its force be doubled.

To the men assigned to PEP, the squad is more than just an experiment to bring about greater understanding of the policeman's role in the community and to reduce crime. It is also a chance to do something concrete about the slum problems the PEP members themselves faced while growing up in the city.

The unit patrols the entire area covered by Chief Waith's command—Borough Patrol Manhattan North, North of 59th Street river to river—and concentrates on visible street crime.

Chief Waith said that the idea for the Squad had come as a result of hundreds of community meetings that he and other police officials attended.

"Everywhere we went, minority people complained that the police were insensitive and that they didn't care," he said.

"They said that the police usually went home to Westchester or Long Island and couldn't care less to what happened to the people or to the community."

To 21-year-old Patrolman James Hopper, PEP is a chance to do something about the narcotics problem, which destroys the lives of slum youths.

"I had a buddy of mine die of an overdose," he said, "and I know there is a job to be done here. We're needed."

He then told of working more than 28 hours, without a break, to help crack a narcotics case that added to the more than 1,000 decks of heroin seized by the unit since it went on the street.

"Gentlemen, I suggest you move off this corner," he called out through the patrol-car window to a group of about 20 black men drinking wine outside a liquor store at 128th Street and Lenox Avenue.

"You're not moving fast enough," the young patrolman told the men, almost all of them old enough to be his father.

"I didn't know that, brother," one of the men called out as they moved.

One of the men, younger than the rest, wearing a black leather coat and a black fedora, started to protest to his friends. Suddenly Sgt. Howard Sheffey, who has spent more than 13 years on the force, jumped out of the car and approached the man as Patrolman Trimingham moved toward him from around a parked car.

The sergeant asked the man to show him what he had in his hip pocket. It was a rolled up magazine.

"The bulge could have been a gun," Sergeant Sheffey told Patrolman Trimingham and Patrolman Waverly Logan as he got back into the squad car. "It wasn't, but he's moving."

On-the-job instruction is part of Sergeant Sheffey's concept of PEP. He has 20 young men—the average age is 25—all with less than two years on the force, to mold into sensitive, effective policemen.

"This is the best thing that ever happened," the sergeant said of PEP. "I'm crazy about it. You have to have lived in and around Harlem to see what people feel about police. I try to make the men more aware of what to look for. They are already sensitive to the problems in the area and to the people here."

Sergeant Sheffey said that the men were receiving special training in police work and were learning more in three weeks than many patrolmen learned in three years.

For example, the men have been receiving special instruction from the narcotics unit of the Police Department on recognizing different types of narcotics and have attended a criminal-investigation course usually attended only by detectives.

Each afternoon they have a critique of the operation by their superiors, in which they go over the previous day's work, discussing what went right and what went wrong.

However, not everything turns out the way they expect.

From the back seat of the slowly cruising patrol car, Patrolman Waverly, 28, spotted a youth staggering up 118th Street the other day under the load of two heavily laden shopping bags.

The youth put the bags down, got a better grip, then moved off quickly.

"Let's see what he's got," Sergeant Sheffey said.

The patrol car was blocked by traffic, then moved ahead of the youth.

"He'll catch up to us," Patrolman Logan said.

Suddenly the youth ducked into a hallway. The three policemen jumped from the car and ran toward the doorway.

As they entered, a woman followed behind them and looked up, perplexed by all the police activity. The boy was her son, it turned out, he was carrying home the groceries.

"That'll probably be the last time he does that," Sergeant Sheffey said sheepishly as he got back into the patrol car.

Patrolman Trimingham stayed behind to talk to the woman.

"He's rapping," the sergeant explained. "He's telling her about our unit and what we're all about. You just can't stop someone and then just walk away. This way they understand what we're trying to do."

Patrolman Trimingham slid behind the wheel of the patrol car.

"She said the kids shoot up [use narcotics] every afternoon about 4 o'clock," he told the sergeant. "At least we got something."

Sergeant Sheffey made a notation in a notebook. The day unit would be asked to give the location special attention.

Even when an arrest is made, the men of PEP use the opportunity to talk to the community residents about their work.

"We get less hostile reactions from the community because of this," noted Lieut. Hamilton Robinson, 37, who grew up in the Bedford-Stuyvesant section of Brooklyn. "The people see that we care and they accept what we have to do. They see that the unit is really meant to serve them."

Lieutenant Robinson said that in addition to fighting crime, the unit concentrates on conditions that lead to the decay of a community—stores that pile garbage in the streets, prostitutes who congregate in certain areas or street dice games.

The street dice games accounted for almost half of the squad's 132 arrests between Oct. 23 and Nov. 15. There also were 61 arrests for narcotics, four for street muggings, one for auto theft and 11 for assault, during which two loaded revolvers were seized.

Sergeant Sheffey pointed out that much of the unit's effectiveness stemmed from the fact that it did not have to answer routine precinct calls, such as family disputes, fires, crank calls or ambulance calls.

The arrest process itself, paradoxically, appears to be one of the unit's biggest problems. Because of the time the men must spend in court or in processing prisoners, the unit, which works two shifts—10 a.m. to 6 p.m. and 6 p.m. to 2 a.m., Tuesday through Saturday—is often undermanned.

Last Friday, for instance, there were more men in court or processing prisoners than were available to go out on patrol.

JULES B. GERARD

St. Louis Police Plays Politics with Law

Free speech and peaceable assembly are in clear and present danger of being extinguished in St. Louis.

Over the past three years, the Metropolitan Police Department has arrested more than 100 people for exercising First Amendment rights, 12 of them in the last three months.

The most recent incident occurred December 8, 1967. Vice President Hubert H. Humphrey was in the city to preside at a fundraising dinner. During the day, he visited a Head Start Program at the Centennial Christian Church. Nine people were arrested at the Church before he was due to appear. Six of them were carrying standard political signs in support of Senator Eugene J. McCarthy's campaign for president. They were walking unobtrusively on a public sidewalk across the street from the Church. Two spectators also were seized, apparently for standing too close to the sign carriers. The ninth victim was taken into custody for calling the arrests to the attention of the crowd.

No charges were filed against the nine individuals. But they were held in the Deer Street station for approximately three hours before being released.

This procedure follows a pattern devised by the Department three years ago. In early 1964, on the occasion of President Lyndon B. Johnson's first visit to St. Louis after assuming office, 87 persons were rounded up in Forest Park. The group had gathered for the purpose of marching to the Chase Hotel where Johnson was speaking. The assassination of President John Kennedy having occurred only a few months earlier, leaders of the group realized that they would not be permitted to get close to Johnson. So they planned to march as far as the police would allow and to picket at that point. They had gone less than a block when they were taken into custody, still more than a mile from the hotel. They were held at Central District station until Johnson had departed, a period of almost four hours.

No charges were filed against them either. But they were interrogated

From *Focus/Midwest*, Vol. VI, No. 40, p. 15. Reprinted by permission of the author and Focus/Midwest magazine.

during their unlawful detention with such questions as, "What organizations do you belong to? Are you a member of NAACP or CORE?"

The procedure of making groundless arrests without filing charges is know as "rousting." (The St. Louis Department's quaint term for it is "sausage pinch.") When employed against known hoodlums, its primary purpose is to force an individual out of a geographical area. Tired of being rousted, the hoodlum will move on, the police believe, and his crimes will become the responsibility of some other department. *When used against groups, its primary purpose is to sweep the streets clean of people the police look upon as troublemakers, although its secondary purpose of intimidation is never far beneath the surface.*

The roust has important tactical advantages for the police. First, since no charges are filed, they are relieved of the necessity of proving that there were reasonable grounds to believe the person had committed a crime. Thus, the Department does not end up with egg on its face by having a case thrown out of court.

The procedure imposes onerous burdens upon the person rousted for speaking. The most oppressive is that he has been deprived of his right of speech at the only time his speech could have been effective. Free speech necessarily includes the right to communicate, for speech which no one is permitted to hear is not free speech. The purpose of these two assemblies was to communicate ideas to Johnson and Humphrey. Preventing their communication while Johnson and Humphrey were present was just as effective as suppressing the ideas themselves.

The redress available to the citizen for this invasion of his rights is limited. Theoretically, he has the right to file a formal complaint of misbehavior with the Police Department; secondly, to file criminal charges with the FBI; and, thirdly, to file a suit for money damages against the offending officers. The first has become a bad joke. Exercising the second option rarely results in activity. When it does, the activity, as often as not, is an indictment against the victim for filing false charges! (Those who believe that federal and local agencies always work at cross purposes should investigate the co-operation between the FBI and local law enforcement bodies in discouraging, if not suppressing, complaints of police misbehavior.) The third possibility is also illusory. Such suits are expensive, and few lawyers will undertake them without being paid in advance.

Being arrested is a frightening, humiliating experience. No doubt some victims of a roust will be intimidated. Many will take to heart the message which comes through loud and clear: keep your ideas to yourself.

The roust is kept alive by the existence of loosely-defined laws which creep as close to the forbidden boundaries of uncertainty as the Constitution permits. Laws, for example, prohibiting disturbance of the peace, loitering, and failing to obey the reasonable request of a police officer, have one element in common: whether or not they were violated is more a matter of opinion than it is a question of fact. For instance, whether the defendant was making noise is a question of fact, but whether he was making enough noise to unreasonably disturb the peace of the community is often a matter of opinion. The crucial opinion, of course, is the policeman's. He is given, in effect, power to make crimes on the spot.

This power of curbstone legislation shields the policeman from liability in the event a person he has rousted decides to seek redress. The officer can always claim he had reasonable grounds to believe the person had committed some crime, since the question then is, not whether the person did or did not commit the crime, but whether the officer had reasonable grounds to believe he did; the protection is nearly perfect.

In summary, 28 people have been arrested in recent months for exercising what they believed to be their First Amendment rights. No charges were ever filed against 10 of them, and those filed against 3 others were later withdrawn. Of the remaining 15 arrests, that of the student seized at the hotel was of dubious legality. The 12 which occurred at the police headquarters may or may not have been constitutional; but it is certain in either event that they showed the Department's callous indifference to the need of First Amendment freedoms for breathing space. Only 2 of the 28 arrests, then, were free of constitutional doubt. And 12 of them—2 at the Veiled Prophet Ball, and 9 at the Centennial Church—were clearly unlawful under *any* view of the Constitution.

That St. Louis should present such a discouraging picture is surprising. It has not been racked with the violence of Watts, Newark, and Detroit. Compared to other cities with large university populations, its peace demonstrations have been well-tempered and orderly. So there can be no claim that the Department's unlawful activities resulted from over-reaction to dangerous situations. In addition, the Department's "community relations" program enjoys the reputation of being one of the finest in the country.

Instead of guaranteeing some measure of protection to First Amendment freedoms, both of these facts, ironically, contribute to their current perilous state. A determination to prevent riots in St. Louis leads the Department into taking increasingly precipitous action every time more than two people congregate. And the reputation of its community relations program is used to fend off complaints about such behavior, assuring that nothing will be done about it. . . .

Ameliorating this kind of direct hostility is the primary purpose of the community relations program. In its preventive aspect, this program attempts to create a favorable image of the policeman both by implanting such an image in the minds of those without preconceptions, and by changing the minds of those who hold unfavorable pictures. The success of the former depends upon reaching enough of the right people. The success of the latter depends upon convincing the citizen with real or imagined grievances that the Department is making a sincere effort to deal with them. Sincerity is also the keynote to success in the pathological aspect of community relations, that which deals with instances of misbehavior once they have occurred.

The reputation of St. Louis' program is built almost entirely upon preventive community relations. That its reputation is impressive cannot be doubted. Michigan State University praised it as "one of the first in the country and one of the most extensive." Inside the closed society of "the thin blue line," other departments have studied and imitated the program, San Francisco among them. Such is its prestige that when the Department conducted a three-day workshop on community relations in January without appreciable advance publicity, delegates attended from 41 cities all over the country, and Attorney General Ramsey Clark interrupted his schedule to make the convocation address.

The grassroots of the St. Louis program are its district (precinct) committees. The word "committee" is something of a misnomer, for there is no city-wide organization. The district committees operate independently, under the guidance, but not necessarily the control, of a civilian employee of the Department, who is given the title of Director of Police Community Relations. Each committee is divided into a formidable array of subcommittees, such as Businessmen's, Juvenile, Sanitation, etc. These subcommittees perform a variety of valuable tasks, even if one assumes the normal amount of slippage between objective and achievement which is common among volunteer groups. The Businessmen's Subcommittee, for example, arranges for detectives to inspect premises for the purpose of recommending safeguards that might be taken against burglaries. The Juvenile Subcommittee solicits residents to act as "block watchers"—people who watch the streets while children are going to and from school. It also arranges "cruiser tours" for high school students; students spend an evening riding in unmarked cars answering calls, thus getting a first-hand picture of the life of a patrolman.

Although this sampling is totally inadequate to convey the range of activities pursued, it does accurately reflect their tenor, which is wholly preventive. They are aimed at promoting understanding of policemen. Some of them are also designed to prove that the policeman recognizes the problems society creates for the individual, and that he is an ally in efforts to solve them. Valuable as these programs are, they do not touch the citizens' grievances against the police themselves. And a few of them smack of the

Madison Avenue practice of selling the same old product in a glossy new package. In his address opening the workshop in January, Attorney General Clark warned that "police community relations has nothing to do with public relations." The available evidence tends to show that merely preventive efforts will fail to mitigate hostility towards police, at least in the short run.

The point was emphasized graphically by two speakers at the workshop. Detroit Police Inspector Carl Heffernan described a program which had been modeled upon St. Louis', and remarked ruefully that it had failed to prevent riots. Newark Police Captain Edward Williams, a Negro, told of attending district committee meetings in that city for a year prior to last summer. Arriving at a station which was under siege after the riots began, Williams said he had hoped to stop the disorder by talking to people he had met through the community relations program. "I looked into that crowd and didn't recognize anyone. I had not touched the real rioters. They are not coming to any meeting. You've got to go out and find them." Whether St. Louis will heed these warnings remains to be seen.

There are a few hopeful signs. The Department opened four "storefront centers" in high crime areas last year. Each center is staffed by a policeman whose job it is to get to know the members of the community. The centers are used as meeting places by local residents. Their most important function, however, is to give policemen a base where residents can come to make complaints and discuss problems outside the unwelcome atmosphere of the district station.

Membership on the committees is now open to all residents of a district instead of being confined to people the Department considers "responsible." This change was made after two years of badgering by the Executive Committee of the St. Louis Council on Police Community Relations. The Executive Committee is an unofficial group of citizens drawn from throughout the community. Since its founding in 1955, its chairman has been Virgil Border, local director of the National Conference of Christians and Jews. Over the years, the Executive Committee has suggested much of what now is the community relations program. Sensitivity training of police officers in human relations is one of its more recent accomplishments. Such training is now given all police cadets, and is a required part of the in-service training of all officers.

The Executive Committee meets regularly with the Board of Police Commissioners and Chief of Police Curtis Brostron. Although it was not designed that way, the Committee does in fact comprise at least one representative of every major civil rights organization in the city. Half its members are Negroes. It is probably true, therefore, as Mayor Alfonso J. Cervantes said while testifying before the President's National Advisory Committee on Civil Disorders, that "lines of communication are open every day, in many, many ways."

But are open lines of communication enough? Hostility towards policemen is largely the result of experience. These experiences can be classified in terms of whether the person was subjected to police contact lawfully or unlawfully, and whether he was treated reasonably or abusively. The preventive aspect of community relations has relatively slight impact in this area. Academy training teaches policemen when an arrest is lawful. But a roust does not result from ignorance; rather it follows from an officer's deliberate decision to violate a person's rights for reasons which seem to him sufficient at the time. Sensitivity training can teach an officer the kinds of insults most deeply resented by Negroes, but it cannot force him to be polite. When prevention fails, is it enough to give the citizen a place to complain?

For some people, the willingness of the Department to listen to complaints of misbehavior will be proof enough that it is sincerely interested in bettering community relations. But a growing number insist that action be taken against offending officers. They will be convinced by deeds, not by words. Newark Police Captain Williams made it frighteningly, but unmistakably clear: "The platitudes don't stop them any more. They say, 'I'm tired of waiting. I think I'll throw a few bricks'."

Consider the Department's response to the nine arrests at the Centennial Church. Shortly after the people were taken into custody, an onlooker called a number of faculty members at the university to inform them of the arrests. One faculty member went immediately to the station, arriving approximately 30 minutes after the students. Upon inquiring why the students were being held, he has told, "For investigation." When he asked, "Investigation of what?" he was told to sit down and shut up. During the next half hour, further inquiries concerning the charge resulted in his being referred to three other officers, none of whom would answer his question. Finally the district commander, a captain, appeared. The faculty member asked him. The commander conferred privately with a lieutenant and some other officers, told the man to "wait here," and drove off with the lieutenant. Returning in less than half an hour, the captain told the faculty member that the students had been arrested for disturbing the peace on the complaint of the Rev. S. W. Hylton, Jr., pastor of the Centennial Church. The police then gave "courtesy summonses" to those arrested, and released them, after a minor delay.

In the meantime, another faculty member had been on the telephone since learning of the arrests. He first called the district station, asking for the commander. Informed the commander was not in, he asked for the officer in charge, and got the desk sergeant. The sergeant confirmed that students were in custody. Asked on what charge, the sergeant replied, "I don't know. They were arrested on the orders of the Intelligence Unit." The professor then asked to speak to someone from the Intelligence Unit. He was told they were all at the Centennial Church. He then asked whether the students were going to be booked, and if so, when. The sergeant replied, "I don't know. My orders are to hold them until the Intelligence Unit gets back here."

Wholly dissatisfied with this answer, the faculty member called a highly placed friend in police headquarters. The friend said, "Our Intelligence Unit works closely with the Secret Service. What probably happened is the Secret Service told our men that Humphrey didn't want to see any demonstrators." When the faculty member vehemently protested that the Secret Service had no more authority to violate the constitution than anyone else, his friend replied that he would check into the matter and call back. The return call came two hours later, at about the same time the students were being released. The friend reported the students had been arrested on complaint of the minister.

On December 12, the following Tuesday, *Student Life*, the campus newspaper, carried a front page story which read in part:

"The St. Louis Police Department claimed it had acted on the phone call complaint of S. W. Hylton, pastor of the church. . . . Pastor Hylton denied calling police in an interview . . . last Saturday, December 9. 'I was inside the building and did not see the people,' Pastor Mylton said. He added that the police had not contacted him about the matter."

Norm Pressman, the student whose byline appeared on this story, affirmed that he had talked to the Reverend Hylton, and that Hylton was quoted accurately. Asked in early January to comment on the conflict between the police report and the student story, Hylton said, "I do not wish to make any further statement on the matter because I understand the matter may become the subject of a lawsuit. If asked the question on the stand, I will answer it."

In late December, the St. Louis Civil Liberties Committee, the local affiliate of the A.C.L.U., held a press conference in which it condemned the "unconstitutional abuses of the Metropolitan Police Department," citing the incidents discussed here as examples. The Department's response to this criticism was a series of three statements. In the first, Edward L. Dowd, president of the Board of Police Commissioners, was reported on television to have said, "The students were arrested on the complaint of the minister, who was afraid they might create a disturbance." But since fear of what a person might do would not pass constitutional muster, a revision was not long in coming. The revised version, issued later in the day, was that the persons had been arrested on the minister's complaint that they were disturbing the peace. But that was no good either, since, even if there is a complaint, a policeman is not entitled to make an arrest if he can see with his own eyes that no law has been violated. Hence, another modification was required. The Official Truth, Third Edition, now is that the persons were taken into custody solely because they refused to give their addresses *while at the Church,* and thus prevented the officer from completing the blanks in the summonses, which he felt obliged to give in order to placate the minister. By such *ex post facto* corrections is the infallibility of police officers publicly maintained.

Following the events of December 8, a group of citizens, calling itself The Ad Hoc Committee to Insure Constitutional Rights organized to support the 25 individuals who had been arrested. The defense fund established by the Ad Hoc Committee included on its board of trustees such people as James F. Hornback, the leader of the Ethical Society; William Kahn, executive director of the Jewish Community Centers Association; Jack L. Pierson, local president of Americans for Democratic Action; and Harold Gibbons, president of Teamsters Union Joint Council 13.

After the routine press conference to announce its formation, the Committee sponsored an open meeting. The meeting was timed to coincide with the banquet commencing the Department's workshop on police-community relations. About 200 people attended in sub-zero weather to voice approval of a series of resolutions. One called upon the Police Commissioners to accept financial responsibility for the medical expenses of the person who was beaten in the lobby of police headquarters. Another demanded that all charges pending against those arrested that day be dismissed. Still another called upon Attorney General Clark "to take such action as is necessary to insure that local police officials will not be subject to pressures by federal police agencies, such as the Secret Service or FBI, that may encourage exaggerated or brutal reactions by these local officials during the visits of national figures."

After the meeting ended, a delegation of the Ad Hoc Committee attempted to present this resolution to Clark personally. Management personnel at the banquet turned them away. Delegations reduced to five people, and finally to a single individual, were also rebuffed.

One of the Ad Hoc Committee's resolutions asked for a *public* investigation of the arrests. Ever since cries of "police brutality" at the scene of an arrest led to the bombardment of a district station in late 1964, and the shooting of an unarmed burglary suspect precipitated a series of demonstrations in July 1965, the St. Louis Council on Police Community Relations and the St. Louis Civil Liberties Committee also have been apprehensive that the standard investigation of such incidents would prove ineffective to ward off serious violence.

The two groups had different anxieties. The Council's concern was the need to publish a thorough investigation speedily. The Civil Liberties Committee's concern was the need that the investigation be credible to the community. Neither group, however, has succeeded in securing the adoption of any major change. At the most critical stage in the pathology of community relations—where a citizen has been seriously wounded or killed, allegedly by police misbehavior—the Board of Police Commissioners apparently remains unconvinced that there is a serious problem. It seems doubtful that the Ad Hoc Committee's resolution will persuade it.

At some other time, the outlook for the preservation of First Amendment freedoms under these conditions would only be distressing. In this election year, it is positively grim.

The overriding issues in the coming election will be the war in Vietnam and the drive for meaningful racial equality. Historically, demonstrations are an inevitable part of all election campaigns. In the past few years, opponents of the war and supporters of civil rights, by and large, have become convinced that the most effective way they have of wielding political power lies in demonstrations.

At the same time, when more demonstrations can be expected, the police are reacting with increasing intolerance to groups in the streets. The groups are biracial, for opposition to the war and support of civil rights have fused into a single cause in the minds of many, in St. Louis as elsewhere. This increases the likelihood that the police will view any political demonstration as a potential race riot. *It also means that significant portions of the white middle-class community are experiencing lawless police tactics for the first time. They are being rousted in "an early show of force." They are being arrested instead of the brick throwers because they are some of "the leaders who must be gotten early." Hostility towards police grounded in personal experience is, thus, spreading to parts of the community where it never existed.*

The Police Department's inadequate response to these developments has been two-pronged. On the one hand, it has developed worthwhile programs to train its officers in human relations, and to devise means to help citizens adjust to the cruelties of the urban environment. But, outside the area of preventive community relations, it has steadfastly refused to come to grips with the citizens' legitimate grievances about the misbehavior of its own few bigots and bullies.

On the other hand, its standard response to all criticism is a lamentation about the supposed widespread disrespect for law and order. The lamentation is usually supported with statistics showing the number of policemen killed in the line of duty, as though being shot by an armed robber justifies suppressing the peaceful citizen's right of free speech. It may be that disrespect for law and order is engendered in the disadvantaged by laws which favor the more powerful; but it seems equally probable that disrespect for law is the inevitable lesson learned by people whose rights are trampled by policemen whose duty should be to protect them.

Perhaps Mayor Cervantes is correct in believing that St. Louisans will be satisfied with open channels of communication. Perhaps the Board of Police Commissioners is correct in believing that the problem can be resolved by the established practices which have worked in the past. Perhaps the police are correct in believing that the situation can be controlled by a deft combination of suppression and public relations.

But if they are not . . . ?

DAVID FELTON

Rock Festival Called Learning Experience by Chief of Police

Some called it a gas, a beautiful happening of the Aquarian Age. Others called it the world's largest traffic jam or a disaster area.

But to Police Chief Joseph Paul Kimble of Beverly Hills, last weekend's Woodstock Music and Art Fair in New York's Catskills was a "learning experience."

"I think it was a tremendous learning experience for the policemen who participated. It was for me," said Kimble.

"These were people who have a different life style than mine, different values, certainly a different appearance.

"One thing I learned was that not all hippies can be stereotyped. That's a pretty uncomfortable revelation for most policemen. There were a lot there who didn't drink, didn't smoke pot. A lot got high just from the emotional experience of the festival."

Kimble, 43, has gained a national reputation as an expert on civil disorders and one of the new breed" of highly educated policemen. He became chief in Beverly Hills four months ago.

He is a large, round-faced man with twinkly eyes and a soft, good-natured voice. As he spoke, he cut out newspaper stories of the giant rock festival.

"I went back there originally as an observer," explained Kimble. "The hippie movement, rather than dying out, has, if anything, increased. I wanted to learn first-hand about the hippie phenomenon."

But Kimble's observer status was converted quickly to that of participant when the New York police commissioner—at the last minute—forbade several hundred of his policemen to work off-duty at the festival.

As a result, Kimble was asked to help supervise what may become a turning point in police crowd control.

Not only was it one of the largest crowds ever assembled for one of the longest periods—400,000 for three days and nights—it was controlled by a combination of radically new police methods and attitudes.

No weapon of any kind was allowed in the festival area.

"I still have a strong conviction that traditional police methods are not necessarily the best methods," said Kimble.

"The promoters decided to approach the problem in a nontraditional way. The police wore bright red windbreaker jackets with the word 'peace' silkscreened where the badge is usually worn.

"On the back of the jackets was the emblem of Woodstock Ventures, the promoters. It consisted of a guitar with a dove sitting on it, which I think is kind of nice."

Kimble said the officers also wore blue jeans, pith helmets and red T-shirts with emblems similar to those on their jackets. The "uniforms" were designed by Wesley A. Pomeroy, security coordinator of the festival and an old friend of Kimble.

"It was something that caught on with the people attending," the chief said. "It didn't take long to learn there was not any fuzz around with guns, Mace or riot sticks."

Kimble said the security plan worked for four reasons.

"First was the attitude of the people who came there. They came with the idea it was a groovin' thing and they wanted to enjoy every moment of it.

"I've never seen that many people in so small an area who acted so peacefully.

"It proves something I've believed for a long time—that people are capable of policing themselves if they want to."

The second reason, said Kimble, was the "subprofessional" police work of members of the Hog Farm, a commune of hippies from Taos, N.M.

"This group more than any other group helped keep things cool," he said. "They worked around the clock with various militant groups or individuals with emotional problems.

"And let me clue you, there were a lot of very radical groups there. Abbie Hoffman was there with his people. A revolutionary gang group from New York was there. A very small group of black militants was there.

"They not only showed up, they brought their printing presses."

He said whenever a radical group attempted some kind of confrontation—tried to storm the stage or "liberate" the food from concessionaries—the police would drop back and let the Hog Farm people cool things down.

"The third reason the plan worked was the professional services that we provided," continued Kimble.

"We had a Legal Aid trailer with attorneys from New York offering free legal advice. We had a counseling service run by ministers and social workers.

"And we had a complete medical setup of doctors and nurses. They treated 3,000 people."

He said the medical facilities included three trailers and two tent infirmaries. One infirmary, located in the Hog Farm compound, was called the "pig hospital."

"Walking barefooted down the Sunset Strip is a lot different than walking barefooted in a rural area," said Kimble. "There were cuts, bruises, cases of sunburn and exposure, and certainly a lot of narcotics cases."

He said five helicopters were used to bring in food, medical supplies and sometimes performers. On Saturday, the National Guard provided two additional helicopters.

"There was some exaggeration about the shortage of food and water," Kimble said. "We had some short-term shortages for maybe a few hours, but then we'd airlift a ton of bread or bring in two truckloads of Cokes."

No one expected the crowd to be as large as it was, he said.

"A lot came as early as Tuesday. I talked to kids from Denver, Portland, Los Angeles, New Orleans and Chicago.

Kimble said the fourth reason the security plan succeeded was the attitude of the 300 off-duty policemen hired by the festival promoters.

"They were there to keep the peace. We called them peace corpsmen instead of policemen. That sounds hokey, I know, but we were trying to semantically drill the idea into them.

"We told them just to walk through the crowd and listen to people who wanted to ventilate their feelings against the police. If it got extremely bad, they were to radio the Hog Farm."

As for the ticklish problem of mass drug usage, he said police were instructed to report "obvious use of hard drugs—heroin, speed, that sort of thing"—to a command post outside the festival area, where uniformed sheriff's deputies or state troopers could decide what action to take.

About 80 drug arrests were reported.

According to Kimble, beer and wine drinkers were left alone if they were not disturbing anyone, and "this appeared to be the policy" toward marijuana smokers.

Had police tried to arrest pot smokers, said the chief, "they would have generated a riot, in my personal opinion."

Of his experience, Kimble said:

"I've found there's no correlation between a clean-shaven cheek and morality, and conversely, there's no correlation between long hair and immorality.

"Whether we like it or not, the hippie movement is a reality. So rather than ranting and raving about it, we must simply deal with it in the most effective way."

GOVERNOR'S SELECT COMMISSION
ON CIVIL DISORDER OF NEW JERSEY

New Municipal Court System

I. *The Municipal Courts should be abolished and their functions absorbed by the State judicial system.*

The recommended change would mean that cases now heard by magistrates would be heard by State judges. State judges are more insulated politically than magistrates, who must rely on a continuing relationship with the local political system for reappointment. Giving jurisdiction to the State courts would mean that the policies and administration of the courts would be uniform throughout the State. It would also put these cases throughout the State in the hands of fulltime personnel, thus allowing a higher standard of professionalism. Finally, transfer of jurisdiction to the State courts would allow more flexibility in assignment of personnel, taking account of caseloads on a county-wide basis. Suitable revenue adjustments should be made between the State and the municipalities.

II. *The present volunteer program of release on recognizance should be expanded through the use of interviewers on court staffs.*

Nonprofessional staff can be trained easily to be interviewers. An interviewer should be on hand at any time of the day and night. Arrested persons should be interviewed as soon as possible. When the court is not sitting, arrangements should be made for a judge to call in and pass on cases recommended for release on recognizance. Release on recognizance should be

From *Report For Action,* Governor's Select Commission on Civil Disorder of New Jersey, 1968, pp. 165-66.

the usual disposition of a case pending trial both for indictable and non-indictable offenses. Monetary bail should be used only when there is reason to believe that there is an unusual risk that the defendant will not return for trial.

III. *The procedure of issuing summons in lieu of arrest, which has already been worked out and accepted in principle by the police and the courts, should be implemented forthwith.*

Municipal Court Bulletin Letter 119 of the Administrative Office of the Courts suggested that, instead of arresting a person charged with nonindictable offenses, a policeman should have the discretion to issue a summons to him to appear in court at a specified time. The use of summons instead of arrest would save police time in booking the person and holding him for bail. It would save the person charged from being arrested and held in custody or for bail.

IV. *County jails should be organized so as to recognize that those prisoners who are not convicted criminals are treated accordingly.*

All jail facilities should be re-examined in that light with special emphasis on relaxing restraints on communication between prisoners and the outside world.

V. *The act establishing the Office of the Public Defender should be amended to broaden the range of cases that office handles.*

The Public Defender should be responsible for representing indigents in Municipal Court in all nontraffic cases where there is a possibility of a jail sentence, and in Juvenile Court in all cases.

VI. *While it continues in existence, the Municipal Court should keep a record of its proceedings.*

At present, the Municipal Court is not a court of record, although either party may make a record if it chooses. The making of a record would formalize the proceedings and simplify the appeal procedure. A record can be made by a mechanical device or court reporters. Either way, a system should be established.

MARVIN E. WOLFGANG

Corrections and the Violent Offender

Current methods of treating offenders who are violent are less efficient than could be devised. Our discussion here is mostly theoretical and confined to those persons who are convicted of a crime, or, if juveniles, who are treated as delinquents. The right of organized society to intervene in the lives of persons who are arrested but not yet convicted of a crime is not established and is not discussed here.

Even the limits of intervention after conviction are not clear, but there is reason to believe that more legal tests of those limits will occur in the near future as ethical values are raised about the control and manipulation of persons who have violated the law. When one steps over the threshold from law-abiding to law-violating behavior, he does not yield control over his life, even a time-segment of his life, or over his corporeal substance. Just as we may frown on Rousseau's dictum to force men to be free, so we retreat from the notion of utter control over the criminal offender for the sake of the probability of rehabilitation by means of such control.

Let us consider how persons who are violent come into the system of justice and how they are handled. Because of faulty statistics, the picture portrayed may be a slight descriptive distortion of reality, but the basis for the presentation comes from the best available data crowned with the assumptions that logic suggests.

LABELING PROBLEMS

In law enforcement and the administration of justice, we label a set of people as violent offenders when they have committed acts defined as assaultive (that is, criminal homicide, rape, aggravated or simple assault, and, usually, robbery). There are obviously violent people who do not commit crimes. There are violent offenders who commit assaultive crimes who are not convicted, and there are essentially nonviolent offenders who are convicted for assaultive crimes. Finally there are violent people who commit nonassaultive

From *The Annals* of the American Academy of Political and Social Science, Vol. 381, January 1969, pp. 119-24. Reprinted by permission.

crimes who are or who are not convicted for these crimes. A tabular display
appears as follows:

CRIMINAL STATUS OF VIOLENT OFFENDERS

| | | CRIMINAL STATUS | |
PERSONS	None	Convicted of Violent Crime	Convicted of Nonviolent Crime
Violent	x	a	c
Nonviolent	y	b	d

By "essentially nonviolent" I mean to suggest that because a person has
been arrested and convicted for an act defined as assaultive, he should not
absolutely and categorically be labeled forever as violent. A situationally induced act of assault in an otherwise nonviolent life pattern preceding the
incident does not clinically or statistically produce a prognosis or prediction
of repeated violence. This description refers to b in the table. We do not
know the proportion that b represents among all persons $(x + y)$, among all
nonviolent persons (y), or even among all convicted persons $(a + b + c + d)$.
Yet, as we shall see, the distortion that occurs from misplacing this group in
the criminal-justice system has deleterious effects on the entire system.

In the table, c and d probably constitute higher proportions of both x and y,
respectively. There simply are more nonviolent offenses possible in the statutes. Moreover, considering the informal institutional process of plea-
bargaining, the difficulties of getting convictions on more controversial evidence in assaultive crimes, and so forth, it is not unexpected that c/x and d/y
are larger than a/x, or certainly b/y, by definition.

We may assume that among all persons convicted of violent crimes $(a + b)$,
that a is larger than b, but this assumption is not tested by data. We may
also assume that the proportion of violent criminals among violent people
(a/x) is greater than the proportion of violent offenders among nonviolent
people (b/y). Because we do not know the distribution of x and y in the
general population, we cannot pursue these assumed proportions any further.

What we do further assert, however, is that many convicted offenders are
improperly disposed of by the courts and improperly handled by correctional
authorities because improper classifications are made of the offenders. Offenders commonly are responded to by agents of social control, based on the
label which the agent's own social organization places on those in their
charge. Improper classification or labeling can thus produce inappropriate
role-response by those agents (probation and parole officers, guards, prison
administrators). Even a treatment staff that has become addicted to the

process of routine, and thereby themselves become administratively institutionalized, tend to respond to the inmate's label rather than to the totality or to large portions of his personality.

Because the gravity of the offense is an important and heavily weighted ingredient in the determination of sentence, a serious assaultive crime (like homicide) committed by an essentially nonviolent person (b of y) will commonly be sent to a state or federal prison for some period of time beyond two years. Acquisitive crimes like burglary, grand larceny, auto theft, embezzlement, and even some robbery, may be committed by persons who are essentially nonviolent. Yet many of these persons are sentenced to prison (d of y). Of course, violent offenders who are violent people (a of x) and violent people who are convicted of nonviolent crimes (c of x) are also sent to these same prisons, but our focus is on the b and d groups. . . .

Once sentenced to prison, these offenders are diagnosed and classified in ways that are not always or, perhaps, even primarily designed to separate violent from nonviolent persons. The labels previously sewn to the biographies of the incoming inmates become convenient categories at classification time. And men who can work in kitchens or in fields, who can learn in print shops or on work details are often sent to specific correctional facilities on these bases. Maximum, medium, minimum custody, open or closed facility, are choices made for prisoners by reason of their offense labels or labels assigned for reasons other than careful diagnoses to determine the violence proclivity of prisoners. It may be that the state of our diagnostic art is still quite imprecise or poorly invalidated, but even in its present condition, it could be used to better advantage.

We do not know that proportionate distribution of a, b, c, and d, of our model who are in prison. Nor do we know their mix in specific types of institutions. Whatever that mix might be, there is reason to believe that most correctional institutions are managed from the focal concern with persons presumed to be violent: that is, the presence of nonviolent b's mixed with violent a's, and of nonviolent d's mixed with violent c's, causes the control and management of prisoners to be performed as if the b's and d's were like a's and c's.

In other words, the pivotal perceptual framework for running a correctional institution is the existence of some a's and c's or persons who are indeed violent. These offenders are likely to be disruptive of the prison regime, may need close custody, and may require careful control for screening of letters, kitchen utensils, and contraband, and to prevent escapes. But in the process of designing a social organization to regulate the routine of these men, the essentially nonviolent inmates are required to undergo the same regime.

Thus, we are confronted with the paradoxical situation in which the concern with violence versus nonviolence is primary with respect to the risks of being victims of crime and to the length and type of sentence, but virtually ignored—or at least confounded—in the subsequent correctional process. The dynamics of daily life under incarceration, of who cellmates are, of how the weight of time and the interactional social system of an institution function as part of the rehabilitation process, are not perceived in relation to a violence-nonviolence division of the prisoner population.

Relative to the classification of violent offenders in prison, many false positives are confused with true positives, and the latter function to promote the kinds of prison organization we are accustomed to construct. Major decisions about conjugal visits or (better, I think) furloughs for prisoners to spend time free in the community, about work-release programs, or about extending the limits of inmate responsibility in general are still being made with the case of the violent prisoner in mind.

As a basis for judging how a prison should be managed, the violent offender in prison functions as a restraint on the freedom that could otherwise be afforded the nonviolent inmates. The unknown way in which violent and nonviolent inmates are imprisoned together has thus promoted and perpetuated a whole set of rubrics about prison management that may be not only unnecessary but quite dynfunctional for most of the persons sent to prison. The presence of truly violent prisoners and the dominance of the image of prisoners which they promote in the minds of laymen as well as prison administrators have had systemic effects on all persons processed through prison.

There are some violent offenders who are docile and conforming while in prison but who have high probabilities for recidivism upon release. These constitute another group who may not need the heavy burden of close custody and the other accouterments of most prison regimes. Although they may be difficult to reform, there is no reason for their being managed in prison as if they were there committing the offenses they may commit outside, when their records inside show little need for disciplinary action. . . .

STEVEN A. WALDHORN

Legal Intervention

Legal intervention in social institutions can affect all of the features which contribute to pathological bureaucracies. As value-interpretive institutions, however, courts have a special competence not only to hold bureaucracies to their commitments but also to elucidate what these commitments mean. Public-serving bureaucracies are often most affected when courts act in this educative role. On the other hand, judicial intervention in bureaucracies seems to be most limited by the problems connected with expertise, where courts have to determine in which areas they should or should not defer to bureaucracies and their special kinds of knowledge.

Courts intervene in bureaucratic decision-making on a number of grounds. As pointed out above, public-serving bureaucracies are often so pathological that they not only cease to perform their assigned tasks adequately, but actually violate statutory or constitutional mandates which are supposed to govern their behavior. One way courts enter areas where they have previously been inactive is first to deal with explicit statutory violations, such as the denial to welfare recipients of emergency benefits to which they are statutorily entitled. Only later do courts move to more subtle questions concerning the abuse of discretion. In virtually all of their activities, however, courts must necessarily have a continuing concern with the meaning of the goals which are supposed to inform the institutions under consideration.

Courts also often initially intervene in public-serving bureaucracies on issues related to procedural due process or equal protection. In this way, they may deal with such questions as school suspensions or public housing admission or eviction procedures. This approach allows courts to sidestep some difficult issues concerning the aims these bureaucracies should pursue. Yet while general standards of fairness apply to all cases, the "differing rules of fair play" encompassed by the concept of due process "vary according to specific factual context . . . and differing types of proceedings." What due process means in a particular case can be determined by a court only if it explores and understands the substantive goals which the bureaucracy is supposed to be maximizing.

From Parts II and III of a paper given at the American Political Science Association Convention, September 1969, New York. Reprinted by permission of the author.

Another way courts often become concerned with questions of bureaucratic values is through their traditional concern with protection of the individual. As pointed out above, the tension between property and equality implicit in the goals of most public-serving institutions is often resolved against the individual who is supposed to be helped, and in favor of the policies which perpetuate the property-oriented *status quo*. Where advocates can show that their clients have interests which should be recognized by these institutions but, in fact, are not, courts will often intervene to redress the balance. As the Supreme Court has indicated, however, the process of determining the protection meant to be given individuals by a statute necessitates an inquiry into the broad social purposes for which the statute was intended.

In elucidating what values mean in order to reach decisions, courts lay out for bureaucracies—and for the wider society as well—the goals bureaucracies should pursue. The changes in institutions which result from these authoritative pronouncements on values often exceed anything which courts could have directly ordered. As a result of court decisions, for instance, which have revealed many public housing management practices to be arbitrary and capricious, the Department of Housing and Urban Development issued new regulations concerning eviction procedures which were more sweeping than a court could ever have ordered. Nevertheless, courts often experience definite limitations when they move too far beyond their educative and value-interpretive roles and attempt to prescribe detailed administrative reforms. As Herbert Packer has pointed out with regard to the police:

> The Supreme Court is not in the business of running police departments. It has not direct disciplinary powers over the police (or anyone else, for that matter). Its sole occasion for dealing with police conduct comes when it reviews state criminal convictions in which questions have been raised about the admissibility under the Fourteenth Amendment standards of evidence obtained by the police in asserted violation of those standards. It cannot discipline the offending police officer; it cannot direct his superiors to discontinue the illegal search or the third-degree interrogation; it can only set aside the conviction so obtained and hope that both its action and the expression of its disapproval will have some exemplary effect on the police. The same is true of all other courts in the judicial hierarchy, state and federal. . . . [The Court] cannot independently inform itself about the dimensions of the general law enforcement problem, or identify and choose among the range of particularized solutions that may be available. It cannot frame a program, much less carry one out.[1]

1. Herbert Packer, "Policing the Police," *New Republic* (Sept. 4, 1965), p. 18.

By promoting adherence to organizational aims and by insuring that administrators follow generally accepted standards of fairness in interpreting and applying these organizational aims, courts also advance an overarching goal which is important for its own sake, the ideal of legality. In a democratic society, a broad end is sought by all the groups which participate together in the political system in addition to the specialized ends which each individual group legitimately pursues. This overall end is legality, or the rule of law. Legality fundamentally involves the control of power through the use of agreed-on standards. Where bureaucracies displace their assigned values and pursue different ends, where bureaucrats have unchecked power to do as they please, and where individuals have no recourse when they are harmed by bureaucracies, not only does society lose the intended benefits from these institutions, but the whole concept of legality suffers as well. . . .

An area where courts have a particularly significant impact on bureaucracies is in helping define the limits of organizational autonomy. One way courts accomplish this is by increasing the visibility of decisions made in bureaucracies. An example of this was a New York decision forcing the local housing authority to make public its arbitrary and previously secret standards for admission to public housing.[2] As a result of this visibility, fairer and more binding standards were promulgated. Similarly, a California case declaring that midnight raids[3] of welfare recipients' homes by welfare officials were unconstitutional was the first of a series of such cases which gave nationwide publicity to the ways in which the rights to privacy of low-income persons were being violated. Another way courts can curb the autonomy of bureaucracies is by recognizing the rights of outside groups to check bureaucratic abuses by ensuring that official public policy is enforced. This is done when courts accord standing to persons affected by administrative actions, such as urban renewal displacees, and conservation organizations, thus allowing them to seek redress for their grievances.

The range of forms of relief open to courts basically defines their power to affect the internal penalty and reward structures of bureaucracies. In general, courts can enjoin certain activities, e.g., stop an urban renewal project, and can make certain previously discretionary activities illegal, e.g., third-degree police confession techniques. They can also fine individuals or organizations; and, when criminal intent is found, they can jail persons. Quite often, the court's effectiveness in this area is limited by the essentially negative tools at its disposal and its hesitancy to enter into an area in which it has limited competence. In the *Norwalk-CORE* case,[4] for

2. *Holmes v New York Housing Authority*, 398 F. 2d Cir. (1968).
3. *Parrish v Alameda Civic Service Commission* (Cal. Sup. Ct. 1967) 57 Cal. Reporter 623, 425 R. 2d 223.
4. 395 F. 2d 920 (2d Cir. 1968).

example, the court had no way of improving the plight of urban renewal displacees whose homes had been destroyed, because the project was virtually completed, and the court could not find a way to order the construction of more low-income housing. In the *WACO* case,[5] the court temporarily enjoined further displacement of urban renewal area residents because of inadequacies in the relocation plan, but it still could not order what the revised relocation should include, e.g., a specific number of additional low-income units. In one recent case, however, a court has taken a clearly affirmative posture and stipulated, among other things, in its judgment order that the Chicago Housing Authority:

> . . . shall use its best efforts to increase the supply of Dwellings Units as rapidly as possible in conformity with the provisions of this judgment order and shall take all steps necessary to that end, including making applications for allocations of federal funds and carrying out all necessary planning and development. . . .[6]

Courts have had varying degress of success in affecting bureaucracies in all these areas—goals, resources, autonomy, penalty and reward structures, and information. Yet in almost every case they face a recurring problem: given their own competence, how should they deal with technical issues complex enough to have necessitated the establishment of a special agency to deal with them in the first place. They face this problem most directly when determining what scope of review they should undertake. . . .

CITIZEN PARTICIPATION

Citizen participation presents a second important strategy of intervention for affecting bureaucratic behavior. Like legal intervention, citizen participation affects all the aspects of bureaucracies which contribute to their pathological behavior, but seems to be able to affect certain characteristics of public-serving institutions more than others. While citizen groups have special qualifications for affecting the goals of bureaucracies, they are often not able to affect them in a direct way. Because they are given less deference, citizen groups, unlike courts, must often force their interpretation of goals on bureaucracies, rather than educate them. They can, however, affect bureaucracies by curbing their autonomy and reorienting their penalty and reward structure, and thereby indirectly influence institutional goals. Citizen participation also differs from legal intervention in that a number of or-

5. 294 F. Supp. 433 (ND Cal. 1968).
6. Judgment Order dated July 1, 1969, at page 9, Gautreaux v. The Chicago Housing Authority, Civil Action No. 66 C 1459 (ND I) E. Div.

ganizational requisites for its effective implementation must be present. Citizen groups themselves have institutional needs which must be met in order for them to function effectively.

What is particularly important from the standpoint of strategies of intervention in pathological bureaucracies is that legal intervention and citizen participation often complement each other, with one strategy pressing on bureaucracies in areas where the other is not effective. This intermingling of the two strategies results not only from their differing competencies and roles, but also from the institutional needs and limitations of each. As has been pointed out with regard to welfare, for instance, legal action concerning eligibility, terminations, and other aspects of welfare has more clearly outlined the purposes of public assistance and thus sharpened the targets for attack by recipient organizations. Equally important, the pressure placed on attorneys by their welfare organization clients has, in turn, spurred them on to more radical and aggressive attacks through the courts.

Similar to courts, citizen groups have particular qualifications to evaluate, criticize, and often change the goals—and thereby other features—of public-serving institutions. Citizens such as welfare recipients, public housing tenants, and urban renewal area residents are acutely aware of the problems which these institutions were established to ameliorate. This is the traditional qualification of knowing "where the shoe pinches." Low-income persons know they are poor and that the welfare department should provide them with sufficient resources to support their families; slum dwellers know that public housing should provide them with adequate shelter and that urban renewal should—along with other purposes—improve their living conditions. Not only are citizens who are clients of public-serving institutions aware of the problems which these institutions should be solving, but they are also particularly qualified to judge the efficacy of the institutions' efforts for accomplishing their goals. This is what Jean and Edgar Cahn have called the "consumer perspective, the perspective of the persons who must live day to day with the end results of those efforts."[7] While courts have a special competence to elucidate institutional goals, clients of these organizations have a special competence to understand the problems with which these bureaucracies must deal and to evaluate their success in doing so. The competence of courts is based primarily on an understanding of broad social policy and of legal rights and procedural standards of fairness. The competence of client-citizens, on the other hand, is based on an intimate involvement with bureaucratic policies and procedures which touch almost every aspect of their daily lives.

7. "Citizen Participation," in Hans B. C. Spiegel (ed.), *Citizen Participation in Urban Development*, Vol. 1 (Washington, D.C.: NTL Institute for Applied Behavioral Science, 1968), p. 220.

Citizen groups usually accept the broad goals of the bureaucracies they are trying to affect. Their objective is to operationalize what have become merely rhetorical goals because of the pathological nature of public-serving institutions. Thus, parents and teachers in slum schools agree—at least in principle—that the goal is education; the police as well as ghetto residents recognize the need for protection against crime. They often disagree, however, as to what are proper and efficacious means of achieving these goals. Where citizen groups reject even the broadly-accepted rhetorical goals of institutions, they have to seek changes by affecting the broader political environment, and they are not pursuing an interventionist strategy.

Courts are often limited in how far they can go in laying out bureaucratic goals in a detailed fashion because of their lack of information and special kinds of technical competence. Citizen groups are not only subject to these limitations but also to those caused by the difficulties they encounter in trying to penetrate the bureaucratic system. One of the accepted roles of courts is to police bureaucracies and to hear grievances of persons who allege wrong-doings by these institutions. The accepted doctrine of judicial review provides courts with access to the bureaucratic system, and the writing of legal opinions provides an institutional and authoritative forum for their interpretation of organizational goals. Citizen groups, on the other hand, have often been forced to resort to much more *ad hoc* means to express their criticisms of institutional goals—newspaper articles, testimony before public hearings, public protests, etc. The legitimacy—as well as the validity—of their criticisms has often been open to question. The increasing role now being accorded citizen participation in a wide range of Federal programs, however, is providing citizens with an opportunity to move into public-serving institutions and to affect their resources, autonomy, and penalty and reward structures. Moreover, the growing acceptance of the right of citizens to present their grievances before administrative hearings and courts is affording them a more institutionalized means of expounding upon organizational goals through written complaints and court suits.

On another level, citizen groups can reduce the autonomy of bureaucracies by closely monitoring their day-to-day actions. This is a role which is uniquely suited to citizen groups and one which often follows through on reforms initiated by courts. The WACO court, for instance, ordered the San Francisco Redevelopment Agency to prepare a more adequate relocation plan, and as a result the Agency committed itself to the subsidization of 49 per cent of all moderate-income housing units in the project in order to increase the amount of low-income housing available for relocation purposes. The court did not have the competence, however, to specify precisely how this new goal should be achieved. The responsibility for continuing surveillance of the implementation of this commitment has fallen on WACO, which had been designated the Project Area Committee (WAPAC) for the Western Addition A-2 project. WAPAC, and not the court, has the role of negotiating with the Redevelopment Agency on each individual housing development within the project to ensure that the plan approved by the court is actually implemented. While courts can elucidate goals and hold bureaucracies to their commitments on a general basis, they are in many cases unable to specify in a detailed way how these goals should be reached. This lack of specificity sometimes means that administrative agencies can flaunt the court's orders by being purposefully vague as to how goals will be implemented. It is often uniquely the role of citizen groups, by virtue of sustained involvement, to ensure compliance on a detailed basis. . . .

Three conditions are crucial to continuing effective citizen participation. First, citizen groups, especially the poor, need clear incentives to act; they must be able to expect adequate short-range—as well as long-range—benefits from their activities. Inside bureaucracies, goals and the penalty and reward structure are usually easy to distinguish. For teachers, the goal is education; the penalty and reward structure involves seniority, promotion, etc. For citizen groups, the distinction between goals and the penalty and reward structure is often less clear. For instance, in urban renewal, the incentives to act for individual citizens are often short-range aspects of the project's broader goals, e.g., a particular individual might become involved in redevelopment issues in an attempt to save his house from demolition or to get an urban renewal connected job. It is the translation of broad goals into more specific, immediate gains that is so important to mobilizing the poor and sustaining their activities to affect bureaucracies.

Second, citizen groups need legal or political entitlements to legitimize their participation in bureaucracies. Very few community groups have adequate resources both to struggle for the right to be heard and then, once recognized, to fight over the issues in contention. Federal citizen participation requirements, requiring "maximum feasible participation," as in OEO programs, giving citizens "clear and direct access to decision-making," as in Model Cities, and requiring "close consultation and cooperation," as in HUD's Workable Program, can help overcome this problem. These federal standards not only legitimize citizen participation but also provide community groups with access to public-service institutions. Past experience has shown, however, that these requirements by themselves do not automatically open the doors to bureaucratic innersanctums. Given the inherent difficulties in legislative attempts to force bureaucracies to accept citizen groups and because federal commitments to enforce these requirements are often lacking, citizen groups trying to take advantage of these requirements must still have the ability to mobilize their forces and aggressively press for more than rhetorical commitments to their participatory rights. One tactic upon which citizen groups are beginning to rely is recourse to the courts for re-affirmation of their rights to participate in federal programs.

Finally, citizen groups need technical assistance in order to be able to identify issues, formulate alternative proposals, and understand rules, which are so important in a bureaucratic context. This kind of resource is particularly crucial to citizen participation in public-serving institutions because part of the very nature of bureaucracies which separates them from the rest of society is their virtual monopoly on technical competence. Without the ability to understand administrative regulations and the technical tools used to implement these regulations, citizens are often unaware that their rights have been violated, much less that they may have some means to correct these abuses. Technical assistance enables citizen groups to participate in a dialogue with bureaucrats, where otherwise understanding on both sides might break down.

A major aspect of the emerging new federalism of the late 1960's has been the addition of citizen participation requirements in federal grant-in-aid programs assisting local bureaucracies, such as schools, community action agencies, housing authorities, redevelopment agencies, welfare departments, etc. These programs have been largely responsible for nurturing the growth of citizen groups at the bottom of the bureaucratic system which can then use program standards promulgated from the top of the system to affect local institutions. Conventionally, federalism has relied on administrative superintendence alone to enforce program standards. Such superintendence has often been vitiated, however, by problems connected with paper compliance. Bureaucrats have been unable to ensure compliance due to staff limitations, lack of information, and the general difficulty of evaluating real life through written reports. Furthermore, political constraints have often prevented conscientious enforcement of standards and prevented available information from being gathered. With the growing role of citizen groups in federal programs, however, the technical competence of administrators to police local administration of projects is bolstered by the role citizen groups can play in monitoring them on a sustained basis. Citizen groups' continuing involvement in local projects and their consequent ability to report violations of program standards to federal officials provides administrators with the detailed information they need to perform their jobs adequately. Furthermore, while the role of citizen groups in enforcement of federal standards does not lessen the political constraints on federal officials, these considerations can often no longer be given such high priority when administrators are confronted with official complaints as to noncompliance with laws and administrative regulations governing the programs. Thus, citizen groups form the other half of the bureaucratic scissors which can be used to reform public-serving institutions.

The increasing growth of federal programs and their encouragement of citizen participation is also important because federal standards are usually of much higher quality than those developed in the localities. This is because federal standards are made in response to a broader constituency and because it is often much easier to make high rhetorical commitments on one level of government when those who must actually carry out these commitments are on another level of government. High federal standards to which citizen groups—as well as courts—can appeal gives them additional leverage in trying to reduce the gap between operational and rhetorical program goals.

The experience of citizen participation in federal redevelopment programs exemplifies the ways in which citizen groups can intervene in bureaucracies, the prerequisites they need for doing this, and the limitations on their effectiveness. . . .

Both citizen participation and court action as strategies of intervention in pathological bureaucracies represent a new form of politics. The reliance of both strategies on the importance of goals to affect bureaucratic behavior points out the importance of normative analysis in political science. Both strategies demonstrate the complexity of goals and hint that political philosophy may sometimes be as important as organizational theory in understanding why public-serving institutions become pathological.

Anderson v. Sills

Matthews, J. S. C. Plaintiffs are adult citizens and a civil rights organization of Hudson County. They have instituted this action seeking a declaratory judgment that the use of a reporting system by local and county officials to gather and compile information relating to potential and actual civil disorders violates the United States Constitution. They also seek injunctive relief against the continuance of such reporting system and for the termination thereof.

On or about April 23, 1968 defendant Attorney General Sills distributed a memorandum entitled "Civil Disorders—the Role of Local, County and State Government" to municipal and county officials within New Jersey. A letter accompanying the memorandum, signed by the Attorney General,

Superior Court of New Jersey, Chancery Division, July 30, 1969, pp. 545-66.

indicated that it was being distributed pursuant to a conference held between Governor Hughes and the mayors of various municipalities of the State on April 16, 1968.

The memorandum deals with many aspects of the problem of civil disorder, including methods of advance planning, mutual assistance between municipalities, summoning assistance from State Police and National Guard, legal steps to be taken in proclaiming an emergency, and the control of false rumors which may escalate a civil disorder.

Plaintiffs here seek review of and relief from only a small segment of the 43-page memorandum. The matter at issue is contained in a portion of the memorandum, printed on page 19 therefore, which is entitled "Potential Problems" and which read as follows:

> "Our State Police have been working closely with local police in various communities throughout the State in a continuing effort to keep abreast of potential civil disorder problems. In that respect, therefore, we are already familiar generally with basic problems in these communities. However, these problems change and we should never become over confident to the end that we lose sight of the cause, as well as the effect of civil disturbances. The State Police Central Security Unit has distributed Security Summary Reports (Form 421) and Security Incident Reports (Form 420) . . . to each police department. It is necessary that these reports be used routinely to inform the State Police of the situation in your community. We urge you to see that this vital intelligence is communicated to this central bureau for evaluation and dissemination."

·   ·   ·

Form 420, the Security Incident Report Form, refers in paragraph 9 to a civil disturbance, riot, rally, protest, demonstration, march and confrontation as being illustrative of incidents which are urged to be reported. Paragraphs 4 through 6 indicate that anticipated incidents, incidents still in progress and completed incidents all fall within the scope of the reporting system. The report is designed to determine the names of organizations or groups involved, leaders, the type of organization and the nature of the incident. It also requests the reporting authority to identify the source of information concerning the incident. Form 421, the Security Summary Report, is designed to obtain information concerning individuals who may be connected with potential civil disorder problems. Various information is solicited concerning the subject of Form 421 report and also the sources of information.

Generally, plaintiffs submit that the intelligence system urged by the

Attorney General is so broad and sweeping that any gathering or event could qualify for a write-up, entry of a report into central State files, evaluation and dissemination. Broadly, they urge that this system, considering its scope, can only have a deterring effect on the exercise of First Amendment rights not only by them but also by all citizens.

This matter is presently before the court on a motion by the Attorney General to dismiss the complaint as failing to state a cause of action. Plaintiffs have answered this motion by moving for summary judgment. Concededly, there are no relevant issues of fact which must be determined by the court.

The first issue raised by the Attorney General on his motion is that the complaint does not allege facts indicating that any of the plaintiffs has been aggrieved by the intelligence reporting system challenged herein. Since it is contended that none of the plaintiffs has demonstrated or indicated that they have been aggrieved in any way by the intelligence reporting system, their standing to press the constitutional claims made in the complaint are challenged. The Attorney General further alleges that the failure to allege facts which would confer standing on any of the plaintiffs represents something more than a mere technical defect in pleading; he questions whether anyone would genuinely be deterred from exercising First Amendment rights because of the knowledge of the existence of the State Police intelligence system; he urges that the vital role that this intelligence system plays in the affairs of the State should require this court to adhere strictly to the doctrine of standing and only entertain an action by someone who can particularize the manner in which he has been harmed.

[1] I believe that the Attorney General has oversimplified the problem. This is an action for declaratory judgment under N. J. S. 2A:16-50 et seq. Decisions of our courts have indicated that one need not wait until he has been found to violate the law before seeking judicial relief as to the applicability of statutes. . . . In the area of constitutional litigation the United States Supreme Court has in recent decisions shown a marked relaxation of standards of justiciability where governmental action inhibits the exercise of First Amendment rights. See, e. g., Dombrowski v. Pfister, 380 U. S. 479, 85 S. Ct. 1116, 14 L. Ed. 2d 22 (1965); Lamont v. Postmaster General, 381 U. S. 301, 85 S. Ct. 1493, 14 L. Ed. 2d 398 (1965). . . .

In Straut v. Calissi, three members of a peace movement sought a declaration of unconstitutionality of a dormant sedition statute (N. J. S. 2A:148-22) which had been cited in a speech by defendant county prosecutor as a potential weapon against "peaceniks." None of the plaintiffs was personally threatened with prosecution. Judge Forman, in writing the opinion of the court, stated:

"The importance of the constitutional right here being asserted, however, overrides the substantiality or insubstantiality of the threats in this
case. . . . Where, as here, suit is brought by plaintiffs whose activities
apparently fall within the statute's broad inhibitions, federal jurisdiction
exists." (at *pp.* 1342-1343; emphasis added)

This court observes that plaintiff Anderson has been involved in a "sit-in" at
St Peter's College, Jersey City, and that she was a defendant in litigation
subsequently instituted by the college in this court. Plaintiff Castle is well-
known throughout Hudson County for his civil rights activities, and the
court takes notice of such activities.

[2] Under the federal cases the concepts of standing in First Amendment
cases have had the effect of constituting individual litigants *quasi*-attorneys
general for large classes of citizens whose rights might otherwise be oppressed.
I have no difficulty in accepting the standing of plaintiffs to maintain this
action. The question of standing as posed, however, is related to the substantive question as to whether the State Police intelligence gathering system results in a denial of constitutional rights. The answer to this question
must be resolved by turning to plaintiffs' motion for summary judgment.

The State urges that the public purposes of the State Police intelligence
gathering system is apparent from an examination of the memorandum in
which it is presented. The Attorney General points out that in the last four
years one civil disorder after another has occurred in cities of the United
States; hundreds of citizens have been killed and hundreds of millions of
dollars in property have been destroyed. It is pointed out that in the summer of 1967, serious civil disorders broke out in this State in Newark and
Plainfield, and that less serious disorders broke out in many other cities.
Following the trouble occurring in the summer of 1967, Governor Hughes
and President Johnson both appointed select commissions to study the causes
of the disorders and to make recommendations. Both commissions submitted
reports calling for massive programs to deal with the root problems of unrest
in the black ghettos in big cities. The reports also recommended that careful planning be conducted, first, to prevent the outbreak of future disorders
and, second, to minimize the effect of disorders as they occur. The Attorney
General further informs us that the President's Commission specifically
directed its attention to the role of police intelligence in preventing civil
disorders, and quotes from a supplement to the Commission's report:

"Intelligence—The absence of accurate information both before and
during a disorder has created special control problems for police. Police
departments must develop means to obtain adequate intelligence for planning purposes, as well as on-the-scene information for use in police operations during a disorder.

An intelligence unit staffed with full-time personnel should be established to gather, evaluate, analyze, and disseminate information on potential as well as actual civil disorders. It should provide police administrators and commanders with reliable information essential for assessment and decision-making. It should use undercover police personnel and informants but it should also draw on community leaders, agencies, and organizations in the ghetto." *Report of the National Advisory Commission on Civil Disorders*, at p. 487 (1968).

The inference to be drawn is that the State Police intelligence reporting system was created, if not in compliance with the Commission's Report, at least by following its suggestion.

This court is not unmindful of the concern of the Governor, the Legislature and the Attorney General over the danger to life and property presented by the advent of civil disorders and riots. Neither is it unaware of the obligation cast upon the Executive and Legislative Branches of the State Government to protect the life and property of *all* the citizens of the State. It may be conceded that the objects of the actions of the Attorney General taken here are well within the established police power of the State. However, when a state official, in exercising his powers, comes in conflict with those individual liberties protected by the Bill of Rights, it is the delicate and difficult task of the courts to determine whether the resulting restriction on freedom can be tolerated. . . .

Form 421, the Security Summary Report, requests local police or law enforcement officials to include basic personal data on the subject of the report, such as date and place of birth, marital status, name of spouse, age, race, physical description, occupation, and employer, motor vehicle record, as well as names and addresses of associates, and a narrative which should include, according to instructions, among other items, citizenship, habits or traits, places frequented, financial status, and past activities, findings and/or observations. There is no indication or inference to be drawn that the purpose of the Attorney General in obtaining such information is to stop people from expressing political views. Clearly, his aim is to prevent civil disorders and apprehend perpetrators thereof. The civil disorders memorandum prepared by the Attorney General makes its apparent that he believes there is a relationship between individuals and organizations who engage in protest demonstrations, and the civil disorders which are the object of his concern. He does not, however, in any manner, make clear in the memorandum how the gathering of the data called for in Form 421 will be helpful in preventing civil disorders. It may very well be that some protestors and their activities have had some relationship to some unlawful occurrences, but what can be the effect of the knowledge of the existence of such an intelligence gathering system upon those of our fellow citizens who have the desire and the right to demonstrate both physically and vocally in a lawful manner their opposition to governmental policy or political activity?

Over the past decade the Supreme Court of the United States has significantly developed the content and meaning of First Amendment rights and the availability of remedies for infringement thereof. If any case is to be singled out as being a landmark in this development it is *Dombrowski v. Pfister*, 380 *U. S.* 479, 85 *S. Ct.* 1116, 14 *L. Ed. 2d* 22 (1965). There, threatened state criminal proceedings were enjoined, despite the traditional federal abstention doctrine and the burden of proof required to obtain injunctive relief. The court found that as long as the statue under which the criminal proceedings were threatened existed, the threat of prosecutions of protected areas of expression was a real and substantial one. It found that even the prospect of ultimate failure of such prosecutions did not serve to dispel their chilling effect on protested expression.

In *Lamont v. Postmaster General*, 381 *U.S.* 301, 85 *S. Ct.* 1493, 14 *L. Ed. 2d* 398 (1965), the court struck down a governmental scheme which required addressees of foreign communist propaganda to return a reply card if they wanted such material delivered by the Post Office Department. In doing so, the court made it clear that it was not the minimal burden of returning the card that was at fault, but that this requirement was "almost certain to have a deterrent effect, especially as respects those who have sensitive positions." (*At p.* 307, 85 *S. Ct., at p.* 1496) To the same effect is *NAACP v. Button*, 371 *U. S.* 415, 83 *S. Ct.* 328, 9 *L. Ed. 2d* 405 (1963), which found the challenged Virginia regulation invalid because its mere existence might deter the exercise of delicate and valuable First Amendment rights.

[3, 4] The constitutional doctrine which is found as a common thread in the cases just cited rests on the premise that First Amendment rights are of transcendental value to all society and not merely to those exercising their rights. *Dombrowski v. Pfister, supra*. Thus, the injury to be remedied is considered not only personal but also as one affecting society as well. Such injury must be measured by the impact the given inhibitory regulation, law, or official act may have on those who will not complain because of the chilling effect that even that action might have on their otherwise absolute right to do so. Of course, whether a given regulation, law or official act will have a chilling effect on the First Amendment rights of an individual probably cannot be proved in any objective, measurable manner in any given case. Accordingly, I believe that the constitutional doctrine requires that we consider any burden placed upon First Amendment rights that might reasonably be expected to interfere or to prevent their exercise as constituting an impermissible infringement on those rights. See *Dombrowski v. Pfister*, and *Lamont v. Postmaster General, supra*.

[5] It is apparent, therefore, that where First Amendment rights are in-

volved, mere judicial recognition of the legitimacy of governmental goals in controlling unprotected and illegal conduct cannot be sufficient to support any given regulation, law or official act. Nor should it be the task of the judiciary to balance governmental need against First Amendment rights when the regulation, law or official act goes beyond areas reasonably necessary to reach the permissible governmental goal, and thereby inhibits the rights of persons who otherwise would not be affected by more narrow efforts on the part of the government to control unlawful conduct. See *United States v. Robel,* 389 *U. S.* 258, 266, 88 *S. Ct.* 419, 19 *L. Ed.* 2d 508 (1967). *Robel* involved a federal statute making it a crime for communists to work in designated defense plants, once they had knowledge that they were members of an organization designated as communistic by the Subversive Activities Control Board. In holding the statute unconstitutional, the court recognized that the purpose of the statute involved a legitimate governmental interest in protecting against sabotage in defense facilities; nevertheless, the court said:

> ". . . It is not our function to examine the validity of that congressional judgment. Neither is it our function to determine whether an industrial security screening program exhausts the possible alternatives to the statute under review. We are concerned solely with determining whether the statute before us has exceeded the bounds imposed by the Constitution when First Amendment rights are at stake. The task of writing legislation which will stay within those bounds has been committed to Congress. Our decision today simply recognizes that, when legitimate legislative concerns are expressed in a statute which imposes a substantial burden on protected First Amendment activities, Congress must achieve its goal by means which have a 'less drastic' impact on the continued vitality of First Amendment freedoms. . . . The Constitution and the basic position of First Amendment rights in our democratic fabric demand nothing less." (At *pp.* 267-268, 88 *S. Ct.* at 425)

In *Robel* the court refused to balance the obviously legitimate governmental interest against First Amendment rights. Instead, it confined its analysis to whether Congress had adopted constitutional means in achieving its concededly legitimate legislative goal. Consequently, the court held only that the congressional power and individual rights be accommodated by legislation drawn more narrowly to avoid the conflict. 389 *U. S.,* at *p.* 268, 88 *S. Ct.* 419.

The related constitutional concepts of vagueness and overbreadth have been established in many decisions of the United States Supreme Court. Pertinent citations, in addition to *Robel,* include *Schneider v. Smith,* 390 *U. S.* 17, 88 *S. Ct.* 682, 19 *L. Ed.* 2d 799 (1968); *Keyishian v. Board of Regents of New York,* 385 *U. S.* 589, 87 *S. Ct.* 675, 17 *L. Ed.* 2d 629 (1967); *Elfbrandt v. Russell,* 384 *U. S.* 11, 86 *S. Ct.* 1238, 16 *L. Ed.* 2d 321 (1966); *Lamont v. Postmaster General,* and *Dombrowski v. Pfister, supra.* Consideration should also be given to the decisions of the three-judge panels in *Straut v. Calissi, supra,* and *Heilberg v. Fixa,* 236 *F. Supp.* 405 (*N. D. Cal.* 1964).

I find that the directive in question, and Forms 420 and 421 as used therewith, are violative of the First Amendment of the United States Constitution in that they overreach in their attempt to achieve what is probably a legitimate governmental goal. At the risk of oversimplification, it is not too difficult to imagine the reluctance of an individual to participate in any kind of protected conduct which seeks publicly to express a particular or unpopular political or social view because of the fact that by doing so he might now have a record, or because his wife, his family or his employer might also be included in the data bank created by the State through the forms in question. While it might be argued that the directive, and the forms accompanying it, relate only to mass type action conduct, and not to anyone who expresses a radical, political or social opinion—or that the directive and its forms are not concerned with the content of expression, but rather with the preservation of public order and, therefore, only an indirect infringement of speech—such arguments are refuted by the all encompassing nature of the content of the two forms in question. The Security Summary Report (Form 421) is not restricted to something that a law enforcement officer would normally consider an improper incident. The form is related to people and not to activities, and the probability that it will be interpreted by some as requesting investigations of political troublemakers is too apparent. What, for example, is to prevent a report being rendered on one who opposes an existing political regime in a city, county or the state. In addition, insofar as the procedures would inhibit freedom of association, they are clearly impermissible.

I conclude that plaintiffs' complaint, that they do not want to be investigated and the subject of central surveillance as potential problems, bears merit. The far-reaching nature of the forms in question, together with the apparent lack of standards for the use thereof, indicates strongly that plaintiffs and others may well be subjected to abuse as a result of this intelligence system. The secret files that would be maintained as a result of this intelligence gathering system are inherently dangerous and by their very existence tend to restrict those who would advocate, within the protected areas, social and political change. Accordingly, I determine that a judgment should be entered declaring that the completion, maintenance and distribution of Forms 420 and 421, under the directive aforementioned, is violative of the First Amendment to the Constitution of the United States. Further, that the Attorney General be directed to issue a communication rescinding the directive aforementioned and the use of Forms 420 and 421 thereunder. Finally, that the Attorney General produce and destroy all forms and files connected therewith, and any other information concerning the activities of plaintiffs and other similarly situated, collected under the directive aforementioned, except where such information will be used to charge persons with specifically defined criminal conduct.

No costs to any party.

APPENDIX

INSTRUCTIONS FOR PREPARING THE SECURITY INCIDENT REPORT, SP FORM 420, AND CONTINUATION PAGE, SP FORM 420 A.

The numbers on the Security Incident Report, SP Form 420 and continuation page, SP Form 420A, have been inserted to simplify filling out the report. They correspond with the following numbers and titles:

1. DEPARTMENT OR AGENCY—Enter Department or Agency reporting.
2. CASE NUMBER—Type Case Number, if applicable.
3. REFERENCE NUMBER—Leave Blank.
4. ANTICIPATED INCIDENT—Check box if reporting an anticipated incident.
5. INCIDENT IN PROGRESS—If reporting on an incident still in progress, check box.
6. INCIDENT COMPLETED—Check box if reporting an incident that has occurred.
7. DATE OR DATES—Enter date of incident. Use numbers for month, day and year. If incident is anticipated, include expected date. In reporting incident spanning several days, list date started and date ended. EXAMPLE: 8-4-68 to 8-7-68
8. TIME—If the exact time of the incident is known, type the time. Use "AM" and "PM". In reporting incident covering several hours, list time started and time completed. EXAMPLE: 10:00 A.M. to 2:00 P.M.
9. TYPE OF INCIDENT—Enter the type of incident. EXAMPLES: Civil disturbance, riot, rally, protest, demonstration, march, confrontation, etc.
10. LOCATION—Type the location of the incident. If business or residence, the number and name of street, road, lane or avenue. If open area, give approximate distance to a known geographic location.
11. REASON OR PURPOSE OF INCIDENT—Enter reason for incident or alleged purpose.
12. NUMBER OF PARTICIPANTS—List estimated or announced number of participants or anticipated participants.
13. ORGANIZATIONS AND/OR GROUPS INVOLVED—Give full names and addresses of organizations and/or groups involved. If more space is needed, use Narrative.

14. LEADERS—Enter names, addresses and titles, if any, of leaders of organizations and/or groups involved. Include nicknames, aliases, and other identifying data.

15. EVALUATION OF SOURCE—Evaluate the source by checking the box which most nearly describes the informant:
Completely Reliable
Fairly Reliable
Unreliable
Reliability Unknown

16. EVALUATION OF INFORMATION—Evaluate information by checking the box which most nearly describes the contents:
Confirmed by Other Source
Possibly True
Improbable
Cannot be Judged

17. NARRATIVE
   a. Information previously included elsewhere on this report need not be repeated in the Narrative.
   b. If an organization and/or group is involved in the incident reported, include type and how involved.
      EXAMPLES OF TYPES: Left wing, Right wing, Civil Rights, Militant, Nationalistic, Pacifist, Religious, Black Power, Ku Klux Klan, Extremist, etc.
      EXAMPLES OF HOW INVOLVED: Sponsor, co-sponsor, supporter, assembled group, etc.
   c. Use this section to furnish additional information.
   d. If additional space is required, use Continuation Page, SP Form 420A.

18. REPORTING DATE—Type date this report was prepared using numbers for month, day and year.

19. NAME—Type rank and name in block. (Sign above block)

20. BADGE NUMBER—Type badge number in block, if any.

21. PAGE OF PAGES—May be filled in with ball point pen when report is completed.

STATE OF NEW JERSEY — SECURITY INCIDENT REPORT

(1) DEPARTMENT OR AGENCY	(2) CASE NUMBER	(3) REFERENCE NUMBER

(4) Anticipated Incident	(5) Incident In Progress	(6) Incident Completed	(7) DATE OR DATES	(8) TIME OR TIMES

(9) TYPE OF INCIDENT	(10) LOCATION OF INCIDENT

(11) REASON OR PURPOSE OF INCIDENT	(12) NUMBER OF PARTICIPANTS

(13) ORGANIZATIONS AND/OR GROUPS INVOLVED (NAMES—ADDRESSES)

(14) LEADERS (NAMES—ALIASES/NICKNAMES—ADDRESSES)

(15) EVALUATION OF SOURCE	Completely Reliable		Fairly Reliable		Unreliable		Reliability Unknown	
(16) EVALUATION OF INFORMATION	Confirmed by Other Source		Possibly True		Improbable		Cannot be Judged	

(17) Narrative: OTHER FINDINGS AND OBSERVATIONS — INCLUDE PRIOR ACTIVITIES OF ORGANIZATIONS AND/OR GROUPS AND SOURCE OF INFORMATION, IF OTHER THAN CONFIDENTIAL.

(18) REPORTING DATE	(19) NAME	(20) BADGE NUMBER	(21)
			PAGE OF PAGES

NJSP 420 (2-68)

MAIL TO: Central Security Unit, New Jersey State Police, Box 68, West Trenton, N.J. 08625

STATE OF NEW JERSEY

CONTINUATION PAGE

(1) DEPARTMENT OR AGENCY	(2) CASE NUMBER	(3) REFERENCE NUMBER

(18) REPORTING DATE	(19) NAME	(20) BADGE NUMBER	(21)
			PAGE OF PAGES

RON EINSTOSS

Officer Indicted on Charges of Excessive Force

A Los Angeles police officer was indicted Tuesday for allegedly using excessive force on a man who is said to have verbally abused him during an unsuccessful search for a machine gun used in a series of bank robberies.

The indictment was the first returned against a policeman for alleged brutality in *several years.* *

Much of the evidence reportedly was supplied by other police officers.

Officer John R. Salyer, 30, attached to the Foothill Division as a detective at the time of the incident last November 1, was charged by the County Grand Jury with assault with a deadly weapon and with assaulting a person in his custody. He is accused of striking Eddie J. Tunstall Jr., 35-year-old former tavern owner, who lives at 13118 Daventry St., Pacoima.

Tunstall, a Negro, allegedly was hit with a shotgun butt in the face and groin by Salyer, who is white. The officer, a veteran of eight years on the force and with a clean record, previously was suspended without pay for thirty days after an investigation of the incident by the Police Department's Internal Affairs Division.

Acting Police Chief Roger Murdock said after the indictment that no further action would be taken against Salyer because he already has served a suspension. Any further action, the chief said, would follow the outcome of the court proceedings.

According to the investigation, Salyer was one of about ten plainclothes detectives and uniformed patrolmen who responded to an informant's late evening tip that a machine gun, used in many recent bank robberies in the city, was secreted somewhere on the premises of an unoccupied building in Pacoima.

When the police arrived at 11 p.m. they herded together for questioning more than a dozen persons present in the dimly lit building and at the same time began their unsuccessful search for the weapon. Witnesses indicated that Tunstall allegedly was struck by Salyer when he became abusive and shouted obscenities at the officer, who was one of those questioning the persons found in the building.

Salyer reportedly admitted striking Tunstall in the face, but only after the suspect, in addition to his alleged remarks, whirled around and appeared to be reaching in his belt for a weapon.

Tunstall, later found to be unarmed, was arrested and charged with interfering with an officer. He was acquitted.

The investigation of the incident by the Internal Affairs Division was launched after a complaint by Tunstall, charging police brutality. The matter later was referred to Dis. Atty. Evelle J. Younger's Special Investigations Division, which handles cases involving alleged misconduct by public officials, including police officers.

Tunstall, who reportedly was hospitalized for three days, has filed a claim against the city and Police Department in which he is seeking $100,000 damages for his injuries.

The indictment was returned before Superior Judge William B. Keene.

Ex-Arkansas Prison Head Fined for Cruel Treatment of Inmates

James L. Bruton, former superintendent of Tucker State Prison Farm, has drawn a $1,000 fine and a suspended one-year prison sentence on a charge of brutality against inmates. Federal Judge J. Smith Henley said he refused to send the defendant to prison because it was likely that Mr. Bruton would be murdered there.

Mr. Bruton, 56 years old, pleaded no contest. The judge imposed the maximum penalty, but said he wished that the law permitted a heavier fine.

"Quite frankly, Mr. Bruton, the court thinks that if it sentenced [you] to a year in prison and requested you to serve it at this time, the chances of your surviving that year would not be good," Judge Henley said. "I don't believe you could live 60 days in a Federal penitentiary or a jail."

"I think that long before that time, some one or more of these persons or their friends with whom you have dealt in the past as inmates of the Arkansas Penitentiary will kill you," he said. "The court doesn't want to give you a death sentence."

Mr. Bruton was to face trial Tuesday on a charge that he administered cruel and unusual punishment to two inmates in 1964. He was accused of torturing them with an old crank wall telephone that was used to send electrical shocks through an inmate's genitals.

A jury acquitted Mr. Bruton on eight counts of brutality in November, but issued no verdict on another count involving two inmates who said they were tortured. Judge Henley had scheduled another trial on that count.

The judge said Friday that after hearing the testimony in Mr. Bruton's trial in November, he regretted that he could not punish him more severely.

United States Attorney W. H. Dillahunty said Mr. Bruton's conviction on the single charge vindicated the prosecution's efforts last fall.

A Federal jury empaneled by Judge Henley in July indicted 15 persons for brutality in Arkansas prisons. Six have been acquitted and one former trusty guard pleaded guilty and received a suspended sentence. Mr. Dillahunty said charges may be dropped against several others next week.

BEN DOVER

People's Defenders Organize To Resist Oppression

People are getting scared. They have a good right to be—especially young people. Police harassment directed by the Establishment power structure is only one form of repression now coming down.

People are acting scared. They shouldn't be. Either you back down in the face of repression and become more repressed, or else you stand up and fight, and at least in fighting, declare your freedom.

The Los Angeles People's Defenders, an action caucus of the Coalition Against Repression, has begun fighting and is proving to be a group where people can fight repression without having to act scared.

The first public action of the Los Angeles People's Defenders began on Independence Day, July 4th, 1969. A love-in planned by Green Power for the Venice beach had all the makings of the big kind of bust that the Free Press Love-ins, Devonshire Downs, and the Shrine-Cheetah-Bank-type concert halls had—lots of kids out to have a good time, lots of music, and lots of grass and wine.

Over the past year the Police Department has been mounting its activities

From the Los Angeles *Free Press*, July 18, 1969, p. 3. Reprinted by permission.

aimed at doing away with all peaceful activities designed to provide a pleasurable atmosphere for kids. The police have beaten people, falsely arrested people, and brought fear to masses of people out picnicking.

The Los Angeles People's Defenders suspected the planned Love-In on July 4th would be the target of another police field day. The questions the Defenders wanted to deal with were how to make the kids at the Love-In relate their repression coming down on the campuses, the Black and Brown communities, the Panthers, the Anti-War movement, etc.; and when the bust came, how to help the people there? The most important thing to be communicated to the kids was that they should not just sit back and be repressed, but should begin to organize and fight.

Members of the People's Defenders began arriving at Venice beach early Friday morning prepared to talk with the people at the Love-In. A leaflet was to be passed out telling people about political repression and police harassment, and giving advice on what to do when the police began busting people—how to help the crowd from panicking, and where to get legal and medical aid.

It had been announced some days before by Captain Sillings of the Venice Police Division that they were mobilizing all available men to deal with what was projected to be mass crowds at the beach, that the tactical Metro Squad from Downtown would be there, that the streets near the beaches would be manned by police who would then close them off when the initial parking lots were filled up, and that they were pressing the Green Power people not to hold their Love-in and the Free Venice Committee from holding a scheduled Independence Day Free Venice parade.

Free Venice had been denied a permit to hold their parade the same day that a conservative group in Pacific Palisades was granted a permit to hold a Patriotic July 4th parade. The Free Venice Committee decided to call off their parade and distributed a leaflet urging people to go instead to a silent vigil at the Venice Police Station to demonstrate the community's anger at the police harassment.

By 10 a.m. the police began showing up. Paddywagons, police cars, and police buses pulled up to the ruins of Pacific Ocean Park and turned the old Cheetah into an instant-arrest-and-booking station. Down the way, the Venice Pavillion had become a mass mobilization point for the forces of "law and order." As the people began to arrive at the beach they found uniformed police with walkie-talkies being guided by groups of police stationed on beachfront rooftops armed with high-powered binoculars and telescopic lenses. Dozens of plainclothesmen clad unnoticeably in khaki pants, tee-shirts, sneakers, straw beach hats, and sunglasses milled through the young crowd.

The food was there and being prepared, the bands were arriving to play and the People's Defenders were going to groups of kids (actually, the crowd was quite small), passing out leaflets, and discussing the issue of repression. The reception from the kids was fairly enthusiastic. "Hell," the general attitude was expressed by one fellow, "there are more cops than people here today. Looks like another big bust. For what? Why the hell can't we come out here to the beach and enjoy ourselves? Pretty soon we won't be able to go anywhere and do anything. The cops said they'll even bust anyone with a dog here today. What the hell can we do to stop these motherfuckers?"

The dozen or so members of the People's Defenders, many of whom are students at UCLA, talked to the kids and told them to organize politically. Sure, Love, Peace and Flowers are great, but what the hell do you do when the Man's coming down on your brothers and sisters?

And so the Man began to come down on these kids—began to pick them off one by one or two by two. One for a bottle of wine, another for empty beer cans filled with sand near their beach blanket, another for possession.

A long-haired (down to his shoulders) freak walked up to two kids, showed him his badge under his shirt and arrested them for having wine.

And the Man was being led by Big Brother on the rooftops with the telescopic lenses and binoculars and walkie-talkie communication. And the kids were letting their brothers and sisters be taken without protest or fight! One member of the People's Defenders, Ed Pearl, took the microphone and talked about repression and the need to organize, talked about the "pigs hassling you kids," and the kids gave him a round of applause, perhaps because he had the guts to say it in the face of the Man, maybe because somebody had to say something.

Then one of the Defenders, Jerry Kay, was busted. He had seen a kid busted and handed him a leaflet that had a telephone number for legal aid on it. He was arrested for handing out leaflets in a public park. The other Defenders saw this and surrounded the two officers demanding to know why they were busting him.

"What has he done? You can't bust him you pig!"

"One more step and I'll arrest you for interfering with an arrest!"

The busted Defender turned to the officer and began yelling at him that he had earlier called up the Venice Police Station who said it was legal to hand out leaflets. The officers were hassled. They became nervous and uptight about the people talking back to them. The two people were handcuffed and marched off to be booked and tossed into a paddy wagon (the wagons were conveniently marked for "Adult Male," "Adult Female," "Juvenile Male," and "Juvenile Female!") awaiting transport to the Venice Jail.

One of the Defenders, Gordon Alexandre, got up to the microphone and said one of our Brothers has been arrested, all his friends should go to the jail and demand he be released. Then Cleo Knight, guiding guru of Green Power, told the crowd, "No, don't hassle the police. We should thank them for letting us hold this love-in. It's just a small group of radicals who are causing all the trouble. Let the police take the people they arrest quietly." Sure! And next 4th of July we can all celebrate in the concentration camps.

And while Cleo Knight was celebrating the rebirth of fascism in America, the People's Defenders went to the Venice Jail to demand the release of their brother.

Now, the Venice police are considered by many to be some of the most brutal in the city, and the police station in Venice is considered to be almost an impregnable fortress. The Free Venice Committee had earlier called for a silent vigil at the station and when the 50-or-so of them solemnly approached the police station with signs reading "Silence NO Violence," they met about 20 members of the People's Defenders militantly besieging the police station. Free Venice rigidly took its position outside the station, while the People's Defenders entered it demanding that their brother be released.

Meanwhile outside, the cops had brought in a fellow with an American flag painted on the trunk of his car. Instead of stars, he had a peace symbol. The People's Defenders told the cops that that wasn't against the law. The cops took the kid into the station and he came out again with the intention of painting over the flag. Ed Pearl stormed into the station again and demanded to see the captain, claiming that it was illegal for the police to force the kid to do that, and that he'd file a citizen's complaint if he did. Meanwhile outside John Donaldson of the People's Defenders told a cop he couldn't hold the kid.

After some debate, the captain finally agreed to let the kid go. He left, hopefully realizing that he CAN fight for his rights.

The jailed Defender was booked for handing out handbills in a public park. Bail was set at $125. He was immediately bailed out. The Free Venice vigil had broken up and they had left. Members of the People's Defenders were on the beachfront that evening helping people who were being busted by the continued police repression.

People are getting scared. They have a good right to be. People are acting scared. They shouldn't be. Contact the Los Angeles People's Defenders at 653-8516.

ALLAN KATZMAN

Community Action

The aftermath of the Tompkins Square debacle on Memorial Day is just beginning to be felt in the East Village community. June 1, the next morning after the brutality spree, a meeting was held at the Brotherhood of Man, between Avenues C and D, on 3rd Street. Present were members of the neighborhood Churches, Hippies, representatives of the Negro community, the Straight community, Captain Fink of the 9th Precinct and Lt. Lipsky of Community Relations. The main concern of the discussion was on how to prevent such an occurrence from happening again. A representative of the Communications Company, Bill Principe, reminded everyone that "we could expect fifty thousand hippies here this summer, and if we don't settle what happened at Tompkins Square Park, we can expect to have a riot situation on our hands."

Captain Fink was quite perturbed as he tried to explain the need for a dialogue to be thoroughly established between the police and the rest of the community: Negro, Puerto Rican, Ukrainian, Italian and Hippie. Everyone agreed that a meeting should be called between the police and the community, and that it should be limited to thirty people, representatives from different parts of the community. It was decided that the Lutheran church on 9th Street and Ave. B., Friday at 7:30, was the best time and place.

Larry and Pat Pool, of the Tompkins Square Press, walked in just after the decision had been made. Larry was quite upset, and, in no uncertain terms, let everyone know what he felt. "Look," he began, "I have been up all night, walking around, talking to people, and I'm telling you, there are people around who are pushing to see this turn into a full-fledged riot. They got blood in their eyes and in their hands; and I'm telling you, they're calling for the revolution." He refused to name names, but told us, "you know who they are." There was silence; no one wanted to say what they feared, but the few minutes' empty silence seemed to answer, as if we knew who they were.

Larry was filled in on what had occurred before he arrived, and this calmed him down. He offered to help in any way he could. The meeting broke up at 2 o'clock.

I arrived back at my office to find a woman waiting for me, who was looking for a lawyer and bail money for the hippies who were still in jail. "My God," I said, "don't you know of the bail and lawyer fund set up by the Jade Companions of the Flowered Dance, set up by the Hippie community." She shook her head. She was a hippie living in the neighborhood for over a year, but she had never heard of them.

I gave her the number of the Jade Companions, who had already been contacted when the incident happened, and were out raising the rest of the bail money.

I left my office to attend a press conference that the hippie community had called for 5 o'clock today at Pablo, an artists' commune at 9 Bleeker Street. When I arrived, newsmen were hanging around, and T.V. cameras were being set up. Five of the hippies who had been arrested were sitting in chairs, waiting to be interviewed. Jim Fouratt, of the Communications Company, was trying to get the newsmen and cameras trained on the people who were involved. But they wouldn't listen, they interviewed whomever they wanted, took pictures of the weirdest-looking people they could find. It was their show, and they were determined to create the news according to their own preconceived, imaginary script. As it turned out, I found myself the next day in a photograph in the *New York Times*, identified as one of the hippies who had been arrested. What a farce! I had come to the press conference, not only as an involved member of the community, but also as a newspaper man covering an event, and found myself involved in the script. It's as if the entire news media was acting out of its own hallucinations, its own lies. It was the pseudo-event of the week.

I arrived back at my office to find that a meeting of the hippie community had been called for 9 o'clock tonight, at the Forum restaurant, on Avenue A between 10th and 11th Streets. The Forum was packed when I arrived, and Jim Nash, of the newly established Community Defense Committee, was chairing the meeting. He began the meeting by reiterating the proposals that the new committee had written up the night of the Memorial Day incident. There was much pushing and shoving up front, and it was hard to hear what the proposals were. They seemed to deal with setting up a bail fund and lawyers, and communications with the police. The atmosphere became heavy with anger when a few radicals tried to break up the meeting by shouting everyone else down. Jim Nash deferred the meeting over to Captain Fink, who had been invited to the meeting by the Defense Committee.

Fink began his plea by stating, "Look, I have come here to answer your complaints and hear your grievances." But he was cut off before he could finish. The radicals started shouting "Fascist" and "The revolution is here, and this time it's your blood that's going to flow!" Then all hell broke loose. People were pushing and shouting. A woman next to me cried out, "I don't believe it! I don't believe it! I'm going to be sick." My stomach was churning, too. I looked around and realized that the majority of the hippie community had not attended.

By this time, Captain Fink had to leave the meeting, with hostility and abuse following his footsteps. Jim Nash tried to get back control of the meeting, but he was shouted down with invectives of "Stool Pigeon," "Informer." Nash left the Forum, taking his committee to a secret location on the East Side, to work out the problems. The radicals remained in the coffee house, shouting their abuses, rallying their hatred against the entire world. It became all too evident to the other people who were wandering around bewildered, that these radicals were no different than the people who had tarred and feathered a flower child at the recent loyalty-day parade, except that they were using venom and words, instead of fists and clubs. They were calling for blood, everyone's blood.

I attended a meeting the next day, called by the Communications Company, at the Family Store, on 6th Street between 2nd and 3rd Avenues. Everyone felt a little better now. Frank Wise, the last remaining hippie, had been released on $50 bond. Most of the representatives of the hippie communities were in attendance, including Andy Kent, a member of Jim Nash's newly formed Community Defense Committee. It was agreed by all present, that we had to consolidate the entire hippie community in one organization; otherwise, everyone would be working at cross purposes. Everyone agreed the best organization would be a tribal council modeled after the American Indians, where representatives from every part of the community would be sent, to sit in council and decide issues. All decisions would be made in the name of the council, and no one person would be responsible for making any decision without consulting the council first.

I left the meeting and headed over to the Village Theater, where the fashion show of East Village boutiques, "Trips to Wear," was in progress. Earlier, a rumor was heard that there might be a bust by the police, on possible nudity in the fashion show. I knew the rumor had to be ridiculous, but couldn't help feeling that everything that had happened in the past two days was nothing short of unbelievable. I waited, and it happened, the ridiculous, but not in the theater, in Tompkins Square Park. A riot was in progress while we all watched the transitory happening of Fashion. WINS and WMCA reported the events as they were happening. "Anti-Hippie elements had started a riot in Tompkins Square Park," the radio blared. The ridiculous had been made real. The World had now been divided into Hippie and Anti-Hippie. The situation had worsened. We were now made fully aware that the situation had to be dealt with, dealt with now, or else.

CESAR CHAVEZ

Nonviolence: Nonviolence Still Works

At a time when many American radicals are saying that nonviolence—as an instrument for social change—died with Martin Luther King, it is reassuring to meet a man of faith who preaches compassion rather than bloody confrontation, practices what he preaches and gets results.

At 42, Cesar Chavez, the head of the United Farm Workers Organizing Committee, is soft-spoken but tough. This man has had to be. The self-educated son of a migrant family, he has worked hard at stoop labor since the age of ten.

For the past seven years, he has been the leader and guiding spirit of *La Causa,* a movement that is not just a union but also a civil rights group and self-help association run by and for the poor, and dedicated to militant nonviolence.

Today, Chavez's movement is nearing the end of a four-year struggle for union recognition from California's $140 million-plus grape-growing industry. Contracts have been signed with 11 companies, including all the major wine-grape growers. Somehow, *La Causa* has succeeded where many other union movements over many years have tried and failed.

Here are the highlights of a recent conversation with Look in which Chavez tells why:

Nonviolence can only be used by those whose cause is strong. It is very hard, and man's self-control is very weak. I am not completely nonviolent yet, and I know it. That is why I fasted; I felt it was a very personal form of self-testing and of prayer. Anyone could be nonviolent in a monastery, after all, but that is easy, and that was not the way of Christ. What's difficult is to be nonviolent in the cause, in the battle for social justice; knowing what violence can be done to ourselves, knowing—and this is even more difficult —what violence can be done to our family and brothers and our cause.

This requires training. Soldiers must be trained in techniques of war, and fighters for social justice must be trained in nonviolence. Even after the basic discipline is learned, there is never a time you can say you've arrived. The training must be kept up every day.

We must respect all human life, in the cities and in the fields and in Vietnam. Nonviolence is the only weapon that is compassionate and recognizes each man's value. We want to preserve that value in our enemies—or in our adversaries, as President Kennedy said more gently, more rightly. We want to protect the victim from being the victim. We want to protect the executioner from being the executioner.

This Christmas was sad for many of our workers who were a long way from their families, without money to come home. They were in many big cities—New York, Boston, Detroit—working on the boycott. You see, the wine companies have recognized our union, but the table-grape growers still have not. They will not sit down to talk with us, and they use strike-breakers illegally, because the Immigration Service and the Department of Justice and the Border Patrol all conveniently look the other way. In our negotiations with the big corporate farms, we find we have to strike just to get an election. This may sound ridiculous to anyone who knows anything about labor relations, but it is a fact.

So the only other nonviolent and economically just instrument we have is a consumer boycott. We do not want to damage the grape industry by this boycott—that would only be taking jobs away from ourselves—but we feel we must tell the consumer that those who sell scab grapes are supporting poverty, supporting injustice.

To do this, small groups of three or four of us go into the cities, living on $5-a-week strike benefits and staying with union or church groups. Then we start the long process of picketing markets and handing out leaflets to explain why. It has been successful because many leaders of both parties have supported us—Senator McCarthy, Humphrey, Ted Kennedy, Senator Javits and many mayors of big cities—but it takes a very long time.

Some stores lie to the customers and say the grapes aren't from California. Some big chains just don't want to understand.

So there are still many lonely Farm Workers far from home, picketing in the cold, telling their story to passers-by who will listen. The love of justice in the hearts of other Americans is still our last and best hope.

Well, we took a vote on whether to go out on strike or not, even though we might not be ready. We were unanimous on two things—we would strike, and we would keep the strike nonviolent.

We have won many victories during this long struggle; the fourth year of the strike began in September. In 1966, we marched 300 miles to Sacramento, the state capital, to put our problems before Governor Brown. All through the little towns in the heart of the Central Valley, we marched—singing union songs and workers' songs and songs of joy.

Each night, we held a rally for farm workers nearby, and each morning, there was a joyful Mass. We began with 75 workers, and we carried the Virgin of Guadalupe, the union flag, and the flags of Mexico and the United States. Our theme was "Penitence, Pilgrimage, and Revolution."

When we got to Sacramento on Easter Sunday, the farm workers and the city friends who had joined us along the way had increased our march to 8,000. The night before we arrived, one big company agreed to negotiate with us, and all the tired workers sang for joy.

It is times like those when we know there is hope to end our suffering.

It may be a long time before we get justice under the law, because the law is on the side of the growers. As Robert Kennedy said to the Delano sheriff during Senate hearings on migrant labor—he was amazed to find that our people were arrested because they *might* commit a crime—"I suggest that the sheriff read the Constitution of the United States."

It may be a long time before the growers see us as human beings.

It may be a long time before there is no threat of violence to our workers on the picket line, no intimidation by the growers, no allowing strikebreakers to cross the border.

But we will win, we *are* winning, because ours is a revolution of mind and heart, not only of economics.

We have helped people to lose the fear that has been instilled in them.

When a man or woman, young or old, takes a place on the picket line for even a day or two, he will never be the same again. He has confirmed his own humanity. Through nonviolence, he has confirmed the humanity of others.

CARROL W. CAGEL AND HARRY P. STUMPF

Citizen Arrest: The Trial of Reies Lopez Tijerina

On June 5, 1967, a band of armed men swept into a remote northern New Mexico courthouse in search of a hated district attorney. The district attorney was not present but two officers were wounded, the courthouse shot up, and a newsman and deputy kidnaped. Before nightfall, armored, troop-

From *Political Trials*, edited by Theodore Becker, pp. 183, 192-199. Copyright © 1971 by The Bobbs-Merrill Company, Inc. Reprinted by permission.

carrying vehicles of the New Mexico National Guard had fanned out across the vast, mountainous area in search of the "insurrectionists." The date has since become the most discussed and debated in the state's history. The "courthouse raid," as it is now known simply, brought national reporters into Rio Arriba County in force for the first time, and focused national attention on the land grant issue, fiery land grant leader Reies Lopez Tijerina, and the plight of New Mexico's Hispanic population. Tensions produced by the violent event were to simmer without letup until November 13, 1968—the day the authorities moved the continuing struggle with the Hispanic militants into the Establishment's own arena of the courtroom. There, the mercurial Tijerina—eloquent but with little formal education and unversed in the law—confronted the man he had sought to "arrest" a year and a half earlier—District Attorney Alfonso Sanchez. The trial, whether evoking memories of Pancho Villa or Zapata or capturing the imagination of black separatists and campus revolutionaries, was to become the non-violent equivalent of the confrontation which never occurred at the court-house.

.   .   .   .

What the Albuquerque Journal called "one of the state's most noted criminal cases" got under way on November 12, 1968. The scene: a paneled, carpeted, heavily-guarded courtroom of the modernistic Bernalillo County Courthouse in downtown Albuquerque. Reporters, visiting high school classes, hangers-on and Alianza sympathizers packed the galleries. District Court Judge Paul Larrazolo, a slight, nervous man whose father had once been governor of New Mexico, was plainly ill at ease. He had reason to be. Assembled before him were District Attorney Sanchez and his assistants, Tijerina and nine of his co-defendants, and a diverse array of defense lawyers. In addition to court-appointed New Mexico attorneys, there were legal counsel of the nation's radical community whose attention Tijerina had drawn: Beverly Axelrod, one-time defender of Eldridge Cleaver, and beaded, booming, California civil liberties lawyer John Thorne.

It was obvious from the first that confusion would reign. . . .

. . . Tijerina and the other nine defendants were to be tried on three charges each: kidnaping (which carries a possible death penalty), assault on the Rio Arriba County jail, and false imprisonment of Deputy Sheriff Daniel Rivera.

. . . The trial was important beyond the specific charges involved. First, it pitted Tijerina and his archenemy Sanchez in direct battle. Sanchez had long been the most vociferous critic of Tijerina and his Alianza, having called loudly and frequently for the land grant leader's detention and maintaining through the news media his belief that Communistic influences were at work. Tijerina, for his part, regarded Sanchez (and U.S. Senator Joseph

Montoya) as the Hispano who had "sold out," who had abandoned his heritage to "make it" in the Anglo Establishment. Worse, he had turned on *los pobres* (poor Hispanos) rather than championing their cause. Second, public opinion throughout the state was enraged by the raid. Editorial writers and citizens in the street called for Tijerina to be "locked up," legal niceties and procedural detail notwithstanding. Tijerina received the brunt of reaction from law officers, public officials and citizens to urban and campus rebellion elsewhere around the country. He was the local manifestation of hated and feared revolution, the antithesis of law, order and complacency. Having declined to petition for grievances within normal channels, Tijerina must now submit to the awesome judgment of the Law. Thus, the trial became the arena for the protectors of the status quo to assert their full authority over the unregenerate minority.

The trial, then was for Reies Tijerina a personal confrontation (with Sanchez) and another contest in his continuing struggle against the "Establishment." Placed in formal, almost austere surroundings, denied the friendly atmosphere of rural Rio Arriba County, denied, even his most formidable weapon—the use of fiery Spanish-language rhetoric—Tijerina obviously did not relish the encounter.

The confrontation became direct four days after the trial opened as Judge Larrazolo announced his decision to sever Tijerina's trial from those of the nine co-defendants. . . .

. . . Tijerina, it should be noted, preferred the severance. Although he did not say so publicly, he indicated indirectly that he was beginning to feel more confident. After four days of watching the powerful legal apparatus of the state become entrapped in a morass of technical confusion, Tijerina appeared to be gaining confidence that he could, just perhaps, beat the State with the force and clarity of his own eloquence. . . .

Severing of the trial, he announced, had made his attorneys "obsolete." But he insisted that he needed "a few days" to prepare his case.

. . . With the judge's approval, the trial emerged as a head-to-head confrontation between Tijerina and the State. Surprisingly, Alfonso Sanchez did not seem to welcome this change. . . .

Peter Nabokov, the journalist who is writing a book on the raid and who knows both Tijerina and Sanchez well, described the confrontation this way:

> To appreciate the irony of Tijerina and Sanchez confronting each other, it must be recalled that . . . the "citizens' arrest" of Sanchez had been the sole reason for the courthouse blitz.
>
> The district attorney apparently had inflamed some local citizens by threatening imprisonment to anyone attending an Alianza "convention" the weekend before. In hot retaliation for his . . . "persecution" the raid was staged, and Tijerina was fingered as its architect.

> Now the two men, the . . . raid's object and its . . . alleged perpetrator, were facing each other in the polite and equal footing of opposing barristers—arguing a case from which they were anything but removed and cool legal minds.

After the stage was set for direct battle, the trial took a meandering course.

.   .   .

In a more interesting theme, he continually pushed the contention that citizens may make "arrests" of guilty persons—even authorities themselves (such as Sanchez). His deeper point was not missed by the intent Hispanos who sat in the gallery: that, in the land grant areas, the Alianza—not the State—is the law. If men got shot and a courthouse damaged in the process of making a legitimate "arrest," too bad.

Tijerina drew out this contention further when cross-examining State Policeman Juan Santistevan. The officer had testified he was approaching the courthouse on June 5 when men started shooting at him. A bullet hit the windshield of his car, he backed the vehicle behind a house and ran for cover.

"Did you know that citizens of the United States could arrest an officer if they believed they had a grievance against him?" Tijerina asked. "No," replied Santistevan. "Isn't it possible," asked Tijerina further, "these people pushed to the brink of desperation, had to teach you a lesson, teach you what you were not taught by your superiors?"

Undaunted, Tijerina did not miss an opportunity to pursue this point throughout the trial. He knew that if the "citizens' arrest" theory could be vindicated, it would have the short-range practical effect of making the raid —in search of Sanchez—plausible. Further, it would secure him a valuable legal weapon in his efforts to secure Alianza hegemony over territory within the "free city-states." So as every witness ascended to the paneled witness stand, he hammered home his point as to the plight of a people "pushed to the brink of desperation" and using the common law right available to every citizen to obtain redress.

To make matters worse for Sanchez and the prosecution, witnesses at the courthouse failed to come through with the clear-cut, dramatic testimony that was expected. On December 3, in fact, when the state rested its case, a Rio Arriba County undersheriff seemed to take the steam out of an already-sputtering prosecution case. The undersheriff, 68-year-old Daniel Rivera, told the jury he had not heard Tijerina order him to be pistol-whipped. Then he told Tijerina: "I'm not blaming you for anything, sir."

As the trial proceeded into December and neared a close, it became even more difficult to predict the outcome. National attention was focused on the trial. The state press, particularly the Albuquerque dailies and television stations, had extensive and daily coverage. Although editorial comment was not forthcoming, those familiar with New Mexico newspaper know there was strong sentiment among editors for a conviction on all three counts. New Mexico reporters at the scene, if hallway talk was a fair indication, seemed to feel the State could get a conviction on only one or possibly two charges —not all three. Meanwhile, the underground and left-wing press nationally was keeping a close eye on Albuquerque. The *National Guardian*, a leftist publication, wrote on December 14: ". . . the trial of Tijerina for crimes supposedly committed in the Tierra Amarilla courthouse 'raid' of June 5, 1967, finally got down to the real issues: the oppression and exploitation of the Indo-Hispano people."

. . .

Finally, on Friday the 13th, Dec., after a month of seemingly inconclusive testimony, Judge Larrazolo prepared to instruct the jury. His instructions, although perhaps not directly affecting the jury's verdicts, certainly were regarded with amazement by New Mexico legal practitioners and with delight by Tijerina and his sympathizers in the state and around the country. The instructions seemed to give particular sanction to the concept of "citizens' arrest."

Those instructions read:

> The Court instructs the Jury that citizens of New Mexico have the right to make a citizen's arrest under the following circumstances:
> (1) If the arresting person reasonably believes that the person arrested, or attempted to be arrested, was the person who committed, either as a principal or as an aider and abettor, a felony; or
> (2) If persons who are private citizens reasonably believe that a felony has been committed, and that the person who is arrested or attempted to be arrested was the person committing, or aiding and abetting, said felony.
>
> The Court instructs the Jury that a citizen's arrest can be made even though distant in time and place from the acts constituting or reasonably appearing to constitute the commission of the felony. The Court further instructs the Jury that a citizen's arrest may be made whether or not law enforcement officers are present, and, further, may be made in spite of the presence of said law enforcement officers.
>
> The Court instructs the Jury that anyone, including a State Police Officer, who intentionally interferes with a lawful attempt to make a citizen's arrest does so at his own peril, since the arresting citizens are entitled under the law to use whatever force is reasonably necessary to defend themselves in the process of making said citizen's arrest.

These words were startling enough to the courtroom observers, but in a few hours they were overshadowed by the surprise verdict: "not guilty" on all three counts.

Tijerina, his young wife Patsy, and the devoted Hispano followers who had sat through the trial, were elated. The vigorous land grant leader immediately began bubbling over with future plans. Among other things, he would write a book, a "New Science" on how the "browns" (Hispanos) could bridge the widening gap between whites and blacks in America. Shortly, he announced plans to "organize" Albuquerque's garbage collectors and to sue the Albuquerque Board of Education for discrimination against "Indo-Hispano" students.

When Tijerina first returned to Tierra Amarilla after the trial, he told his followers: "When the jury brought in its verdict that Tijerina was innocent, the justice of God and of you who struggle fell on the heads of the powerful . . . the sky fell on their heads!" Noting national publicity of the verdict, he added: "Many of you, who are not lawyers, may not realize the effect of this victory on the judges, officials, everyone." He later told the audience, "We don't believe in violence, but we believe in Jesus Christ. The revolution of Tierra Amarilla was like Christ entering the temple and cleaning out the Pharisees."

Later, in a talk with one of the authors at a Santa Fe cafe, Tijerina talked further about his court victory:

"First, it was a great example for a terrified people who had been in captivity for more than 470 years." The State, he said, "threw all the organized power that the taxpayers have built up to crack the people of the mountains. They got me into court. I took it on myself to beat them in their own game. Now everyone knows that the cops are subject to citizens' arrest, just like criminals. The Establishment is cracked already—it's like the liberty bell. They thought I was going to break down under court entanglements, court threats, court action. But I didn't. I go for court action now. I love it!"

He vowed to carry on with his land grant activities, claiming his (almost) single-handed victory in the courts had increased his popularity among northern Hispanos. He told *The New York Times* gleefully: "My philosophy is that of the cricket against the lion. The cricket is the king of the insects and the lion is the king of the beasts. The cricket had no chance against the lion, so he jumped into the lion's ear and tickled him to death. That's what we're going to do to the United States—we're going to tickle him to death."

Tijerina's friends and associates were likewise jubilant. *El Grito del Norte* (The Cry from the North), an unofficial publication of the Alianza published in Espanola, noted the expressions of shock from officialdom. It quoted Jack Love as saying, "the verdict came as a complete shock. Never can I remember so completely misreading what the mood of a jury seemed to be." It also mentioned comments by Rio Arriba County Sheriff Benny Naranjo and others, then commented: "These men just couldn't tolerate the fact that Reies Lopez Tijerina, a man with few years of formal education behind him and many years of poverty, had defeated the power structure on its own grounds, by its own rules, and in its own language—which is his second language."

Anti-Establishment, underground publications elsewhere also applauded the acquittal. Typical was the *Berkeley Barb:* " 'Amazing, amazing and beautiful,' is how San Francisco lawyer Harold McDermid described the freeing of Reis Tijerina from the manacles of New Mexican pigs. Tijerina, Mexican-American leader of the liberation struggle of the brown people from the repressive economic and educational system in New Mexico, was charged with kidnapping District Attorney Alfonso Sanchez. . . . Actually, Tijerina was making a citizen's arrest of Sanchez. . . . The beauty of the decision that freed Tijerina is that it upholds the right of a citizen to make an arrest of anyone, even the police, who deprives him of his constitutional rights."

LEROI JONES

Violence: Up Against the Wall Mother Fucker

What about that bad short you saw last week on Frelinghuysen, or those stoves and refrigerators, record players, shotguns, in Sears, Bambergers, Klein's, Hahnes', Chase, and the smaller joosh enterprises? What about that bad jewelry, on Washington Street, and those couple of shops on Spring-field? You know how to get it, you can get it, no money down, no money never, money dont grow on trees no way, only whitey's got it, makes it with a machine, to control you you cant steal nothin from a white man, he's already stole it he owes you anything you want, even his life. All the stores will open if you will say the magic words. The magic words are: Up against the wall mother fucker this is a stick up! Or: Smash the window at night (these are magic actions) smash the windows daytime, anytime, together, lets smash the window drag the shit from in there. No money down. No time to pay. Just take what you want. The magic dance in the street. Run up and down Broad Street niggers, take the shit you want. Take their lives if need be, but

From *Evergreen Review*, December 1967. Copyright © 1967 by LeRoi Jones. Reprinted by permission of The Sterling Lord Agency.

get what you want what you need. Dance up and down the streets, turn all the music up, run through the streets with music, beautiful radios on Market Street, they are brought here especially for you. Our brothers are moving all over, smashing at jellywhite faces. We must make our own World, man, our own world, and we can not do this unless the white man is dead. Let's get together and kill my man, lets get to gather the fruit of the sun, let's make a world we want black children to grow and learn in do not let your children when they grow look in your face and curse you by pitying your tomish ways.

A License To Kill?

What Ronald August really wanted to be when he was mustered out of the Navy in 1963 was a carpenter or plumber or electrician. But back home in Detroit he found all the apprenticeship programs closed, so August became a policeman. Then came the chaos of Detroit's 1967 summer riot. It swept him briefly inside a shady hostelry called the Algiers Motel, from there to the nation's front pages and, finally, to the defendant's box in a sandstone courthouse. August was charged with murdering a black teenager, and to many the case epitomized the nonstop confrontation between white cops and the black community.

At the Algiers, August and other lawmen had encountered a group of ten black youths whiling away the riotwracked hours with two white prostitutes. The cops battered the blacks with pistol barrels and rifle butts, threatened to kill them, then led them off to side rooms and blasted away at the walls. It was part of the "game" designed to elicit information about suspected snipers in the motel. No snipers were ever turned up, but three of the youths were left dead or dying when the cops pulled out. At the trial, a parade of 42 prosecution witnesses suggested that August had gone beyond the rules of the game and actually killed one of the three, 19-year-old Auburey Pollard, in cold blood.

At first, August and his fellow officers had not even bothered to report the deaths. When the bodies were discovered, the cops reported that the boys were already dead when they entered the motel. "I didn't tell the truth at that time," August later admitted from the witness stand. "A half hour later

From *Newsweek*, June 23, 1969, pp. 32-33. Copyright 1969 by Newsweek, Inc. Reprinted by permission.

... I asked ... if I could have my statement back." In his revised statement
—and his testimony in court—August said he had taken quick-tempered
young Pollard into a motel room, then killed him with a single shotgun blast
in self-defense. "I told him, 'Don't touch the gun'," said the officer. "He came
at me again. I fired."

Thus, after 22 days of testimony, the case came down to a relatively simple
question. Would the word of the white police officer be believed by the all-
white jury (11 women, one man). Judge William J. Beer instructed the jury
it had only two choices for its verdict—either first-degree murder or acquittal
—thus eliminating the possibility the jury might find August guilty of the
lesser counts of second-degree murder or manslaughter. The jurors deliber-
ated two hours and 35 minutes, then announced that they had found August
innocent. On his way out of court, the patrolman told reporters simply, "I'm
going to pray."

August's prayers may be needed. He still faces Federal charges of conspir-
ing to deprive Pollard and the others of their civil rights. And despite the
personal verdict of Mrs. Rebecca Pollard, Auburey's mother, that her son
had received a "fair trial," Detroit's Negro population was boiling. Around
the ghetto, hundreds of posters showed August's picture and the words
"MURDERER—WANTED DEAD." But there was fear in the black community as
well as anger. Said a Negro state senator, "The inevitable result of the trial
... has granted a license to kill to the Detroit Police Department as far as
black men are concerned."

STUART S. NAGEL

Ombudsmen Among the Poor

In the 1968 Law Day edition of *The Chicago Daily Law Bulletin*, this
writer prepared an article entitled, "The Poor, Too, Want Law and Order."
It concluded that "there is indeed a need for greater law and order especially with regard to stricter enforcement of housing codes and anti-discrimination legislation and more objective standards in the operations of public
housing, the setting of bail, the appointing of the public defender, and the
relief work of the township supervisors." The purpose of this present article

From *Chicago Daily Law Bulletin*, Law Day Edition, April 25, 1969. Reprinted by
permission.

is to describe one new approach to promoting some aspects of this kind of law and order, namely having ombudsmen among the poor.

An ombudsman is an individual whose job is to *mediate* complaints received from people against governmental personnel or activities with the exception of complaints against judges, legislators, and chief executives. Unlike an arbitrator or a judge, he has no power to hand down decisions binding on the parties. Unlike an attorney, he is not an advocate for either the complainants or respondents.

The idea first came into formal existence in the Scandinavian countries at the national level. It has since spread to Britain and some of the Commonwealth countries. It is now being considered for adoption in various American states and cities including Illinois where both the Republicans and Democrats have introduced ombudsmen bills in the state legislature. A recent boost to the ombudsman idea came on Jan. 27, 1969, when the House of Delegates of the American Bar Association resolved "that state and local governments of the United States should give consideration to the establishment of an ombudsman."

An ombudsman for the poor would specialize in the complaints of the poor either as a separately authorized ombudsman or as a special division within a general ombudsmen program. He would arrange for one or more neighborhood offices or some other outreach devices designed to facilitate use of his services by the poor. Such specialization is needed in view of the fact that (1) the complaints of the poor against governmental officials tend to be different than middle class complaints, (2) the poor are more apathetic and pessimistic about the utility of complaining, and (3) the frustrations of the poor are threatening to boil over into anti-social aggression.

The complaints processed can deal with government personnel who administer *federal* social security, *state* public aid, or *city* housing codes, or just one of the levels of government if it is deemed that the program should be more narrowly focused. Complaints can come from people living or working in the area to be served and also from legislators who represent the area and who want the ombudsmen to aid the legislators in processing complaints. Complaints against the police can be excluded from the jurisdiction in order to remove the ombudsman from the emotionality, workload, and overlapping of police review agencies and in order to make his establishment more politically realistic. Complaints against judges are logically excluded because of the availability of appellate courts and judicial fitness commissions. Likewise legislators and chief executives are better subject to political and electoral processes than the more narrowly directed redress provided by the ombudsman.

The processing can involve such things as referring citizens to the correct agencies or to an attorney, clarifying unclear communications between citizens and officials, rectifying mistakes, or making policy recommendations to resolve numerous complaints that have a common cause. The ombudsmen can also be given subpoena power to question persons or examine records as the ABA recommends. Complaints and inquiries can be received and relayed by phone, mail, or in person with a heavy emphasis on informal mediation rather than formalized procedures.

Existing legal aid programs do not adequately fulfill the functions of an ombudsman mainly because they are so busy processing complaints against private parties especially against husbands and wives of clients that they have little time for processing complaints against government officials. Their role is also that of an advocate not a mediator which handicaps their ability to serve as a neutral go-between. Furthermore, they are generally confined to concrete cases as contrasted to the ombudsman who can, for example, look into the problem of improving relations between the fire department and the poor on the basis of reading newspaper articles which mention the stoning of firemen without waiting for a client who wants to bring a lawsuit against the fire department. The ombudsman can also ethically encourage people to tell him what, if anything, is troubling them (or is deserving of praise) without being accused of stirring up litigation.

Like legal aid offices, existing city hall complaint receiving offices also do not represent a complete substitute for the ombudsman concept. They probably tend, in the eyes of the potential complainants especially poor complainants, to be too much associated with the government personnel against whom the complaints might be directed. City hall complaint offices also tend to lack the neighborhood decentralization associated with the ombudsmen among the poor.

The Buffalo Ombudsmen Project is an existing program roughly approximating what this article has in mind. It was established on an experimental basis in 1967 with a grant from the Office of Economic Opportunity that is scheduled to expire in 1969. The director of the project is a distinguished practicing attorney who was chosen by the University of Buffalo with publicized assurances of cooperation from the Mayor of Buffalo. The director might have been even more effective, however, if he were jointly chosen by representatives of the city council and the mayor and also representatives of the poor analogous to the way the steel companies and the steelworkers choose a labor arbitrator. With two neighborhood offices and a small staff, he has been processing over 100 complaints a month.

With the endorsement of the American Bar Association and other organizations, the ombudsman idea seems destined to spread in America. It is arriving at an opportune time in view of (1) increased government activity, (2) increased feelings of ineffectiveness on the part of the individual citi-

zens, and (3) increased sensitivity to real and imagined injustices and in-
equalities. Within the general ombudsman concept, it is hoped that provisions
will be made for ombudsmen among the poor so as to promote greater
justice, equality, and tranquility where many feel those things have been
especially lacking.

Let's Have Trial by Television

Politicians, civil rights leaders, lawyers, newspapers, and the liberal community have called and called for an "official investigation" of the Fred
Hampton case by many kinds of jurisdictional and fact-finding bodies.

The request comes from a conviction that the Hampton killing has divided
the community so deeply that only an official report can soothe the emotions
and relax the social tensions.

The hope is, either Hanrahan's version of the events will prove to be correct or, if murder by the police is proved, the guilty ones will be indicted
for murder and the normal legal processes will take control.

The real issue, however, is the fear that the normal legal processes are
responsible for the deaths of Hampton and Mark Clark.

If the facts prove that this is the case, how reliable are the legal remedies?
Revolution, the Black Panther Party maintains, is the only answer to a fascist
state.

And if the facts support the contention raised by many that this is a conspiracy by the law enforcement apparatus to do away with revolutionaries,
would be a responsible fact-finding body say so? "Responsible" people are
against revolution—by definition.

It's hard to escape the feeling that the legal system from the local police
level to the Justice Department is on trial here. It's hard to escape the feeling that something in the system might be very wrong.

Here is a list of suggested investigative groups and their hang-ups in
judging a case involving revolutionaries—plus a new suggestion from CJR:

1. National Commission on the Causes and Prevention of Violence—It's

From *Chicago Journalism Review*, Vol. 2, No. 12, December 1969, p. 13. Reprinted by
permission.

life has expired. A majority opinion opposed even non-violent civil disobedience, much less the position of an avowedly revolutionary group like the
Black Panther Party.

2. Afro-American Patrolmen's League—No longer impartial. It has made
an investigation and turned its information over to the defense attorneys.

3. Illinois Attorney General's Office—Has no jurisdiction and would not
be assumed impartial by the Panthers and their supporters.

4. Blue Ribbon Coroner's Jury—County Coroner Andrew J. Toman has
become an issue in the case because of the disputed autopsy report issued by
his office, and cannot subpoena evidence in any case.

5. Chicago Commission on Human Relations—Cannot subpoena evidence,
has not proved itself effective or impartial and does not command sufficient
respect from either side.

6. Illinois Bureau of Investigation—The "Little FBI" works with the Federal Bureau of Investigation, is largely composed of former FBI agents and
can be expected to have strong feelings in the case.

7. Police Department's Internal Investigations Division—Considered the
police department's "whitewash machine," the IID has already proved most
reluctant to look into the affair.

8. Atty. Gen. John F. Mitchell—Listed the Black Panther Party as "subversive," thus triggering increased FBI surveillance. Even moderate Democrats don't trust him.

9. Federal Bureau of Investigation—Has led raids against the Panthers;
director J. Edgar Hoover called the Panthers "the greatest threat to the
internal security of the country." FBI information may be linked to the
Hampton case.

10. U.S. Civil Rights Commission—Led by the Rev. Theodore M. Hesburg,
whose strong anti-student-demonstrator position (suspension if administration orders at Notre Dame are not heeded) has attracted the applause of
law-and-order proponents. Quite a respector of authority himself and un-
sympathetic to Panther philosophies.

11. The United Nations—No jurisdiction over the internal affairs of a
sovereign state and could expect no cooperation from the U.S. government.

12. The panel to be financed by a $100,000 grant from the Ford Founda-
tion, headed by former Supreme Court Justice Arthur J. Goldberg, including
Ramsey Clark, Sam Brown, Roy Wilkins. Perhaps the best bet, although no
revolutionaries are included.

13. The Blue-Ribbon Grand Jury—Since public lines of communication—
print and electronic media—have already done their inevitable part in communicating the facts and fears which set this social crisis, the *Review* suggests they do their part to solve the matter one way or another. We propose
that under the rules established by an independent (perhaps foreign) judge,

Hanrahan and the Panthers be allowed to present their evidence with full subpoena power, cross-examination, etc., in fully televised hearings, broadcast throughout the community.

Most of us are asking ourselves if it's true. Let's find out.

TOM WOLFE

Excerpts from *The Electric Kool-Aid Acid Test:* Copping Out

. . . The big rally had been going on all day. They were out on a big lawn, or plaza, on the campus, about fifteen thousand of them, the toggle-coat bohemians, while the P.A. loudspeakers boomed and rabbled and raked across them. There was a big platform set up for the speakers. There had been about forty of them, all roaring or fulminating or arguing cogently, which was always worse. The idea at these things is to keep building up momentum and building up momentum and tension and suspense until finally when it is time for action—in this case, the march—the signal launches them as one great welded body of believers and they are ready to march and take billy clubs upside the head and all the rest of it.

All the shock workers of the tongue were there, speakers like Paul Jacobs, and M. S. Arnoni, who wore a prison uniform to the podium because his family had been wiped out in a German concentration camp during World War II—and out before them was a great sea of students and other Youth, the toggle-coat bohemians—toggle coats, Desert Boots, civil rights, down with the war in Vietnam—". . . could call out to you from their graves or from the fields and rivers upon which their ashes were thrown, they would implore this generation of Americans not to be silent in the face of the genocidal atrocities committed on the people of Vietnam . . ." and the words rolled in full forensic boom over the P.A. systems.

The first person in the Vietnam Day Committee circle to notice Kesey approaching the speaker's platform was Paul Krassner, the editor of *The Realist* magazine. Most of the Pranksters were still on the bus, fooling around with the guns for the befuddlement of the gawkers who happened by. Kesey, Babbs, Gretchen Fetchin and George Walker came on over the platform, Kesey in his orange Day-Glo coat and World War I helmet. Krassner ran his magazine as pretty much a one-man operation and he knew Kesey subscribed to it. So he wasn't so surprised that Kesey knew him. What got him was that Kesey just started talking to him, just like they had been having a conversation all along and something had interrupted them and now they were resuming. . . . It is a weird thing. You feel the guy's charisma, to use that one, right away, busting out even through the nutty Day-Glo, or maybe sucking one in, the way someone once wrote of Gurdjieff: "You could not help being drawn, almost physically, towards him . . . like being sucked in by a vast, spiritual vacuum cleaner." At the time, however, Krassner thought of Flash Gordon.

"Look up there," Kesey says, motioning up toward the platform.

Up there is Paul Jacobs. Jacobs tends toward the forensic, anyway, and the microphone and loudspeakers do something to a speaker. You can hear your voice rolling and thundering, powerful as Wotan, out over that ocean of big ears and eager faces, and you are omnipotent and more forensic and orotund and thunderous minute by minute—*It is written, but I say unto you . . . the jackals of history-ree-ree-ree-ree.* . . . From where they are standing, off to the side of the platform, they can hear very little of what Jacobs is actually saying, but they can hear the sound barking and roaring and reverberating and they can hear the crowd roaring back and baying on cue, and they can see Jacobs, hunched over squat and thick into the microphone, with his hands stabbing out for emphasis, and there, at sundown silhouetted against the florid sky, is his jaw, jutting out, like a cantaloupe . . .

Kesey says to Krassner: "Don't listen to the words, just the sound, and the gestures . . . who do you see?"

And suddenly Krassner wants very badly to be right. It is the call of the old charisma. He wants to come up with the right answer.

"Mussolini . . . ?"

Kesey starts nodding. Right, right, but keeping his eye on the prognathous jaw.

By this time more of the Pranksters have come up to the platform. They have found some electrical outlets and they have run long cords up to the platform, for the guitars and basses and horns. Kesey is the next to last speaker. He is to be followed by some final Real Barnburner of a speaker and then—the final surge and the march on Oakland.

From the moment Kesey gets up there, it is a freaking jar. His jacket glows at dusk, and his helmet. Lined up behind him are more Day-Glo crazies, wearing aviator helmets and goggles and flight suits and Army tunics, Babbs, Gretch, Walker, Zonker, Mary Microgram, and little Day-Glo kids, and half of them carrying electric guitars and horns, mugging and moving around in Day-Glo streaks. The next jar is Kesey's voice, it is so non-forensic. He comes on soft, in the Oregon drawl, like he's just having a conversation with 15,000 people:

You know, you're not gonna stop this war with this rally, by marching . . . That's what they *do . . . They hold rallies and they march . . . They've been having wars for ten thousand years and you're not gonna stop it this way . . . Ten thousand years, and this is the game they play to do it . . . holding rallies and having marches . . . and that's the same game you're playing . . . their game . . .*

Whereupon he reaches into his great glowing Day-Glo coat and produces a harmonica and starts playing it right into the microphone, *Home, home on the range,* hawonking away on the goddamn thing—*Home . . . home . . . on the ra-a-a-a-ange hawonkawonk . . .*

The crowd stands there in a sudden tender clump, most of them wondering if they heard right, cocking their heads and rolling their heads to one another. First of all, that conversational tone all of a sudden, and then random notes from the Day-Glo crazies behind him ripped out often the electric guitars and the general babble of the place feeding into the microphone—did anybody hear right—

—all the while Kesey is still up there hawonking away on the freaking harmonica, *Home, home on the ra-a-a-a-a-a-ange*—

—ahhhh, that's it—they figure it's some calculated piece of stage business, playing *Home, home on the range*—building up to something like Yah! We know about that *home!* We know about that *range!* That rotten U.S. home and that rotten U.S. range!—

—but instead it is the same down-home drawling voice—

I was just looking at the speaker who was up here before me . . . and I couldn't hear what he was saying . . . but I could hear the sound of it . . . and I could hear your *sound coming back at him . . . and I could see the gestures—*

—and here Kesey starts parodying Paul Jacobs' stabbing little hands and his hunched-over stance and his—

—and I could see his jaw sticking out like this . . . silhouetted against the sky . . . and you know who I saw . . . and who I heard? . . . Mussolini . . . I saw and I heard Mussolini here just a few minutes ago . . . Yep . . . you're playing their game . . .

Then he starts hawonking away again, hawonking and hawonking *Home, home on the range* with that sad old setter harmonica-around-the-campfire pace—and the Pranksters back him up on their instruments. Babbs, Gretch, George, Zonker, weaving up there in a great Day-Glo freakout.

—and what the hell—a few boos but mainly confusion—what in the name of God are the ninnies—

—We've all heard all this and seen all this before, but we keep on doing

it . . . I want to see the Beatles last month . . . And I heard 20,000 girls screaming together at the Beatles . . . and I couldn't hear what they were screaming, either . . . But you don't have to . . . They're screaming Me! Me! Me! Me! . . . I'm Me! . . . That's the cry of the ego, and that's the cry of this rally! . . . Me! Me! Me! Me! . . . And that's why wars get fought . . . ego . . . because enough people want to scream Pay attention to Me . . . Yep, you're playing their game . . .

—and then more *hawonkawonkawonkawonkawonka—*

—and the crowd starts going into a slump. It's as if the rally, the whole day, has been one long careful inflation of a helium balloon, preparing to take off—and suddenly somebody has pulled the plug. It's not what *he* is saying, either. It's the sound and the freaking sight and that goddamn mournful harmonica and that stupid Chinese music by the freaks standing up behind him. It's the only thing the martial spirit can't stand—a put-on, a prank, a shuck, a goose in the anus.

—Vietnam Day Committee seethe together at the edge of the platform: 'Who the hell invited this bastard!" "*You* invited him!" "Well, hell, we figured he's a writer, so he'll be against the war!" "Didn't you have enough speakers?" says Krassner. "You need all the big names you can get, to get the crowd out." "Well, that's what you get for being celebrity fuckers," says Krassner. If they had had one of those big hooks like they had on amateur night in the vaudeville days, they would have pulled Kesey off the podium right then. Well, then, why doesn't somebody just go up there and edge him off! He's ruining the goddamn thing. But then they see all the Day-Glo crazies, men and women and children all weaving and electrified, clawing at guitars, blowing horns, all crazed aglow at sundown . . . And the picture of the greatest anti-war rally in the history of America ending in a Day-Glo brawl to the tune of Home, home on the range . . .

—suddenly the hawonking on the freaking harmonica stops. Kesey leans into the microphone—

There's only one thing to do . . . there's only one thing's gonna do any good at all . . . And that's everybody just look at it, look at the war, and turn your backs and say . . . Fuck it . . .

—*hawonkawonkawonkawonka—*

—They hear that all right. The sound of the phrase—*Fuck it*—sounds so weird, so shocking, even here in Free Speech citadel, just coming out that way over a public loudspeaker, rolling over the heads of 15,000 souls—

Home, home on the range hawonkawonkawonka, and the Pranksters beginning to build up most madly on their instruments now, behind the harmonica, sounding like an insane honky-tonk version of Juan Carrillo who devised 96 tones on the back seat of a Willys Jeep, saved pennies all through the war to buy it, you understand, zinc pennies until the blue pustules formed under his zither finger nether there, you understand . . .

—Just look at it and turn away and say . . . Fuck it

—say . . . Fuck it . . .

hawonkawonkawonka blam

—Fuck it—

Hawonkafuckit . . . friends . . .